ILLEGAL DRUGS
AMERICA'S ANGUISH

ILLEGAL DRUGS
AMERICA'S ANGUISH

Curtis Jackson-Jacobs

INFORMATION PLUS® REFERENCE SERIES
Formerly published by Information Plus, Wylie, Texas

GALE GROUP
THOMSON LEARNING

Detroit • New York • San Diego • San Francisco
Boston • New Haven, Conn. • Waterville, Maine
London • Munich

ILLEGAL DRUGS: AMERICA'S ANGUISH

Curtis Jackson-Jacobs, *Author*

The Gale Group Staff:

Editorial: Ellice Engdahl, *Series Editor*; John F. McCoy, *Series Editor*; Charles B. Montney, *Series Associate Editor*; Andrew Claps, *Series Associate Editor*; Jason M. Everett, *Series Associate Editor*; Michael T. Reade, *Series Associate Editor*; Heather Price, *Series Assistant Editor*; Teresa Elsey, *Editorial Assistant*; Debra M. Kirby, *Managing Editor*; Rita Runchock, *Managing Editor*

Image and Multimedia Content: Barbara J. Yarrow, *Manager, Imaging and Multimedia Content* ; Robyn Young, *Project Manager, Imaging and Multimedia Content*

Indexing: Susan Kelsch, *Indexing Supervisor*

Permissions: Margaret Chamberlain, *Permissions Specialist*; Maria Franklin, *Permissions Manager*

Product Design: Michelle DiMercurio, *Senior Art Director and Product Design Manager*; Michael Logusz, *Cover Art Designer*

Production: Evi Seoud, *Assistant Manager, Composition Purchasing and Electronic Prepress*; NeKita McKee, *Buyer*; Dorothy Maki, *Manufacturing Manager*

Cover photo © AP/World Wide Photos.

ISBN 0-7876-5103-6 (set)
ISBN 0-7876-5397-7 (this volume)
ISSN 1536-5220 (this volume)
Printed in the United States of America
10 9 8 7 6 5 4 3 2 1

TABLE OF CONTENTS

PREFACE

Illegal Drugs: America's Anguish is one of the latest volumes in the Information Plus Reference Series. Previously published by the Information Plus company of Wylie, Texas, the Information Plus Reference Series (and its companion set, the Information Plus Compact Series) became a Gale Group product when Gale and Information Plus merged in early 2000. Those of you familiar with the series as published by Information Plus will notice a few changes from the 1999 edition. Gale has adopted a new layout and style that we hope you will find easy to use. Other improvements include greatly expanded indexes in each book, and more descriptive tables of contents.

While some changes have been made to the design, the purpose of the Information Plus Reference Series remains the same. Each volume of the series presents the latest facts on a topic of pressing concern in modern American life. These topics include today's most controversial and most studied social issues: abortion, capital punishment, care for the elderly, crime, health care, the environment, immigration, minorities, social welfare, women, youth, and many more. Although written especially for the high school and undergraduate student, this series is an excellent resource for anyone in need of factual information on current affairs.

By presenting the facts, it is Gale's intention to provide its readers with everything they need to reach an informed opinion on current issues. To that end, there is a particular emphasis in this series on the presentation of scientific studies, surveys, and statistics. These data are generally presented in the form of tables, charts, and other graphics placed within the text of each book. Every graphic is directly referred to and carefully explained in the text. The source of each graphic is presented within the graphic itself. The data used in these graphics is drawn from the most reputable and reliable sources, in particular the various branches of the U.S. government and major independent polling organizations. Every effort has been made to secure the most recent information available. The reader should bear in mind that many major studies take years to conduct, and that additional years often pass before the data from these studies is made available to the public. Therefore, in many cases the most recent information available in 2001 dated from 1998 or 1999. Older statistics are sometimes presented as well, if they are of particular interest and no more recent information exists.

Although statistics are a major focus of the Information Plus Reference Series, they are by no means its only content. Each book also presents the widely held positions and important ideas that shape how the book's subject is discussed in the United States. These positions are explained in detail and, where possible, in the words of their proponents. Some of the other material to be found in these books includes: historical background; descriptions of major events related to the subject; relevant laws and court cases; and examples of how these issues play out in American life. Some books also feature primary documents, or have pro and con debate sections giving the words and opinions of prominent Americans on both sides of a controversial topic. All material is presented in an even-handed and unbiased manner; the reader will never be encouraged to accept one view of an issue over another.

HOW TO USE THIS BOOK

Prescription and over-the-counter drugs can cure people of illnesses or relieve their pain, but there are other drugs that serve no medical purpose, or for which the risks outweigh the benefits. These substances, though illegal, are prevalent in modern-day America, and can pose major health risks to individuals, including psychological and/or physical dependence. The U.S. government has tried to control the spread of illegal drugs through such strategies as stiff criminal penalties for drug offenses and an ongoing battle against drug producers known as the "war on drugs." This book provides an overview of illegal drugs, including their history, health impact, addictive nature, and potential for abuse. Also discussed are the political and economic ramifications of illegal drugs, their use by youth, treatment programs for drug abuse, drug production and distribution, the relationship of drugs to criminal behavior, and public opinions about illicit drugs.

Illegal Drugs: America's Anguish consists of eleven chapters and three appendices. Each of the chapters is devoted to a particular aspect of illegal drugs or related issues. For a summary of the information covered in each chapter, please see the synopses provided in the Table of Contents at the front of the book. Chapters generally begin with an overview of the basic facts and background information on the chapter's topic, then proceed to examine sub-topics of particular interest. For example, Chapter 9: AIDS and Intravenous Drug Use begins with a discussion of what AIDS is, its symptoms, the ways it is transmitted, and the race, ethnicity, and gender of AIDS victims. It then examines the way drug use behaviors can contribute to the spread of AIDS, including perinatal transmission and the sharing of equipment. Also discussed at length are needle exchange programs (NEPs), including their goal (to help IV drug users avoid AIDS), the political controversies that surround them, various support for them, the banning of federal funds for NEPs, and the American Bar Association's recommendations for the deregulation of NEPs and syringe sales. Readers can find their way through a chapter by looking for the section and sub-section headings, which are clearly set off from the text. Or, they can refer to the book's extensive index if they already know what they are looking for.

Statistical Information

The tables and figures featured throughout *Illegal Drugs: America's Anguish* will be of particular use to the reader in learning about this issue. These tables and figures represent an extensive collection of the most recent and important statistics on illegal drugs, as well as related issues—for example, graphics in the book cover the use of illicit drugs among pregnant and nonpregnant women, annual positivity rates for employee drug testing programs, the percentage of high school students who have used marijuana in the past year, the number of substance references in popular movies and songs, drug use among arrestees in several U.S. cities, federal drug trafficking penalties, price ranges for various amounts of heroin, the percentage change in drug use of participants in various types of drug treatment programs, and American attitudes toward the legalization of marijuana. Gale believes that making this information available to the reader is the most important way in which we fulfill the goal of this book: to help readers understand the issues and controversies surrounding illegal drugs in the United States and reach their own conclusions.

Each table or figure has a unique identifier appearing above it, for ease of identification and reference. Titles for the tables and figures explain their purpose. At the end of each table or figure, the original source of the data is provided.

In order to help readers understand these often complicated statistics, all tables and figures are explained in the text. References in the text direct the reader to the relevant statistics. Furthermore, the contents of all tables and figures are fully indexed. Please see the opening section of the index at the back of this volume for a description of how to find tables and figures within it.

In addition to the main body text and images, *Illegal Drugs: America's Anguish* has three appendices. The first is the Important Names and Addresses directory. Here the reader will find contact information for a number of government and private organizations that can provide information on illegal drugs. The second appendix is the Resources section, which can also assist the reader in conducting his or her own research. In this section, the author and editors of *Illegal Drugs: America's Anguish* describe some of the sources that were most useful during the compilation of this book. The final appendix is the index. It has been greatly expanded from previous editions, and should make it even easier to find specific topics in this book.

COMMENTS AND SUGGESTIONS

The editors of the Information Plus Reference Series welcome your feedback on *Illegal Drugs: America's Anguish*. Please direct all correspondence to:

Editor
Information Plus Reference Series
27500 Drake Rd.
Farmington Hills, MI, 48331-3535

ACKNOWLEDGEMENTS

Photographs and illustrations appearing in Information Plus Illegal Drugs 2001, *were received from the following sources:*

American Management Association. Illustration from *Workplace Drug Testing and Drug Abuse Policies*. Reproduced by permission.

Bureau of Justice Statistics. Illustrations from *Prisoners in 1999, Sourcebook of Criminal Justice Statistics 1999*. (2000), *Substance Abuse and Treatment, State and Federal Prisoners* (1997). Reproduced by permission.

Centers for Disease Control and Prevention. Illustrations from *HIV/AIDS Surveillance Report* (2000); *Morbidity and Mortality Weekly Report;* (1997), *Youth Risk Behavior Surveillance-United States, 1999* (2000). All courtesy of the Centers for Disease Control and Prevention.

Department of Justice. Illustrations from *Correctional Populations in the United States, 1997*. (2000)

Department of State. Illustration from: *International Narcotics Control Strategy Report*.

Drug Enforcement Administration. Illustrations from *Drugs of Abuse*, (1996) Courtesy of the U.S. Food and Drug Administration. *Illegal Drug Price/Purity Report; Major Coca & Opium Producing Nations: Cultivation and Production Estimates*, (1994 & 1998). All reproduced by permission.

Federal Bureau of Investigation. Illustrations from *Crime in the United States, 1999*. (2000)

Government Accounting Office. Illustrations from *Drug Abuse: Research Shows Treatment is Effective but Benefits May be Overstated*, (1998); *Drug Control: U.S. Assistance to Colombia Will Take Years to Produce Results* (2000); *Drug Control: U.S. Counternarcotics Efforts in Columbia Face Continuing Challenges; Drug control: U.S.-*

Mexican Counternarcotics Efforts Face Difficult Challenges, (1990 and 1997); *Drug Control: Update on U.S. Interdiction Efforts in the Caribbean and Eastern Pacific*, (1997). All reproduced by permission.

The Higher Education Center for Alcohol and Other Drug Prevention. Illustration by Joel Epstein *The Higher Education Amendments*. Reproduced by permission.

Institute of Medicine. Illustration edited by Janet E. Joy, Stanley J. Watson, Jr., and John A. Benson, Jr.: *Marijuana and Medicine: Assessing the Science Base*. Reproduced by permission.

Institute for Social Research, University of Michigan, and the National Institute on Drug Abuse, U.S. Department of Health and Human Services. Illustrations from *Monitoring the Future: National Results on Adolescent Drug Use—Overview of Key Findings, 2000*. (2001).

The National Center on Addiction and Substance Abuse at Columbia University. Illustration from *Back to School National Survey of American Attitudes on Substance Abuse IV: Teens, Teachers and Principals*. Reproduced by permission.

National Conference of State Legislatures. Illustrations by Robert E. Frohling and Eric Staton *NCSL Legisbrief*. Courtesy of the National Conference of State Legislatures.

National Institute of Justice. Illustrations from *Arrestee Drug Abuse Monitoring Program*. All reproduced by permission.

National Institute on Drug Abuse. Illustrations from *Anabolic Steroid Abuse*. Courtesy of the National Institute on Drug Abuse. All reproduced by permission.

National Narcotics Intelligence Consumers Committee. Illustrations from *The NNICC Report 1997: The Supply of Illicit Drugs to the*

United States. Courtesy of the National Narcotics Intelligence Consumers Committee.

Office of National Drug Control Policy. Illustrations from *The National Drug Control Strategy, 2000*. (April 2001)

Office of National Drug Control Policy and Substance Abuse and Mental Health Services Administration. Illustration from *Substance Use in Popular Movies and Music*. Reproduced by permission.

Partnership for a Drug-Free America. Illustrations from *1998 Partnership Attitude Tracking Study*. (1998) All reproduced by permission.

PRIDE Surveys. Illustrations from *PRIDE National Summary 1999-00* (1999), *Pride Questionnaire Report: 1997-98 National Summary, Grades 6 through 12*. Reproduced by permission.

RAND. Illustration by Jonathan P. Caulkins, C. Peter Rydell, William L. Schwabe *Mandatory Minimum Drug Sentences: Throwing Away the Key or the Taxpayers' Money?* Reproduced by permission.

SmithKline Beecham Clinical Laboratories. Illustrations from *SmithKline Beecham Drug Testing Index*. Both reproduced by permission.

Southern Illinois University, Core Institute. Illustration by C.A. Presley, J. S. Leichliter, P. W. Meilman *Alcohol and Drugs on American College Campuses: A Report to College Presidents: Findings from 1995, 1996, and 1997*. Reproduced by permission.

Substance Abuse and Mental Health Services Administration. Illustrations from *The DAWN Report: Club Drugs; National Household Survey on Drug Abuse: Population Estimates 1998; The National Treatment Improvement Evaluation Study; Preliminary Results from the 1997 National Household Survey on Drug Abuse; Services Research Outcomes*

Study; Treatment Episode Data Set (TEDS): 1993–1998; Summary Findings from the 1999 National Household Survey on Drug *Abuse; Uniform Facility Data Set Data for 1980 and 1996.* (1980 and 1996); *Uniform Facility Data Set (UFDS): 1998* (2000); and *Year-End 1999 Emergency Department Data from the Drug Abuse Warning Network,* All reproduced by permission.

CHAPTER 1
DRUGS—A LONG AND VARIED HISTORY

Since before recorded history, people have experimented with drugs other than alcohol. Ancient cultures found relief from physical pain through narcotic plants and similar agents. For centuries, others have used drugs for everything from relaxation and recreation to sharing in religious events, escaping the pressures of reality, and altering their life perspective.

NARCOTICS

Opium

Medically, the term "narcotic" refers to opium and opium derivatives or synthetic substitutes. A plant named *Papaver somniferum* is the main source of nonsynthetic narcotics. Records from Mesopotamia (5000–4000 B.C.E.) refer to this poppy. The ancient Greek and Egyptian societies used extracts from the opium poppy to soothe their children. The Greek physician Galen prescribed opium for headaches, deafness, epilepsy, asthma, coughs, fevers, "women's problems," and for just feeling bad. Hippocrates (c. 400 B.C.E.), widely considered the father of modern medicine, used medicinal herbs, including opium. In those days, opium cakes and candles were sold in the streets. The Romans undoubtedly learned of opium from their eastern Mediterranean conquests.

The Islamic civilization preserved the medical arts after the decline of the Roman Empire and by the tenth century had established trade and an interchange of medical knowledge among Persia, China, and India. Sometime in the sixteenth century, laudanum, the modern form of opium, was introduced, and it was widely used in Europe for the next two hundred years. In the early 1700s a professor of chemistry at the University of Leyden in the Netherlands discovered a pain reliever called paregoric, a combination of camphor and tincture of opium.

COMMONLY USED. In the eighteenth century the British Society of Arts awarded prizes and gold medals for growing the most attractive *Papaver somniferum*. By the nineteenth century most babies in the United Kingdom were being soothed to sleep with a sleeping preparation containing laudanum. British prime minister William Gladstone (1809–98) put laudanum in his coffee so that he could speak better in front of Parliament. British writers Samuel Taylor Coleridge and Elizabeth Barrett Browning were addicted to opiates like laudanum, while author Charles Dickens calmed himself with opium. Novelist Arthur Conan Doyle's most famous literary creation, Sherlock Holmes, even used opium.

The great British trader William Jardine considered the sale of opium "the safest and most gentleman-like speculation I am aware of." At the height of the opium trade, the "noble house" of Jardine and his partner had 18 well-fitted opium clipper ships and 14 receiving ships along the Chinese coast to help unload opium shipments.

Perhaps because so few other painkillers and therapeutics were available until the nineteenth century, there appears to have been little real concern about excessive use of opium in many parts of the world. An exception was China: In 1729 the Manchu dynasty (1644–1912), in an attempt to discourage the importation and use of opium in that country, passed laws directing that opium dealers be strangled.

Since Great Britain then held a monopoly on the importation of opium into China, the British fought to keep their highly profitable trade. The British defeated the Chinese in the Opium War (1839–42) to guarantee their right to continue to sell opium to the Chinese people. The illegal opium trade that developed in China to avoid tariffs led to gangsterism—not unlike the growth of the underworld in the United States during Prohibition.

In 1805 a German pharmacist's assistant discovered how to isolate morphine, the primary active agent in opium—and ten times as potent as opium. In 1832 codeine, another product of opium, was isolated. The development of the hypodermic needle in the early 1850s made it easier to use morphine. It became a common medicine for pain, especially from war injuries, in both Europe and the United States. During the American Civil War, so many soldiers became addicted to morphine that the addiction was later called "soldier's disease."

In 1874 a medical scientist at St. Mary's Hospital in Paddington, England, discovered how to turn opium into heroin, a far more powerful and dangerous drug. In 1898 the Bayer Company began marketing heroin as a cough remedy and painkiller.

Coca

The ancient South American rite of burying coca with the dead dates back more than four thousand years. The deceased were buried in a sitting position, wrapped in cloths and surrounded by pottery containing artifacts, maize, and bags of coca to sustain them on their way to the afterlife. Even then, the Incas knew that cocaine, extracted from coca leaves, was capable of producing euphoria, hyperactivity, and hallucinations. After the Spanish conquest, coca was grown on plantations and used as wages to pay workers. The drug seemed to negate the effects of exhaustion and malnutrition, especially at high altitudes. In fact, many South Americans still use coca to alleviate the effects of high altitudes.

In the 1850s, Paolo Mantegazza, an Italian doctor, became enamored by the "restorative" powers of coca while living in Lima, Peru. In 1859 he published a book praising the drug, which led to interest in coca in the United States and Europe. While William Hammond, U.S. surgeon general under President Abraham Lincoln, was impressed with the drug, most doctors were unsure. Popular response, on the other hand, was very favorable, and extracts from coca leaves found their way into wines, chewing gum, teas, home remedies, and throat lozenges. Even Pope Leo XIII and Thomas A. Edison endorsed products containing coca.

A developing temperance (anti-alcohol) movement helped fuel the public's fondness for nonalcoholic products containing coca. In the mid-1880s Atlanta, Georgia, became one of the first major American cities to forbid the sale of alcohol. It was there that pharmacist John Pemberton first marketed Coca-Cola, a syrup that then contained extracts of both coca and the kola nut, as a "temperance drink."

Most doctors of the time generally felt uncomfortable with cocaine, for the most part limiting its use to eye and nose procedures. They were not alone. In 1914, when Congress outlawed the sale of narcotics (with the Harrison Narcotic Act), cocaine was included, even though it is a stimulant and not a narcotic. The government considered cocaine a social danger—particularly among southern blacks—rather than a physically dangerous drug.

Hallucinogens

For over two thousand years Native American societies often used naturally occurring hallucinogens, such as the "sacred" mushroom of Mexico and the peyote cactus of the Southwest, in religious ceremonies. Until recently, the use of peyote, while illegal, was acceptable under federal law when used in "bona fide religious rites" by members of the Native American Church only. Although scientists were slow to discover the medicinal possibilities of hallucinogens, by 1919 they had isolated mescaline from the peyote cactus and recognized its resemblance to the adrenal hormone epinephrine.

Cannabis

Cannabis is the term generally applied to the Indian hemp plant *Cannabis sativa*, from which marijuana, hashish, ganja, and bhang are derived. This ancient plant dates back more than five thousand years to central Asia and China, from where it quickly spread to India and the Near East.

Cannabis was highly regarded as a medicinal plant used in folk medicines. It was long valued as an analgesic, topical anesthetic, antispasmodic, antidepressant, appetite stimulant, antiasthmatic, and antibiotic. But by the mid-twentieth century its use as a "recreational drug" had spread, eclipsing its traditional medicinal uses.

DRUGS EASILY AVAILABLE

In late nineteenth-century America it was possible to buy, in a store or by mail order, many medicines (or alleged medicines) containing morphine, cocaine, and even heroin. Until 1903 the soft drink Coca-Cola contained cocaine. The cocaine was then replaced with another drug, caffeine. Pharmacies sold cocaine in pure form, as well as many drugs made from opium, such as morphine and heroin.

Beginning in 1898 heroin became widely available when the Bayer Company marketed it as a powerful cough suppressant. Physician prescriptions of these drugs increased from 1 percent of all prescriptions in 1874 to 20–25 percent in 1902. These drugs were not only available but also widely used, with little concern for any health consequences.

Cocaine, heroin, and other drugs were taken off the market for a number of reasons. A growing awareness of the dangers of drug use and food contamination led to the passage of such laws as the Pure Food and Drug Act of 1906 (PL 59-384), which, among other things, required the removal of false claims from patent medicines. The label also had to state the amount of any narcotic ingredient the medicine contained and whether that medicine was habit forming. A growing temperance movement, the development of safe, alternative painkillers (such as aspirin), and more alternative medical treatments contributed to the passage of laws limiting drug use, although these laws did not completely outlaw the drugs.

By the turn of the century, narcotic use was considered an international problem. In 1909 the International Opium Commission met to discuss drugs. This meeting led to the signing of a treaty two years later in the Netherlands, requiring all signatories to pass laws limiting the use of narcotics for medicinal purposes. After nearly three years of debate, in 1914 Congress passed the Harrison Narcotic Act (PL 63-223), which called for the strict control of opium and coca.

A CONNECTION BETWEEN DRUGS, IMMIGRANTS, AND MINORITIES?

By the mid- to late 1800s drug use had come to be associated with "undesirables." These "undesirables" usually included poorer Americans, often black, and immigrants, especially from southern Europe and Asia, who were arriving in ever-greater numbers in the United States.

In the United States especially, narcotic use was thought to be confined to the poor and disadvantaged, while evidence of use among higher classes was conveniently overlooked. When drug users were thought to live only in the slums, drug use was considered solely a criminal problem; but when it was finally recognized in middle-class neighborhoods, it became seen as a mental health problem.

Regulating Drugs

The passage of the Harrison Narcotic Act reflected, in part, a growing belief that opium and cocaine were medicines to be taken only when a person was sick (and then only when prescribed by a doctor). In addition, many people were beginning to believe that these drugs caused insanity or led to crime, particularly among foreigners and minorities. For example, opium use was strongly associated with Chinese immigrants. Many Americans also believed that cocaine affected blacks more powerfully than it did whites, frequently inciting them to violence.

"The Cocaine Habit," an article published in 1900 in the *Journal of the American Medical Association* (vol. 34), claimed that southern blacks were the major purchasers of an inexpensive form of cocaine known as the "5-cent sniff." Because temperance laws had led to an increase in the price of alcohol, it was thought that many poorer Americans, especially blacks, were turning to less expensive drugs. In addition, many observers claimed that the "drug-habit menace" had led to increased crime, particularly among blacks.

During the 1920s the federal government regulated drugs through the Treasury Department. In 1930 President Herbert Hoover created the Federal Bureau of Narcotics, headed by Commissioner of Narcotics Harry Anslinger. For the next 32 years, Anslinger, believing all drug users were deviant criminals, vigorously enforced the law. Marijuana, for example, was presented as a "killer weed" that threatened the very fabric of American society.

Marijuana was believed to have been brought into the country and promoted by Mexican immigrants and then picked up by black jazz musicians. These beliefs played a part in the passage of the 1937 Marijuana Tax Act (PL 75-238), which tried to control the use of marijuana. The act made the use or sale of marijuana without a tax stamp a federal offense. Since by this time the sale of marijuana was illegal in most states, buying a federal tax stamp would alert the police in a particular state to who was selling drugs. Naturally, no marijuana dealer wanted to buy a stamp and expose his/her identity to the police. (The federal tax stamp for gambling serves the same purpose.)

From the 1940s through the 1960s, the Food and Drug Administration (FDA), based on the authority granted by the 1938 Food, Drug, and Cosmetic Act (52 Stat. 1040), began to police the sale of certain drugs. The act had required the FDA to stipulate that specific drugs, such as amphetamines, barbiturates, and sulfa drugs, were safe for self-medication.

After studying most amphetamines and barbiturates, the agency concluded that it simply could not declare them safe for self-medication. Therefore, it ruled that these drugs could only be used under medical supervision; that is, with a physician's prescription. For all pharmaceutical products other than narcotics, this marked the beginning of the distinction between prescription and over-the-counter drugs.

For 25 years undercover FDA inspectors tracked down pharmacists who sold amphetamines and barbiturates without a prescription and doctors who wrote illegal prescriptions. In the 1950s, with the growing sale of amphetamines, barbiturates, and, eventually, LSD and other hallucinogens at cafes, truck stops, flophouses, and weight-reduction salons, and by street-corner pushers, FDA authorities went after these other illegal dealers. In 1968 the drug-enforcement responsibilities of the FDA were transferred to the U.S. Department of Justice.

THE WAR ON DRUGS

From the mid-1960s to the late 1970s, the demographic profile of drug users changed dramatically. Previously, drug use had generally been associated with minorities, lower classes, or young "hippies" and "beatniks." However, during this period, drug use among middle-class whites became widespread and more generally accepted. Cocaine, an expensive drug, began to be used by middle-

and upper-class whites, many of whom looked upon it as a nonaddictive recreational drug and status symbol.

During the 1960s many young people began using drugs, including marijuana and heroin. During the Vietnam War, many servicemen and servicewomen were exposed to drugs. Drugs in Vietnam were cheap and plentiful, and many soldiers used them. When they returned to the United States, these soldiers became a vivid symbol of the changing demographics of drug use.

For the first time, a large segment of the American population came to feel that drug use was a threat to their communities. Drugs not only symbolized poverty by this time but were deeply tied to antiwar and antiestablishment movements. Drugs presented a practical threat to families: their children might become users. They also presented a moral and symbolic threat to conventional American values. By the end of the 1960s there was enough fear surrounding drugs to fuel new political antidrug movements.

When he ran for president in 1968, Richard Nixon included a strong antidrug plank in his law-and-order platform, calling for a "War on Drugs." As president, Nixon created the President's National Commission on Marijuana and Drug Abuse. Ever since the Nixon administration, the U.S. government has been waging a war on drugs in some form or another. In 1973 the Drug Enforcement Administration (DEA) was formed to reduce the supply of drugs. A year later, in 1974, the National Institute on Drug Abuse (NIDA) was created to lead the effort to reduce the demand for drugs and to direct research and federal prevention and treatment services.

Under the Nixon, Ford, and Carter administrations, federal spending tended to emphasize the treatment of drug abusers. Meanwhile, a growing number of parents, fearing that their children were being exposed to drugs, began to pressure elected officials and government agencies to do more about the growing use of drugs. In response, NIDA began widely publicizing the dangers of marijuana and other drugs once thought not to be particularly harmful.

The Reagan administration favored a strict approach to drug use and increased enforcement. The budget to fight drugs rose from $1.5 billion in 1981 to $4.2 billion in 1989. By the end of the Reagan administration, two-thirds of all drug-control funding went for law enforcement and one-third went for treatment and prevention. First Lady Nancy Reagan vigorously campaigned against drug use, urging children to "Just say no!" The Crime Control Act of 1984 (PL 98-473) dramatically increased the penalties for drug use and drug trafficking.

THE APPEARANCE OF CRACK COCAINE

Cocaine use increased dramatically in the 1960s and 1970s, but the drug's high cost restricted its use to the more affluent. In the early 1980s cocaine dealers discovered a way to prepare the cocaine so that it could be smoked in small and inexpensive, but very powerful and highly addictive, amounts. The creation of this so-called crack cocaine meant that poorer people could now afford to use the drug, and a whole new market was opened up. In addition, the AIDS epidemic caused some intravenous (IV) drug users to switch to smoking crack to avoid HIV exposure from sharing needles.

Battles for control of the distribution and sale of the drug led to a violent black market. The easy availability of sophisticated firearms and the huge amounts of money to be made selling crack and other drugs transformed many areas of the nation—but particularly the inner cities—into dangerous places.

The widespread fear of crack cocaine led to increasingly harsh laws and penalties. Authorities warned that crack was instantly addictive and spreading rapidly, and they predicted a subsequent generation of crack babies. Later, however, attitudes toward the use of crack changed and the market for the drug declined.

THE RETURN OF HEROIN

The 1990s witnessed the return of heroin as a major drug of choice. Heroin, while always present, had become less popular in the 1980s. The large number of deaths from heroin overdoses had lessened the attraction of the drug. In addition, heroin use had generally involved the use of a syringe to intravenously inject the drug into the body. Concerns about HIV, which could be passed through shared syringes, led many abusers to turn to "safer," smokable drugs.

In later years, however, because of increased competition among suppliers, heroin not only became purer but also cheaper and more available. It is no longer necessary to take the drug intravenously—it can be sniffed much like cocaine, although many users continue to use syringes.

A CONTINUING EFFORT

The Anti-Drug Abuse Act of 1988 (PL 100-690) created the Office of National Drug Control Policy (ONDCP), to be headed by a director—popularly referred to as the "drug czar"—who would coordinate the nation's drug policy. Spending for drug control rose from $4.2 billion under President Reagan to $12.2 billion in the last year of the elder President George Bush's term. As was the case during the Reagan administration, the monetary split was roughly two-thirds for law enforcement and one-third for treatment and prevention. By 1990 every state that had once decriminalized the use of marijuana had repealed those laws.

When he took office in 1993, President Bill Clinton cut the ONDCP staff from 146 to 25, while at the same time raising the director of the ONDCP to cabinet status. Clinton called for 100,000 more police officers on the streets and advocated drug treatment on demand. In 1998 drug-control spending totaled $16.1 billion, with the split remaining at about two-thirds for law enforcement and one-third for treatment and prevention.

Taking office in 2001, President George W. Bush promised to continue national efforts to eradicate illegal drugs in the United States and abroad. On May 10, 2001, Bush appointed John Walters the new drug czar. Together they pledged to continue "an all-out effort to reduce illegal drug use in America." Their proposed goals include increased spending on treatment, intensified work with foreign nations, and an adamant opposition to the legalization of any currently illegal drugs.

CHAPTER 2
DRUGS OF ABUSE—ORIGINS, USES, AND EFFECTS

SCHEDULING OF DRUGS

The federal strategy to reduce illicit drug use is based on the Comprehensive Drug Abuse Prevention and Control Act of 1970, Title II (PL 91-513)—commonly called the Controlled Substances Act. This act establishes the criteria for "scheduling," or categorizing, all substances regulated under existing federal law. (See Table 2.1.)

- Schedule I—These drugs have a high potential for abuse and have no currently accepted medical use in treatment in the United States. Included in this class are heroin; most hallucinogens, such as LSD and methaqualone; and the members of the cannabis family, including marijuana and hashish.

- Schedule II—These drugs also have a high potential for abuse but have been accepted for medical use in the United States, with severe restrictions. Abuse of these drugs may lead to severe psychological or physical dependence. Opium, morphine, PCP, methamphetamine, methadone, certain barbiturates, and cocaine are some of the drugs in this schedule.

- Schedule III—The drugs in this class have less potential for abuse than those in the first two schedules. They are currently accepted for medical use in the United States, but abuse may lead to moderate or low physical dependence or high psychological dependence. Included in this category are anabolic steroids, codeine, hydrocodone, and some barbiturates.

- Schedule IV—These drugs have even less potential for abuse than those in Schedule III and are currently accepted for medical use in the United States. Abuse may lead to limited physical and psychological dependence. Darvon, Equanil, Valium, and Xanax are included here.

- Schedule V—These drugs have a lower potential for abuse than those in Schedule IV. They are accepted for medical use, but abuse may lead to limited physical or psychological dependence. Some narcotics used for antidiarrheal or antitussive purposes are included here.

While less addictive than Schedule I and II drugs, Schedule III, IV, and V drugs can be very dangerous to an abuser's health. A significant black market has developed in these drugs. Drug abusers visit their doctors complaining of a problem they know will likely be treated by a drug they desire. If the physician is fooled, he or she writes a prescription, which the drug abuser has filled at a pharmacy. The abuser then either uses the drugs personally or sells them to another drug addict.

Considerations in Determining the Schedule

In structuring the regulatory requirements shown in Table 2.2, federal agencies must first consider eight specific factors:

- The drug's actual or relative potential for abuse.

- Scientific evidence of its pharmacological effect, if known.

- The state of current scientific knowledge about the drug.

- Its history and current pattern of abuse.

- The scope, duration, and significance of abuse.

- The risk, if any, to public health.

- The drug's psychological or physiological "dependence liability" (the chance that the user may become addicted to it).

- The substance's potential to be a source for a drug already regulated under federal law.

NATURAL NARCOTICS

Narcotics are opium and opium derivatives, or synthetic substitutes, used medically to relieve intense pain.

TABLE 2.1

Uses and abuses of controlled substances

Drugs	CSA Schedules	Trade or Other Names	Medical Uses	Physical Dependence	Psychological Dependence	Tolerance	Duration (Hours)	Usual Method	Possible Effects	Effects of Overdose	Withdrawal Syndrome
Narcotics											
Heroin	I	Diacetylmorphine, Horse, Smack	None in U.S., Analgesic, Antitussive	High	High	Yes	3-6	Injected, sniffed, smoked	Euphoria; Drowsiness; Respiratory depression; Constricted pupils; Nausea	Slow and shallow breathing; Clammy skin; Convulsions; Coma; Possible death	Watery eyes; Runny nose; Yawning; Loss of appetite; Irritability; Tremors; Panic; Cramps; Nausea; Chills and sweating
Morphine	II	Duramorph, MS-Contin, Roxanol, Oramorph SR	Analgesic	High	High	Yes	3-6	Oral, smoked, injected			
Codeine	II, III, V	Tylenol w/Codeine, Empirin w/Codeine, Robitussin A-C, Fliorinal w/Codeine, APAP w/Codeine	Analgesic, Antitussive	Moderate	Moderate	Yes	3-6	Oral, injected			
Hydrocodone	II, III	Tussionex, Vicodin, Hycodan, Lorcet	Analgesic, Antitussive	High	High	Yes	3-6	Oral			
Hydromorphone	II	Dilaudid	Analgesic	High	High	Yes	3-6	Oral, injected			
Oxycodone	II	Percodan, Percocet, Tylox, Roxicet, Roxicodone	Analgesic	High	High	Yes	4-5	Oral			
Methadone and LAAM	I, II	Dolophine, Methadose, Levo-alpha-acetylmethadol, Levomethadyl acetate	Analgesic, Treatment of Dependence	High	High	Yes	12-72	Oral, injected			
Fentanyl and Analogs	I, II	Innovar, Sublimaze, Alfenta, Sufenta, Duragesic	Analgesic, Adjunct to Anesthesia, Anesthetic	High	High	Yes	10-72	Injected, Trans-dermal patch			
Other Narcotics	II, III, IV, V	Percodan, Percocet, Tylox, Opium, Darvon, Talwin[2], Buprenorphine, Meperdine (Pethidine), Demerol	Analgesic, Antidiarrheal	High–Low	High–Low	Yes	Variable	Oral, injected			
Depressants											
Chloral Hydrate	IV	Noctec; Somnos; Felsules	Hypnotic	Moderate	Moderate	Yes	5-8	Oral	Slurred speech; Disorientation; Drunken behavior without odor of alcohol	Shallow respiration; Clammy skin; Dilated pupils; Weak and rapid pulse; Coma; Possible death	Anxiety; Insomnia; Tremors; Delirium; Convulsions; Possible death
Barbiturates	II, III, IV	Amytal; Florinal; Nembutal; Seconal; Tuinal; Phenobarbital; Pentobarbital	Anesthetic, Anticonvulsant; Sedative; Hypnotic; Veterinary euthanasia agent	High-Moderate	High-Moderate	Yes	5-8	Oral, injected			
Benzodiazepines	IV	Ativan; Dalmane; Diazepam; Librium; Xanax; Serax; Valium; Tranxene; Verstran; Versed; Halcion; Paxpam; Restoril	Anti-Anxiety; Sedative: Anti-convulsant; Hypnotic	Low	Low	Yes	4-8	Oral, injected			
Glutethimide	II	Doriden	Sedative; Hypnotic	High	Moderate	Yes	4-8	Oral			
Other depressants	I, II, III, IV	Equanil; Mlltown; Noludar; Placidyl; Valmid; Methaqualone	Anti-anxiety, Sedative; Hypnotic	Moderate	Moderate	Yes	4-8	Oral			

TABLE 2.1

Uses and abuses of controlled substances [CONTINUED]

Drugs	CSA Schedules	Trade or Other Names	Medical Uses	Physical Dependence	Psychological Dependence	Tolerance	Duration (Hours)	Usual Method	Possible Effects	Effects of Overdose	Withdrawal Syndrome
Stimulants											
Cocaine[1]	II	Coke, Flake, Snow, Crack	Local anesthetic	Possible	High	Yes	1-2	Sniffed, smoked, injected	Increased alertness; Excitation; Euphoria; Increased pulse rate & blood pressure; Insomnia; Loss of appetite	Agitation; Increased body temperature; Hallucinations; Convulsions; Possible death	Apathy; Long periods of sleep; Irritability; Depression; Disorientation
Amphetamine/Methamphetamine	II	Biphetamine, Desoxyn, Dexedrine, Obetrol, Ice	Attention deficit disorder; Narcolepsy; Weight control	Possible	High	Yes	2-4	Oral, injected, smoked			
Methlphenidate	II	Ritalin	Attention deficit disorder; Narcolepsy; Weight control	Possible	High	Yes	2-4	Oral, injected			
Other stimulants	I, II, III, IV	Adipex, Didrex, Ionamin, Melfiat, Plegine, Captagon, Sanorex, Tenuate, Tepanil, Prelu-2, Preludin	Attention deficit disorder; Narcolepsy; Weight control	Possible	High	Yes	2-4	Oral, injected			
Cannabis											
Marijuana	I	Pot, Acapulco Gold, Grass, Reefer, Sinsemilla, Thai Sticks	None	Unknown	Moderate	Yes	2-4	Smoked, oral	Euphoria; Relaxed inhibitions; Increased appetite; Disorientation	Fatigue; Paranoia; Possible psychosis	Occasional reports of insomnia; Hyperactivity; Decreased appetite
Tetrahydrocannabinol	I, II	THC, Marinol	Antinauseant	Unknown	Moderate	Yes	2-4	Smoked, oral			
Hashish and Hashish Oil	I	Hash, Hash oil	None	Unknown	Moderate	Yes	2-4	Smoked, oral			
Hallucinogens											
LSD	I	Acid, Microdot	None	None	Unknown	Yes	8-12	Oral	Illusions and hallucinations; Altered perception of time and distance	Longer; More intense "trip" episodes; Psychosis; Possible death	Unknown
Mescaline and Peyote	I	Mescal, Buttons, Cactus	None	None	Unknown	Yes	8-12	Oral			
Amphetamine Variants	I	2, 5-DMA, STP, MDA, MDMA, Ecstasy, DOM, DOB	None	Unknown	Unknown	Yes	Variable	Oral, injected			
Phencyclidine and Analogs	I, II	PCE, PCPy, TCP, PCP, Hog, Loveboat, Angel Dust	None	Unknown	High	Yes	Days	Oral, smoked			
Other Hallucinogens	I	Bufotenine, Ibogaine, DMT, DET, Psilocybin, Psilocyn	None	None	Unknown	Possible	Variable	Smoked, oral, injected, sniffed			
Anabolic Steriods											
Testosterone (Cypionate, Enanthate)	III	Depo-Testosterone, Delatestryl	Hypogonadism	Unknown	Unknown	Unknown	14-28 days	Injected	Virilization; Acne; Testicular atrophy; Gynecomastia; Agressive behavior; Edema	Unknown	Possible depression
Nandrolone (Decanoate, Phenpropionate)	III	Nortestosterone, Durabolin, Deca-Durabolin, Deca	Anemia; Breast cancer	Unknown	Unknown	Unknown	14-21 days	Injected			
Oxymetholone	III	Anadrol-50	Anemia	Unknown	Unknown	Unknown	24	Oral			

1 Designated a narcotic under the CSA
2 Not designated a narcotic under the CSA

SOURCE: "Controlled Substances Uses and Abuses," in *Drugs of Abuse*, U.S. Drug Enforcement Agency, Arlington, VA, 1996

TABLE 2.2

Regulatory requirements for controlled substances

	Schedule I	Schedule II	Schedule III	Schedule IV	Schedule V
Registration	Required	Required	Required	Required	Required
Recordkeeping	Separate	Separate	Readily retrievable	Readily retrievable	Readily retrievable
Distribution Restrictions	Order forms	Order forms	Records required	Records required	Records required
Dispensing Limits	Research use only	Rx: written; no refills	Rx: written or oral; refills Note 1	Rx: written or oral; refills Note 1	OTC (Rx drugs limited to MD's order)
Manufacturing Security	Vault/safe	Vault/safe	Secure storage area	Secure storage area	Secure storage area
Manufacturing Quotas	Yes	Yes	No, but some drugs limited by Schedule II	No, but some drugs limited by Schedule II	No, but some drugs limited by Schedule II
Import/Export Narcotic	Permit	Permit	Permit	Permit	Permit to Import; declaration to export
Import/Export Non-Narcotic	Permit	Permit	Note 2	Declaration	Declaration
Reports to DEA by Manufacturer/Distributor Narcotic	Yes	Yes	Yes	Manufacturer only	Manufacturer only
Reports to DEA by Manufacturer/Distributor Non-Narcotic	Yes	Yes	Note 3	Note 3	No

Note 1: With medical authorization, refills up to 5 in 6 months
Note 2: Permit for some drugs, declaration for others
Note 3: Manufacturer reports required for specific drugs

SOURCE: "Regulatory Requirements: Controlled Substances," in *Drugs of Abuse*, U.S. Drug Enforcement Agency, Arlington, VA, 1996

The main source of nonsynthetic narcotics is resin from the poppy *Papaver somniferum*. (See Figure 2.1.) Opium gum is produced from the resin, which is scraped by hand from cut, unripe seedpods and air-dried.

A more modern method of harvesting, known as the industrial poppy straw process, involves extracting alkaloids (organic compounds found in living organisms) from the mature dried plant. The extract may be in a number of forms. Most poppy straw concentrate made available commercially is a fine brownish powder with a distinct odor.

Opium

Opium can come in several forms, but it usually appears as dark brown chunks or powder that can be either smoked or eaten. The Drug Enforcement Administration (DEA) claims that there is little opium abuse in this country because of laws governing the production and distribution of narcotic substances. Numerous drugs derived from, or chemically similar to, opium, however, are popular in the United States.

At least 25 alkaloids, which are divided into two general categories, can be extracted from opium. Drugs of the first type, represented by morphine and codeine, are used as analgesics (pain relievers) and cough suppressants, and are known as phenanthrene alkaloids. Those in the second group, isoquinoline alkaloids, are used as intestinal relaxants and also as cough suppressants.

Isoquinoline alkaloids have no significant influence on the central nervous system and are not regulated under the Controlled Substances Act. Virtually all of the opium imported into this country is broken down into alkaloid constituents—principally morphine and codeine.

Morphine

Morphine is one of the most effective drugs known for pain relief, as well as the principal ingredient of opium. It is marketed in a variety of forms, including oral solutions, sustained-release tablets, and injectable preparations. It is odorless and bitter, and darkens with age. Morphine can be administered orally, subcutaneously, intramuscularly, or intravenously—the latter method being the one most frequently used by drug addicts. Tolerance and dependence develop rapidly in the user.

Morphine is used legally only in hospitals or hospices, usually to control the terrible pain resulting from such illnesses as cancer. Only a small portion of the morphine obtained from opium is used medicinally; most is converted to codeine and, secondarily, to hydromorphone.

Codeine

Codeine is found in raw opium. Although it occurs naturally, most is produced from morphine. Compared with morphine, codeine produces less pain relief, but it also produces less sedation and respiratory depression. It is used for moderate pain relief by itself or combined with other products, such as aspirin or acetaminophen (Tylenol). Robitussin A-C and Cheracol are examples of liquid codeine preparations. Codeine is the most widely used naturally occurring narcotic in medical treatment.

SEMISYNTHETIC NARCOTICS

Semisynthetic narcotics are derived by altering chemicals contained in opium. The two most commonly produced are heroin and hydromorphone.

Heroin

Heroin was first synthesized from morphine in 1874 but was not used extensively until the Bayer Company of Germany first began commercial production in 1898. It was widely accepted as a painkiller for years, with the medical profession largely unaware of its potential for addiction. The Harrison Narcotic Act of 1914 established control of heroin in the United States.

Pure heroin, a bitter white powder, is usually dissolved and injected. Heroin found "on the street" may vary in color from white to dark brown, depending on the amount of impurities left from the manufacturing process or the presence of additives, such as food coloring, cocoa, or brown sugar.

For many years, the typical "bag" (single dose) of street heroin weighed about 100 milligrams and frequently contained less than 10 percent actual heroin, with the remainder made up of sugar, starch, powdered milk, or quinine. By the 1990s, however, the national average of heroin purity ranged between 35 and 40 percent. In 1997 the highest-purity heroin was reported in cities in the Northeast, such as Philadelphia (79.5 percent) and New York City (62.5 percent).

"Black tar" heroin is popular in the western United States. A crudely processed form of heroin, black tar is manufactured illegally in Mexico and derives its name from its sticky, dark brown or black appearance. Black tar is often sold on the street in its tarlike state and can have purities ranging from 20 to 80 percent. It can be diluted with substances such as burnt cornstarch or converted into a powder. It is most commonly injected.

Until recently, heroin was usually injected—intravenously (the preferred method), subcutaneously ("skin popping"), or intramuscularly. The increased availability

FIGURE 2.1

Opium poppies. *(© Galen Rowell/CORBIS.)*

of high-purity heroin, however, meant that users could snort or smoke the drug, which contributed to an increase in heroin use. Snorting or smoking is likely more appealing to many abusers because it removes both the fear of contracting diseases through shared syringes (mainly HIV/AIDS and hepatitis) and the historical stigma attached to heroin use. However, once hooked, many abusers who started by snorting or smoking shift to intravenous use.

Because of the increased availability of heroin, the price of the drug has dropped—street-level prices are generally $10 to $20 a bag, or even less. As noted in Chapters 3 and 4, heroin abuse has risen markedly in recent years. Officials believe that this increase is primarily due to lower prices, easy availability, and higher purity.

SYMPTOMS AND RELATED PROBLEMS. Symptoms and signs of heroin use include euphoria, drowsiness, respiratory depression, constricted pupils, and nausea. Withdrawal symptoms include watery eyes, runny nose, yawning, loss of appetite, tremors, panic, chills, sweating, nausea, diarrhea, muscle cramps, and insomnia. Elevations in blood pressure, pulse, respiratory rate, and temperature occur as withdrawal progresses. Because heroin abusers are often unaware of the actual strength of the drug and its true contents, they are at risk of overdose.

Symptoms of overdose, which may result in death, include shallow breathing, clammy skin, convulsions, and coma. According to medical examiners, heroin is the second most frequently reported drug in drug-abuse deaths.

Sharing unsterilized needles with other addicts increases the risk of exposure to HIV (human immunodeficiency virus), the virus that causes AIDS (acquired immunodeficiency syndrome). The use of heroin, as well as the self-abusing lifestyle that often accompanies its use, may compromise the body's ability to withstand infection, compounding the devastating effects of HIV. As a result, drug abusers have become one of the fastest-growing groups of HIV sufferers in the United States.

Pregnant women addicted to heroin often give birth to babies addicted to heroin. These babies must go through painful withdrawal and may not develop normally. Some women give birth to children carrying HIV, some of whom will eventually develop AIDS. In addition, children born to addicted mothers are at greater risk of SIDS (sudden infant death syndrome), a disorder in which infants suddenly and inexplicably stop breathing and die.

Hydromorphone

Commonly called Dilaudid, hydromorphone is the second-oldest semisynthetic narcotic painkiller. It is shorter acting, more sedating, and two to eight times more intense than morphine. Highly abusable, it is highly sought after by addicts—usually through theft or fraudulent prescriptions. Hydromorphone tablets, which are stronger than liquid forms of the drug, may be dissolved and injected.

SYNTHETIC NARCOTICS

Unlike products derived directly or indirectly from narcotics of natural origin, synthetic narcotics are produced entirely in the laboratory. The primary objective of laboratory production is to produce a drug that will have the analgesic properties of morphine while minimizing the potential for addiction. The two products most widely available are meperidine and methadone, although both are still addictive.

Hydrocodone and Oxycodone

Hydrocodone and oxycodone are two of the most commonly prescribed narcotic painkillers in the United States. Although they are designed to have less euphoric effect than morphine, they are still highly sought after by recreational users and addicts. Like morphine, these drugs have enough potential for abuse that they are classified as Schedule II substances. (See Table 2.1.)

In 2001 the drug OxyContin, produced by Purdue Pharma L.P., received an enormous amount of media attention. Although the active ingredient, oxycodone, has been around for a long time in drugs such as Percocet and

Percodan, media and law enforcement seized on a new wave of use. OxyContin, which is sold in high-dosage time-release pills, can be easily swallowed, chewed, or even crushed and injected, for a heroin-like high. The manufacturer, after DEA pressure, agreed to try to produce its product in ways that had less potential for abuse.

Meperidine (Pethidine)

First introduced in the 1930s, meperidine parallels morphine's pain-relieving strength. It is the most widely used drug for relief of moderate to severe pain and is frequently used during childbirth and after operations. Tolerance and dependence develop with chronic use, and large doses can result in convulsions. Demerol and Pethadal are meperidine products.

Methadone and Related Drugs

Methadone was first synthesized by German scientists during World War II because of a shortage of morphine. Although its chemical makeup is unlike that of morphine or heroin, it produces many of the same effects as those drugs. It was introduced to the United States in 1947 and became widely used in the 1960s to help treat narcotic addicts.

The effects of methadone last up to 24 hours, and the drug is almost as effective when administered orally as by injection. Tolerance and dependence can develop, and in some metropolitan areas, methadone has become just another illegal drug. It has also emerged as an important cause of overdose deaths.

Levo-alpha-acetylmethadol (LAAM) is a closely related synthetic compound with an even longer duration of action (48–72 hours), allowing for fewer clinic visits and eliminating take-home medication. In 1994 it was approved for use in the treatment of narcotic addiction. Another close relative of methadone is propoxyphene, first marketed in 1957 under the trade name Darvon for the relief of mild to moderate pain. There is less chance of dependence, but also less pain relief. It has one-half to one-third the potency of codeine but is about ten times stronger than aspirin. Because of misuse, propoxyphene was placed in Schedule IV. (See Table 2.1.)

DEPRESSANTS

The Controlled Substances Act regulates depressants because they have a high potential for abuse and are associated with both physical and psychological dependence. Taken as prescribed by a physician, depressants may be beneficial for the relief of anxiety, irritability, and tension, as well as for the symptomatic relief of insomnia. When taken in excessive amounts, however, they produce a state of intoxication very similar to that of alcohol. Unlike most other illegal drugs, depressants (except for methaqualone) are rarely produced in secret laboratories. Instead, they are generally obtained through theft and fraudulent prescriptions and sold illegally on the black market.

Chloral Hydrate

The oldest of the hypnotic (sleep-inducing) drugs, chloral hydrate was first synthesized in 1832 and soon replaced alcohol, opium, and cannabis for bringing about sedation and sleep. Its effects are particularly similar to those of alcohol, and withdrawal symptoms resemble delirium tremens (the "DTs"). Cases of poisoning have occurred from mixing chloral hydrate with alcohol. Older adults are the most common abusers of this drug; it is not a street drug of choice.

Barbiturates

About 2,500 derivatives of barbituric acid have been synthesized, but only 15 are used medically. Small therapeutic doses calm nervous conditions, and larger doses cause sleep within a short period of time. A feeling of excitement precedes the sedation. Too large a dose can bring a person through stages of sedation, sleep, and coma to death caused by respiratory failure and cardiovascular complications.

Barbiturates are classified as ultrashort-, short-, intermediate-, and long-acting. Ultrashort-acting barbiturates produce anesthesia within one minute of intravenous delivery into the system. Pentathol, Brevital, and Surital are among those currently in medical use. Because of the rapid onset and brief duration of effect, these drugs are usually undesirable for purposes of abuse.

Short-acting and intermediate-acting barbiturates, including Nembutal, Seconal, and Amytal, with durations up to six hours, are very highly sought after by abusers. Long-acting barbiturates, such as Veronal, Luminal, and Mebaral, have onset times up to 1 hour and durations up to 16 hours. These are used medicinally as sedatives, hypnotics, and anticonvulsants.

Glutethimide and Methaqualone

Glutethimide (Doriden) was introduced in 1954 and methaqualone (Quaalude, Sopor) in 1965 as safe barbiturate substitutes. Usually prescribed for pain and sleep disturbance, in medically-approved doses they cause a feeling of calmness, drowsiness, and euphoria. They are administered orally and, in large doses, can cause tremors and altered sleep patterns.

Not long after its introduction, methaqualone became a drug of choice among drug users, who thought it was both nonaddictive and an aphrodisiac. Extensive use and abuse of methaqualone can cause hallucinations, anxiety, numbness, tingling, and even serious poisoning. In 1984 the United States stopped production and distribution of methaqualone pharmaceutical products because of growing abuse, and the drug was transferred to Schedule I of the Controlled Substances Act. Counterfeit copies containing diazepam (Valium), flurazepan, and phenobarbital are prevalent on the U.S. illicit drug market. In 1991 glutethimide was transferred to Schedule II because of its potential for abuse.

Benzodiazepines

Benzodiazepines are depressants that relieve anxiety, tension, and muscle spasms; produce sedation; and prevent convulsions. They have a relatively slow onset but long duration of action. They also have a greater margin of safety than other depressants. Benzodiazepines are among the most widely prescribed medications in the United States. Xanax (alprazolam), Librium (zepoxide), and Valium (diazepam) are in this group.

Prolonged use of excessive doses may result in physical and psychological dependence. Because benzodiazepines are eliminated from the body slowly, withdrawal symptoms generally develop slowly, usually 7 to 10 days after continued high doses are stopped. When these drugs are used illicitly, they are often taken with alcohol or marijuana to achieve a euphoric "high." Since benzodiazepines are generally legal, they are usually obtained by getting prescriptions from doctors or forging prescriptions. They are also bought illegally on the black market.

Rohypnol (flunitrazepam), another benzodiazepine, has become increasingly popular among young people. The drug, manufactured as a short-term treatment for severe sleeping disorders, is not marketed legally in the United States and must be smuggled in. It is widely known as a "date-rape drug" because rapists frequently drop it secretly into a woman's drink to facilitate sexual assault. Several states—including Florida, Idaho, Minnesota, New Mexico, North Dakota, Oklahoma, and Pennsylvania—placed the drug under Schedule I control, and the United States has banned its importation and imposed stiff federal penalties for its sale. Responding to pressure from the American government, the Mexican producer of Rohypnol, Roche, began putting a blue dye in the pill so that it could be seen when dissolved in a drink.

STIMULANTS

Potent stimulants make users feel stronger, more decisive, and self-possessed. Because of the buildup effect, chronic users often develop a pattern of using "uppers" in the morning and "downers," such as alcohol or sleeping pills, at night. Such manipulation interferes with normal body processes and can lead to mental and physical illness. Large doses can produce paranoia and auditory and visual hallucinations.

Overdoses can also produce dizziness, tremors, agitation, hostility, panic, headaches, flushed skin, chest pain with palpitations, excessive sweating, vomiting, and abdominal cramps. Chronic high-dose users exhibit profound depression, apathy, fatigue, and disturbed sleep for

FIGURE 2.2

Refined cocaine. (© *Francoise de Mulder/CORBIS.*)

commonly, it is mixed with water and injected—which brings a more intense high because the drug reaches the brain more quickly.

For some time, people thought cocaine was relatively safe from undesirable side effects. This is not true for those who become heavy users. Cocaine produces a very short but extremely powerful rush of energy and confidence. Because the pleasurable effects are so intense, cocaine can lead to severe mental dependency, destroying a person's life as the need for the drug supersedes any other considerations. Physically, cocaine users risk permanent damage to their noses by exposing the cartilage and dissolving the nasal septum, resulting in a collapsed nose. Cocaine significantly increases the risk of heart attack in the first hour after use. Heavy use (two grams or more a week) impairs memory, decision making, and manual dexterity.

In the 1970s cocaine was popularly accepted as a recreational drug—particularly by the wealthy, who were among the few who could afford to use it. The coming years, however, would see a development that would bring cocaine to the masses: "crack."

Crack

Freebasing is a process in which dissolved cocaine is mixed with ether or rum and sodium hydroxide, or baking powder. The salt base dissolves, leaving granules of pure cocaine, which are then heated in a pipe until they vaporize. The vapor is inhaled directly into the lungs, causing an immediate high that lasts about 10 minutes.

There is a danger of being badly burned if the open flame gets too close to the ether or the rum and ignites. The dangers inherent in freebasing may have been the catalyst for the development of crack cocaine. When actor-comedian Richard Pryor set himself on fire while freebasing in 1980, many users started to search for a safer way to achieve the same high.

Cocaine hydrochloride, the powdered form of cocaine, is soluble in water, can be injected, and is fairly insensitive to heat. When cocaine hydrochloride is converted to cocaine base, it yields a substance that becomes volatile when heated. "Crack" is processed by mixing cocaine with baking soda and heating it to remove the hydrochloride rather than by the more volatile method of using ether. The resultant chips, or "rocks," of pure cocaine are usually smoked in a pipe or added to a cigarette or marijuana joint. (See Figure 2.3 and Figure 2.4.)

Crack gets its name from the "cracking" sound it makes when smoked. Inhaling the cocaine fumes produces a rapid, intense, and short-lived effect. This incredible intensity is followed within minutes by an abnormally disconcerting and anxious "crash," which leads almost

up to 20 hours when going through withdrawal, which may last for several days.

Cocaine

Cocaine, the most potent stimulant of natural origin, is extracted from the leaves of the coca plant (*Erythroxylon coca*), which has been cultivated in the Andean highlands of South America since prehistoric times. The coca leaves are frequently chewed for refreshment and relief from fatigue—in much the same way some North Americans chew tobacco.

Pure cocaine was first isolated in the 1880s and used as a local anesthetic in eye surgery. In the late nineteenth and early twentieth centuries it became popular in this country as an anesthetic for nose and throat surgery. Since then, other drugs, such as lidocaine and novocaine, have replaced it as an anesthetic.

Illicit cocaine is distributed as a white crystalline powder, often contaminated, or "cut," with sugars or local anesthetics. (See Figure 2.2.) The drug is commonly sniffed, or "snorted," through the nasal passages. Less

FIGURE 2.3

FIGURE 2.4

Crack pipe. *(Corbis Corporation (Bellevue).)*

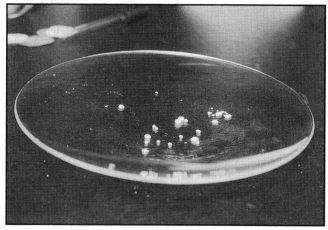

Crack granules. *(© Roger Ressmeyer/CORBIS.)*

inevitably to the need for more of the drug—and a great likelihood of addiction.

MARKETING CRACK. The mass marketing of crack began in the early 1980s. A glut of powdered cocaine had saturated the market, driving down prices and cutting into dealers' profits. This coincided with the discovery of a new form of cocaine—one that was highly addictive and could easily "hook" a user after just a few tries.

Experimenters in the Caribbean developed the first prototypes of crack by mixing cocaine with baking soda, water, and rum. At that time, most cocaine was being shipped to the United States through the extensive islands and cays of the Bahamas, and a sizable portion of it was being diverted to the local population.

When dealers saw the attraction that this new product had for Bahamian users, they were quick to realize the potential profits that could be made by introducing it on the streets of the United States—first in Miami, Los Angeles, and New York. Pushers in those cities began to offer crack at low prices, knowing that users would quickly become addicted and come back for more.

Once introduced in the mid-1980s, crack spread rapidly. The most convenient distribution method was to use inner-city street gangs, because they were located in areas with the heaviest concentration of drug users. Also, since crack sold for only $5 to $10 a hit, it could easily be sold to poor people living in these areas. Expanding from the three source cities (Miami, Los Angeles, and New York), interstate and intrastate transport spread crack across the nation.

Although crack spread rapidly in the early 1980s and received a lot of attention from the media and government, it faded from view somewhat in the 1990s. Crack use dropped throughout the 1990s, news stories stopped appearing, and the government began to focus its attention on other drugs, such as methamphetamine and ecstasy.

Amphetamines

The history of the illicit use of amphetamines is very much like that of cocaine. Amphetamines were first marketed in the 1930s, under the name Benzedrine, in an over-the-counter inhaler to treat nasal congestion. Abuse of these inhalers soon became popular among teenagers and prisoners. In 1937 Benzedrine became available in pill form, and the number of abusers quickly increased.

Medically, amphetamines are used mainly to treat depression, narcolepsy (a rare disorder resulting in an uncontrollable desire to sleep), hyperactive disorders in children (now called attention deficit hyperactivity disorder), and certain cases of obesity. During World War II pilots took Benzedrine to stay awake.

"Speed freaks," who injected amphetamines, became famous in the drug culture for their strange and often violent behavior. In 1965 federal food and drug laws were amended to curb the growing black market in amphetamines. Many legal drugs using amphetamines were removed from the market, and doctors began prescribing them less frequently. As a result, clandestine laboratories increased their production to meet the growing black-market demand. Today, most amphetamines are produced in these clandestine laboratories.

Extended amphetamine use can lead to a number of health problems. Short-term effects include sleeplessness, which can lead to, and compound, psychotic episodes brought on by heavy use. Long-term effects are unknown, although it is suspected that chronic amphetamine use may contribute to neurological damage, such as the development of Parkinson's disease.

Methamphetamines

Methamphetamines were first developed by a Japanese pharmacologist in 1919. The drug came to market during the 1930s as a treatment for narcolepsy, attention deficit disorder, and obesity. A form of the drug often referred to as "speed" became popular during the 1960s and led to government control over the manufacture of the drug. Methamphetamine abuse fell off in the 1970s as cocaine became increasingly available. In later years, however, its use increased dramatically.

Methamphetamines have traditionally been distributed by outlaw motorcycle gangs and other independent producers. While these groups still play a role in the drug's sale, traffickers operating out of Mexico have taken over major distribution. Using money raised from the sale of other drugs, they have built sophisticated new laboratories that produce large quantities of the drug. At first, these traffickers limited distribution to the western United States, but they have since expanded their distribution channels well into the Midwest.

Methamphetamines can be either injected or inhaled. To make the drug more attractive, Mexican traffickers have increased its purity. This has made it easier to inhale and, therefore, more attractive to potential users who might be concerned about the dangers of using syringes.

The effects of methamphetamines are similar to those of cocaine, but their onset is slower and they last longer. Abusers frequently become paranoid, pick at their skin, and suffer from auditory and/or visual hallucinations. Chronic abusers may exhibit violent and erratic behavior. Methamphetamines are associated with such health conditions as memory loss and heart and brain damage. Crystallized methamphetamine hydrochloride, or "ice," is a smokable form of methamphetamine.

Methcathinone—"Cat"

"Cat," or methcathinone, a more recent drug of abuse in the United States, was placed into Schedule I of the Controlled Substances Act in 1993. "Cat" is produced in clandestine laboratories and is usually snorted, although it can be mixed in a beverage and taken orally or diluted in water and injected intravenously.

Methcathinone has about the same abuse potential as methamphetamine and produces similar results: excessive energy, hyperactivity, extended wakefulness, and loss of appetite. The user feels both euphoric and invincible. At the same time, use of "cat" can lead to anxiety, tremors, insomnia, weight loss, sweating, stomach pains, a pounding heart, nose bleeds, and body aches. Excessive use can lead to convulsions, paranoia, hallucinations, and depression.

Phenmetrazine (Preludin) and Methylphenidate (Ritalin)

Abuse patterns of these drugs are similar to those of other stimulants. Preludin is used medically as an appetite suppressant, and Ritalin, frequently prescribed by physicians, is used mainly to treat children with attention deficit disorders. These drugs are most subject to abuse in countries where they are easily available, such as in the United States.

Recent debates have arisen regarding the overprescription of Ritalin. Some estimates have concluded that in the United States alone, 3 million children are being treated with some amphetamine—usually Ritalin—for attention deficit disorders. Opponents of Ritalin prescription argue that the diagnosis of attention deficit hyperactivity disorder (ADHD) is simply a way of labeling children who make classroom management difficult and medicating them so they will stop acting out. Proponents argue that ADHD is a very serious medical condition and that stimulant drugs are necessary in helping children with the condition develop correctly. Experts on both sides, though, agree that the ADHD diagnosis is sometimes applied, and medication prescribed, in cases where it is unnecessary.

Anorectic Drugs

These drugs are relatively recent attempts to replace amphetamines as appetite depressants. They produce many of the same effects but are generally less potent. Abuse patterns have not been determined, but all drugs in this group are classified as controlled substances because of their similarity to amphetamines. They include Didrex, Pre-Sate, Tenuate, Tepanil, Pondimin, Mazanor, Ionamin, Adipex-P, and Sanorex.

Khat

Khat is a natural substance that comes from the fresh young leaves of the *Catha edulis* shrub, which grows primarily in East Africa and the Arabian peninsula. People in these areas have been chewing khat for centuries, often in communal social situations—the same way Americans drink coffee or tea. Chewed in moderation, khat alleviates fatigue and reduces appetite. Excessive use may result in paranoia and hallucinations. Khat contains many chemicals that are controlled substances, including cathinone (Schedule I) and cathine (Schedule IV).

HALLUCINOGENS

Hallucinogenic drugs, or psychedelics, are natural or synthetic substances that distort the appearance of reality. They cause excitation, which can vary from a sense of well-being to severe depression. Time may appear to stand still, and forms and colors seem to change and take on new meaning. The heart rate may increase, blood pressure rise, and pupils dilate. The experience may be pleasurable or extremely frightening. The effects of hallucinogens are unpredictable each time they are used.

The most common danger of using hallucinogens is impaired judgment, which can lead to rash decisions and accidents. Long after hallucinogens have been eliminated from the body, users may experience "flashbacks," such as perceived intensity of color, the apparent motion of fixed objects, or the mistaking of one object for another.

Some hallucinogens come from natural sources, such as mescaline from the peyote cactus, and some, such as LSD, are synthetic. The abuse of hallucinogens in the United States peaked in the late 1960s, but the 1990s saw a resurgence in the use of these drugs.

Peyote and Mescaline

Mescaline is the primary active ingredient of the peyote cactus, *Lophophor williamsii*, a small, spineless plant native to Mexico and the southwestern United States. The top of the cactus, often called the crown, is made up of disk-shaped buttons that can be cut off and dried. These buttons are generally chewed or soaked in water to produce an intoxicating liquid. A dose of 350 to 500 milligrams produces hallucinations lasting from 5 to 12 hours. Mescaline can be extracted from peyote or produced synthetically.

Peyote and mescaline have long been used by American Indians in religious ceremonies. Recently, however, this use has come into serious question. In 1990 the U.S. Supreme Court, in *Employment Division, Department of Human Resources v. Smith* (494 US 872), ruled that the state of Oregon could bar the Native American Church from using peyote in its religious ceremonies. The passage of the Religious Freedom Restoration Act of 1993 (PL 103-141) allowed the church to use peyote in those ceremonies; but in 1997 the Supreme Court, in *Boerne v. Flores* (65 LW 4612), declared the Religious Freedom Restoration Act unconstitutional.

Arizona law allows the use of peyote in connection with the practice of a religious belief if it is an integral part of a religious exercise and if it is used in a manner not dangerous to public health. In general, the Native American Church is the only recognized organization with a bona fide claim that peyote is a sacrament in its rituals.

DOM, DOB, MDA, MDMA, and "Designer Drugs"

DOM (4-methyl-2,5-mimethoxyamphetamine), DOB (4-bromo-2,5-dimethoxyamphetamine), MDA (3,4-methylenedioxyamphetamine), MDMA (3,4 methylenedioxymethamphetamine), and "designer drugs" are chemical variations of mescaline and amphetamines that have been synthesized in the laboratory. They differ from one another in speed of onset, duration of action, and potency. They are usually taken orally, and sometimes snorted, but rarely injected intravenously.

Because they are produced illegally, these drugs are seldom pure, and dosage quantity and quality vary considerably. These drugs are often used at "raves"—large, all-night dance parties once held in unusual places such as warehouses or railroad yards. Although many raves are now mainstream events, professionally organized and held at public venues, the underground style and culture of raves remains an alluring draw to many teenagers. Part of the allure is the drug use.

The most noted designer drug, MDMA (also called ADAM, ecstasy, or X-TC) was first banned by the DEA in 1985. Widespread abuse placed it in Schedule I of the Controlled Substances Act. Early proponents of MDMA believed it was not harmful—and even helped break down barriers between therapists and patients and between family members—but this has been found to be untrue.

Users of MDMA have been known to suffer serious psychological effects—including confusion, depression, sleep problems, drug craving, severe anxiety, and paranoia—both during, and sometimes weeks after, taking the drug. Physical symptoms include muscle tension, involuntary teeth clenching, nausea, blurred vision, rapid eye movement, faintness, and chills or sweating.

MDA, the parent drug of MDMA, has been found to destroy serotonin-producing neurons, which play a direct role in regulating aggression, mood, sexual activity, sleep, and pain sensitivity. This may explain the sense of heightened sexual experience, tranquility, and conviviality said to accompany MDA use. The Anti-Drug Abuse Act of 1986 (PL 99-570) made all designer drugs illegal.

LSD (LSD-25, Lysergide)

LSD, an abbreviation of the German term for lysergic acid diethylamide, is one of the most potent mood-changing chemicals in existence. Odorless, colorless, and tasteless, it is produced from a substance derived from ergot fungus or from a chemical found in morning glory seeds. Both chemicals are found in Schedule III of the Controlled Substances Act.

LSD is usually sold in tablets ("microdots"), thin squares of gelatin ("window panes"), or impregnated paper ("blotter acid"). Effects of doses higher than 30 to 50 micrograms can persist for 10 to 12 hours, severely impairing judgment and decision making. Tolerance develops rapidly, and more of the drug is needed to achieve the desired effect.

Dr. Albert Hoffman originally synthesized LSD in 1938, but it was not until 1943 that he accidentally took the drug and recorded his "trip." He was aware of vertigo and an intensification of light. During the two-hour experience, he also saw a stream of fantastically vivid images, coupled with an unusual play of colors.

Because of its structural similarity to a chemical present in the brain, LSD was originally used as a research tool to study the mechanism of mental illness. It was later adopted by the drug culture of the 1960s. During the 1960s LSD use was seen by users and nonusers alike as central to full participation in the emerging counterculture movement. Such major icons as author Ken Kesey and Harvard professor Timothy Leary began to promote a culture in which certain political values and drug use were almost synonymous.

FIGURE 2.5

Budding cannabis plant. (© Bill Lisenby/CORBIS.)

LSD use dropped in the 1980s but showed a resurgence in the 1990s. It is inexpensive ($2 to $10 for 80 micrograms) and nonaddictive, and one hit can last for 8 to 12 hours. Many young people have rediscovered the drug, taking it in a liquid form dropped on the tongue or in the eyes with an eye dropper, or by placing impregnated blotter paper on their tongues.

Phencyclidine (PCP) and Related Drugs

Many drug-treatment professionals believe that phencyclidine (PCP) poses greater risks to the user than any other drug. PCP was originally investigated in the 1950s as an anesthetic but was discontinued for human use because of its side effects, which included confusion and delirium. The drug is still occasionally used on animals, but even many veterinarians are now turning away from it.

In the United States, virtually all PCP is manufactured in clandestine laboratories and sold on the black market. This drug is sold under at least 50 different names, many of which reflect its bizarre and volatile effects: Angel Dust, Crystal, Supergrass, Killer Weed, Embalming Fluid, Rocket Fuel. It is often sold to users who think they are buying mescaline or LSD.

In its pure form, PCP is a white crystalline powder that readily dissolves in water. It can also be taken in tablet or capsule form. It can be swallowed, sniffed, smoked, or injected. It is commonly applied to a leafy material, such as parsley, mint, oregano, or marijuana, and smoked.

Because PCP is an anesthetic, it produces an inability to feel pain, which can lead to serious bodily injury. Unlike other hallucinogens, PCP produces depression in some individuals. Regular use often impairs memory, perception, concentration, motor movement, and judgment. PCP can also produce a psychotic state in many ways indistinguishable from schizophrenia, or lead to hallucinations, mood swings, paranoia, and amnesia.

Because of the extreme psychic disorders associated with repeated use, or even one dose, of PCP and related drugs, Congress passed the Psychotropic Substances Act of 1978 (PL 95-633). The penalties imposed for the manufacture or possession of these chemicals are the stiffest of any nonnarcotic violation under the Controlled Substances Act.

CANNABIS

Cannabis sativa, the hemp plant from which marijuana is made, grows wild throughout most of the world's tropic and temperate regions, including Mexico, the Middle East, Africa, and India. (See Figure 2.5.) For centuries, its therapeutic potential has been explored, including uses as an analgesic and anticonvulsant. But with the advent of new, synthetic drugs and the passage of the Marijuana Tax Act of 1937, interest in marijuana—even for medicinal purposes—faded. In 1970 the Controlled Substances Act classified marijuana as a Schedule I drug, having "no currently accepted medical use in treatment in the United States."

Cannabis plants are usually smoked in the form of loosely rolled cigarettes ("joints") or in various kinds of pipes. The effects are felt within minutes, usually peaking in 10 to 30 minutes and lingering for two to three hours. Low doses induce restlessness and an increasing sense of well-being, followed by a dreamy state of relaxation and, frequently, hunger. Changes in sensory perception—a more vivid sense of sight, smell, touch, taste, and hearing—may occur, with subtle alterations in thought formation and expression. Drugs made from the cannabis plant are widely distributed on the U.S. black market.

Marijuana

Marijuana is a tobacco-like substance produced by drying the leaves and flowery top of the cannabis plant. Its potency varies considerably, depending on how much of the chemical THC (delta-9-tetrahydrocannabinol) is present. Most wild U.S. cannabis, with a THC content of less than 0.5 percent, is considered inferior to Jamaican, Colombian, and Mexican varieties, whose THC content ranges between 0.5 and 0.7 percent.

The most potent form of marijuana is *sinsemilla* (Spanish for "without seed"), which comes from the unpollinated female cannabis plant and can contain up to 17 percent THC. Another potent form, Southeast Asian "Thai stick" (marijuana buds bound into short sections of bamboo), is not often found in the United States.

Marijuana is grown illegally throughout the United States, both indoors and outdoors. Growers generally try to achieve the highest possible THC content in order to produce the greatest possible effect. It is thought that most marijuana smoked in the United States is grown in the United States. Street names for marijuana include "pot," "grass," "weed," "Mary Jane," and "reefer."

USE AND EFFECTS. Marijuana is the most extensively used illicit drug in this country. During the 1960s and 1970s it was as common at many parties as beer and wine. In 1997 an estimated 71 million Americans—or about one-third of the population age 12 and over—had tried marijuana.

Extensive research by the National Institute on Drug Abuse (NIDA) uncovered the effect that THC has on the hippocampus, a part of the brain that is crucial for learning, memory, and the integration of sensory experiences with emotions and motivation. Many feel that these studies, when taken together, may explain the euphoria and memory loss induced by marijuana, as well as provide definitive proof of the drug's toxic effect on brain nerve cells.

UCLA scientists found that smoking one to three marijuana cigarettes produces the same lung damage and potential cancer risk as smoking five times as many cigarettes. NIDA reports that marijuana adversely affects reproductive function, potentially causing sterility.

The immediate physical effects of marijuana include a faster heartbeat (by as much as 50 percent), bloodshot eyes, and a dry mouth and throat. It can reduce short-term memory, alter one's sense of time, and reduce concentration and coordination. Some users experience light-headedness and giddiness, while others feel depressed and sad. Many users have also reported experiencing severe anxiety attacks.

Although symptoms usually disappear in about four to six hours, it takes about three days for 50 percent of the drug to be broken down and eliminated from the body. It takes three weeks to completely excrete the THC from one marijuana cigarette. If a user smokes two joints a week, it takes months for all traces of the THC to disappear from the body.

SUPPORT FOR PATIENT USE. In the past marijuana has been used to treat glaucoma and several neurological disorders. However, an Institute of Medicine (IOM) report concluded that the drug was not useful in glaucoma treatment because its effects were short-lived. The report also indicated that marijuana was ineffective in treating patients suffering from Parkinson's or Huntington's diseases. According to one of the principal investigators for the IOM, John Benson, Jr., the medical effects of marijuana are generally modest, and only patients who do not respond well to other medications should use it. Marijuana appears to be useful in treating conditions such as chemotherapy-induced nausea or the wasting caused by AIDS. It may also help relieve muscle spasms associated with multiple sclerosis.

In May 1991 nearly half of all cancer specialists who responded to an unofficial Harvard University survey said that they would prescribe marijuana for some of their patients if the drug were legal. A somewhat smaller percentage said that despite the drug's illegal status, they had already recommended it to patients as a means of enhancing appetite and relieving chemotherapy-related nausea.

As noted at the beginning of this chapter, one of the criteria used by the Drug Enforcement Administration (DEA) in classifying drugs is whether there is a "currently accepted medical use in treatment in the United States." In 1988 Francis Young, the administrative judge of the DEA, noted that marijuana "in its natural form, is one of the safest therapeutically active substances known to man" and recommended that physicians be authorized to use it. The DEA refused to relax the restrictions.

In 1991 the Massachusetts Supreme Court, in *Massachusetts v. Hutchins* (49 CRL 1442), ruled that society's interest in preventing illegal drug use outweighed a patient's "medical necessity" to use marijuana. The defendant, who began growing his own marijuana when he was unable to get government approval to use the drug to relieve the pain of his chronic illness, had been charged with possession and cultivation of the cannabis plant.

SUPREME COURT UPHOLDS THE DEA ON MARIJUANA RESCHEDULING. Over the past two decades, a number of legal attempts have been made to get marijuana rescheduled from Schedule I, the most restrictive classification, to a less restrictive schedule. The first petition was filed in 1972 and reached the Court of Appeals of the District of Columbia four times: *National Organization for the Reform of Marijuana Laws v. Ingersoll* (497 F.2d 654, 1974), *National Organization for the Reform of Marijuana Laws v. Drug Enforcement Administration* (559 F.2d 735, 1977), *National Organization for the Reform of Marijuana Laws v. Drug Enforcement Administration & Department of Health, Education and Welfare* (No. 79-1660, 1980), and *Alliance for Cannabis Therapeutics and The National Organization for the Reform of Marijuana Laws v. Drug Enforcement Administration* (930 F.2d 936, 1991). All of these petitions failed.

In the latest attempt, *Alliance for Cannabis Therapeutics and Drug Policy Foundation v. Drug Enforcement Administration* (15 F.3d 1131, 1994), the petitioners claimed that the DEA had failed to recognize that "marijuana is misclassified because it has been shown to serve various medicinal purposes . . . marijuana alleviates some side effects of chemotherapy in cancer patients, aids in the treatment of glaucoma and eye diseases, and reduces muscle spasticity in patients suffering from multiple sclerosis and other maladies of the central nervous system."

In support of their case, the petitioners submitted affidavits and testimonials from a number of patients and doctors who said marijuana had been helpful in treatment. The Food and Drug Administration (FDA) claimed that the testimonials were not scientific proof and that no scientific study had shown that marijuana was useful in medical treatment.

The FDA claimed that, when questioned under oath, each witness supporting the rescheduling of marijuana "admitted he was basing his opinion on anecdotal evidence, on stories he heard from patients, and on his impressions about the drug." The appeals court agreed with the FDA that "only rigorous scientific proof can satisfy" the requirements needed to change marijuana's rating and let the FDA's position stand.

THE MEDICAL USE OF MARIJUANA—A POLITICAL ISSUE OR A SCIENTIFIC ISSUE?. By the late 1990s voters in nine states—Alaska, Arizona, California, Colorado, Hawaii, Maine, Nevada, Oregon, and Washington—had approved initiatives intended to make marijuana legal for medical purposes. However, the initiatives were ineffective. The federal government threatened to prosecute doctors who wrote prescriptions for marijuana. And patients found it increasingly difficult to obtain the drug, especially since the federal government started closing down "buyers' clubs," or organizations that distribute medical marijuana to seriously ill patients who wouldn't be able to obtain it otherwise.

In 1997 the White House Office of National Drug Control Policy (ONDCP) made an effort to take the issue out of the political arena and place it in the scientific arena. The ONDCP asked the Institute of Medicine (IOM), a private, nonprofit organization that provides health-policy advice to Congress, to review the scientific evidence on the potential health benefits and risks of marijuana. Following an 18-month study, the investigators concluded that "the future of cannabinoid drugs lies not in smoked marijuana, but in chemically defined drugs that act on . . . human physiology." Rigorous clinical trials, along with the development of new delivery mechanisms for the drug, were among the recommendations of the IOM's report.

Hashish

Hashish is made from the THC-rich resinous material of the cannabis plant. This resin is collected, dried, and compressed into a variety of forms, including balls, cakes, and sticks. Pieces are then broken off and smoked. Most hashish comes from the Middle East, North Africa, Pakistan, and Afghanistan. The THC content of hashish in the United States hovered around 6 percent during the 1990s. Demand in this country is limited.

Hash Oil

Hash oil is not related to hashish. Hash oil is produced by extracting the cannabinoids from the cannabis plant with a solvent. The color and odor of hash oil depend on the solvent used. Most recently, seized hash oil has ranged from amber to dark brown with about 15 percent THC. In terms of effect, a drop or two of hash oil on a cigarette is equal to a single "joint" of marijuana.

ANABOLIC STEROIDS

Anabolic steroids are drugs derived from the male sex hormone testosterone. They are used illegally by some weight lifters, bodybuilders, long-distance runners, cyclists, and others who believe that these drugs can give them a competitive advantage or improve their physical appearance. When used in combination with exercise training and a high-protein diet, anabolic steroids can lead to increased size and strength of muscles, improved endurance, and shorter recovery time between workouts.

Steroids are taken orally or by intramuscular injection. Most are smuggled into the United States and sold at gyms and competitions or by mail-order companies. The most commonly used steroids include boldenone (Equipoise), ethylestrenol (Maxibolin), fluoxymesterone (Halotestin), methandriol, methandrostenolone (Dianabol), methyltestosterone, nandrolone (Durabolin, Deca-Durabolin), oxandrolone (Anavar), oxymetholone (Anadrol), stanozolol (Winstrol), testosterone, and trenbolone (Finajet).

Steroid use was once considered a problem limited to professional athletes, but recent surveys estimate that 5 to 12 percent of male high school students and 1 percent of female students use steroids by the time they are seniors. Concerns about the drug led Congress, in 1991, to place anabolic steroids into Schedule III of the Controlled Substances Act.

Because concern about anabolic steroids is relatively recent, the adverse effects of large doses are not well established. Nonetheless, there is growing evidence of serious health problems, including cardiovascular damage, liver damage, and harm to reproductive organs. Physical side effects include elevated blood pressure and cholesterol levels, severe acne, premature balding, reduced sexual desire, and atrophying of the testicles. Males may develop breasts, while females may experience a deepening of the voice, increased body-hair growth, fewer menstrual cycles, and diminished breast size. Some of these effects can be irreversible. In adolescents, bone development may stop, causing stunted growth. Some users become violently aggressive.

CHAPTER 3
TRENDS IN DRUG USE

The *National Household Survey on Drug Abuse: Population Estimates 1998* (Substance Abuse and Mental Health Services Administration, Washington, D.C., 1999), hereafter referred to as the *National Survey*, is one of two major annual surveys generally considered the primary indicators of drug use in the United States. The other, *Monitoring the Future*, more commonly known as the *National High School Senior Survey,* is an ongoing research project performed by the University of Michigan's Institute of Social Research and funded by the National Institute on Drug Abuse. That survey will be discussed in Chapter 4.

The population surveyed for the *National Survey* consists of noninstitutionalized civilians living in households, college dormitories, homeless shelters, rooming houses, and military installations. The report does not include segments of the U.S. population that contain a substantial number of drug abusers—such as homeless who don't live in shelters and persons in city and county jails or state and federal prisons. Nevertheless, the survey is considered to be the most comprehensive analysis of drug use in America.

HAS THE DECLINE IN DRUG USE STOPPED?

The *National Survey* found that the number of respondents who used any illicit drug in the month prior to the survey (considered current use) began decreasing in 1979, with the decline accelerating between 1985 and 1988. In 1985, 23.3 million people (12 percent of the population aged 12 and over) had current prevalence (use) rates for at least one illicit drug. By 1988 the number had dropped to 15.2 million (7.7 percent of the population), a decline of 35 percent. By 1991 the number had dropped to 13.4 million people (6.6 percent) and, by 1993, 12.3 million (5.9 percent).

However, the 15-year decline in drug use came to an end in 1995, when the *National Survey* reported that 6.1 percent of respondents, or about 12.8 million people, had

used drugs in the month before the survey. By 1998 the figure had climbed slightly, to 6.2 percent, or about 13.6 million people (See Table 3.1.)

The 1998 *National Survey* indicated that close to 78 million Americans age 12 or older (35.8 percent of the population) had tried some illicit drug at least once in their lives. (See Table 3.1.) While the actual number of Americans who have used drugs has increased, the proportion has changed very little over the past few years.

Slightly more than 23 million people (10.6 percent of the population) used an illicit drug at least once during 1998. In all age groups, men were more likely than women to have used drugs, although the differences were considerably smaller in the 12–17 age group. Those over age 35 were much less likely to have used drugs than those in the 18–34 age group. (See Table 3.1.)

Tables 3.2–3.4 illustrate drug use by race and ethnicity. Whites (38.2 percent) were somewhat more likely to have ever used an illicit drug than were blacks (33.2 percent) or Hispanics (26.6 percent), but the study found that the rate of current use was somewhat higher for blacks (8.2 percent) than for whites (6.1 percent) and Hispanics (6.1 percent). The *National Survey* also found that current drug use was highest in the West (7.3 percent) and lowest in the South (5.5 percent). The North Central and Northeast regions had rates of 6.7 percent and 5.8 percent, respectively.

Marijuana Use

PREVALENCE. Marijuana, a Schedule I drug, remains the most commonly used illicit drug in the United States. It is used by 80 percent of current illicit drug users—either alone or with another illicit drug. Often associated with the antiestablishment culture of the 1960s, marijuana is considered by many to be the least objectionable of illicit drugs. Marijuana is almost always smoked in hand-rolled cigarettes or pipes but is occasionally ingested.

TABLE 3.1

Any illicit drug use by gender within age group for total population, 1998

AGE/ GENDER	Ever Used			Used Past Year			Used Past Month		
	Observed Estimate		95% C.I.	Observed Estimate		95% C.I.	Observed Estimate		95% C.I.
			RATE ESTIMATES (Percent)						
12-17	21.3		(19.9 - 22.8)	16.4		(15.1 - 17.7)	9.9		(8.9 - 11.1)
Male	22.1		(20.2 - 24.2)	16.7		(15.0 - 18.6)	10.3		(8.9 - 11.9)
Female	20.5		(18.3 - 22.9)	16.0		(14.2 - 18.0)	9.5		(8.0 - 11.4)
18-25	48.1		(45.9 - 50.3)	27.4		(25.5 - 29.4)	16.1		(14.7 - 17.7)
Male	54.1		(51.1 - 57.2)	32.6		(29.6 - 35.7)	20.5		(18.2 - 22.9)
Female	41.9		(39.2 - 44.7)	22.1		(19.6 - 24.8)	11.7		(10.1 - 13.6)
26-34	50.6		(48.5 - 52.6)	12.7		(11.4 - 14.1)	7.0		(6.0 - 8.2)
Male	56.3		(53.3 - 59.3)	16.2		(14.1 - 18.5)	9.8		(8.1 - 11.8)
Female	44.9		(42.1 - 47.7)	9.3		(7.9 - 10.9)	4.3		(3.4 - 5.5)
≥35	31.8		(29.9 - 33.8)	5.5		(4.8 - 6.3)	3.3		(2.8 - 3.9)
Male	38.4		(35.6 - 41.2)	7.2		(6.0 - 8.5)	4.4		(3.5 - 5.4)
Female	26.0		(23.9 - 28.2)	4.0		(3.3 - 4.9)	2.4		(1.8 - 3.1)
TOTAL	35.8		(34.3 - 37.2)	10.6		(9.9 - 11.3)	6.2		(5.7 - 6.8)
Male	41.6		(39.8 - 43.5)	13.1		(12.1 - 14.2)	8.1		(7.3 - 8.9)
Female	30.3		(28.6 - 32.1)	8.2		(7.5 - 9.0)	4.5		(4.0 - 5.1)
			POPULATION ESTIMATES (In Thousands)						
12-17	4,851		(4,533 - 5,185)	3,727		(3,441 - 4,032)	2,262		(2,020 - 2,529)
Male	2,570		(2,344 - 2,811)	1,944		(1,741 - 2,165)	1,200		(1,038 - 1,384)
Female	2,281		(2,035 - 2,548)	1,783		(1,581 - 2,006)	1,062		(889 - 1,265)
18-25	13,445		(12,839 - 14,053)	7,660		(7,134 - 8,211)	4,513		(4,103 - 4,956)
Male	7,645		(7,213 - 8,074)	4,601		(4,181 - 5,041)	2,890		(2,575 - 3,233)
Female	5,800		(5,427 - 6,180)	3,060		(2,717 - 3,432)	1,623		(1,400 - 1,876)
26-34	17,497		(16,792 - 18,202)	4,397		(3,954 - 4,882)	2,432		(2,085 - 2,831)
Male	9,670		(9,144 - 10,188)	2,778		(2,418 - 3,180)	1,680		(1,392 - 2,020)
Female	7,827		(7,343 - 8,316)	1,620		(1,378 - 1,899)	752		(589 - 957)
≥35	42,330		(39,780 - 44,966)	7,330		(6,394 - 8,395)	4,408		(3,721 - 5,218)
Male	23,897		(22,189 - 25,653)	4,475		(3,760 - 5,314)	2,725		(2,187 - 3,387)
Female	18,433		(16,955 - 19,993)	2,855		(2,343 - 3,474)	1,683		(1,304 - 2,169)
TOTAL	78,123		(74,948 - 81,357)	23,115		(21,588 - 24,737)	13,615		(12,473 - 14,855)
Male	43,782		(41,865 - 45,724)	13,797		(12,777 - 14,886)	8,494		(7,685 - 9,382)
Female	34,341		(32,372 - 36,376)	9,318		(8,487 - 10,223)	5,121		(4,530 - 5,784)

SOURCE: "Table 2A: Any Illicit Drug Use by Gender Within Age Group for Total Population in 1998" in *National Household Survey on Drug Abuse: Population Estimates 1998,* Substance Abuse and Mental Health Services Administration, Washington, D.C., 2000

Some users incorporate the drug into cigars. Several groups long advocated legislation on the state and federal level for the legalization and/or decriminalization of marijuana, and several states now permit its use for prescribed medical purposes.

One-third (33.0 percent) of all Americans 12 and older, or about 72 million people, have used marijuana at least once in their lives. Approximately 17 percent of youths (3.9 million), 44.6 percent of young adults (12.5 million), 47.9 percent of adults age 26–34 (16.6 million), and 29.4 percent of adults 35 and older (39.2 million) have tried the drug. (See Table 3.5.) Except for adults 26–34, a higher percentage of each group reported that they had used marijuana than had in 1995.

As of 1998 marijuana use was heaviest among those 18–25 years old. The figure of 13.8 percent for this age group was up from the 1995 figure of 12 percent but down sharply from 22 percent in 1985. The percentage of 12- to 17-year-olds who used marijuana in the month before the survey rose significantly, from 5 percent in 1993 to 8.3 percent (nearly 1 in 12) in 1998. About 5.5 percent of those 26–34 years old reported current use, compared with 2.5 percent of those 35 and older. (See Table 3.5.)

FREQUENCY OF MARIJUANA USE. The 1998 *National Survey* found that 8.6 percent of respondents (18.7 million people) used marijuana at least once during the previous year. Slightly less than 5 percent (10.5 million) had used marijuana 12 times or more, while more than 3 percent (6.8 million) used it once a week or more. Those 18–25 years old were most likely to use the drug weekly (9.1 percent), with about one in eight males in this age group smoking marijuana once a week or more. (See Table 3.6.)

Cocaine

CURRENT USE AND POPULARITY. Cocaine, a Schedule II drug, is usually sniffed, or "snorted," in doses of 10–40 milligrams and absorbed through the mucous membranes of the nose. It can also be injected or smoked, and it is sometimes used in conjunction with other drugs. The

TABLE 3.2

Any illicit drug use by age group and gender for White, Non-Hispanics, 1998

AGE/ GENDER	Ever Used		Used Past Year		Used Past Month	
	Observed Estimate	95% C.I.	Observed Estimate	95% C.I.	Observed Estimate	95% C.I.
RATE ESTIMATES (Percent)						
AGE						
12-17	21.7	(19.8 - 23.7)	16.9	(15.2 - 18.7)	10.3	(8.9 - 11.8)
18-25	54.2	(51.2 - 57.1)	30.4	(27.7 - 33.3)	17.6	(15.5 - 19.8)
26-34	57.0	(54.2 - 59.7)	13.4	(11.7 - 15.3)	7.1	(5.8 - 8.7)
≥35	33.4	(31.0 - 35.9)	5.2	(4.4 - 6.1)	3.2	(2.6 - 3.9)
GENDER						
Male	43.5	(41.1 - 46.0)	12.6	(11.5 - 13.9)	7.7	(6.8 - 8.7)
Female	33.1	(30.9 - 35.4)	8.4	(7.4 - 9.4)	4.5	(3.9 - 5.3)
TOTAL	38.2	(36.2 - 40.1)	10.4	(9.6 - 11.4)	6.1	(5.4 - 6.8)
POPULATION ESTIMATES (In Thousands)						
AGE						
12-17	3,301	(3,014 - 3,606)	2,564	(2,307 - 2,844)	1,561	(1,356 - 1,794)
18-25	10,157	(9,600 - 10,709)	5,709	(5,195 - 6,250)	3,294	(2,909 - 3,717)
26-34	13,550	(12,885 - 14,204)	3,188	(2,784 - 3,641)	1,693	(1,379 - 2,073)
≥35	34,819	(32,316 - 37,415)	5,433	(4,599 - 6,408)	3,309	(2,686 - 4,070)
GENDER						
Male	34,099	(32,211 - 36,011)	9,894	(9,007 - 10,855)	6,061	(5,361 - 6,845)
Female	27,727	(25,862 - 29,658)	7,000	(6,228 - 7,857)	3,796	(3,256 - 4,421)
TOTAL	61,826	(58,701 - 65,013)	16,894	(15,503 - 18,394)	9,857	(8,819 - 11,009)

SOURCE: "Table 2B: Any Illicit Drug Use by Age Group and Gender for White, Non-Hispanics, in 1998" in *National Household Survey on Drug Abuse: Population Estimates 1998,* Substance Abuse and Mental Health Services Administration, Washington, D.C., 2000

TABLE 3.3

Any illicit drug use by age group and gender for Hispanics, 1998

Age/ Gender	Ever Used		Used Past Year		Used Past Month	
	Observed Estimate	95% C.I.	Observed Estimate	95% C.I.	Observed Estimate	95% C.I.
RATE ESTIMATES (Percent)						
AGE						
12-17	23.0	(20.5 - 25.8)	17.4	(15.1 - 19.9)	9.9	(7.9 - 12.2)
18-25	34.6	(31.3 - 38.1)	19.0	(16.4 - 22.0)	11.1	(9.3 - 13.0)
26-34	29.7	(26.7 - 32.9)	9.1	(7.1 - 11.7)	5.4	(4.0 - 7.3)
≥35	23.2	(20.4 - 26.4)	6.0	(4.5 - 7.9)	3.5	(2.4 - 5.2)
GENDER						
Male	32.6	(30.0 - 35.4)	13.1	(11.2 - 15.2)	7.7	(6.3 - 9.3)
Female	20.3	(18.2 - 22.6)	7.9	(6.6 - 9.4)	4.5	(3.5 - 5.8)
TOTAL	26.6	(24.7 - 28.5)	10.5	(9.4 - 11.7)	6.1	(5.3 - 7.1)
POPULATION ESTIMATES (In Thousands)						
AGE						
12-17	716	(637 - 803)	540	(469 - 619)	307	(247 - 379)
18-25	1,353	(1,224 - 1,488)	744	(640 - 861)	432	(366 - 509)
26-34	1,389	(1,248 - 1,539)	426	(331 - 545)	253	(187 - 341)
≥35	2,475	(2,170 - 2,808)	638	(480 - 845)	376	(256 - 549)
GENDER						
Male	3,696	(3,399 - 4,005)	1,479	(1,266 - 1,722)	869	(718 - 1,050)
Female	2,238	(2,005 - 2,490)	869	(724 - 1,041)	499	(386 - 641)
TOTAL	5,934	(5,515 - 6,372)	2,348	(2,099 - 2,623)	1,368	(1,181 - 1,583)

SOURCE: "Table 2C: Any Illicit Drug Use by Age Group and Gender for Hispanics in 1998" in *National Household Survey on Drug Abuse: Population Estimates 1998,* Substance Abuse and Mental Health Services Administration, Washington, D.C., 2000

most popular and notorious combination of cocaine and another illegal drug is the "speedball," a dangerous mixture of heroin and cocaine.

In 1998, 10.6 percent of respondents (23.1 million people) said they had used cocaine—including crack—at some point in their lives; 1.7 percent (3.8 million)

TABLE 3.4

Any Illicit drug use by age group and gender for Black, Non-Hispanics, 1998

AGE/ GENDER	Ever Used			Used Past Year			Used Past Month		
	Observed Estimate	95% C.I.		Observed Estimate	95% C.I.		Observed Estimate	95% C.I.	
RATE ESTIMATES (Percent)									
AGE									
12-17	19.3	(16.1 - 22.8)		14.0	(11.2 - 17.5)		9.9	(7.6 - 12.8)	
18-25	41.0	(38.0 - 44.1)		26.2	(23.6 - 29.1)		17.1	(14.9 - 19.6)	
26-34	45.3	(41.6 - 49.1)		14.9	(12.5 - 17.7)		9.4	(7.4 - 11.8)	
≥35	30.2	(26.7 - 34.0)		8.2	(6.5 - 10.2)		4.8	(3.5 - 6.5)	
GENDER									
Male	41.5	(37.9 - 45.1)		17.9	(15.6 - 20.5)		12.0	(10.1 - 14.2)	
Female	26.4	(23.6 - 29.3)		9.0	(7.7 - 10.4)		5.2	(4.3 - 6.1)	
TOTAL	33.2	(30.8 - 35.6)		13.0	(11.7 - 14.4)		8.2	(7.2 - 9.3)	
POPULATION ESTIMATES (In Thousands)									
AGE									
12-17	625	(523 - 741)		456	(362 - 568)		320	(245 - 416)	
18-25	1,611	(1,493 - 1,731)		1,031	(926 - 1,142)		671	(583 - 769)	
26-34	1,975	(1,812 - 2,140)		651	(545 - 773)		409	(323 - 516)	
≥35	4,004	(3,540 - 4,501)		1,082	(868 - 1,345)		637	(467 - 865)	
GENDER									
Male	4,618	(4,223 - 5,024)		1,994	(1,738 - 2,279)		1,335	(1,121 - 1,583)	
Female	3,596	(3,224 - 3,994)		1,225	(1,056 - 1,418)		704	(592 - 835)	
TOTAL	8,214	(7,626 - 8,824)		3,219	(2,892 - 3,577)		2,038	(1,793 - 2,314)	

SOURCE: "Table 2D: Any Illicit Drug Use by Age Group and Gender for Black, Non-Hispanics, in 1998" in *National Household Survey on Drug Abuse: Population Estimates 1998,* Substance Abuse and Mental Health Services Administration, Washington, D.C., 2000

had used it in the past year; and less than 1 percent (1.8 million) were current users. (See Table 3.7.) The number of current users dropped dramatically over only a few years—from 5.8 million in 1985 to 1.6 million in 1990—before rising slightly to 1.9 million in 1991, dropping to 1.3 million in 1993, and rising to 1.7 million in 1998.

Frequency-of-use responses indicated that about 0.7 percent (1.5 million) had used cocaine 12 or more days in the past year, while approximately 0.3 percent (595,000) had used the drug once a week or more. (See Table 3.8.)

MINORITY USE. Cocaine use among blacks and Hispanics, once relatively high compared with use among whites, dropped significantly. In 1985, 6.2 percent of black respondents reported using cocaine in the month before the survey; by 1988 the proportion had declined to 4.4 percent; by 1990 it had dropped to 1.8 percent; and by 1995 it was down to 1.1 percent, before rising slightly in 1998 to 1.3 percent.

Past-month use among Hispanics dropped only slightly between 1985 and 1988, from 5.7 percent to 5.1 percent. It tumbled to 1.6 percent in 1991 and 1.1 percent in 1993; dropped further, to 0.7 percent, in 1995; but rose to 1.3 percent in 1998. Whites had a current-prevalence rate of 0.7 percent in 1991, 0.5 percent in 1993, 0.6 percent in 1995, and 0.7 percent in 1998.

In 1997, the proportion of whites who reported ever using cocaine (11.4 percent) was considerably higher than the proportion of Hispanics (8.9 percent) and blacks (8.5 percent) who reported ever using the drug. The proportion for blacks dropped significantly between 1995 and 1997, from 8.1 percent to 6.5 percent, but then it jumped to 8.5 percent in 1999.

CRACK. Crack is a purified, smokable form of cocaine that has undergone chemical conversion. Crack's low price, about $5–$10 per dose, has made cocaine, once considered the drug of the rich and famous, available to all segments of the American population.

In the 1998 *National Survey* 2 percent of respondents (4.5 million people) reported ever using crack; 0.4 percent (971,000) used it in the past year; and 0.2 percent (437,000) used it in the past month. (See Table 3.9.) While only 0.1 percent of whites and 0.3 percent of Hispanics had used crack within the past month, 0.9 percent of blacks had used the drug in the past 30 days.

Heroin

While cocaine/crack use dropped, heroin, a Schedule I drug, made a comeback. A big reason for the resurgence is the drug's increased purity, which made the use of needles largely unnecessary. *National Survey* estimates of heroin users are thought to be on the low side, primarily because of underreporting and undercoverage of this segment of the population. In 1998, 1.1 percent of survey respondents (2.4 million people) reported ever using heroin, while 0.1 percent (253,000)

TABLE 3.5

Marijuana use by gender within age group for total population, 1998

AGE/ GENDER	Ever Used		Used Past Year		Used Past Month	
	Observed Estimate	95% C.I.	Observed Estimate	95% C.I.	Observed Estimate	95% C.I.
			RATE ESTIMATES (Percent)			
12-17	17.0	(15.7 - 18.3)	14.1	(12.9 - 15.3)	8.3	(7.2 - 9.4)
Male	17.7	(16.0 - 19.7)	14.4	(12.8 - 16.2)	8.6	(7.4 - 10.1)
Female	16.1	(14.3 - 18.2)	13.7	(12.0 - 15.6)	7.9	(6.4 - 9.7)
18-25	44.6	(42.5 - 46.7)	24.1	(22.3 - 26.0)	13.8	(12.5 - 15.2)
Male	49.4	(46.1 - 52.6)	28.1	(25.3 - 31.1)	17.2	(15.2 - 19.3)
Female	39.8	(37.1 - 42.4)	20.0	(17.7 - 22.6)	10.3	(8.8 - 12.1)
26-34	47.9	(45.8 - 50.0)	9.7	(8.6 - 11.0)	5.5	(4.6 - 6.5)
Male	53.2	(50.1 - 56.3)	13.0	(11.1 - 15.1)	8.1	(6.6 - 9.9)
Female	42.7	(39.9 - 45.5)	6.5	(5.4 - 7.8)	2.9	(2.2 - 3.8)
≥35	29.4	(27.7 - 31.3)	4.1	(3.5 - 4.7)	2.5	(2.1 - 3.1)
Male	35.8	(33.3 - 38.4)	5.6	(4.6 - 6.8)	3.5	(2.7 - 4.5)
Female	23.8	(21.8 - 25.9)	2.7	(2.2 - 3.5)	1.7	(1.2 - 2.3)
TOTAL	33.0	(31.6 - 34.4)	8.6	(8.0 - 9.2)	5.0	(4.6 - 5.5)
Male	38.5	(36.8 - 40.2)	10.8	(10.0 - 11.6)	6.7	(6.0 - 7.4)
Female	27.9	(26.3 - 29.6)	6.5	(5.9 - 7.2)	3.5	(3.1 - 4.0)
			POPULATION ESTIMATES (In Thousands)			
12-17	3,855	(3,568 - 4,162)	3,197	(2,928 - 3,486)	1,878	(1,639 - 2,148)
Male	2,058	(1,853 - 2,281)	1,670	(1,481 - 1,878)	1,003	(854 - 1,175)
Female	1,797	(1,594 - 2,021)	1,527	(1,336 - 1,742)	875	(709 - 1,075)
18-25	12,474	(11,885 - 13,069)	6,739	(6,242 - 7,261)	3,855	(3,499 - 4,241)
Male	6,973	(6,514 - 7,432)	3,966	(3,568 - 4,389)	2,424	(2,145 - 2,731)
Female	5,502	(5,139 - 5,872)	2,773	(2,444 - 3,134)	1,431	(1,219 - 1,675)
26-34	16,569	(15,850 - 17,290)	3,362	(2,974 - 3,794)	1,894	(1,604 - 2,232)
Male	9,131	(8,595 - 9,662)	2,227	(1,900 - 2,599)	1,390	(1,134 - 1,698)
Female	7,438	(6,948 - 7,937)	1,135	(944 - 1,362)	503	(385 - 656)
≥35	39,171	(36,821 - 41,606)	5,412	(4,651 - 6,293)	3,390	(2,782 - 4,126)
Male	22,310	(20,719 - 23,952)	3,469	(2,853 - 4,209)	2,192	(1,702 - 2,817)
Female	16,861	(15,457 - 18,350)	1,943	(1,532 - 2,460)	1,197	(876 - 1,635)
TOTAL	72,070	(69,122 - 75,080)	18,710	(17,454 - 20,048)	11,016	(10,066 - 12,050)
Male	40,471	(38,682 - 42,291)	11,332	(10,477 - 12,247)	7,010	(6,326 - 7,762)
Female	31,598	(29,748 - 33,518)	7,378	(6,679 - 8,146)	4,006	(3,512 - 4,566)

SOURCE: "Table 3A: Marijuana Use by Gender Within Age Group for Total Population in 1998" in *National Household Survey on Drug Abuse: Population Estimates 1998,* Substance Abuse and Mental Health Services Administration, Washington, D.C., 2000

reported using it in the past year. The rate of heroin use was highest among males, blacks, and 18- to 25-year-olds, although well over two-thirds (70.5 percent) of those who had ever used heroin were 35 and older. (See Table 3.10.)

Between 1994 and 1997, the proportion of heroin users who reported ever smoking or snorting the drug increased from 55 percent to 71 percent. During the same period, the proportion who had ever injected heroin remained about the same—49 percent in 1994 and 55 percent in 1997.

Hallucinogens

Prevalence rates for hallucinogens—which include LSD, PCP, mescaline, and peyote—did not change significantly between 1985 and 1993. However, the 1995 and 1998 *National Surveys* revealed significant increases in past-year and past-month use—especially among young people. In 1998, 9.9 percent of those polled (21.6 million people) had used hallucinogens at some point during their

lives, while an estimated 1.6 percent (3.6 million) had used them during the past year. (See Table 3.11.)

In the 1998 *National Survey* 5.3 percent of youths (12–17 years old) reported ever using hallucinogens—similar to the 5.4 percent in 1995. Lifetime-prevalence rates for young adults (18–25 years old) rose between 1995 and 1998, from 14 percent to 17.4 percent. Rates for adults 26–34 dropped slightly in that same period, from 15 percent to 13.2 percent.

Current use among youths jumped from 0.5 percent in 1993 to 1.8 percent in 1998. Similarly, current use among young adults rose from 1.3 percent to 2.7 percent in the same period. Males in the 18–25 age group were the most likely to be currently using hallucinogens. (See Table 3.11.)

LSD (LYSERGIC ACID DIETHYLAMIDE). LSD is the most commonly used hallucinogen. After 1985, when 4.6 percent of respondents reported ever using the drug, life-time-prevalence rates for LSD steadily increased. In 1998, 7.9 percent (17.2 million) of those interviewed claimed

TABLE 3.6

Frequency of marijuana use during past year by gender within age group for total population, 1998

AGE/GENDER	At Least Once		12 or More Days		51 or More Days	
	Observed Estimate	95% C.I.	Observed Estimate	95% C.I.	Observed Estimate	95% C.I.
Rate Estimates (Percent)						
12-17	14.1	(12.9 - 15.3)	7.6	(6.7 - 8.8)	4.8	(4.0 - 5.8)
Male	14.4	(12.8 - 16.2)	8.2	(6.9 - 9.6)	5.2	(4.2 - 6.5)
Female	13.7	(12.0 - 15.6)	7.1	(5.7 - 8.8)	4.3	(3.2 - 5.8)
18-25	24.1	(22.3 - 26.0)	14.0	(12.7 - 15.4)	9.1	(8.1 - 10.2)
Male	28.1	(25.3 - 31.1)	17.4	(15.4 - 19.5)	12.2	(10.4 - 14.2)
Female	20.0	(17.7 - 22.6)	10.5	(8.9 - 12.3)	6.0	(4.9 - 7.3)
26-34	9.7	(8.6 - 11.0)	4.8	(4.0 - 5.7)	3.2	(2.6 - 3.9)
Male	13.0	(11.1 - 15.1)	6.8	(5.5 - 8.3)	4.5	(3.5 - 5.7)
Female	6.5	(5.4 - 7.8)	2.8	(2.2 - 3.7)	1.9	(1.3 - 2.6)
≥35	4.1	(3.5 - 4.7)	2.4	(1.9 - 2.9)	1.5	(1.2 - 2.1)
Male	5.6	(4.6 - 6.8)	3.3	(2.6 - 4.2)	2.1	(1.5 - 2.9)
Female	2.7	(2.2 - 3.5)	1.6	(1.1 - 2.2)	1.1	(0.7 - 1.7)
TOTAL	8.6	(8.0 - 9.2)	4.8	(4.4 - 5.3)	3.1	(2.7 - 3.5)
Male	10.8	(10.0 - 11.6)	6.3	(5.6 - 7.0)	4.2	(3.6 - 4.8)
Female	6.5	(5.9 - 7.2)	3.4	(3.0 - 3.9)	2.1	(1.8 - 2.5)
Population Estimates (In Thousands)						
12-17	3,197	(2,928 - 3,486)	1,737	(1,514 - 1,990)	1,087	(901 - 1,308)
Male	1,670	(1,481 - 1,878)	946	(800 - 1,116)	608	(491 - 752)
Female	1,527	(1,336 - 1,742)	791	(639 - 976)	478	(351 - 649)
18-25	6,739	(6,242 - 7,261)	3,905	(3,538 - 4,304)	2,549	(2,264 - 2,865)
Male	3,966	(3,568 - 4,389)	2,454	(2,178 - 2,757)	1,721	(1,468 - 2,010)
Female	2,773	(2,444 - 3,134)	1,452	(1,238 - 1,697)	828	(677 - 1,010)
26-34	3,362	(2,974 - 3,794)	1,655	(1,399 - 1,955)	1,096	(899 - 1,335)
Male	2,227	(1,900 - 2,599)	1,160	(941 - 1,425)	769	(602 - 981)
Female	1,135	(944 - 1,362)	495	(376 - 650)	327	(234 - 456)
≥35	5,412	(4,651 - 6,293)	3,166	(2,585 - 3,875)	2,061	(1,540 - 2,754)
Male	3,469	(2,853 - 4,209)	2,047	(1,592 - 2,626)	1,284	(911 - 1,806)
Female	1,943	(1,532 - 2,460)	1,120	(811 - 1,544)	777	(512 - 1,175)
TOTAL	18,710	(17,454 - 20,048)	10,464	(9,523 - 11,493)	6,793	(6,002 - 7,683)
Male	11,332	(10,477 - 12,247)	6,606	(5,917 - 7,370)	4,383	(3,812 - 5,034)
Female	7,378	(6,679 - 8,146)	3,858	(3,377 - 4,403)	2,410	(2,034 - 2,853)

SOURCE: "Table 20A: Frequency of Marijuana Use During Past Year by Gender Within Age Group for Total Population in 1998" in *National Household Survey on Drug Abuse: Population Estimates 1998*, Substance Abuse and Mental Health Services Administration, Washington, D.C., 2000

that they had used LSD at some point in their lives, while 0.8 percent (1.8 million) said they had used it during the past year. White males between the ages of 18 and 25 were the most likely to have ever used LSD. (See Table 3.12.)

PCP (PHENCYCLIDINE). PCP is a very powerful drug that poses great risks to users. It can produce severe depression and/or a psychotic state similar to schizophrenia. In 1998, 3.5 percent (7.6 million) of survey respondents admitted having tried PCP at least once, while 0.2 percent (346,000) had used the drug within the past year. Older, white males over the age of 25 were the most likely to have ever used PCP. (See Table 3.13.)

THE DRUG ABUSE WARNING NETWORK (DAWN)

The Drug Abuse Warning Network (DAWN), a program of the National Institute on Drug Abuse, is a voluntary data-collection system. Under this system medical examiners report deaths due to drug abuse, and hospital emergency rooms report information on drug-related medical crises. Reporting hospitals are nonfederal, short-stay, general hospitals with 24-hour emergency departments. They are located throughout the United States and include 21 metropolitan areas. The figures given below are based on this sampling of emergency rooms and medical examiners and are estimates projected for the entire United States.

Hospital Emergency Rooms

An estimated 554,932 drug episodes—drug-related visits to hospital emergency rooms (ERs)—occurred in 1999, up significantly from the 443,493 in 1992. Between 1992 and 1999 the number of drug episodes was estimated to have increased by 25 percent, while the total number of ER visits for all causes increased by only 6 percent. The number of reported drug episodes rose 50 percent between 1990 and 1999, a period when total ER visits increased by only 11 percent. (See Table 3.14 and Figure

TABLE 3.7

Cocaine use by gender within age group for total population, 1998

AGE/ GENDER	Ever Used			Used Past Year			Used Past Month		
	Observed Estimate		95% C.I.	Observed Estimate		95% C.I.	Observed Estimate		95% C.I.
RATE ESTIMATES (Percent)									
12-17	2.2		*(1.7 - 2.7)*	1.7		*(1.3 - 2.2)*	0.8		*(0.5 - 1.2)*
Male	2.0		*(1.4 - 2.8)*	1.3		*(0.9 - 2.0)*	0.6		*(0.3 - 1.1)*
Female	2.4		*(1.8 - 3.3)*	2.0		*(1.4 - 3.0)*	1.0		*(0.6 - 1.8)*
18-25	10.0		*(8.9 - 11.2)*	4.7		*(3.9 - 5.5)*	2.0		*(1.5 - 2.6)*
Male	12.3		*(10.6 - 14.2)*	5.9		*(4.7 - 7.4)*	2.6		*(1.8 - 3.7)*
Female	7.7		*(6.4 - 9.2)*	3.4		*(2.6 - 4.5)*	1.3		*(0.9 - 2.0)*
26-34	17.1		*(15.6 - 18.7)*	2.7		*(2.1 - 3.5)*	1.2		*(0.8 - 1.7)*
Male	19.3		*(17.0 - 21.9)*	3.6		*(2.6 - 5.0)*	1.4		*(0.8 - 2.4)*
Female	14.8		*(13.0 - 16.9)*	1.9		*(1.3 - 2.6)*	0.9		*(0.6 - 1.5)*
≥35	10.4		*(9.3 - 11.6)*	0.9		*(0.7 - 1.2)*	0.5		*(0.3 - 0.7)*
Male	13.7		*(11.8 - 15.8)*	1.3		*(0.9 - 1.8)*	0.7		*(0.4 - 1.2)*
Female	7.6		*(6.4 - 8.9)*	0.5		*(0.3 - 0.9)*	0.2		*(0.1 - 0.4)*
TOTAL	10.6		*(9.8 - 11.4)*	1.7		*(1.5 - 2.0)*	0.8		*(0.7 - 1.0)*
Male	13.1		*(12.0 - 14.4)*	2.3		*(1.9 - 2.7)*	1.1		*(0.8 - 1.4)*
Female	8.2		*(7.4 - 9.1)*	1.2		*(1.0 - 1.5)*	0.5		*(0.4 - 0.7)*
POPULATION ESTIMATES (In Thousands)									
12-17	497		*(396 - 623)*	379		*(285 - 503)*	186		*(121 - 283)*
Male	227		*(161 - 320)*	151		*(100 - 227)*	72		*(40 - 129)*
Female	270		*(195 - 372)*	228		*(155 - 333)*	114		*(65 - 200)*
18-25	2,805		*(2,502 - 3,140)*	1,306		*(1,097 - 1,552)*	548		*(409 - 733)*
Male	1,737		*(1,500 - 2,006)*	834		*(666 - 1,042)*	364		*(250 - 529)*
Female	1,068		*(890 - 1,278)*	472		*(353 - 628)*	183		*(118 - 283)*
26-34	5,906		*(5,387 - 6,464)*	942		*(731 - 1,211)*	404		*(279 - 584)*
Male	3,318		*(2,924 - 3,752)*	618		*(440 - 863)*	243		*(143 - 411)*
Female	2,588		*(2,266 - 2,948)*	324		*(229 - 457)*	161		*(100 - 258)*
≥35	13,880		*(12,405 - 15,508)*	1,185		*(888 - 1,579)*	612		*(405 - 925)*
Male	8,525		*(7,379 - 9,817)*	796		*(555 - 1,141)*	453		*(270 - 758)*
Female	5,356		*(4,564 - 6,272)*	388		*(242 - 622)*	160		*(84 - 303)*
TOTAL	23,089		*(21,390 - 24,906)*	3,811		*(3,342 - 4,344)*	1,750		*(1,428 - 2,143)*
Male	13,807		*(12,587 - 15,127)*	2,399		*(2,027 - 2,837)*	1,132		*(866 - 1,478)*
Female	9,282		*(8,348 - 10,310)*	1,412		*(1,147 - 1,736)*	618		*(470 - 811)*

SOURCE: "Table 4A: Cocaine Use by Gender Within Age Group for Total Population in 1998" in *National Household Survey on Drug Abuse: Population Estimates 1998,* Substance Abuse and Mental Health Services Administration, Washington, D.C., 2000

3.1.) In 1999 drug episodes accounted for 0.6 percent, or about 1 in 150, of all visits to hospital ERs.

Characteristics of Emergency Room Episodes

In 1999, 23.6 percent of all drug episodes involved persons 26–34 years old, while almost twice that number, 46.7 percent, involved people 35 and older. Nineteen percent involved those in the 18–25 age group, and 9.5 percent involved 12- to 17-year-olds. After 1992 drug-related ER visits were about equally divided between men and women.

The largest increase was for the 35-and-older population. Between 1992 and 1999 the total number of drug episodes increased by more than 120,000. During this same period, the number of episodes involving a patient 35 or older increased by almost 105,000. In fact, most of the 28 percent rise in the number of total drug episodes was due to the increase in drug episodes among the 35-and-older age group. (See Table 3.15.)

About 56 percent of all drug episodes occurred among whites, with 24 percent among blacks and 10 percent among Hispanics. (Race was unknown or "other" for 10 percent.) In 1999 the most common reason claimed for taking a drug was "dependence" (37 percent), surpassing "suicide," which had been the most common drug-use motive since 1992. "Suicide" (32 percent) and "recreational use" (12 percent) were the other major motives for taking a drug. (See Table 3.15.)

The most frequently reported reason for going to the ER was "overdose" (42 percent), followed by "other/ unknown reason" (17 percent), "unexpected reaction" (14 percent), "seeking detoxification" (13 percent), "chronic effects" (9 percent), and "withdrawal" (4.6 percent). (See Table 3.15.)

RATES OF DRUG ABUSE. For the entire U.S. population, 228 per 100,000 people went to hospital ERs because of drug abuse–related episodes. In the 18–25 age group, the number was 388 per 100,000, and among those

TABLE 3.8

Frequency of cocaine use during past year by gender within age group for total population, 1998

AGE/GENDER	At Least Once		12 or More Days		51 or More Days	
	Observed Estimate	95% C.I.	Observed Estimate	95% C.I.	Observed Estimate	95% C.I
	Rate Estimates (Percent)					
12-17	1.7	(1.3 - 2.2)	0.6	(0.3 - 0.9)	0.3	(0.2 - 0.5)
Male	1.3	(0.9 - 2.0)	0.4	(0.2 - 0.8)	0.2	(0.1 - 0.4)
Female	2.0	(1.4 - 3.0)	0.8	(0.4 - 1.4)	0.4	(0.2 - 0.9)
18-25	4.7	(3.9 - 5.5)	1.1	(0.8 - 1.4)	0.5	(0.3 - 0.8)
Male	5.9	(4.7 - 7.4)	1.5	(1.0 - 2.2)	0.6	(0.3 - 1.1)
Female	3.4	(2.6 - 4.5)	0.6	(0.4 - 1.0)	0.4	(0.2 - 0.7)
26-34	2.7	(2.1 - 3.5)	1.0	(0.7 - 1.4)	0.5	(0.3 - 0.7)
Male	3.6	(2.6 - 5.0)	0.9	(0.5 - 1.8)	0.5	(0.2 - 0.9)
Female	1.9	(1.3 - 2.6)	1.0	(0.6 - 1.7)	0.4	(0.2 - 0.8)
≥35	0.9	(0.7 - 1.2)	0.5	(0.3 - 0.8)	0.2	(0.1 - 0.3)
Male	1.3	(0.9 - 1.8)	0.7	(0.4 - 1.2)	0.3	(0.1 - 0.6)
Female	0.5	(0.3 - 0.9)	0.4	(0.2 - 0.7)	0.1	(0.0 - 0.3)
TOTAL	1.7	(1.5 - 2.0)	0.7	(0.5 - 0.8)	0.3	(0.2 - 0.4)
Male	2.3	(1.9 - 2.7)	0.8	(0.6 - 1.1)	0.3	(0.2 - 0.5)
Female	1.2	(1.0 - 1.5)	0.5	(0.4 - 0.7)	0.2	(0.1 - 0.3)
	Population Estimates (In Thousands)					
12-17	379	(285 - 503)	126	(78 - 203)	64	(35 - 115)
Male	151	(100 - 227)	41	(19 - 91)	21	(9 - 46)
Female	228	(155 - 333)	85	(48 - 150)	43	(19 - 95)
18-25	1,306	(1,097 - 1,552)	301	(224 - 403)	133	(83 - 214)
Male	834	(666 - 1,042)	214	(146 - 312)	83	(43 - 161)
Female	472	(353 - 628)	87	(55 - 139)	50	(26 - 96)
26-34	942	(731 - 1,211)	342	(233 - 501)	156	(99 - 245)
Male	618	(440 - 863)	161	(85 - 304)	78	(39 - 157)
Female	324	(229 - 457)	181	(112 - 290)	78	(41 - 147)
≥35	1,185	(888 - 1,579)	683	(451 - 1,031)	243	(136 - 433)
Male	796	(555 - 1,141)	427	(248 - 734)	172	(81 - 365)
Female	388	(242 - 622)	255	(136 - 479)	70	(27 - 185)
TOTAL	3,811	(3,342 - 4,344)	1,452	(1,158 - 1,819)	595	(445 - 797)
Male	2,399	(2,027 - 2,837)	843	(615 - 1,155)	354	(232 - 541)
Female	1,412	(1,147 - 1,736)	608	(443 - 834)	241	(162 - 358)

SOURCE: "Table 21A: Frequency of Cocaine Use During Past Year by Gender Within Age Group for Total Population in 1998" in *National Household Survey on Drug Abuse: Population Estimates 1998*, Substance Abuse and Mental Health Services Administration, Washington, D.C., 2000

26–34 years old, 393 per 100,000. Older people (35 and over) were less than half as likely as young adults to have drug emergencies, with a rate of 193 per 100,000. After 1992 men had a slightly higher rate than women. (See Table 3.16.)

ALCOHOL, COCAINE, AND HEROIN. For each ER drug episode, data were gathered about what specific drugs were involved in the episode. Multiple drugs could be mentioned—and often were. Visits that involved alcohol were not counted, unless the alcohol was used in combination with another drug. In order to properly interpret the percentage of episodes related to a particular drug, it is important to remember that the drug mentioned is often not the only drug related to the episode.

Combining alcohol with other drugs can be very dangerous. Indeed, "alcohol-in-combination" was the leading cause of drug-related episodes between 1992 and 1999, accounting for between 33 percent (in 1992) and 35 percent (in 1999) of all ER visits in which a drug was men-

tioned. (See Table 3.14.) Cocaine was mentioned in 28 percent of episodes in 1992, and 30 percent in 1999. During the 1990s heroin began to account for more ER drug episodes, increasing from 11 percent in 1992 to 15 percent in 1999. (See Table 3.14.)

In 1999, 51 percent of all cocaine-related episodes (168,763) occurred among persons 35 and older, and 39 percent occurred among those 26–34. After 1992, however, cocaine-related episodes among those 35 and older more than doubled, while such episodes for persons 26–34 rose only slightly. In 1999 about 46 percent of cocaine-related episodes occurred among blacks, with 34 percent among whites and 12 percent among Hispanics. (Figure 3.2 shows the number of cocaine mentions by race/ethnicity.) Males accounted for almost two-thirds of cocaine-related episodes.

In 1999, 57 percent of heroin-related episodes occurred among persons 35 and older. After 1990 heroin-related episodes more than tripled for this age group

TABLE 3.9

Crack use by gender within age group for total population, 1998

AGE/ GENDER	Ever Used		Used Past Year		Used Past Month	
	Observed Estimate	95% C.I.	Observed Estimate	95% C.I.	Observed Estimate	95% C.I.
	RATE ESTIMATES (Percent)					
12-17	0.7	(0.5 - 1.2)	0.5	(0.3 - 0.8)	0.2	(0.1 - 0.5)
Male	0.7	(0.4 - 1.3)	0.3	(0.2 - 0.8)	0.2	(0.1 - 0.4)
Female	0.8	(0.4 - 1.4)	0.6	(0.3 - 1.2)	0.3	(0.1 - 1.0)
18-25	2.7	(2.1 - 3.4)	0.8	(0.5 - 1.1)	0.3	(0.2 - 0.6)
Male	3.7	(2.8 - 4.9)	1.0	(0.7 - 1.7)	0.4	(0.2 - 0.9)
Female	1.7	(1.1 - 2.4)	0.5	(0.3 - 0.9)	0.3	(0.1 - 0.6)
26-34	3.9	(3.1 - 4.8)	0.7	(0.5 - 1.1)	0.3	(0.2 - 0.5)
Male	4.5	(3.4 - 6.0)	0.7	(0.4 - 1.3)	0.3	(0.1 - 0.6)
Female	3.2	(2.4 - 4.2)	0.7	(0.4 - 1.2)	0.3	(0.2 - 0.7)
≥35	1.7	(1.3 - 2.1)	0.3	(0.2 - 0.5)	0.1	(0.1 - 0.3)
Male	2.4	(1.8 - 3.2)	0.5	(0.3 - 0.8)	0.2	(0.1 - 0.5)
Female	1.0	(0.7 - 1.4)	0.2	(0.1 - 0.4)	0.1	(0.0 - 0.2)
TOTAL	2.0	(1.8 - 2.3)	0.4	(0.4 - 0.6)	0.2	(0.1 - 0.3)
Male	2.8	(2.3 - 3.3)	0.6	(0.4 - 0.8)	0.2	(0.2 - 0.4)
Female	1.4	(1.1 - 1.7)	0.3	(0.2 - 0.5)	0.2	(0.1 - 0.2)
	POPULATION ESTIMATES (In Thousands)					
12-17	170	(110 - 264)	103	(59 - 178)	56	(26 - 121)
Male	83	(47 - 146)	40	(18 - 89)	18	(7 - 44)
Female	88	(49 - 157)	63	(30 - 132)	38	(13 - 110)
18-25	755	(600 - 950)	220	(154 - 314)	90	(49 - 163)
Male	523	(392 - 696)	148	(93 - 235)	53	(22 - 126)
Female	232	(159 - 339)	72	(42 - 123)	37	(17 - 79)
26-34	1,332	(1,076 - 1,646)	250	(169 - 369)	105	(62 - 179)
Male	780	(592 - 1,024)	128	(75 - 217)	46	(19 - 110)
Female	552	(412 - 739)	122	(70 - 211)	59	(28 - 127)
≥35	2,218	(1,782 - 2,759)	399	(259 - 614)	187	(99 - 351)
Male	1,510	(1,144 - 1,990)	284	(163 - 494)	146	(67 - 316)
Female	708	(495 - 1,012)	114	(50 - 262)	40	(11 - 145)
TOTAL	4,476	(3,913 - 5,119)	971	(770 - 1,225)	437	(324 - 590)
Male	2,896	(2,436 - 3,439)	600	(446 - 808)	263	(179 - 384)
Female	1,580	(1,278 - 1,953)	371	(256 - 537)	175	(108 - 283)

SOURCE: "Table 5A: Crack Use by Gender Within Age Group for Total Population, 1998" in *National Household Survey on Drug Abuse: Population Estimates 1998,* Substance Abuse and Mental Health Services Administration, Washington, D.C., 2000

(15,900 in 1990; 48,104 in 1999). In 1999, 40 percent of heroin-related episodes occurred among whites, with 34 percent among blacks and 14 percent among Hispanics. (See Figure 3.3.) Sixty-seven percent occurred among men. During the 1990s the number of heroin-related episodes increased approximately 250 percent for both women (10,700 in 1990; 27,200 in 1999) and men (22,900 in 1990; 56,600 in 1999).

OTHER DRUGS. Marijuana/hashish-related hospital admissions fell from about 20,000 in 1988 to about 16,000 in 1990 and 1991, before rising sharply to 40,200 in 1994 and 87,150 in 1999. The number of methamphetamine-related episodes dropped between 1988 and 1991, then rose from 4,900 episodes in 1991 to 17,700 in 1994, before falling to 10,500 in 1999. (See Table 3.14.)

PCP admissions fell from more than 8,000 in 1989 to just 3,500 in 1991, but then rose to more than 6,000 between 1993 and 1995, before dropping to 5,000 in 1999. LSD-related admissions remained relatively stable through 1993, at around 3,500 per year, but topped 5,000 in 1994. After 1994, the annual number of LSD episodes hovered around 5,000. (See Table 3.14.)

As can be seen in Table 3.14, legal drugs were also involved in many of these episodes. An apparently safe, over-the-counter or prescription drug can become very dangerous when taken in combination with other drugs, whether legal or illegal. The mixture of legal drugs should be carefully monitored—particularly among older people, whose reactions to drugs and drug combinations can differ dramatically from those of younger people.

DRUG DEATHS

The *Annual Medical Examiner Data 1999*, prepared from DAWN by the Substance Abuse and Mental Health Services Administration (SAMHSA), reported 11,651 drug-abuse deaths in 1999, up from 8,426 in 1995 and 5,628 in 1990. Males accounted for 73.1 percent of these deaths. Sixty percent of the cases involved white victims;

TABLE 3.10

Heroin use by age, gender, race, and region for total population, 1998

	Ever Used			Used Past Year	
	Observed Estimate	95% C.I.		Observed Estimate	95% C.I.
Rate Estimates (Percent)					
AGE					
12-17	0.4	(0.2 - 0.6)		0.3	(0.1 - 0.5)
18-25	1.1	(0.8 - 1.5)		0.4	(0.2 - 0.7)
26-34	0.9	(0.6 - 1.4)		0.1	(0.0 - 0.2)
≥35	1.3	(0.9 - 1.7)		*	*
GENDER					
Male	1.3	(1.0 - 1.8)		0.1	(0.1 - 0.2)
Female	0.8	(0.6 - 1.1)		0.1	(0.1 - 0.2)
RACE/ETHNICITY					
White, non-Hispanic	1.0	(0.8 - 1.3)		0.1	(0.1 - 0.2)
Black, non-Hispanic	1.9	(1.3 - 2.8)		0.2	(0.1 - 0.5)
Hispanic	0.7	(0.5 - 1.0)		0.1	(0.1 - 0.3)
REGION					
Northeast	1.2	(0.8 - 2.1)		0.2	(0.1 - 0.4)
North Central	1.0	(0.6 - 1.7)		0.1	(0.0 - 0.3)
South	0.8	(0.5 - 1.1)		0.1	(0.0 - 0.2)
West	1.5	(1.1 - 2.1)		0.1	(0.1 0.3)
TOTAL	1.1	(0.9 - 1.3)		0.1	(0.1 - 0.2)
Population Estimates (In Thousands)					
AGE					
12-17	80	(48 - 135)		58	(31 - 108)
18-25	303	(214 - 428)		111	(59 - 210)
26-34	315	(211 - 469)		29	(11 - 79)
≥35	1,673	(1,263 - 2,213)		*	*
GENDER					
Male	1,415	(1,048 - 1,908)		142	(81 - 248)
Female	956	(719 - 1,269)		111	(66 - 188)
RACE/ETHNICITY					
White, non-Hispanic	1,633	(1,233 - 2,161)		161	(91 - 286)
Black, non-Hispanic	473	(320 - 697)		61	(32 - 113)
Hispanic	155	(106 - 227)		31	(15 - 62)
REGION					
Northeast	527	(318 - 869)		78	(33 - 186)
North Central	529	(320 - 872)		50	(18 - 140)
South	591	(400 - 871)		56	(25 - 123)
West	724	(523 - 1,001)		69	(38 - 125)
TOTAL	2,371	(1,921 - 2,925)		253	(175 - 365)

* Low precision; no estimate reported.

SOURCE: "Table 18: Heroin Use by Age, Gender, Race, and Region for Total Population in 1998" in *National Household Survey on Drug Abuse: Population Estimate 1998*, Substance Abuse and Mental Health Services Administration, Washington, D.C., 2000

26 percent, black; and 12.4 percent, Hispanic. Nearly 72 percent of the victims were 35 or older. (See Table 3.17.)

In 55 percent of the cases the manner of death was accidental or unexpected, while in 16 percent the victims used the drugs to commit suicide. (The manner of death was unknown in 29 percent of the cases.) Women were more likely to use drugs to commit suicide than men: 21 percent of the female cases were suicides, compared with 14 percent of the male cases.

Cocaine (41.8 percent), heroin/morphine (41.4 percent), and alcohol-in-combination (33.6 percent) were involved in the most drug-related deaths. (See Table 3.18.) The numbers add to more than 100 percent because nearly three-quarters (73.8 percent) of the deaths involved the use of more than one drug. Cocaine was detected in the

bloodstream in 45 percent of male cases and in 33 percent of female cases. Heroin/morphine was a factor in 45 percent of male deaths and 31 percent of female deaths.

Sixty-four percent of drug-related deaths among blacks involved cocaine, while 45 percent of Hispanic deaths and 32 percent of white deaths involved the drug. Forty-seven percent of Hispanic deaths, 41 percent of white deaths, and 39 percent of deaths among blacks involved heroin/morphine. Forty-three percent of Hispanic deaths, 33 percent of white deaths, and 31 percent of deaths among blacks involved alcohol-in-combination.

Medical examiners cited cocaine in 39 percent of the drug-related deaths involving people 18–25 years old; in 49 percent involving 26- to 34-year-olds; and in 41 percent involving those 35 and older. Heroin/mor-

TABLE 3.11

Hallucinogen use by gender within age group for total population, 1998

AGE/ GENDER	Ever Used		Used Past Year		Used Past Month	
	Observed Estimate	95% C.I.	Observed Estimate	95% C.I.	Observed Estimate	95% C.I.
			RATE ESTIMATES (Percent)			
12-17	5.3	(4.6 - 6.2)	3.8	(3.2 - 4.6)	1.8	(1.4 - 2.5)
Male	5.4	(4.4 - 6.7)	4.0	(3.1 - 5.1)	2.1	(1.5 - 3.0)
Female	5.3	(4.1 - 6.8)	3.6	(2.6 - 5.0)	1.6	(0.9 - 2.5)
18-25	17.4	(15.6 - 19.3)	7.2	(6.1 - 8.5)	2.7	(2.0 - 3.6)
Male	20.5	(18.2 - 23.0)	8.8	(7.2 - 10.7)	3.1	(2.2 - 4.5)
Female	14.2	(12.1 - 16.6)	5.6	(4.3 - 7.1)	2.2	(1.3 - 3.5)
26-34	13.2	(11.7 - 14.8)	1.1	(0.8 - 1.7)	0.4	(0.2 - 0.7)
Male	16.2	(13.9 - 18.7)	1.5	(0.9 - 2.4)	0.7	(0.3 - 1.2)
Female	10.2	(8.6 - 12.0)	0.8	(0.4 - 1.5)	0.2	(0.1 - 0.6)
≥35	8.2	(7.2 - 9.4)	0.2	(0.1 - 0.5)	0.2	(0.1 - 0.4)
Male	11.1	(9.4 - 13.1)	0.2	(0.1 - 0.5)	0.1	(0.0 - 0.3)
Female	5.7	(4.8 - 6.8)	0.2	(0.1 - 0.7)	0.2	(0.1 - 0.7)
TOTAL	9.9	(9.1 - 10.7)	1.6	(1.4 - 1.9)	0.7	(0.5 - 0.9)
Male	12.6	(11.5 - 13.8)	2.0	(1.7 - 2.4)	0.8	(0.6 - 1.1)
Female	7.4	(6.5 - 8.3)	1.3	(1.0 - 1.6)	0.6	(0.4 - 0.8)
			POPULATION ESTIMATES (In Thousands)			
12-17	1,217	(1,041 - 1,420)	869	(717 - 1,051)	415	(308 - 558)
Male	631	(514 - 774)	467	(365 - 594)	242	(170 - 343)
Female	585	(453 - 753)	402	(290 - 555)	173	(105 - 283)
18-25	4,858	(4,368 - 5,391)	2,006	(1,693 - 2,372)	742	(552 - 994)
Male	2,895	(2,568 - 3,253)	1,237	(1,012 - 1,507)	443	(307 - 636)
Female	1,963	(1,671 - 2,298)	768	(602 - 977)	299	(183 - 485)
26-34	4,556	(4,047 - 5,119)	392	(264 - 580)	146	(83 - 256)
Male	2,776	(2,392 - 3,208)	253	(154 - 413)	113	(59 - 213)
Female	1,781	(1,506 - 2,099)	139	(76 - 254)	33	(10 - 109)
≥35	10,976	(9,651 - 12,464)	298	(144 - 614)	211	(81 - 550)
Male	6,937	(5,856 - 8,188)	152	(71 - 324)	70	(23 - 213)
Female	4,039	(3,372 - 4,829)	146	(46 - 464)	142	(43 - 466)
TOTAL	21,607	(19,932 - 23,407)	3,565	(3,071 - 4,136)	1,514	(1,192 - 1,921)
Male	13,239	(12,075 - 14,498)	2,109	(1,773 - 2,507)	868	(665 - 1,131)
Female	8,368	(7,407 - 9,443)	1,455	(1,171 - 1,808)	646	(436 - 957)

SOURCE: "Table 7A: Hallucinogen Use by Gender Within Age Group for Total Population in 1998" in *National Household Survey on Drug Abuse: Population Estimates 1998,* Substance Abuse and Mental Health Services Administration, Washington, D.C., 2000

phine was mentioned in 42 percent of the drug-related deaths involving 18- to 25-year-olds; in 41 percent involving 26- to 34-year-olds; and in 45 percent involving those 35 and older. Alcohol-in-combination was noted in 29 percent of the cases involving 18- to 25-year-olds; in 36 percent involving 26- to 34-year-olds; and in 34 percent involving those 35 and older. The cities with the greatest number of reported drug-abuse deaths were Los Angeles (1,896), New York (944), Chicago (879), Philadelphia (860), Detroit (695), Phoenix (561), and Baltimore (557).

DRUG-EXPOSED INFANTS

Background

The demographic profile of, and public concern about, drug use changed dramatically in the 1980s and 1990s. During the 1960s and 1970s, public concern focused primarily on heroin addicts, most of whom were men. The problem, as it was perceived at the time, was

that these addicts contributed greatly to crime and lawlessness, affecting members of society who had no role in the drug trade. In the 1980s and early 1990s, however, a new public concern arose: pregnant women addicted to drugs. A number of national publications, including the *Washington Post*, *New York Times*, and *Newsweek*, ran stories on the problem, and public figures, such as then-"drug czar" William Bennett, began speaking out about "crack babies."

Historically, women have not used drugs as heavily as men. However, this changed dramatically with the appearance of crack cocaine. In 1991, of the more than 4.5 million women of childbearing age who reported that they were using illegal drugs, 610,000 of them were using cocaine.

A REAL RISK. Drug use during pregnancy places both mother and infant at risk for major health problems. Use of illegal drugs during pregnancy has been associated with increased incidences of premature birth, stillbirth and

TABLE 3.12

LSD use by age, gender, race, and region for total population, 1998

	Ever Used		Used Past Year	
	Observed Estimate	95% C.I.	Observed Estimate	95% C.I.
	Rate Estimates (Percent)			
AGE				
12-17	4.2	(3.5 - 5.0)	2.6	(2.1 - 3.3)
18-25	14.0	(12.6 - 15.6)	3.4	(2.7 - 4.3)
26-34	10.6	(9.4 - 12.1)	0.3	(0.2 - 0.6)
≥35	6.5	(5.6 - 7.5)	0.1	(0.0 - 0.3)
GENDER				
Male	10.2	(9.1 - 11.3)	0.9	(0.7 - 1.2)
Female	5.8	(5.1 - 6.5)	0.7	(0.5 - 1.0)
RACE/ETHNICITY				
White, non-Hispanic	9.2	(8.4 - 10.1)	1.0	(0.8 - 1.2)
Black, non-Hispanic	4.0	(2.9 - 5.5)	0.1	(0.1 - 0.3)
Hispanic	4.1	(3.5 - 4.9)	0.5	(0.4 - 0.8)
REGION				
Northeast	6.8	(5.4 - 8.5)	0.7	(0.3 - 1.3)
North Central	8.9	(7.4 - 10.7)	1.3	(0.9 - 1.8)
South	6.1	(5.2 - 7.1)	0.7	(0.5 - 1.0)
West	10.7	(9.2 - 12.4)	0.6	(0.5 - 0.9)
TOTAL	7.9	(7.2 - 8.6)	0.8	(0.7 - 1.0)
	Population Estimates (In Thousands)			
AGE				
12-17	962	(806 -1,148)	601	(475 - 758)
18-25	3,925	(3,522 - 4,365)	944	(746 - 1,192)
26-34	3,684	(3,238 - 4,182)	104	(53 - 204)
≥35	8,652	(7,478 - 9,997)	158	(53 - 466)
GENDER				
Male	10,694	(9,624 - 11,868)	991	(772 - 1,270)
Female	6,529	(5,793 - 7,352)	816	(602 - 1,105)
RACE/ETHNICITY				
White, non-Hispanic	14,897	(13,548 - 16,364)	1,593	(1,276 - 1,987)
Black, non-Hispanic	994	(723 - 1,359)	37	(18 - 77)
Hispanic	925	(783 - 1,092)	120	(81 - 179)
REGION				
Northeast	2,873	(2,276 - 3,614)	280	(148 - 530)
North Central	4,537	(3,759 -5,456)	650	(454 - 930)
South	4,720	(4,043 - 5,502)	574	(410 - 802)
West	5,093	(4,365 - 5,926)	303	(224 - 409)
TOTAL	17,223	(15,783 - 18,783)	1,806	(1,479 - 2,206)

SOURCE: "Table 16: LSD Use by Age, Gender, Race, and Region for Total Population in 1998" in *National Household Survey on Drug Abuse: Population Estimates 1998,* Substance Abuse and Mental Health Services Administration, Washington, D.C., 2000

infant mortality, low birthweight, sudden infant death syndrome (SIDS), and long-term developmental disabilities.

Number of Drug-Exposed Infants Declining

As of 1999 substance abuse among women of childbearing age was declining. Nonetheless, a significant number of women ages 15–44 continued to use alcohol, tobacco, and illegal drugs prior to, and often during, pregnancy. According to the 1999 *National Survey,* 3.4 percent of pregnant respondents were current drug users. This was significantly lower than the 8.1 percent rate for nonpregnant women, suggesting that most women stop or reduce their drug use when they become pregnant.

Drug use was a particular problem among younger mothers: 6.5 percent of pregnant women 18–25 reported using an illicit drug in the month before the interview—

five times the rate reported by those 26–34 (1.3 percent). Marijuana was the most commonly used illicit drug (2.9 percent). Of the 3.4 percent of pregnant respondents who reported using an illicit drug in the month before the survey, only 0.8 percent used a drug other than marijuana. Approximately 0.2 percent of pregnant women reported using cocaine, including crack, but separate estimates of crack use were too low to be reliable. (See Table 3.19.)

"Crack Baby" Scare

Of great concern in the mid-1980s was the future of so-called "crack babies," a generic term for infants whose mothers had used cocaine during pregnancy. Cocaine causes constriction of blood vessels in the placenta and umbilical cord. This constriction can result in a lack of oxygen and nutrients to the fetus, leading to inadequate fetal devel-

TABLE 3.13

PCP use by age, gender, race, and region for total population, 1998

	Ever Used		Used Past Year	
	Observed Estimate	95% C.I.	Observed Estimate	95% C.I.
	Rate Estimates (Percent)			
AGE				
12-17	1.2	(0.9 - 1.7)	0.6	(0.4 - 1.1)
18-25	3.0	(2.4 - 3.7)	0.4	(0.2 - 0.8)
26-34	4.0	(3.2 - 4.9)	*	*
≥35	3.9	(3.2 - 4.7)	0.1	(0.0 - 0.4)
GENDER				
Male	4.4	(3.6 - 5.3)	0.1	(0.1 - 0.2)
Female	2.7	(2.2 - 3.2)	0.2	(0.1 - 0.4)
RACE/ETHNICITY				
White, non-Hispanic	3.9	(3.3 - 4.5)	0.2	(0.1 - 0.3)
Black, non-Hispanic	2.8	(2.0 - 3.8)	0.1	(0.0 - 0.2)
Hispanic	2.0	(1.6 - 2.6)	0.2	(0.1 - 0.3)
REGION				
Northeast	3.6	(2.6 - 5.1)	0.1	(0.1 - 0.4)
North Central	4.1	(3.1 - 5.4)	0.1	(0.1 - 0.3)
South	2.5	(1.9 - 3.2)	0.2	(0.1 - 0.6)
West	4.4	(3.6 - 5.3)	0.1	(0.1 - 0.2)
TOTAL	**3.5**	(3.1 - 4.0)	0.2	(0.1 - 0.3)
	Population Estimates (In Thousands)			
AGE				
12-17	273	(195 - 381)	147	(87 - 246)
18-25	829	(665 - 1,031)	115	(61 - 217)
26-34	1,378	(1,121 - 1,691)	*	*
≥35	5,161	(4,293 - 6,196)	76	(11 - 534)
GENDER				
Male	4,633	(3,820 - 5,609)	140	(85 - 233)
Female	3,007	(2,530 - 3,571)	206	(102 - 415)
RACE/ETHNICITY				
White, non-Hispanic	6,281	(5,383 - 7,323)	277	(159 - 484)
Black, non-Hispanic	688	(503 - 940)	16	(6 - 44)
Hispanic	450	(351 - 578)	36	(20 - 65)
REGION				
Northeast	1,540	(1,100 - 2,145)	62	(25 - 155)
North Central	2,091	(1,592 - 2,739)	73	(30 - 178)
South	1,929	(1,487 - 2,498)	155	(56 - 429)
West	2,081	(1,723 - 2,508)	56	(32 - 99)
TOTAL	**7,640**	(6,710 - 8,694)	346	(208 - 576)

* Low precision; no estimate reported.

SOURCE: "Table 17: PCP Use by Age, Gender, Race, and Region for Total Population in 1998" in *National Household Survey on Drug Abuse: Population Estimates 1998*, Substance Abuse and Mental Health Services Administration, Washington, D.C., 2000

opment and, sometimes, prenatal strokes and hemorrhages in the areas of the brain that control intellectual capacity.

By the mid-1990s, some public health officials began to suggest that observers might have overreacted to the problem. In 1994 Ellen Hutchins, health care administrator of the U.S. Department of Health and Human Services' Office of Maternal and Child Health, noted that medical researchers were beginning to retreat from earlier, dramatic claims about the effects of cocaine on fetuses. The effects of cocaine on such factors as birthweight and head circumference "are very minimal," Hutchins claimed.

In 2001 the *Journal of the American Medical Association* (JAMA) published a review of 36 scientific studies that tested the effects of cocaine exposure before birth on later development ("Growth, Development, and Behavior in Early Childhood Following Prenatal Cocaine Exposure," Frank et al., *JAMA*, March 28, 2001). In this article a group of Boston University medical and public health researchers concluded that there was no convincing evidence that prenatal cocaine exposure has an effect on physical growth; cognitive, language, or motor development; or behavioral or emotional outcomes in early childhood. The early reports of such findings, the authors concluded, often confused the effects of cocaine, alcohol, and tobacco. Because cocaine users are also more likely to smoke and drink alcohol, the use of these substances may account for some of the early findings that children of cocaine users suffer many ill effects.

PROSECUTING PREGNANT ADDICTS

In addition to the effects of prenatal drug exposure on infants, women who use illicit drugs during their pregnan-

TABLE 3.14

Estimated number of emergency department drug episodes, drug mentions, mentions of selected drugs, and total visits, 1992–99

	Total 1992	Total 1993	Total 1994	Total 1995	Total 1996	Total 1997	Total 1998	Total 1999	p-value 1998, 1999[1,2]	p-value 1997, 1999[1,3]
DRUG EPISODES	433,493	460,910	518,521	513,633	514,347	527,058	542,544	554,932	0.610	0.373
DRUG MENTIONS	751,731	796,762	900,317	901,206	907,561	943,937	982,856	1,015,206	0.488	0.245
Alcohol-in-combination	141,772	143,574	160,744	166,925	166,185	171,982	185,002	196,277	0.476	0.232
Cocaine	119,843	123,423	142,878	135,801	152,433	161,087	172,014	168,763	0.767	0.573
Heroin/morphine	48,003	63,232	64,013	70,838	73,846	72,010	77,645	84,409	0.191	0.073
Acetaminophen	31,355	34,033	38,674	36,563	38,265	35,448	32,257	28,258	0.013 -	0.000 -
Aspirin	18,834	18,958	19,358	16,729	15,854	14,623	15,457	12,815	0.007 -	0.148
Ibuprofen	16,400	17,534	19,031	21,250	16,979	17,070	17,146	14,400	0.009 -	0.017 -
Alprazolam	16,498	16,832	17,183	17,082	16,655	17,468	17,833	20,484	0.124	0.110
Marijuana/hashish	23,997	28,873	40,183	45,271	53,789	64,744	76,870	87,150	0.108	0.009 +
Diazepam	13,947	12,409	13,568	14,248	13,601	13,367	12,758	11,406	0.196	0.092
Amitriptyline	10,132	9,863	11,297	8,898	8,874	8,445	6,710	5,716	0.296	0.004 -
Acetamin./codeine	7,094	7,655	6,849	6,829	5,832	6,589	5,045	3,721	0.012 -	0.000 -
OTC sleep aids	7,034	5,380	6,890	6,794	7,628	6,084	5,750	4,986	0.232	0.120
Lorazepam	8,925	10,191	12,248	11,256	10,035	10,818	10,472	10,692	0.873	0.936
d-Propoxyphene	6,551	8,039	7,478	7,015	6,780	7,614	6,885	6,252	0.440	0.103
Fluoxetine	8,327	7,537	9,123	9,499	9,596	10,495	9,812	9,379	0.669	0.293
Diphenhydramine	7,861	7,442	9,537	8,685	9,406	8,804	6,110	5,468	0.326	0.000 -
Methamphetamine/speed	6,563	9,926	17,665	15,936	11,002	17,154	11,491	10,447	0.389	0.002 -
Oxycodone	.3,750	3,395	4,084	3,393	3,190	4,857	5,211	6,429	0.062	0.070
PCP/PCP combinations	5,282	6,614	6,019	6,237	3,924	4,195	4,033	4,969	0.134	0.293
Lithium carbonate	4,653	5,327	5,964	6,707	4,678	4,864	3,481	3,867	0.513	0.224
Clonazepam	8,220	10,175	12,158	12,802	13,375	14,597	17,450	16,584	0.514	0.224
Hydantoin	3,879	3,528	3,276	3,576	2,935	2,434	2,976	2,887	0.885	0.535
Hydrocodone	6,105	6,115	8,478	8,977	10,473	10,705	12,568	14,639	0.158	0.026 +
LSD	3,499	3,422	5,150	5,681	4,569	5,219	4,982	5,126	0.868	0.904
Triazolam	1,666	1,264	997	776	726	322	537	560	0.916	0.207
Phenobarbital	3,220	3,021	2,471	2,888	2,335	1,830	2,545	1,493	0.020 -	0.413
Doxepin	3,605	3,351	4,268	2,726	2,402	2,091	1,537	1,552	0.962	0.186
Cyclobenzaprine	2,731	2,647	3,130	2,924	3,599	3,626	2,967	2,761	0.677	0.114
Haloperidol	2,896	3,301	3,072	2,718	3,311	2,306	2,131	1,183	0.040 -	0.020 -
mphetamine	3,713	5,538	9,664	9,380	9,308	10,235	11,751	11,954	0.887	0.275
Trazodone	4,640	5,682	7,293	9,455	9,210	8,733	9,674	9,853	0.863	0.322
Carisoprodol	5,922	6,570	6,571	7,771	7,279	6,133	8,454	8,829	0.728	0.008 +
Naproxen	2,690	3,125	4,302	5,253	4,546	5,330	5,549	4,610	0.129	0.295
Imipramine	4,371	3,295	2,764	2,482	1,837	1,383	717	751	0.871	0.033
Carbamazepine	3,319	4,823	3,881	3,633	3,740	3,471	3,219	3,052	0.799	0.573
Thioridazine	2,881	3,017	3,190	2,567	2,243	1,727	1,227	478	0.004 -	0.001
TOTAL ED VISITS**	85,944	87,651	89,629	88,548	91,189	89,720	89,683	91,100	0.000 +	0.000 +

** Drug Abuse Warning Network estimates of emergency department (ED) visits (in 1,000s) should be close to but will not necessarily equal totals from previous year's American Hospital Association (AHA) Annual Survey.

[1] In this column, "+" and "-" denote statistically significant increases and decreases, respectively, between estimates for periods noted. For the purposes of this report, p-values less than 0.05 are considered to be statistically significant.

[2] This column compares 1998 to 1999.

[3] This column compares 1997 to 1999.

NOTE: These estimates are based on a representative sample of non-Federal, short-stay hospitals with 24-hour emergency departments in the coterminous U.S.

SOURCE: "Table 2—Estimated number of emergency department drug episodes, drug mentions, mentions of selected drugs, and total visits for coterminous U.S. by year: 1992–1999," in *Year-End 1999 Emergency Department Data from the Drug Abuse Warning Network,* Substance Abuse and Mental Health Services Administration, Washington, D.C., 2000.

cy often do not seek or receive proper health care and tend to suffer from many social, psychological, and economic problems. Many women fear criminal prosecution, incarceration, and/or losing their children to foster care.

Since 1987 a growing number of cases have been brought against women for abusing drugs during pregnancy. The charges range from criminal child abuse to assault with a deadly weapon and manslaughter. In a 1991 case the Michigan Court of Appeals (*People v. Hardy*, 469 NW 2d 50) rejected the state's argument against Kimberly Hardy of Muskegon. The state accused Hardy, who had smoked crack hours before her son was born, of passing

cocaine to her child prenatally, in a manner that constituted criminal delivery of drugs.

Delivering Drugs to a Minor

In a 1991 Florida case Jennifer Clarise Johnson was sentenced to 14 years probation and mandatory participation in a drug-treatment program for using cocaine the night before her son was born in 1987. In 1989 Johnson gave birth to a second child, telling the obstetrician she had used drugs that morning. She was convicted of delivering drugs to a minor by passing cocaine through the umbilical cord in the minutes after her daughter's birth but before the cord was clamped. Legally, the state felt it had a better chance of convicting Johnson of delivering drugs to a minor (after the child was born) than of charging her with abuse of a fetus (before the child was born).

In 1992 the Supreme Court of Florida, in *Johnson v. State* (602 So. 2d 1288, 1290), overturned Johnson's conviction on the grounds that the state legislature did not intend "to use the word 'delivery' in the context of criminally prosecuting mothers for delivery of a controlled substance to a minor by way of the umbilical cord."

Sometimes a Fetus Is Not a Child

In 1997, in a 4–3 decision, the Wisconsin Supreme Court ruled that a fetus was not a child under the state's welfare laws and, therefore, the drug-abusing mother could not be incarcerated to guarantee the safety of the fetus. M. W. was a woman who had been using cocaine and other drugs. After she tested positive for drugs for three months, her obstetrician urged her to enter drug treatment. She did not, and the doctor reported her to the county authorities. They went to juvenile court to request an order that would remove the "unborn child from his or her present custody and placing the unborn child" in protective custody.

The juvenile court agreed and ordered the sheriff to take the child to the local hospital for proper treatment. "Such detention," observed the court, "will, by necessity, result in the detention of the unborn child's mother." M. W. went into treatment, and the court allowed her to stay in the local hospital as long as she continued treatment.

FIGURE 3.1

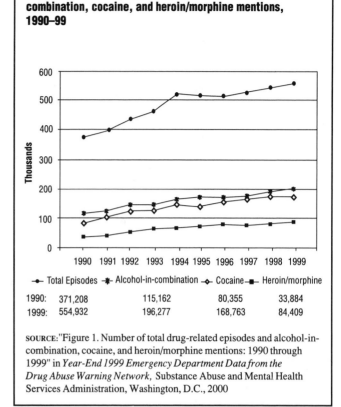

Number of total drug-related episodes and alcohol-in-combination, cocaine, and heroin/morphine mentions, 1990–99

	Total Episodes	Alcohol-in-combination	Cocaine	Heroin/morphine
1990:	371,208	115,162	80,355	33,884
1999:	554,932	196,277	168,763	84,409

SOURCE:"Figure 1. Number of total drug-related episodes and alcohol-in-combination, cocaine, and heroin/morphine mentions: 1990 through 1999" in *Year-End 1999 Emergency Department Data from the Drug Abuse Warning Network,* Substance Abuse and Mental Health Services Administration, Washington, D.C., 2000

FIGURE 3.2

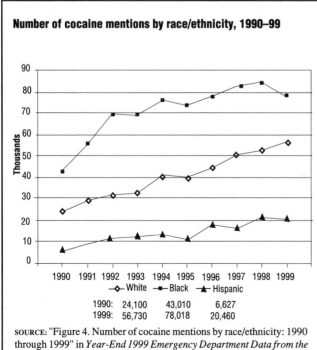

Number of cocaine mentions by race/ethnicity, 1990–99

	White	Black	Hispanic
1990:	24,100	43,010	6,627
1999:	56,730	78,018	20,460

SOURCE: "Figure 4. Number of cocaine mentions by race/ethnicity: 1990 through 1999" in *Year-End 1999 Emergency Department Data from the Drug Abuse Warning Network,* Substance Abuse and Mental Health Services Administration, Washington, D.C., 2000

FIGURE 3.3

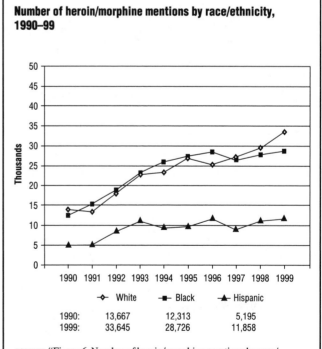

Number of heroin/morphine mentions by race/ethnicity, 1990–99

	White	Black	Hispanic
1990:	13,667	12,313	5,195
1999:	33,645	28,726	11,858

SOURCE: "Figure 6. Number of heroin/morphine mentions by race/ethnicity: 1990 through 1999" in *Year-End 1999 Emergency Department Data from the Drug Abuse Warning Network,* Substance Abuse and Mental Health Services Administration, Washington, D.C., 2000

TABLE 3.15

Emergency department drug episodes by age, gender, race/ethnicity, hospital location, drug use motive, and reason for emergency department contact, 1992–99

DRUG EPISODES

	Total 1992	Total 1993	Total 1994	Total 1995	Total 1996	Total 1997	Total 1998	Total 1999	p-value 1998, 1999[1,2]	p-value 1997, 1999[1,3]
TOTAL U.S.*	433,493	460,910	518,521	513,633	514,347	527,058	542,544	554,932	0.610	0.373
AGE										
6-34	277,887	288,332	324,933	309,937	303,384	306,709	301,960	294,804	0.551	0.450
12-17	46,822	50,039	60,472	60,722	63,949	61,437	59,086	52,783	0.009 -	0.008 -
18-25	96,307	98,276	112,262	103,708	98,625	104,647	103,438	109,580	0.280	0.509
26-34	133,506	138,634	151,195	144,003	139,634	138,897	138,483	131,256	0.240	0.329
35+	154,570	171,257	190,145	202,316	210,105	218,630	239,172	259,318	0.122	0.014 +
GENDER										
Male	219,607	231,721	263,334	256,137	257,658	269,965	281,355	292,085	0.505	0.278
Female	210,051	224,526	250,333	252,162	251,072	252,229	256,230	258,079	0.842	0.630
RACE/ETHNICITY										
White	235,643	245,243	279,312	277,637	274,057	284,242	295,447	310,072	0.437	0.298
Black	122,880	126,929	141,171	139,389	135,332	134,896	136,481	132,983	0.669	0.840
Hispanic	42,174	48,233	50,438	47,360	55,032	52,707	57,162	56,891	0.938	0.569
Other race	4,892	5,844	6,050	5,536	6,020	6,097	5,382	5,585	0.709	0.471
Race unknown	27,905	34,660	41,550	43,709	43,905	49,115	48,072	49,401	0.723	0.964
FACILITY LOCATION										
Central city	158,892	162,210	170,269	171,372	171,926	163,581	165,660	162,466	0.436	0.864
Outside central city	70,445	74,542	82,063	81,587	81,766	81,096	81,860	79,212	0.298	0.602
National Panel	204,155	223,256	266,189	260,674	260,654	282,380	295,023	313,254	0.446	0.314
DRUG USE MOTIVE										
Recreational use	35,008	36,421	43,948	46,207	53,873	56,075	57,035	66,351	0.183	0.142
Dependence	135,280	144,152	165,541	163,991	167,470	178,561	189,094	202,692	0.312	0.183
Suicide	172,403	180,212	199,773	201,120	191,410	191,481	189,897	174,857	0.048 -	0.135
Other/unknown motive	90,801	100,125	109,259	102,315	101,595	100,941	106,518	111,031	0.512	0.234
REASONS FOR ED CONTACT										
Unexpected reaction	52,588	54,569	66,595	57,382	61,902	68,687	71,180	78,342	0.115	0.110
Overdose	232,674	243,765	269,573	271,722	252,915	244,924	245,164	232,283	0.112	0.179
Chronic effects	46,865	50,180	56,010	60,166	53,467	49,273	50,110	49,945	0.963	0.883
Seeking detox	44,815	47,398	52,213	50,483	59,923	67,888	73,043	72,960	0.991	0.678
Withdrawal	9,851	11,125	14,025	15,127	15,013	15,176	17,979	25,910	0.176	0.102
Other/unknown reason	46,700	53,872	60,105	58,754	71,127	81,110	85,068	95,493	0.330	0.325

*** Total includes patients whose gender or age was unknown.

[1] In this column, "+" and "-" denote statistically significant increases and decreases, respectively, between estimates for periods noted. For the purposes of this report, p-values less than 0.05 are considered to be statistically significant.

[2] This column compares 1998 to 1999.

[3] This column compares 1997 to 1999.

NOTE: These estimates are based on a representative sample of non-Federal, short-stay hospitals with 24-hour emergency departments in the coterminous U.S.

SOURCE: "Table 18—Estimated number of emergency department drug episodes, by age, gender, race/ethnicity, hospital location, drug use motive, and reason for emergency department contact: 1992–1999," in *Year-End 1999 Emergency Department Data from the Drug Abuse Warning Network,* Substance Abuse and Mental Health Services Administration, Washington, D.C., 2000.

M. W. appealed the case, claiming that the fetus was not a child with rights and, therefore, the court had no jurisdiction over her. An appeals court disagreed, but the state supreme court did not. As the case was making its way to the Wisconsin Supreme Court, M. W. delivered the child. The Wisconsin Supreme Court ruled that the fetus was, indeed, not a child and, therefore, had no rights. Consequently, the welfare authorities could not order that the mother be incarcerated in order to protect the fetus.

And Sometimes It Is

In South Carolina a woman named Cornelia Whitner had used crack during the final trimester of her pregnancy, and as a result, her baby was born with cocaine residue in its blood. Whitner was charged with child neglect. She pleaded guilty and was sentenced to eight years in prison. After 19 months of incarceration, Whitner challenged her conviction. Whitner's lawyers argued that the relevant statute punished the unlawful neglect of a child, not a fetus, and the conviction was overturned in 1993.

In 1996, however, in *Whitner v. South Carolina* (No. 24468, 1996 WL 393164), the Supreme Court of South Carolina reinstated Whitner's conviction:

South Carolina law has long recognized that viable fetuses are persons holding certain legal rights and privileges. We do not see any rational basis for finding a viable fetus is not a "person" in the present context. It would be absurd to recognize the viable fetus as a per-

TABLE 3.16

Estimated rate of emergency department drug episodes per 100,000 population by age and gender, 1992–99

DRUG EPISODES

	Total 1992	Total 1993	Total 1994	Total 1995	Total 1996	Total 1997	Total 1998	Total 1999
TOTAL U.S.*	**191**	**201**	**225**	**221**	**219**	**222**	**225**	**228**
AGE								
6-34	256	266	300	287	281	284	279	272
12-17	228	238	280	275	286	272	258	229
18-25	345	356	402	375	358	381	372	388
26-34	353	371	416	403	396	400	406	393
35+	131	142	156	162	165	168	181	193
GENDER								
Male	201	209	237	228	227	235	242	249
Female	179	190	210	210	207	205	206	205

*** Total includes patients whose gender or age was unknown.

NOTE: These estimates are based on a representative sample of non-Federal, short-stay hospitals with 24-hour emergency departments in the coterminous U.S.

SOURCE: "Table 46: Estimated rate of emergency department drug episodes per 100,000 population by age, gender: 1992-1999" in *Year-End 1999 Emergency Department Data from the Drug Abuse Warning Network,* Substance Abuse and Mental Health Services Administration, Washington, D.C., 2000

TABLE 3.17

Drug abuse deaths by selected demographic characteristics according to gender, 1999

	TOTAL[1]		Male		Female	
Race/ethnicity and age	Number	Percent	Number	Percent	Number	Percent
GENDER						
Male	8,516	73.1				
Female	3,083	26.5				
Unknown/no response	52	0.4				
TOTAL	**11,651**	**100.0**				
RACE/ETHNICITY						
White	7,042	60.4	5,036	59.1	1,975	64.1
Black	3,023	25.9	2,212	26.0	807	26.2
Hispanic	1,286	11.0	1,060	12.4	221	7.2
Other	167	1.4	113	1.3	54	1.8
American Indian/Alaskan Native	52	0.4	33	0.4	19	0.6
Asian/Pacific Islander	115	1.0	80	0.9	35	1.1
Unknown/no response	133	1.1	95	1.1	26	0.8
TOTAL	**11,651**	**100.0**	**8,516**	**100.0**	**3,083**	**100.0**
AGE						
6-17 years	128	1.1	84	1.0	44	1.4
6-11 years	14	0.1	9	0.1	5	0.2
12-17 years	114	1.0	75	0.9	39	1.3
18-25 years	1,008	8.7	771	9.1	232	7.5
18-19 years	198	1.7	145	1.7	52	1.7
20-25 years	810	7.0	626	7.4	180	5.8
26-34 years	2,122	18.2	1,568	18.4	538	17.5
26-29 years	792	6.8	607	7.1	178	5.8
30-34 years	1,330	11.4	961	11.3	360	11.7
35 years and older	8,355	71.7	6,069	71.3	2,263	73.4
35-44 years	4,163	35.7	3,075	36.1	1,076	34.9
45-54 years	2,951	25.3	2,176	25.6	766	24.8
55 years and older	1,241	10.7	818	9.6	421	13.7
Unknown/no response	38	0.3	24	0.3	6	0.2
TOTAL	**11,651**	**100.0**	**8,516**	**100.0**	**3,083**	**100.0**

Excludes data on homicides, deaths in which AIDS was reported, and deaths in which "drug unknown" was the only substance mentioned.

[1] Includes episodes for which age was unknown or not reported.

SOURCE: "Table 2.01—Distribution of drug abuse deaths by selected demographic characteristics according to gender: 1999," in *Year-End 1999 Emergency Department Data from the Drug Abuse Warning Network,* Substance Abuse and Mental Health Services Administration, Washington, D.C., 2000.

TABLE 3.18

Drugs mentioned most frequently by medical examiners, 1999

Rank	Drug name[1]	Number of mentions	Percent of total episodes	Rank	Drug name[1]	Number of mentions	Percent of total episodes
1	Cocaine	4,864	41.75	44	Valproic Acid	61	0.52
2	Heroin/morphine [2]	4,820	41.37	45	Ephedrine	59	0.51
3	Alcohol-in-combination	3,916	33.61	46	Imipramine (Tofranil)	56	0.48
4	Codeine	1,395	11.97	47	Desipramine (Norpramin)	55	0.47
5	Diazepam (Valium)	811	6.96	48	Oxazepam	54	0.46
6	Methamphetamine/speed	690	5.92	49	Fentanyl	53	0.45
7	Marijuana/hashish	670	5.75	50	Benztropine	51	0.44
8	Methadone	643	5.52	51	Lorazepam (Ativan)	50	0.43
9	Diphenhydramine (Benadryl)	641	5.50	52	Thioridazine (Mellaril)	48	0.41
10	Amitriptyline (Elavil)	477	4.09	53	Hydromorphone (Dilaudid)	46	0.39
11	d-Propoxyphene (Darvocet N, Darvon)	466	4.00	54	MDM	42	0.36
12	Amphetamine [3]	452	3.88	55	Metoprolol	41	0.35
13	Hydrocodone	447	3.84	56	Chlorpromazine (Thorazine)	39	0.33
14	Acetaminophen (Tylenol)	427	3.66	57	Pentobarbital	37	0.32
15	Nortriptyline	424	3.64	58	Ibuprofen	35	0.30
16	Unspec. benzodiazepine	409	3.51	59	Secobarbital	32	0.27
17	Lidocaine	384	3.30	60	Mesoridazine	32	0.27
18	Fluoxetine (Prozac)	305	2.62	61	Phenylpropanolamine	29	0.25
19	Oxycodone (Percocet 5, Percodan, Tylox)	262	2.25	62	Butabarbital	28	0.24
20	Alprazolam (Xanax)	252	2.16	63	Brompheniramine maleate	26	0.22
21	Quinine	250	2.15	64	Trimethoprim/sulfamethox	26	0.22
22	Phenobarbital	232	1.99	65	Propanolol HCl	24	0.21
23	Doxepin (Sinequan)	212	1.82	66	Dihydrocodeine	24	0.21
24	Trazodone (Desyrel)	172	1.48	67	Phentermine	22	0.19
25	Meprobamate	170	1.46	68	Haloperidol	22	0.19
26	Hydantoin (Dilantin)	166	1.42	69	Metoclopramide	22	0.19
27	Carisoprodol	165	1.42	70	Procaine HCl	21	0.18
28	Dextromethorphan	132	1.13	71	Ketamine HCl	21	0.18
29	Chlorpheniramine	117	1.00	72	Flurazepam (Dalmane)	20	0.17
30	Doxylamine succinate	107	0.92	73	Clomipramine	18	0.15
31	Aspirin	104	0.89	74	Naproxen (Naprocyn)	18	0.15
32	Meperidine HCl (Demerol)	103	0.88	75	Oxymorphones	15	0.13
33	Promethazine	100	0.86	76	Theophylline	14	0.12
34	PCP/PCP combinations	98	0.84	77	Hydrocarbon	13	0.11
35	Carbamazepine	98	0.84	78	Hyoscyamine	12	0.10
36	Clonazepam (Klonopin)	96	0.82	79	Methylphenidate	12	0.10
37	Temazepam	92	0.79	80	Insulin	12	0.10
38	Phenaglycodol	88	0.76	81	Amantadine HCl	11	0.09
39	Cyclobenzaprine	84	0.72	82	Quinidine Sulfate	11	0.09
40	Butalbital	78	0.67	83	Levorphanol	11	0.09
41	Chlordiazepoxide (Librium)	75	0.64	84	Papaverine	10	0.09
42	Pseudoephedrine	67	0.58	85	Prochlorperazine	10	0.09
43	Hydroxyzine	63	0.54				

[1] Drugs with fewer than 10 mentions are excluded. Excludes data on homicides, deaths in which AIDS was reported, and deaths in which "drug unknown" was the only substance.
[2] Includes opiates not specified as to type.
[3] Does not include methamphetamine or other unspecified amphetamines.
NOTE: Percentages are based on a total raw medical examiner drug abuse case count of 11,651.

SOURCE: "Table 2.06a—Drugs mentioned most frequently by medical examiners: 1999," in *Year-End 1999 Emergency Department Data from the Drug Abuse Warning Network,* Substance Abuse and Mental Health Services Administration, Washington, D.C., 2000.

son for purposes of homicide and wrongful death statutes, but not for purposes of statutes proscribing [forbidding] child abuse.

The Court emphasized how important it was that the state protect the child from abuse—and the earlier the better:

> The abuse or neglect of a child at any time during childhood can exact a profound toll on the child as well as on society. The consequences of abuse or neglect after birth often pale in comparison to those resulting from abuse suffered by the viable fetus before birth. This policy of prevention supports a reading of the word "person" to include viable fetuses.

Drug Testing Pregnant Women

On March 22, 2001, though, the U.S. Supreme Court ruled that mothers had been identified as drug users unconstitutionally. A case was brought against the city of Charleston, South Carolina, where public hospital personnel—in cooperation with the local police department—were drug testing pregnant patients without their explicit consent. The Court overturned earlier decisions, such as a 1999 decision in the U.S. Court of Appeals for the Fourth Circuit in Richmond, Virginia, that drug testing of pregnant women was justified by a "special needs" condition. (This "special needs" condition has been invoked to justify drug testing of student athletes, customs officials, and people who have a particularly important role in public health and safety.) The Supreme Court found that nonconsensual testing of mothers served law-enforcement purposes at least as much as it did public health—and might even be counterproductive to public health.

The American Medical Association and Public Health Association both argue that nonconsensual testing will frighten pregnant women away from the medical help they need. Studies of fetal alcohol syndrome and prenatal crack exposure suggest that the consequences for babies may be minimized, or even prevented, by ensuring proper health care and nutrition for drug-dependent mothers. The best approach, these organizations feel, is to improve the health of drug-dependent mothers by ensuring access to health care and drug-treatment services.

ANABOLIC STEROIDS AND OTHER PERFORMANCE-ENHANCING DRUGS

Different substances have long been used to try to increase muscular strength. Greek wrestlers reportedly ate 10 pounds of lamb a day to increase strength, while others drank a mixture of strychnine and wine or ate hallucinogenic mushrooms. The earliest recorded charges of drug use by athletes in competition were against swimmers in

TABLE 3.20

Anabolic steroid users' perceptions and behaviors

	Frequency	Percent
Use of injectable AS		
Yes	80	38.3
No	129	61.7
Use of more than one AS at one time ("stacking")		
Yes	93	43.7
No	120	56.1
Personal strength perceptions		
Greater than average	126	57.3
Average	67	30.9
Less than average	13	5.9
Personal health perceptions		
Excellent	89	39.7
Very good	71	31.7
Good	39	17.4
Fair	14	6.3
Poor	11	4.9
I would like to see the use of AS to improve performance in sports stopped.		
Strongly agree	38	17.0
Agree	25	11.2
Undecided	71	31.7
Disagree	35	15.6
Strongly disagree	55	24.6
I would stop using AS if I were absolutely convinced my fellow competitors no longer used them.		
Definitely yes	37	17.0
Probably yes	28	12.8
Unsure	69	31.7
Probably no	33	15.1
Definitely no	51	23.4

SOURCE: "Table 3.25: AS users' perceptions and behaviors," in *Anabolic Steroid Abuse,* National Institute on Drug Abuse, Washington, DC, 1990

TABLE 3.19

Percentages reporting past month use of illicit drugs among females aged 15–44, by pregnancy status, 1999

		PREGNANCY STATUS	
Drug	Total[1]	Pregnant	Not Pregnant
Any Illicit Drug[2]	7.9	3.4	8.1
Marijuana and Hashish	5.8	2.9	5.9
Cocaine	0.8	0.2	0.9
Crack	0.2	*	0.2
Heroin	0.1	*	0.1
Hallucinogens	0.6	*	0.6
LSD	0.3	*	0.3
PCP	0.0	*	0.0
Inhalants	0.4	0.1	0.4
Nonmedical Use of			
Any Psychotherapeutic[3]	2.4	0.6	2.5
Pain Relievers	1.6	0.1	1.6
Tranquilizers	0.7	0.3	0.8
Stimulants	0.7	0.2	0.7
Methamphetamine	0.2	0.2	0.2
Sedatives	0.1	0.2	0.1
Any Illicit Drug Other			
Than Marijuana[2]	3.6	0.8	3.7

*Low precision; no estimate reported.

[1] Estimates in the total column are for all females aged 15 to 44, including those with missing pregnancy status.
[2] Any Illicit Drug indicates use at least once of marijuana/hashish, cocaine (including crack), inhalants, hallucinogens (including PCP and LSD), heroin, or any prescription-type psychotherapeutic used nonmedically. Any Illicit Drug Other Than Marijuana indicates use at least once of any of these listed drugs, regardless of marijuana/hashish use; marijuana/hashish users who also have used any of the other listed drugs are included.
[3] Nonmedical use of any prescription-type pain reliever, tranquilizer, stimulant, or sedative; does not include over-the-counter-drugs.

SOURCE: "Percentages Reporting Past Month Use of Illicit Drugs Among Females Aged 15 to 44, by Pregnancy Status: 1999" in *Summary Findings from the 1999 National Household Survey on Drug Abuse,* Substance Abuse and Mental Health Services Administration, Washington, D.C., 2000

TABLE 3.21

Consequences that would cause anabolic steroid users to discontinue use

	Frequency	Percent
I would stop using AS if it was *proven* beyond doubt that they would . . .		
a. lead to permanent sterility		
Definitely yes	69	31.4
Probably yes	48	21.8
Unsure	46	20.9
Probably no	21	9.5
Definitely no	36	16.4
b. greatly increase my risk of liver cancer		
Definitely yes	69	31.1
Probably yes	59	26.6
Unsure	40	18.0
Probably no	26	11.7
Definitely no	28	12.6
c. greatly influence my risk of a heart attack before age 40		
Definitely yes	69	31.5
Probably yes	60	27.4
Unsure	39	17.8
Probably no	21	9.6
Definitely no	30	13.7

SOURCE: "Table 3.26: AS users' perceptions and behaviors," in *Anabolic Steroid Abuse,* National Institute on Drug Abuse, Washington, DC, 1990

TABLE 3.22

Anabolic steroid users' perceptions of health risk, by number of cycles of steroids taken

Percentage of users who believed that steroid use carried a risk of certain health conditions.

Number of Cycles	Definitely Yes (%)	Probably Yes (%)	Undecided (%)	Probably No (%)	Definitely No (%)
Sterility					
1	50.0	30.0	17.5	2.5	0
2–4	29.9	32.0	23.7	10.3	4.1
≥5	24.4	4.9	19.5	12.2	39.0
Cancer					
1	35.0	32.5	22.5	10.0	0
2–4	34.0	33.0	17.5	12.4	3.1
≥5	26.2	15.5	16.7	11.9	29.8
Heart Attack					
1	35.9	33.3	23.1	5.1	.6
2–4	37.5	33.3	15.6	10.4	3.1
≥5	22.9	16.9	18.1	10.9	31.3

SOURCE: "Table 3.27: Health risk," in *Anabolic Steroid Abuse,* National Institute on Drug Abuse, Washington, DC, 1990

canal races in Amsterdam in 1865. In 1869 bicycle-racing coaches were widely known to administer a heroin and cocaine mixture, known as a "speedball," to increase the cyclists' endurance. The first recorded drug-related sports death involved a European cyclist in an 1886 race.

Types of Drugs Used

The American Osteopathic Academy of Sports Medicine, in *Anabolic Androgenic Steroids and Substance Abuse in Sport* (Middleton, WI, 1989), lists two classes of sports drugs. The first class is restorative drugs, which help an individual recover to his/her previous state of health and performance. They help the athlete compete despite injuries. Restorative drugs include painkillers, aspirin, morphine, muscle relaxants, topical anesthetics, and anti-inflammatory medications.

The other class of drugs is ergogenic substances, which allow the athlete to perform beyond what would normally be possible but which also can be highly addictive. Examples include anabolic steroids, amphetamines, cocaine, caffeine, and blood doping (exchanging an athlete's blood with fresh blood with a high oxygen content). Other performance-enhancing drugs include human growth hormone (used to increase muscle mass), erythropoietin (used to increase the oxygen-carrying capacity of blood), and over-the-counter diet supplements such as creatine and androstenedione.

ANABOLIC STEROIDS. Present-day anabolic steroids, powerful synthesized derivatives of the male hormone testosterone, were developed in Europe in the 1930s. Among their other qualities, steroids build body tissue, helping athletes increase muscle strength and mass. Because the technology for timing in races has become so precise, the difference between winning and losing has been reduced to a fraction of a second—making steroids an irresistible temptation for many professional and amateur athletes.

Steroid use, though, is not limited to athletes. In today's society there is such a premium on physical appearance, and self-esteem is so closely linked to perceived attractiveness, that many users have no athletic goal in mind. Instead they are trying to overcome perceived physical and emotional limitations by "bulking up."

Anabolic steroids can either be taken orally or injected. They are usually taken in periods of weeks or months (known as "cycling") rather than continuously. Cycling involves taking multiple doses of steroids over a specific time period, stopping for a period, and then starting again. Users often combine different types of steroids—a process known as "stacking"—to increase effectiveness while decreasing negative effects.

PSYCHOLOGICAL RISKS OF STEROIDS. Steroids can be highly addictive. The enhanced sense of self-esteem that one gains with steroids plays a major role in their addictive quality. Users become convinced that they need the drugs to look good and perform well. This often leads them to seek out steroids on the black market.

Several psychological attitudes associated with steroid use are the same as those associated with drug dependence in general. One such attitude is a tendency to overlook, disbelieve, or argue against the physical risks of drug use and to perceive the benefits as outweighing the risks.

C. E. Yesalis et al. studied high school seniors and their attitudes toward steroids ("Indications of Psychological Dependence Among Anabolic-Androgenic Steroid Abusers," *Anabolic Steroid Abuse*, National Institute on Drug Abuse, Washington, D.C., 1990). They found that of 226 users, 57.3 percent thought their personal strength was "greater than average," and 71.4 percent thought their health was "excellent" or "very good." (See Table 3.20.) Approximately one in four "definitely" intended to continue use, regardless of possible consequences such as liver cancer, heart attack, or sterility. (See Table 3.21.)

The researchers noted that the more steroids the youths used, the more distorted their perceptions became. Among those who had taken five or more cycles of steroids, 51 percent thought there was "probably" or "definitely" no risk of sterility; 42 percent did not believe there was a risk of cancer; and 42 percent doubted their chances of a heart attack. In contrast, 80 percent of those who had completed only one cycle of steroids feared sterility; 67.5 percent were concerned about cancer; and 69 percent thought they might be risking heart attacks. (See Table 3.22.)

Another serious psychological effect of steroid use is known as "roid rage." The individual may become extremely aggressive and hostile—sometimes to the point of violence. This rage can be so powerful that several homicides and many other senseless, violent crimes have been committed under the influence of steroids. When steroid use is stopped, the user can suffer suicidal depression.

Health Risks of Performance-Enhancing Drugs

Recent research indicates that, despite their widespread use, anabolic steroids do not necessarily improve athletic performance (although they can) and actually have many serious side effects. These include elevated blood pressure; higher cholesterol levels; increased risk of heart attack; enlargement of the male prostate; liver cancer; infertility; kidney disease; severe acne; stunted growth; breast development in men; facial hair, male pattern baldness, and birth abnormalities in women; and diminished sexual desire.

Human growth hormone (hGH) can cause muscle and bone disfigurement, such as a jutting forehead and elongated jaw. Heart and metabolic problems have also been associated with the use of hGH. Erythropoietin (EPO) increases the number of red blood cells. The extra cells can make blood the consistency of yogurt, possibly leading to a clot, heart attack, or stroke. In addition, since EPO must be injected, there is the added risk of contracting or transmitting hepatitis or HIV. Studies suggest that androstenedione may be linked to heart disease and stroke, and even to aggressive behavior.

Despite the dire consequences of using performance-enhancing drugs, some young athletes are willing to take the risks to ensure 10–20 years of increased athletic ability. Some use steroids with the knowledge and consent, or even insistence, of their coaches and trainers, although increased education about steroids has made this far less common. In 1991 former professional football player Lyle Alzado went public about the dangers of steroids, describing and showing the ill effects that long-term steroid use had had on his physical and emotional state. He insisted that his coaches knew of, and encouraged, his steroid use. He died in 1992 from a rare form of cancer that he attributed to his abuse of steroids and hGH.

Drug Testing in Professional Sports

The use of steroids in sports probably began in the 1950s, and many attribute its origin to weight lifters from Eastern Europe. Whatever its origins, it quickly spread to the United States. Anabolic steroids were officially outlawed in Olympic competition in 1973, but at the 1988 Olympic games, mandatory testing revealed that many world-class athletes were still using them.

Perhaps the most publicized figure to use steroids in the 1988 Olympic games was Ben Johnson of Canada, whose steroid use cost him his gold medal in track. In 1993 Johnson tried to make a comeback, and although he was competitive, he could not place in the top three. He returned to steroid use and was again caught and expelled from competition.

Olympic officials estimate that 10 percent of top athletes are using, or have used, performance-enhancing drugs. Some veteran athletes say that 30 percent or higher is more accurate. World records are now looked upon with suspicion rather than amazement. Helmut Digel, president of the German Athletic Federation, even proposed wiping clean all world records in track and field at the end of 1999 and starting over. Nothing became of this proposal.

Drug testing in athletics has been inadequate. Until the mid-1990s, most athletes were tested only during competition, producing positive results in only about 2 percent or less of the athletes. Athletes learned to beat the system, either by reducing or eliminating use just before competition or by using masking agents such as Probenecid. (Probenecid inhibits substances from reaching the urine.) Some countries have instituted frequent, random, out-of-competition testing—effective because most performance-enhancing drugs are used during training. The International Olympic Committee (IOC), however, has only recently begun to mandate out-of-competition testing.

In addition, drug tests cannot keep pace with new drugs. According to Hein Verbruggen, head of the International Cycling Union, "Undetectable drugs are 90 percent of estimated doping cases." Drug concentrations are higher in blood, making drugs easier to detect, but many sports federations, including the IOC, do not test blood. It is considered invasive, and religious issues could also be involved. Instead, urine testing is commonly used to screen athletes. Because urine samples are less concentrated, doping is easier to hide.

Added amounts of hGH do not show up in blood or urine tests. EPO is also difficult to detect because the blood cells that the drug adds are the athlete's own. Water-based steroids (the most common) are undetectable in urine after several weeks.

At the 1998 World Conference on Doping in Sport, some efforts were made to strengthen antidoping measures, but aside from the creation of a $25 million World Anti-Doping Agency (WADA) and the extension of an antidoping code to coaches, officials, and medical staff, very little was accomplished. In 2000 WADA began plans to implement out-of-competition testing for the first time.

In response to growing pressure from around the world, the IOC, with the aid of WADA, launched its most stringent crackdown on drug-using athletes ever at the 2000 Summer Olympics in Sydney, Australia. For the first time, the IOC required athletes to submit to random blood tests. According to WADA, numerous athletes were caught using drugs and prohibited from competing. Nonetheless,

FIGURE 3.4

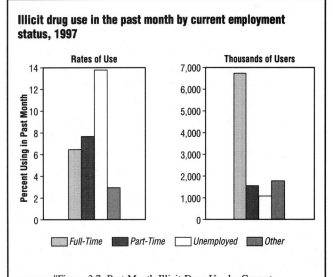

Illicit drug use in the past month by current employment status, 1997

SOURCE: "Figure 3.7: Past Month Illicit Drug Use by Current Employment Status, 1997," in *Preliminary Results from the 1997 National Household Survey on Drug Abuse,* Substance Abuse and Mental Health Services Administration, Washington, DC, 1998

TABLE 3.23

States with laws promoting a drug-free workplace, 1999

	Drug-free workplace laws	Workers' comp. discount for drug-free workplaces	Reduced benefits if injury is due to alcohol or drugs
Alabama		x	x
Alaska			x
California	x		x
Colorado			x
Connecticut			x
Florida	x	x	x
Georgia	x	x	x
Hawaii		x	x
Idaho	x		x
Illinois	x		
Indiana			x
Iowa			x
Kansas			x
Kentucky			x
Louisiana			x
Maine			x
Maryland			x
Minnesota			x
Mississippi		x	x
Missouri			x
Nebraska			x
Nevada			x
New Hampshire			x
New Jersey			x
New Mexico			x
New York			x
North Carolina			x
North Dakota			x
Ohio		x	x
Oklahoma			x
Oregon			x
Pennsylvania			x
Rhode Island			x
South Carolina	x	x	x
South Dakota			x
Tennessee		x	x
Texas	x		x
Utah			x
Virginia		x	x
Washington		x	
West Virginia			x
Wisconsin			x
Wyoming			x

SOURCE: Kelly Fox, "Drug-Free Workplaces," in *NCSL Legisbriefs,* vol. 7, no. 11, February 1999

critics argue that testing will never be able to keep up with new technologies in performance-enhancing drugs.

A Changing Source of Supply

Until recently, most black-market steroids were legitimately manufactured drugs that ended up on the street through theft or fraudulent prescriptions. But more effective law enforcement, coupled with greater demand, has forced black marketeers to seek new sources of production. Currently, a significant percentage of steroids are made overseas and smuggled into the United States or are produced in clandestine laboratories in this country. This new source of steroid production may likely put users at even greater risk than stolen but legally manufactured steroids, because drugs manufactured in these secret labs may be impure, mislabeled, or not even steroids at all.

Extent of Use

In the 1999 *Youth Risk Behavior Surveillance* 3.7 percent of students reported having used illegal steroids in their lifetime. In this survey, males were twice as likely as females to have ever used steroids. The 2000 *Monitoring the Future* survey found that 3.0 percent of eighth-graders, 3.5 percent of tenth-graders, and 2.5 percent of twelfth-graders reported using steroids at least once in their lifetime. In the *Core Alcohol and Drug Survey* 0.8 percent of college students said they had used steroids in 1997. There was no question in this survey about lifetime use. (See Chapter 4 for more on youth drug surveys.)

According to recent studies, the use of steroids by girls is increasing. "Girls on Steroids" (*Time*, August 10, 1998) reported that a survey conducted at Pennsylvania

State University estimated that the number of 14- to 18-year-old girls using steroids could be as high as 175,000. A study of four Massachusetts middle schools found that girls as young as 10 were taking steroids at about the same rate as boys. The reason for the increase, according to the article, is the higher number of girls competing in sports and vying for athletic scholarships. Females face an even longer list of health risks than males.

Nutritional Supplements

During the past few years there has been a growing market for nutritional supplements such as creatine and androstenedione—especially among teenagers. Nutritional supplements are not regulated by the Food and Drug Administration (FDA) in the same ways that over-the-counter and prescription medications are. As long as the manufacturers do not claim any medical value for their products, the FDA does not regulate them. This means that they do not have to pass rigorous trials and tests to determine benefits and possible harm.

One of the most controversial supplements has been androstenedione, a substance naturally produced by the body and involved in testosterone production. It made headlines in 1998 when Mark McGwire announced that he had used it in training in 1997, the year he broke Major League Baseball's all-time home run record. McGwire and many others attributed his success to the supplement.

Although there has been little testing, some research indicates that the effects of androstenedione may be overblown. While creatine may improve performance on some tasks, no medical research supports the claim that androstenedione does the same. The side effects of these substances are also largely unknown. Researchers suspect that androstenedione may cause many of the same health troubles as anabolic steroids. They are especially concerned that adolescents who use creatine and androstenedione may be particularly susceptible to harmful side effects.

DRUG USE IN THE WORKPLACE

Because a significant number of Americans have used, or do use, illegal drugs and alcohol, it should not be surprising that drug and alcohol abuse play a role in the nation's workplaces. The 1997 *National Survey* found that 73 percent of all adults (age 18 and over) who reported current use of illegal drugs were employed, either full-time or part-time—a total of 8.3 million people. This number was slightly higher than the 8.1 million employed adults who reported current drug use in 1996. Of unemployed adults, 13.8 percent reported current illicit-drug use, compared with 6.5 percent of full-time-employed adults. (See Figure 3.4.)

Drug and alcohol abuse result in a multitude of workplace problems. In "Drugs in the Workplace" (*Human Resource Magazine*, February 1998) Mark de Bernardo, executive director of the Institute for a Drug-Free Workplace, identifies these problems as tardiness, absenteeism, turnover, attitude problems, employee theft, accidents, product defects, decreased productivity, crime, and violence.

The U.S. Department of Labor estimates that drug use in the workplace costs employers between $75 billion and $100 billion annually in lost time, health care, accidents, and workers' compensation costs. Sixty-five percent of all workplace accidents can be traced to drugs or alcohol. Substance abusers have three times the absenteeism, and 16 times the number of health-care claims, as nonabusers. The U.S Department of Health and Human Services reports that substance abusers are six times more likely to file a workers' compensation claim.

FIGURE 3.5

Percentage of companies affiliated with the American Management Association who drug-test applicants or employees, 1986–95

SOURCE: "Drug testing becoming more common: Percentage of companies affiliated with the American Management Association who drug-test applicants or employees, 1986–1995," in *Workplace Drug Testing and Drug Abuse Policies,* American Management Association, April 1996

States are responding by passing laws that provide guidelines for promoting drug-free workplaces. Most states allow an employer to deny or reduce benefits to employees who are injured or terminated because of substance-abuse problems. Some states offer premium reductions for employers who comply with the regulations of drug-free-workplace programs. (See Table 3.23.) In a few states, such as California, there is growing conflict between an employee's right to privacy and an employer's right to test for drugs—making it difficult to implement random testing except in safety or security positions.

Drug Testing in the Workplace

Drug testing of job applicants and current employees has become much more common in recent years. Of the companies affiliated with the American Management Association (primarily large companies), 81 percent tested applicants or employees for drugs in 1995, compared with 21.5 percent in 1986. (See Figure 3.5.) Almost 98 percent of Fortune 500 companies now conduct pre-employment drug screening. But, according to Beth Lindamood, senior market analyst for Great American Insurance Companies and nationally recognized expert on workplace drug abuse, 60 percent of employed drug users work for small companies.

Drug use in the workplace seems to be declining, at least based on the percentage of positive employee drug tests. According to the semiannual drug-testing index published by SmithKline Beecham Clinical Laboratories, fewer than 5 percent of employee drugs tests in 1998 came back positive, down significantly from 13.6 percent

FIGURE 3.6

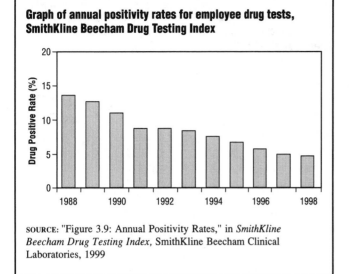

Graph of annual positivity rates for employee drug tests, SmithKline Beecham Drug Testing Index

SOURCE: "Figure 3.9: Annual Positivity Rates," in *SmithKline Beecham Drug Testing Index,* SmithKline Beecham Clinical Laboratories, 1999

TABLE 3.24

Annual positivity rates for employee drug tests, SmithKline Beecham Drug Testing Index

Year	Drug Positivity Rate
1988	13.6%
1989	12.7%
1990	11.0%
1991	8.8%
1992	8.8%
1993	8.4%
1994	7.5%
1995	6.7%
1996	5.8%
1997	5.0%
1998	4.8%

SOURCE: "Table 3.29: Annual Positivity Rates," in *SmithKline Beecham Drug Testing Index,* SmithKline Beecham Clinical Laboratories, 1999

in 1988. (See Figure 3.6 and Table 3.24.) Because more employers are testing for drugs, some observers feel that the decline in the number of positive tests may be a result of more non-drug users being tested. In addition, a growing number of drug users are learning how to evade urinalysis, still the most common form of drug testing.

In the late 1990s, with the unemployment rate at a 25-year low and the economy continuing to grow, some human-resource managers said they were starting to see an increase in the number of job applicants who failed drug screening. One reason for the increase, they believe, was that as the supply of potential employees continued to shrink, those with substance-abuse problems came to represent a larger portion of the labor pool.

Despite having the support of many employers, workplace drug testing also has numerous critics. One of the most vocal is the American Civil Liberties Union (ACLU), which claims that not only have recent scientific studies found few benefits to drug testing, but there are also several serious drawbacks to the procedure, including invasion-of-privacy issues and "false positive" results.

CHAPTER 4

DRUGS AND YOUTH

The annual *Monitoring the Future* survey, prepared by the University of Michigan's Institute for Social Research, monitors drug use among students in the United States. This series, often referred to as the *National High School Senior Survey,* is directed by Dr. Lloyd D. Johnston and is prepared for the National Institute on Drug Abuse (NIDA). It is considered the most authoritative source on drug use among students.

Each year since 1975, the Institute for Social Research has surveyed seniors (in this chapter, alternatively referred to as "twelfth-graders") in high schools nationwide, using self-completed, confidential questionnaires. Since 1991 the Institute has also surveyed similar samples of eighth- and tenth-graders. In 2000 the survey interviewed approximately 50,000 students in more than four hundred public and private secondary schools.

Table 4.1 and Table 4.2 provide an overview of survey findings from 1991 to 2000 for eighth, tenth-, and twelfth-graders. Table 4.3–Table 4.9 illustrate trends in the rates of "annual use" (drug use in the past year) for selected illicit drugs. These findings indicate that during the 1990s use of virtually every type of drug increased. Though the resurgence in drug use did not come near to returning to the levels of a generation ago, it was still a matter of concern. However, the 2000 survey showed that illicit drug use among American secondary school students may have stabilized.

MARIJUANA

After peaking in 1979 and 1980, marijuana use among high school seniors gradually declined until 1992. In 1979 and 1980, three out of five seniors (60.4 percent) reported that they had used marijuana—the most widely used of the illicit drugs—at least once in their lifetimes (defined as "lifetime use" or "lifetime prevalence"). By 1992 the lifetime-prevalence rate had fallen to about one-third (32.6 percent). Then, however, lifetime marijuana use began to rise, reaching 49.6 percent in 1997 and 48.8

percent in 2000. (See Table 4.10.) In 1979 half (50.8 percent) of high school seniors used marijuana at least once during the year of the survey, but by 1992 the proportion had dropped to 21.9 percent. It rose again, though—to 38.5 percent in 1997 and 36.5 percent in 2000. (See Table 4.11 and Table 4.4.)

In 1978, 37.1 percent of surveyed seniors claimed to have smoked marijuana within the past 30 days (defined as "30-day use"); by 1992 this figure had dropped to 11.9 percent. After that, however, the proportion nearly doubled—to 23.7 percent in 1997 and 21.6 percent in 2000. (See Table 4.12.)

Daily use plummeted from 10.7 percent in 1978 to 1.9 percent in 1992, and then began to rise, reaching 6 percent in 1999 and 2000. (See Table 4.13.) These were significant increases over a very short period of time.

Marijuana use among eighth- and tenth-graders also increased dramatically during the 1990s. Between 1991 and 2000, lifetime use among eighth-graders doubled, from 10.2 percent to 20.3 percent; annual use more than doubled, from 6.2 percent to 15.6 percent; and 30-day use nearly tripled, from 3.2 to 9.1 percent. (See Table 4.1 and Table 4.2.)

Among tenth-graders lifetime use rose from 23.4 percent in 1991 to 40.3 percent in 2000. In that same period, annual use nearly doubled, from 16.5 percent to 32.2 percent, and 30-day use more than doubled, from 8.7 percent to 19.7 percent. (See Table 4.1 and Table 4.2.)

INHALANTS

Inhalants are chemicals usually sold and intended for normal everyday use, such as model-airplane glue, gasoline, paint, and turpentine. Young people are the primary abusers of inhalants, often because these products are inexpensive and easy to get. Among eighth-, tenth-, and twelfth-graders, rates of lifetime, annual, and 30-day use have been dropping since 1995. (See Table 4.1 and Table 4.2.) Until

TABLE 4.1

Trends in lifetime prevalence of use of various drugs for eighth, tenth, and twelfth graders

(Entries are percentages)

					Lifetime						
	1991	1992	1993	1994	1995	1996	1997	1998	1999	2000	'99–'00 change
Any Illicit Drug[a]											
8th Grade	18.7	20.6	22.5	25.7	28.5	31.2	29.4	29.0	28.3	26.8	-1.5
10th Grade	30.6	29.8	32.8	37.4	40.9	45.4	47.3	44.9	46.2	45.6	-0.6
12th Grade	44.1	40.7	42.9	45.6	48.4	50.8	54.3	54.1	54.7	54.0	-0.7
Any Illicit Drug Other Than Marijuana[a]											
8th Grade	14.3	15.6	16.8	17.5	18.8	19.2	17.7	16.9	16.3	15.8	-0.6
10th Grade	19.1	19.2	20.9	21.7	24.3	25.5	25.0	23.6	24.0	23.1	-0.9
12th Grade	26.9	25.1	26.7	27.6	28.1	28.5	30.0	29.4	29.4	29.0	-0.3
Any Illicit Drug Including Inhalants[a,b]											
8th Grade	28.5	29.6	32.3	35.1	38.1	39.4	38.1	37.8	37.2	35.1	-2.0
10th Grade	36.1	36.2	38.7	42.7	45.9	49.8	50.9	49.3	49.9	49.3	-0.6
12th Grade	47.6	44.4	46.6	49.1	51.5	53.5	56.3	56.1	56.3	57.0	+0.8
Marijuana/Hashish											
8th Grade	10.2	11.2	12.6	16.7	19.9	23.1	22.6	22.2	22.0	20.3	-1.8
10th Grade	23.4	21.4	24.4	30.4	34.1	39.8	42.3	39.6	40.9	40.3	-0.7
12th Grade	36.7	32.6	35.3	38.2	41.7	44.9	49.6	49.1	49.7	48.8	-0.9
Inhalants[b,c]											
8th Grade	17.6	17.4	19.4	19.9	21.6	21.2	21.0	20.5	19.7	17.9	-1.8s
10th Grade	15.7	16.6	17.5	18.0	19.0	19.3	18.3	18.3	17.0	16.6	-0.4
12th Grade	17.6	16.6	17.4	17.7	17.4	16.6	16.1	15.2	15.4	14.2	-1.2
Nitrites[d]											
8th Grade	—	—	—	—	—	—	—	—	—	—	—
10th Grade	—	—	—	—	—	—	—	—	—	—	—
12th Grade	1.6	1.5	1.4	1.7	1.5	1.8	2.0	2.7	1.7	0.8	-0.8
Hallucinogens[c]											
8th Grade	3.2	3.8	3.9	4.3	5.2	5.9	5.4	4.9	4.8	4.6	-0.1
10th Grade	6.1	6.4	6.8	8.1	9.3	10.5	10.5	9.8	9.7	8.9	-0.8
12th Grade	9.6	9.2	10.9	11.4	12.7	14.0	15.1	14.1	13.7	13.0	-0.7
LSD											
8th Grade	2.7	3.2	3.5	3.7	4.4	5.1	4.7	4.1	4.1	3.9	-0.2
10th Grade	5.6	5.8	6.2	7.2	8.4	9.4	9.5	8.5	8.5	7.6	-1.0
12th Grade	8.8	8.6	10.3	10.5	11.7	12.6	13.6	12.6	12.2	11.1	-1.1
Hallucinogens Other Than LSD											
8th Grade	1.4	1.7	1.7	2.2	2.5	3.0	2.6	2.5	2.4	2.3	-0.1
10th Grade	2.2	2.5	2.8	3.8	3.9	4.7	4.8	5.0	4.7	4.8	+0.1
12th Grade	3.7	3.3	3.9	4.9	5.4	6.8	7.5	7.1	6.7	6.9	+0.2
PCP[d]											
8th Grade	—	—	—	—	—	—	—	—	—	—	—
10th Grade	—	—	—	—	—	—	—	—	—	—	—
12th Grade	2.9	2.4	2.9	2.8	2.7	4.0	3.9	3.9	3.4	3.4	-0.1
MDMA (Ecstasy)[d]											
8th Grade	—	—	—	—	—	3.4	3.2	2.7	2.7	4.3	+1.6ss
10th Grade	—	—	—	—	—	5.6	5.7	5.1	6.0	7.3	+1.3
12th Grade	—	—	—	—	—	6.1	6.9	5.8	8.0	11.0	+3.0s
Cocaine											
8th Grade	2.3	2.9	2.9	3.6	4.2	4.5	4.4	4.6	4.7	4.5	-0.2
10th Grade	4.1	3.3	3.6	4.3	5.0	6.5	7.1	7.2	7.7	6.9	-0.9
12th Grade	7.8	6.1	6.1	5.9	6.0	7.1	8.7	9.3	9.8	8.6	-1.2
Crack											
8th Grade	1.3	1.6	1.7	2.4	2.7	2.9	2.7	3.2	3.1	3.1	0.0
10th Grade	1.7	1.5	1.8	2.1	2.8	3.3	3.6	3.9	4.0	3.7	-0.3
12th Grade	3.1	2.6	2.6	3.0	3.0	3.3	3.9	4.4	4.6	3.9	-0.7s
Other Cocaine[e]											
8th Grade	2.0	2.4	2.4	3.0	3.4	3.8	3.5	3.7	3.8	3.5	-0.3
10th Grade	3.8	3.0	3.3	3.8	4.4	5.5	6.1	6.4	6.8	6.0	-0.8
12th Grade	7.0	5.3	5.4	5.2	5.1	6.4	8.2	8.4	8.8	7.7	-1.1
Heroin[f]											
8th Grade	1.2	1.4	1.4	2.0	2.3	2.4	2.1	2.3	2.3	1.9	-0.4
10th Grade	1.2	1.2	1.3	1.5	1.7	2.1	2.1	2.3	2.3	2.2	-0.1
12th Grade	0.9	1.2	1.1	1.2	1.6	1.8	2.1	2.0	2.0	2.4	+0.4

TABLE 4.1

Trends in lifetime prevalence of use of various drugs for eighth, tenth, and twelfth graders [CONTINUED]

(Entries are percentages)

					Lifetime						
	1991	1992	1993	1994	1995	1996	1997	1998	1999	2000	'99–'00 change
With a needle[g]											
8th Grade	—	—	—	—	1.5	1.6	1.3	1.4	1.6	1.1	-0.5ss
10th Grade	—	—	—	—	1.0	1.1	1.1	1.2	1.3	1.0	-0.2
12th Grade	—	—	—	—	0.7	0.8	0.9	0.8	0.9	0.8	-0.1
Without a needle[g]											
8th Grade	—	—	—	—	1.5	1.6	1.4	1.5	1.4	1.3	-0.1
10th Grade	—	—	—	—	1.1	1.7	1.7	1.7	1.6	1.7	0.0
12th Grade	—	—	—	—	1.4	1.7	2.1	1.6	1.8	2.4	+0.6
Other Narcotics[h]											
8th Grade	—	—	—	—	—	—	—	—	—	—	—
10th Grade	—	—	—	—	—	—	—	—	—	—	—
12th Grade	6.6	6.1	6.4	6.6	7.2	8.2	9.7	9.8	10.2	10.6	+0.4
Amphetamines[h]											
8th Grade	10.5	10.8	11.8	12.3	13.1	13.5	12.3	11.3	10.7	9.9	-0.8
10th Grade	13.2	13.1	14.9	15.1	17.4	17.7	17.0	16.0	15.7	15.7	+0.1
12th Grade	15.4	13.9	15.1	15.7	15.3	15.3	16.5	16.4	16.3	15.6	-0.7
Methamphetamine[i,j]											
8th Grade	—	—	—	—	—	—	—	—	4.5	4.2	-0.3
10th Grade	—	—	—	—	—	—	—	—	7.3	6.9	-0.5
12th Grade	—	—	—	—	—	—	—	—	8.2	7.9	-0.3
Ice[j]											
8th Grade	—	—	—	—	—	—	—	—	—	—	—
10th Grade	—	—	—	—	—	—	—	—	—	—	—
12th Grade	3.3	2.9	3.1	3.4	3.9	4.4	4.4	5.3	4.8	4.0	-0.8
Barbiturates[h]											
8th Grade	—	—	—	—	—	—	—	—	—	—	—
10th Grade	—	—	—	—	—	—	—	—	—	—	—
12th Grade	6.2	5.5	6.3	7.0	7.4	7.6	8.1	8.7	8.9	9.2	+0.2
Tranquilizers[h]											
8th Grade	3.8	4.1	4.4	4.6	4.5	5.3	4.8	4.6	4.4	4.4	0.0
10th Grade	5.8	5.9	5.7	5.4	6.0	7.1	7.3	7.8	7.9	8.0	+0.1
12th Grade	7.2	6.0	6.4	6.6	7.1	7.2	7.8	8.5	9.3	8.9	-0.5
Rohypnol[d,k]											
8th Grade	—	—	—	—	—	1.5	1.1	1.4	1.3	1.0	-0.3
10th Grade	—	—	—	—	—	1.5	1.7	2.0	1.8	1.3	-0.5
12th Grade	—	—	—	—	—	1.2	1.8	3.0	2.0	1.5	-0.6
Alcohol[l]											
Any use											
8th Grade	70.1	69.3	67.1	—	—	—	—	—	—	—	—
			55.7	55.8	54.5	55.3	53.8	52.5	52.1	51.7	-0.4
10th Grade	83.8	82.3	80.8	—	—	—	—	—	—	—	—
			71.6	71.1	70.5	71.8	72.0	69.8	70.6	71.4	+0.9
12th Grade	88.0	87.5	87.0	—	—	—	—	—	—	—	—
			80.0	80.4	80.7	79.2	81.7	81.4	80.0	80.3	+0.2
Been Drunk[j]											
8th Grade	26.7	26.8	26.4	25.9	25.3	26.8	25.2	24.8	24.8	25.1	+0.3
10th Grade	50.0	47.7	47.9	47.2	46.9	48.5	49.4	46.7	48.9	49.3	+0.4
12th Grade	65.4	63.4	62.5	62.9	63.2	61.8	64.2	62.4	62.3	62.3	0.0
Cigarettes											
Any use											
8th Grade	44.0	45.2	45.3	46.1	46.4	49.2	47.3	45.7	44.1	40.5	-3.6sss
10th Grade	55.1	53.5	56.3	56.9	57.6	61.2	60.2	57.7	57.6	55.1	-2.5s
12th Grade	63.1	61.8	61.9	62.0	64.2	63.5	65.4	65.3	64.6	62.5	-2.1
Smokeless Tobacco[d]											
8th Grade	22.2	20.7	18.7	19.9	20.0	20.4	16.8	15.0	14.4	12.8	-1.6
10th Grade	28.2	26.6	28.1	29.2	27.6	27.4	26.3	22.7	20.4	19.1	-1.3
12th Grade	—	32.4	31.0	30.7	30.9	29.8	25.3	26.2	23.4	23.1	-0.4
Steroids[j]											
8th Grade	1.9	1.7	1.6	2.0	2.0	1.8	1.8	2.3	2.7	3.0	+0.3
10th Grade	1.8	1.7	1.7	1.8	2.0	1.8	2.0	2.0	2.7	3.5	+0.8ss
12th Grade	2.1	2.1	2.0	2.4	2.3	1.9	2.4	2.7	2.9	2.5	-0.4

NOTES: Level of significance of difference between the two most recent classes: s = .05, ss = .01, sss = .001.

'—' indicates data not available. '*' indicates less than .05 percent but greater than 0 percent.

Any apparent inconsistency between the change estimate and the prevalence of use estimates for the two most recent classes is due to rounding error.

TABLE 4.1

Trends in lifetime prevalence of use of various drugs for eighth, tenth, and twelfth graders [CONTINUED]

(Entries are percentages)

Approximate Weighted Ns	1991	1992	1993	1994	1995	1996	1997	1998	1999	2000
8th Grade	17,500	18,600	18,300	17,300	17,500	17,800	18,600	18,100	16,700	16,700
10th Grade	14,800	14,800	15,300	15,800	17,000	15,600	15,500	15,000	13,600	14,300
12th Grade	15,000	15,800	16,300	15,400	15,400	14,300	15,400	15,200	13,600	12,800

[a] For 12th graders only: Use of "any illicit drug" includes any use of marijuana, LSD, other hallucinogens, crack, other cocaine, or heroin, or any use of other narcotics, amphetamines, barbiturates, or tranquilizers not under a doctor's orders. For 8th and 10th graders: The use of other narcotics and barbiturates has been excluded, because these younger respondents appear to overreport use (perhaps because they include the use of nonprescription drugs in their answers).

[b] For 12th graders only: Data based on five of six forms in 1991-98; N is five-sixths of N indicated. Beginning in 1999, data based on three of six forms; N is three-sixths of N indicated.

[c] Inhalants are unadjusted for underreporting of amyl and butyl nitrites; hallucinogens are unadjusted for underreporting of PCP.

[d] For 8th and 10th graders only: MDMA data based on one form in 1996; N is one-half of N indicated. Beginning in 1997, data based on one-third of N indicated due to changes on the questionnaire forms. Rohypnol data based on one-third of N indicated due to changes on the questionnaire forms. Smokeless tobacco data based on one of two forms for 1991–96 and on two of four forms beginning in 1997; N is one-half of N indicated. For 12th graders only: Data based on one form; N is one-sixth of N indicated.

[e] For 12th graders only: Data based on four of six forms; N is four-sixths of N indicated.

[f] In 1995, the heroin question was changed in three of six forms for 12th graders and in one of two forms for 8th and 10th graders. Separate questions were asked for use with injection and without injection. Data presented here represent the combined data from all forms. In 1996, the heroin question was changed in all remaining 8th and 10th grade forms.

[g] For 8th and 10th graders only: Data based on one of two forms in 1995; N is one-half of N indicated. For 12th graders only: Data based on three of six forms; N is three-sixths of N indicated.

[h] Only drug use which was not under a doctor's orders is included here.

[i] For 8th and 10th graders only: Data based on one of four forms; N is one-third of N indicated.

[j] For 12th graders only: Data based on two of six forms; N is two-sixths of N indicated.

[k] For 8th and 10th graders only: Data based on one of two forms in 1996–97; N is one-half of N indicated. Data based on three of four forms in 1998; N is two-thirds of N indicated. Beginning in 1999, data based on two of four forms; N is one-third of N indicated.

[l] For all grades: In 1993, the question text was changed slightly in half of the forms to indicate that a "drink" meant "more than a few sips." The data in the upper line for alcohol came from forms using the original wording, while the data in the lower line came from forms using the revised wording. In 1993, each line of data was based on one of two forms for the 8th and 10th graders and on three of six forms for the 12th graders. N is one-half of N indicated for all groups. Beginning in 1994, data were based on all forms for all grades.

SOURCE: Lloyd D. Johnston, Patrick M. O'Malley, and Jerald G. Bachman, "Table 1: Trends in Lifetime Prevalence of Use of Various Drugs for Eighth, Tenth, and Twelfth Graders," in *Monitoring the Future: National Results on Adolescent Drug Use—Overview of Key Findings, 2000,* Institute for Social Research, University of Michigan, and the National Institute on Drug Abuse, U.S. Department of Health and Human Services, 2001

---

the sharp increase in marijuana use that began in 1996, inhalants were the most widely used "drug" among eighth-graders. (Note that although referred to here as a drug, inhalants are technically not drugs.)

HALLUCINOGENS

Lifetime use of hallucinogens—most notably LSD and PCP—among high school seniors dropped from an all-time high of 16 percent in the mid-1970s to 9.2 percent in 1992. After that hallucinogen use rose, reaching 15.1 percent in 1997 and dropping to 13.0 percent in 2000. Similarly, annual and 30-day hallucinogen use increased markedly in 1995. Annual use rose to 10.1 percent in 1996 before falling to 8 percent in 2000. In 1995, 30-day use reached its highest level (4.4 percent) in more than 20 years, but then dropped slightly, to 3.5 percent in 1999 and 2.6 percent in 2000. (See Table 4.1, Table 4.2, Table 4.10, Table 4.11, and Table 4.12.) Hallucinogen use among eighth- and tenth-graders also increased dramatically during the 1990s. (See Table 4.1.) Unlike prevalence rates for other drugs, the rate of hallucinogen use at the turn of the century was very similar to what it was in the 1970s.

ECSTACY

In 1996 *Monitoring the Future* began asking students about their use of methylenedioxy-methampheta-

mine (MDMA)—popularly known as "ecstasy." MDMA use among eighth-, tenth-, and twelfth-graders fell each year between 1996 and 1999, but then rose significantly in 2000. In 2000 about 1 in 9 twelfth-graders (11 percent), 1 in 14 tenth-graders (7.3 percent), and 1 in 23 eighth-graders (4.3 percent) reported that they had used MDMA in their lifetimes. Among seniors, the rates of annual and 30-day use were 8.2 percent and 3.6 percent, respectively—up dramatically from 3.6 and 1.5 percent, respectively, in 1998. (See Table 4.1 and Table 4.2.)

AMPHETAMINES

In 2000 annual use of amphetamines among high school seniors increased to 10.5 percent, while it increased to 11.1 percent for tenth-graders and fell to 6.5 percent for eighth-graders. Lifetime use of crystal methamphetamine, or "ice," among seniors increased steadily between 1990 (the first year *Monitoring the Future* asked about the drug) and 1998. However, it fell from 5.3 to 4.0 between 1998 and 2000. (See Table 4.1.)

HEROIN

Between 1998 and 2000 lifetime heroin use dropped among eighth-graders, while it stayed about the same for tenth-graders and rose slightly for twelfth-graders. Life-

TABLE 4.2

Trends in annual and 30-day prevalence of use of various drugs for eighth, tenth, and twelfth graders

	Annual											30-Day										
	1991	1992	1993	1994	1995	1996	1997	1998	1999	2000	'99–'00 change	1991	1992	1993	1994	1995	1996	1997	1998	1999	2000	'99–'00 change
Any Illicit Drug[a]																						
8th Grade	11.3	12.9	15.1	18.5	21.4	23.6	22.1	21.0	20.5	19.5	-1.1	5.7	6.8	8.4	10.9	12.4	14.6	12.9	12.1	12.2	11.9	-0.4
10th Grade	21.4	20.4	24.7	30.0	33.3	37.5	38.5	35.0	35.9	36.4	+0.5	11.6	11.0	14.0	18.5	20.2	23.2	23.0	21.5	22.1	22.5	+0.4
12th Grade	29.4	27.1	31.0	35.8	39.0	40.2	42.4	41.4	42.1	40.9	-1.2	16.4	14.4	18.3	21.9	23.8	24.6	26.2	25.6	25.9	24.9	-1.0
Any Illicit Drug Other Than Marijuana[a]																						
8th Grade	8.4	9.3	10.4	11.3	12.6	13.1	11.8	11.0	10.5	10.2	-0.4	3.8	4.7	5.3	5.6	6.5	6.9	6.0	5.5	5.5	5.6	+0.1
10th Grade	12.2	12.3	13.9	15.2	17.5	18.4	18.2	16.6	16.7	16.7	0.0	5.5	5.7	6.5	7.1	8.9	8.9	8.8	8.6	8.6	8.5	-0.1
12th Grade	16.2	14.9	17.1	18.0	19.4	19.8	20.7	20.2	20.7	20.4	-0.3	7.1	6.3	7.9	8.8	10.0	9.5	10.7	10.7	10.4	10.4	0.0
Any Illicit Drug Including Inhalants[a,b]																						
8th Grade	16.7	18.2	21.1	24.2	27.1	28.7	27.2	26.2	25.3	24.0	-1.4	8.8	10.0	12.0	14.3	16.1	17.5	16.0	14.9	15.1	14.4	-0.7
10th Grade	23.9	23.5	27.4	32.5	35.6	39.6	40.3	37.1	37.7	38.0	+0.3	13.1	12.6	15.5	20.0	21.6	24.5	24.1	22.5	23.1	23.6	+0.5
12th Grade	31.2	28.8	32.5	37.6	40.2	41.9	43.3	42.4	42.8	42.5	-0.3	17.8	15.5	19.3	23.0	24.8	25.5	26.9	26.6	26.4	26.4	0.0
Marijuana/Hashish																						
8th Grade	6.2	7.2	9.2	13.0	15.8	18.3	17.7	16.9	16.5	15.6	-0.9	3.2	3.7	5.1	7.8	9.1	11.3	10.2	9.7	9.7	9.1	-0.6
10th Grade	16.5	15.2	19.2	25.2	28.7	33.6	34.8	31.1	32.1	32.2	+0.2	8.7	8.1	10.9	15.8	17.2	20.4	20.5	18.7	19.4	19.7	+0.3
12th Grade	23.9	21.9	26.0	30.7	34.7	35.8	38.5	37.5	37.8	36.5	-1.3	13.8	11.9	15.5	19.0	21.2	21.9	23.7	22.8	23.1	21.6	-1.6
Inhalants[b,c]																						
8th Grade	9.0	9.5	11.0	11.7	12.8	12.2	11.8	11.1	10.3	9.4	-0.9	4.4	4.7	5.4	5.6	6.1	5.8	5.6	4.8	5.0	4.5	-0.5
10th Grade	7.1	7.5	8.4	9.1	9.6	9.5	8.7	8.0	7.2	7.3	+0.1	2.7	2.7	3.3	3.6	3.5	3.3	3.0	2.9	2.6	2.6	0.0
12th Grade	6.6	6.2	7.0	7.7	8.0	7.6	6.7	6.2	5.6	5.9	+0.3	2.4	2.3	2.5	2.7	3.2	2.5	2.5	2.3	2.0	2.2	+0.2
Nitrites[d]																						
8th Grade	—	—	—	—	—	—	—	—	—	—	—	—	—	—	—	—	—	—	—	—	—	—
10th Grade	—	—	—	—	—	—	—	—	—	—	—	—	—	—	—	—	—	—	—	—	—	—
12th Grade	0.9	0.5	0.9	1.1	1.1	1.6	1.2	1.4	0.9	0.6	-0.3	0.4	0.3	0.6	0.4	0.4	0.7	0.7	1.0	0.4	0.3	-0.1
Hallucinogens[c]																						
8th Grade	1.9	2.5	2.6	2.7	3.6	4.1	3.7	3.4	2.9	2.8	0.0	0.8	1.1	1.2	1.3	1.7	1.9	1.8	1.4	1.3	1.2	-0.1
10th Grade	4.0	4.3	4.7	5.8	7.2	7.8	7.6	6.9	6.9	6.1	-0.9	1.6	1.8	1.9	2.4	3.3	2.8	3.3	3.2	2.9	2.3	-0.6s
12th Grade	5.8	5.9	7.4	7.6	9.3	10.1	9.8	9.0	9.4	8.1	-1.3s	2.2	2.1	2.7	3.1	4.4	3.5	3.9	3.8	3.5	2.6	-0.9ss
LSD																						
8th Grade	1.7	2.1	2.3	2.4	3.2	3.5	3.2	2.8	2.4	2.4	+0.1	0.6	0.9	1.0	1.1	1.4	1.5	1.5	1.1	1.1	1.0	-0.1
10th Grade	3.7	4.0	4.2	5.2	6.5	6.9	6.7	5.9	6.0	5.1	-0.9	1.5	1.6	1.6	2.0	3.0	2.4	2.8	2.7	2.3	1.6	-0.7ss
12th Grade	5.2	5.6	6.8	6.9	8.4	8.8	8.4	7.6	8.1	6.6	-1.5s	1.9	2.0	2.4	2.6	4.0	2.5	3.1	3.2	2.7	1.6	-1.2sss
Hallucinogens Other Than LSD																						
8th Grade	0.7	1.1	1.0	1.3	1.7	2.0	1.8	1.6	1.5	1.4	-0.1	0.3	0.4	0.5	0.7	0.8	0.9	0.7	0.7	0.6	0.6	+0.1
10th Grade	1.3	1.4	1.9	2.4	2.8	3.3	3.3	3.4	3.2	3.1	-0.1	0.4	0.5	0.7	1.0	1.0	1.0	1.2	1.4	1.2	1.2	0.0
12th Grade	2.0	1.7	2.2	3.1	3.8	4.4	4.6	4.6	4.3	4.4	+0.1	0.7	0.5	0.8	1.2	1.3	1.6	1.7	1.6	1.6	1.7	+0.1
PCP[d]																						
8th Grade	—	—	—	—	—	—	—	—	—	—	—	—	—	—	—	—	—	—	—	—	—	—
10th Grade	—	—	—	—	—	—	—	—	—	—	—	—	—	—	—	—	—	—	—	—	—	—
12th Grade	1.4	1.4	1.4	1.6	1.8	2.6	2.3	2.1	1.8	2.3	+0.5	0.5	0.6	1.0	0.7	0.6	1.3	0.7	1.0	0.8	0.9	+0.1

TABLE 4.2

Trends in annual and 30-day prevalence of use of various drugs for eighth, tenth, and twelfth graders [CONTINUED]

Annual

	1991	1992	1993	1994	1995	1996	1997	1998	1999	2000	'99–'00 change
MDMA (Ecstasy)[d]											
8th Grade	—	—	—	—	—	2.3	2.3	1.8	1.7	3.1	+1.4sss
10th Grade	—	—	—	—	—	4.6	3.9	3.3	4.4	5.4	+1.0
12th Grade	—	—	—	—	—	4.6	4.0	3.6	5.6	8.2	+2.6ss
Cocaine											
8th Grade	1.1	1.5	1.7	2.1	2.6	3.0	2.8	3.1	2.7	2.6	-0.1
10th Grade	2.2	1.9	2.1	2.8	3.5	4.2	4.7	4.7	4.9	4.4	-0.5
12th Grade	3.5	3.1	3.3	3.6	4.0	4.9	5.5	5.7	6.2	5.0	-1.3s
Crack											
8th Grade	0.7	0.9	1.0	1.3	1.6	1.8	1.7	2.1	1.8	1.8	0.0
10th Grade	0.9	0.9	1.1	1.4	1.8	2.1	2.2	2.5	2.4	2.2	-0.2
12th Grade	1.5	1.5	1.5	1.9	2.1	2.1	2.4	2.5	2.7	2.2	-0.5s
Other Cocaine[e]											
8th Grade	1.0	1.2	1.3	1.7	2.1	2.5	2.2	2.4	2.3	1.9	-0.4
10th Grade	2.1	1.7	1.8	2.4	3.0	3.5	4.1	4.0	4.4	3.8	-0.6
12th Grade	3.2	2.6	2.9	3.0	3.4	4.2	5.0	4.9	5.8	4.5	-1.4s
Heroin[f]											
8th Grade	0.7	0.7	0.7	1.2	1.4	1.6	1.3	1.3	1.4	1.1	-0.3s
10th Grade	0.5	0.6	0.7	0.9	1.1	1.2	1.4	1.4	1.4	1.4	0.0
12th Grade	0.4	0.6	0.5	0.6	1.1	1.0	1.2	1.0	1.1	1.5	+0.4s
With a needle[g]											
8th Grade	—	—	—	—	0.9	1.0	0.8	0.8	0.9	0.6	-0.3ss
10th Grade	—	—	—	—	0.6	0.7	0.7	0.8	0.6	0.5	-0.1
12th Grade	—	—	—	—	0.5	0.5	0.5	0.4	0.4	0.4	0.0
Without a needle[g]											
8th Grade	—	—	—	—	0.8	1.0	0.8	0.8	0.9	0.7	-0.2
10th Grade	—	—	—	—	0.8	0.9	1.1	1.0	1.1	1.1	0.0
12th Grade	—	—	—	—	1.0	1.0	1.2	0.8	1.0	1.6	+0.6ss
Other Narcotics[h]											
8th Grade	—	—	—	—	—	—	—	—	—	—	—
10th Grade	—	—	—	—	—	—	—	—	—	—	—
12th Grade	3.5	3.3	3.6	3.8	4.7	5.4	6.2	6.3	6.7	7.0	+0.3
Amphetamines[h]											
8th Grade	6.2	6.5	7.2	7.9	8.7	9.1	8.1	7.2	6.9	6.5	-0.4
10th Grade	8.2	8.2	9.6	10.2	11.9	12.4	12.1	10.7	10.4	11.1	+0.7
12th Grade	8.2	7.1	8.4	9.4	9.3	9.5	10.2	10.1	10.2	10.5	+0.3
Methamphetamine[i,j]											
8th Grade	—	—	—	—	—	—	—	—	3.2	2.5	-0.7
10th Grade	—	—	—	—	—	—	—	—	4.6	4.0	-0.6
12th Grade	—	—	—	—	—	—	—	—	4.7	4.3	-0.3
Ice[h]											
8th Grade	—	—	—	—	—	—	—	—	—	—	—
10th Grade	—	—	—	—	—	—	—	—	—	—	—
12th Grade	1.4	1.3	1.7	1.8	2.4	2.8	2.3	3.0	1.9	2.2	+0.3

30-Day

	1991	1992	1993	1994	1995	1996	1997	1998	1999	2000	'99–'00 change
MDMA (Ecstasy)[d]											
8th Grade	—	—	—	—	—	1.0	1.0	0.9	0.8	1.4	+0.7s
10th Grade	—	—	—	—	—	1.8	1.3	1.3	1.8	2.6	+0.8s
12th Grade	—	—	—	—	—	2.0	1.6	1.5	2.5	3.6	+1.1
Cocaine											
8th Grade	0.5	0.7	0.7	1.0	1.2	1.3	1.1	1.4	1.3	1.2	-0.1
10th Grade	0.7	0.7	0.9	1.2	1.7	1.7	2.0	2.1	1.8	1.8	-0.1
12th Grade	1.4	1.3	1.3	1.5	1.8	2.0	2.3	2.4	2.6	2.1	-0.5
Crack											
8th Grade	0.3	0.5	0.4	0.7	0.7	0.8	0.7	0.9	0.8	0.8	-0.1
10th Grade	0.3	0.4	0.5	0.6	0.9	0.8	0.9	1.1	0.8	0.9	+0.1
12th Grade	0.7	0.6	0.7	0.8	1.0	1.0	0.9	1.0	1.1	1.0	-0.1
Other Cocaine[e]											
8th Grade	0.5	0.5	0.6	0.9	1.0	1.0	0.8	1.0	1.1	0.9	-0.2
10th Grade	0.6	0.6	0.7	1.0	1.4	1.3	1.6	1.8	1.6	1.6	0.0
12th Grade	1.2	1.0	1.2	1.3	1.3	1.6	2.0	2.0	2.5	1.7	-0.7s
Heroin[f]											
8th Grade	0.3	0.4	0.4	0.6	0.6	0.7	0.6	0.6	0.6	0.5	-0.2
10th Grade	0.2	0.2	0.3	0.4	0.6	0.5	0.6	0.7	0.7	0.5	-0.2
12th Grade	0.2	0.3	0.2	0.3	0.6	0.5	0.5	0.5	0.5	0.7	+0.2
With a needle[g]											
8th Grade	—	—	—	—	0.4	0.5	0.4	0.5	0.4	0.3	-0.1
10th Grade	—	—	—	—	0.3	0.3	0.3	0.4	0.3	0.3	-0.1
12th Grade	—	—	—	—	0.3	0.4	0.3	0.2	0.2	0.2	0.0
Without a needle[g]											
8th Grade	—	—	—	—	0.3	0.4	0.4	0.3	0.4	0.3	-0.1
10th Grade	—	—	—	—	0.3	0.3	0.4	0.5	0.5	0.4	-0.2
12th Grade	—	—	—	—	0.6	0.4	0.6	0.4	0.4	0.7	+0.3
Other Narcotics[h]											
8th Grade	—	—	—	—	—	—	—	—	—	—	—
10th Grade	—	—	—	—	—	—	—	—	—	—	—
12th Grade	1.1	1.2	1.3	1.5	1.8	2.0	2.3	2.4	2.6	2.9	+0.3
Amphetamines[h]											
8th Grade	2.6	3.3	3.6	3.6	4.2	4.6	3.8	3.3	3.4	3.4	+0.1
10th Grade	3.3	3.6	4.3	4.5	5.3	5.5	5.1	5.1	5.0	5.4	+0.5
12th Grade	3.2	2.8	3.7	4.0	4.0	4.1	4.8	4.6	4.5	5.0	+0.5
Methamphetamine[i,j]											
8th Grade	—	—	—	—	—	—	—	—	1.1	0.8	-0.3
10th Grade	—	—	—	—	—	—	—	—	1.8	2.0	+0.2
12th Grade	—	—	—	—	—	—	—	—	1.7	1.9	+0.2
Ice[h]											
8th Grade	—	—	—	—	—	—	—	—	—	—	—
10th Grade	—	—	—	—	—	—	—	—	—	—	—
12th Grade	0.6	0.5	0.6	0.7	1.1	1.1	0.8	1.2	0.8	1.0	+0.2

TABLE 4.2

Trends in annual and 30-day prevalence of use of various drugs for eighth, tenth, and twelfth graders [CONTINUED]

Annual

	1991	1992	1993	1994	1995	1996	1997	1998	1999	2000	'99–'00 change
Barbiturates[h]											
8th Grade	—	—	—	—	—	—	—	—	—	—	—
10th Grade	—	—	—	—	—	—	—	—	—	—	—
12th Grade	3.4	2.8	3.4	4.1	4.7	4.9	5.1	5.5	5.8	6.2	+0.4
Tranquilizers[h]											
8th Grade	1.8	2.0	2.1	2.4	2.7	3.3	2.9	2.6	2.5	2.6	+0.2
10th Grade	3.2	3.5	3.3	3.3	4.0	4.6	4.9	5.1	5.4	5.6	+0.2
12th Grade	3.6	2.8	3.5	3.7	4.4	4.6	4.7	5.5	5.8	5.7	-0.1
Rohypnol[i,k]											
8th Grade	—	—	—	—	—	1.0	0.8	0.8	0.5	0.5	+0.1
10th Grade	—	—	—	—	—	1.1	1.3	1.2	1.0	0.8	-0.3
12th Grade	—	—	—	—	—	1.1	1.2	1.4	1.0	0.8	-0.2
Alcohol — Any use											
8th Grade	54.0	53.7	51.6	46.8	45.3	46.5	45.5	43.7	43.5	43.1	-0.4
10th Grade	72.3	70.2	69.3	63.9	63.5	65.0	65.2	62.7	63.7	65.3	+1.6
12th Grade	77.7	76.8	76.0	73.0	73.7	72.5	74.8	74.3	73.8	73.2	-0.6
Been Drunk											
8th Grade	17.5	18.3	18.2	18.2	18.4	19.8	18.4	17.9	18.5	18.5	0.0
10th Grade	40.1	37.0	37.8	38.0	38.5	40.1	40.7	38.3	40.9	41.6	+0.7
12th Grade	52.7	50.3	49.6	51.7	52.5	51.9	53.2	52.0	53.2	51.8	-1.4
Cigarettes — Any use											
8th Grade	—	—	—	—	—	—	—	—	—	—	—
10th Grade	—	—	—	—	—	—	—	—	—	—	—
12th Grade	—	—	—	—	—	—	—	—	—	—	—
Smokeless Tobacco[d]											
8th Grade	—	—	—	—	—	—	—	—	—	—	—
10th Grade	—	—	—	—	—	—	—	—	—	—	—
12th Grade	—	—	—	—	—	—	—	—	—	—	—
Steroids[j]											
8th Grade	1.0	1.1	0.9	1.2	1.0	0.9	1.0	1.2	1.7	1.7	0.0
10th Grade	1.1	1.1	1.0	1.1	1.2	1.2	1.2	1.2	1.7	2.2	+0.5s
12th Grade	1.4	1.1	1.2	1.1	1.5	1.4	1.4	1.7	1.8	1.7	-0.1
Approximate Weighted Ns											
8th Grade	17,500	18,600	18,300	18,600	17,500	17,300	17,500	18,100	18,600	16,700	
10th Grade	14,800	14,800	15,300	14,800	15,300	15,800	17,000	15,600	15,500	14,300	
12th Grade	15,000	15,000	15,800	16,300	15,400	15,400	15,400	14,300	15,400	12,800	

30-Day

	1991	1992	1993	1994	1995	1996	1997	1998	1999	2000	'99–'00 change
Barbiturates[h]											
8th Grade	—	—	—	—	—	—	—	—	—	—	—
10th Grade	—	—	—	—	—	—	—	—	—	—	—
12th Grade	1.4	1.1	1.3	1.7	2.2	2.1	2.1	2.6	2.6	3.0	+0.4
Tranquilizers[h]											
8th Grade	0.8	0.8	0.9	1.1	1.2	1.5	1.2	1.2	1.1	1.4	+0.3
10th Grade	1.2	1.5	1.1	1.5	1.7	1.7	2.2	2.2	2.2	2.5	+0.4
12th Grade	1.4	1.0	1.2	1.4	1.8	2.0	1.8	2.4	2.5	2.6	+0.1
Rohypnol[i,k]											
8th Grade	—	—	—	—	—	0.5	0.3	0.4	0.3	0.3	0.0
10th Grade	—	—	—	—	—	0.5	0.5	0.4	0.5	0.4	-0.2
12th Grade	—	—	—	—	—	0.5	0.3	0.3	0.3	0.4	+0.1
Alcohol — Any use											
8th Grade	25.1	26.1	26.2	25.5	24.6	26.2	24.5	23.0	24.0	22.4	-1.7
10th Grade	42.8	39.9	41.5	39.2	38.8	40.4	40.1	38.8	40.0	41.0	+0.9
12th Grade	54.0	51.3	48.6	50.1	51.3	50.8	52.7	52.0	51.0	50.0	-1.0
Been Drunk											
8th Grade	7.6	7.5	7.8	8.7	8.3	9.6	8.2	8.4	9.4	8.3	-1.1
10th Grade	20.5	18.1	19.8	20.3	20.8	21.3	22.4	21.1	22.5	23.5	+1.0
12th Grade	31.6	29.9	28.9	30.8	33.2	31.3	34.2	32.9	32.9	32.3	-0.6
Cigarettes — Any use											
8th Grade	14.3	15.5	16.7	18.6	19.1	21.0	19.4	19.1	17.5	14.6	-2.8sss
10th Grade	20.8	21.5	24.7	25.4	27.9	30.4	29.8	27.6	25.7	23.9	-1.8
12th Grade	28.3	27.8	29.9	31.2	33.5	34.0	36.5	35.1	34.6	31.4	-3.2ss
Smokeless Tobacco[d]											
8th Grade	6.9	7.0	6.6	7.7	7.1	7.1	5.5	4.8	4.5	4.2	-0.3
10th Grade	10.0	9.6	10.4	10.5	9.7	8.6	8.9	7.5	6.5	6.1	-0.5
12th Grade	—	11.4	10.7	11.1	12.2	9.8	9.7	8.8	8.4	7.6	-0.7
Steroids[j]											
8th Grade	0.4	0.5	0.5	0.5	0.6	0.4	0.5	0.5	0.7	0.8	+0.1
10th Grade	0.6	0.6	0.5	0.6	0.6	0.5	0.7	0.6	0.9	1.0	0.0
12th Grade	0.8	0.6	0.7	0.9	0.7	0.7	1.0	1.1	0.9	0.8	-0.1

NOTES: Level of significance of difference between the two most recent classes: s = .05, ss = .01, sss = .001.
"—" indicates data not available. "**" indicates less than .05 percent but greater than 0 percent.
Any apparent inconsistency between the change estimate and the prevalence of use estimates for the two most recent classes is due to rounding error.

TABLE 4.2

Trends in annual and 30-day prevalence of use of various drugs for eighth, tenth, and twelfth graders [CONTINUED]

aFor 12th graders only: Use of "any illicit drug" includes any use of marijuana, LSD, other hallucinogens, crack, other cocaine, or heroin, or any use of other narcotics, amphetamines, barbiturates, or tranquilizers not under a doctor's orders. For 8th and 10th graders: The use of other narcotics and barbiturates has been excluded, because these younger respondents appear to overreport use (perhaps because they include the use of nonprescription drugs in their answers).

bFor 12th graders only: Data based on five of six forms in 1991–98; N is five-sixths of N indicated. Beginning in 1999, data based on three of six forms; N is three-sixths of N indicated.

cInhalants are unadjusted for underreporting of amyl and butyl nitrites; hallucinogens are unadjusted for underreporting of PCP.

dFor 8th and 10th graders only: MDMA data based on one form in 1996; N is one-half of N indicated. Beginning in 1997, data based on one-third of N indicated due to changes on the questionnaire forms. Rohypnol data based on one-third of N indicated due to changes on the questionnaire forms. Smokeless tobacco data based on one of two forms for 1991–96 and on two of four forms beginning in 1997; N is one-half of N indicated. For 12th graders only: Data based on one form; N is one-sixth of N indicated.

eFor 12th graders only: Data based on four of six forms; N is four-sixths of N indicated.

fIn 1995, the heroin question was changed in three of six forms for 12th graders and in one of two forms for 8th and 10th graders. Separate questions were asked for use with injection and without injection. Data presented here represent the combined data from all forms. In 1996, the heroin question was changed in all remaining 8th and 10th grade forms.

gFor 8th and 10th graders only: Data based on one of two forms in 1995; N is one-half of N indicated. For 12th graders only: Data based on three of six forms; N is three-sixths of N indicated.

hOnly drug use which was not under a doctor's orders is included here.

iFor 8th and 10th graders only: Data based on one of four forms; N is one-third of N indicated.

jFor 12th graders only: Data based on two of six forms; N is two-sixths of N indicated.

-For 8th and 10th graders only: Data based on one of two forms in 1996–97; N is one-half of N indicated. Data based on three of four forms in 1998; N is two-thirds of N indicated. Beginning in 1999, data based on two of four forms; N is one-third of N indicated.

lFor all grades: In 1993, the question text was changed slightly in half of the forms to indicate that a "drink" meant "more than a few sips." The data in the upper line for alcohol came from forms using the original wording, while the data in the lower line came from forms using the revisedwording. In 1993, each line of data was based on one of two forms for the 8th and 10th graders and on three of six forms for the 12th graders. N is one-half of N indicated for all groups. Beginning in 1994, data were based on all forms for all grades.

mDaily use is defined as use on twenty or more occasions in the past thirty days except for cigarettes and smokeless tobacco, for which actual daily use is measured, and for 5+ drinks, for which the prevalence or having five or more drinks in a row in the last two weeks is measured.

SOURCE: Lloyd D. Johnston, Patrick M. O'Malley, and Jerald G. Bachman, "Table 2: Trends in Annual and 30-Day Prevalence of Use of Various Drugs for Eighth, Tenth, and Twelfth Graders," in *Monitoring the Future: National Results on Adolescent Drug Use—Overview of Key Findings, 2000,* Institute for Social Research, University of Michigan, and the National Institute on Drug Abuse, U.S. Department of Health and Human Services, 2001

TABLE 4.3

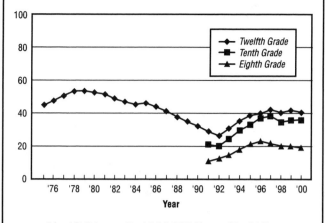

Percentage of eighth, tenth, and twelfth grade students who used any illicit drug in the past year, 1975–2000

SOURCE: Lloyd D. Johnston, Patrick M. O'Malley, and Jerald G. Bachman, "Trends in Illicit Drug Use: Eighth, Tenth, and Twelfth Graders: % who used any illicit drug in the past year," in *Monitoring the Future: National Results on Adolescent Drug Use—Overview of Key Findings, 2000,* Institute for Social Research, University of Michigan, and the National Institute on Drug Abuse, U.S. Department of Health and Human Services, 2001

TABLE 4.4

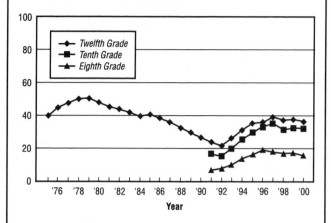

Percentage of eighth, tenth, and twelfth grade students who used marijuana in the past year, 1975–2000

SOURCE: Lloyd D. Johnston, Patrick M. O'Malley, and Jerald G. Bachman, "Marijuana: Trends in Annual Use, Risk, Disapproval, and Availability: Eighth, Tenth, and Twelfth Graders: % who used in the last twelve months," in *Monitoring the Future: National Results on Adolescent Drug Use—Overview of Key Findings, 2000,* Institute for Social Research, University of Michigan, and the National Institute on Drug Abuse, U.S. Department of Health and Human Services, 2001

TABLE 4.5

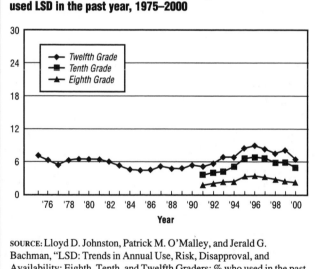

Percentage of eighth, tenth, and twelfth grade students who used LSD in the past year, 1975–2000

SOURCE: Lloyd D. Johnston, Patrick M. O'Malley, and Jerald G. Bachman, "LSD: Trends in Annual Use, Risk, Disapproval, and Availability: Eighth, Tenth, and Twelfth Graders: % who used in the past year," in *Monitoring the Future: National Results on Adolescent Drug Use—Overview of Key Findings, 2000,* Institute for Social Research, University of Michigan, and the National Institute on Drug Abuse, U.S. Department of Health and Human Services, 2001

TABLE 4.6

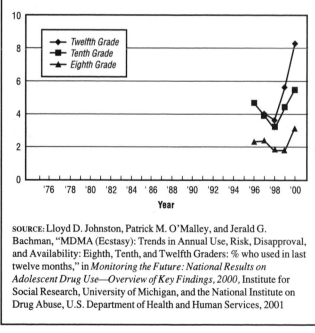

Percentage of eighth, tenth, and twelfth grade students who used MDMA (Ecstasy) in the past year, 1975–2000

SOURCE: Lloyd D. Johnston, Patrick M. O'Malley, and Jerald G. Bachman, "MDMA (Ecstasy): Trends in Annual Use, Risk, Disapproval, and Availability: Eighth, Tenth, and Twelfth Graders: % who used in last twelve months," in *Monitoring the Future: National Results on Adolescent Drug Use—Overview of Key Findings, 2000,* Institute for Social Research, University of Michigan, and the National Institute on Drug Abuse, U.S. Department of Health and Human Services, 2001

time use among twelfth-graders increased significantly between 1991 and 2000, jumping from 0.9 percent to 2.4 percent. Similarly, annual use jumped to 1.5 percent in 2000—the highest rate in more than 25 years. Thirty-day use rose from 0.2–0.3 percent in the 1980s and early 1990s to 0.6 percent in 1995, and reached 0.7 percent in 2000. Daily use stayed relatively constant, at about 0.1

percent. (See Table 4.1, Table 4.2, Table 4.11, Table 4.12, and Table 4.13.)

A notable aspect of the growing use of heroin is that prevalence rates among eighth- and tenth-graders are at least equal to, and often greater than, rates among seniors. (See Table 4.1 and Table 4.2.) Thus, it

TABLE 4.7

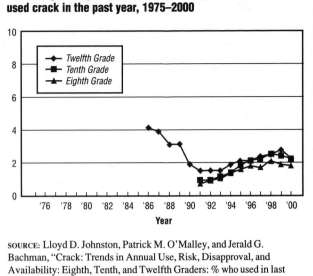

Percentage of eighth, tenth, and twelfth grade students who used crack in the past year, 1975–2000

SOURCE: Lloyd D. Johnston, Patrick M. O'Malley, and Jerald G. Bachman, "Crack: Trends in Annual Use, Risk, Disapproval, and Availability: Eighth, Tenth, and Twelfth Graders: % who used in last twelve months," in *Monitoring the Future: National Results on Adolescent Drug Use—Overview of Key Findings, 2000,* Institute for Social Research, University of Michigan, and the National Institute on Drug Abuse, U.S. Department of Health and Human Services, 2001

TABLE 4.8

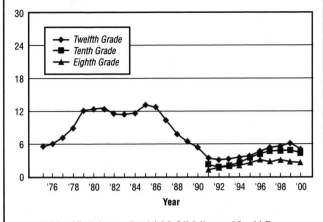

Percentage of eighth, tenth, and twelfth grade students who used cocaine (including crack) in the past year, 1975–2000

SOURCE: Lloyd D. Johnston, Patrick M. O'Malley, and Jerald G. Bachman, "Cocaine (including Crack): Trends in Annual Use, Risk, Disapproval, and Availability: Eighth, Tenth, and Twelfth Graders: % who used in last twelve months," in *<it>Monitoring the Future: National Results on Adolescent Drug Use—Overview of Key Findings, 2000,* Institute for Social Research, University of Michigan, and the National Institute on Drug Abuse, U.S. Department of Health and Human Services, 2001

TABLE 4.9

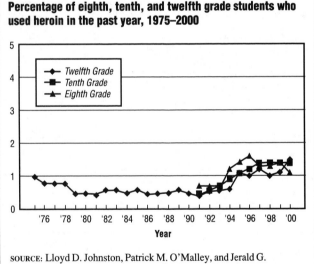

Percentage of eighth, tenth, and twelfth grade students who used heroin in the past year, 1975–2000

SOURCE: Lloyd D. Johnston, Patrick M. O'Malley, and Jerald G. Bachman, "Heroin: Trends in Annual Use, Risk, Disapproval, and Availability: Eighth, Tenth, and Twelfth Graders: % who used in last twelve months," in *Monitoring the Future: National Results on Adolescent Drug Use—Overview of Key Findings, 2000,* Institute for Social Research, University of Michigan, and the National Institute on Drug Abuse, U.S. Department of Health and Human Services, 2001

is very likely that heroin use will continue to grow—especially given the widespread availability of high-quality heroin, which no longer needs to be injected to produce the desired effect. Each year since 1995, the year the survey began asking students how they took heroin, results have shown that at least twice as many

twelfth-graders use heroin without a needle as inject it. (See Table 4.10.)

COCAINE

Cocaine use continues to grow. Lifetime use by high school seniors increased from 6 percent in 1995 to 9.8 percent in 1998, before falling slightly, to 8.6 percent, in 2000. These figures were still well shy of the peak rate of 17.3 percent recorded in 1985. (See Table 4.10.) The percentage of twelfth-graders who reported using cocaine in the year before the survey fell from a high of 13.1 percent in 1985 to a low of 3.1 percent in 1992, but then started rising, reaching 6.2 percent in 2000. (See Table 4.11.) Thirty-day prevalence dropped from 6.7 percent in 1985 to 1.3 percent in 1992 and 1993, but by 2000 had doubled to 2.6 percent. (See Table 4.12.) Daily use, which stayed at a steady 0.1–0.2 percent throughout the 1990s, was 0.2 percent in 2000. (See Table 4.13.)

After increasing in the early 1990s, cocaine use among eighth- and tenth-graders began to level off. Among eighth-graders, annual use dropped from 3.0 percent in 1996 to 2.6 in 2000. Among tenth-graders, annual use in 2000 was 4.4 percent, not significantly different from the previous four years. (See Table 4.2.)

Crack Use

Monitoring the Future first measured crack cocaine use in 1986. Among twelfth-graders, lifetime prevalence decreased from 5.4 percent in 1987 to a low of 2.6 percent

TABLE 4.10

Long-term trends in lifetime prevalence of use of various drugs for twelfth graders

Percent ever used

	Class of 1975	Class of 1976	Class of 1977	Class of 1978	Class of 1979	Class of 1980	Class of 1981	Class of 1982	Class of 1983	Class of 1984	Class of 1985	Class of 1986	Class of 1987	Class of 1988	Class of 1989	Class of 1990	Class of 1991	Class of 1992	Class of 1993	Class of 1994	Class of 1995	Class of 1996	Class of 1997	Class of 1998	Class of 1999	Class of 2000	'99–'00 change
Approx. N (in thousands) =	*9.4*	*15.4*	*17.1*	*17.8*	*15.5*	*15.9*	*17.5*	*17.7*	*16.3*	*15.9*	*16.0*	*15.2*	*16.3*	*16.3*	*16.7*	*15.2*	*15.0*	*15.8*	*16.3*	*15.4*	*15.4*	*14.3*	*15.4*	*15.2*	*13.6*	*12.8*	
Any Illicit Drug[a,b]	55.2	58.3	61.6	64.1	65.1	65.4	65.6	64.4	62.9	61.6	60.6	57.6	56.6	53.9	50.9	47.9	44.1	40.7	42.9	45.6	48.4	50.8	54.3	54.1	54.7	54.0	-0.7
Any Illicit Drug Other Than Marijuana[a,b]	36.2	35.4	35.8	36.5	37.4	38.7	42.8	41.1	40.4	40.3	39.7	37.7	35.8	32.5	31.4	29.4	26.9	25.1	26.7	27.6	28.1	28.5	30.0	29.4	29.4	29.0	-0.3
Marijuana/Hashish[a,b]	47.3	52.8	56.4	59.2	60.4	60.3	59.5	58.7	57.0	54.9	54.2	50.9	50.2	47.2	43.7	40.7	36.7	32.6	35.3	38.2	41.7	44.9	49.6	49.1	49.7	48.8	-0.9
Inhalants[c]	—	10.3	11.1	12.0	12.7	11.9	12.3	12.8	13.6	14.4	15.4	15.9	17.0	16.7	17.6	18.0	17.6	16.6	17.4	17.7	17.4	16.6	16.1	15.2	15.4	14.2	-1.2
Inhalants, Adjusted[c,d]	—	—	—	—	18.2	17.3	17.2	17.7	18.2	18.0	18.1	20.1	18.6	17.5	18.6	18.5	18.0	17.0	17.7	18.3	17.8	17.5	16.9	16.5	16.0	14.6	-1.5
Amyl/Butyl Nitrites[e,f]	—	—	—	—	11.1	11.1	10.1	9.8	8.4	8.1	7.9	8.6	4.7	3.2	3.3	2.1	1.6	1.5	1.4	1.7	1.5	1.8	2.0	2.7	1.7	0.8	-0.8
Hallucinogens[e,f]	16.3	15.1	13.9	14.3	14.1	13.3	13.3	12.5	11.9	10.7	10.3	9.7	10.6	8.9	9.4	9.4	9.6	9.2	10.9	11.4	12.7	14.0	15.1	14.1	13.7	13.0	-0.7
Hallucinogens, Adjusted[d]	16.3	15.1	13.9	14.3	14.1	13.3	13.3	12.5	11.9	10.7	10.3	9.9	10.6	9.2	9.9	9.7	10.0	9.4	11.3	11.7	13.1	14.5	15.4	14.4	14.2	13.6	-0.7
LSD	11.3	11.0	9.8	9.7	9.5	9.3	9.8	9.6	8.9	8.0	7.5	7.2	8.4	7.7	8.3	8.7	8.8	8.6	10.3	10.5	11.7	12.6	13.6	12.6	12.2	11.1	-1.1
Hallucinogens Other Than LSD	14.1	12.1	11.2	11.6	10.7	9.8	9.1	8.0	7.3	6.6	6.5	5.7	5.4	4.1	4.3	4.1	3.7	3.3	3.9	4.9	5.4	6.8	7.5	7.1	6.7	6.9	+0.2
PCP[e,f]	—	—	—	—	12.8	9.6	7.8	6.0	5.6	5.0	4.9	4.8	3.0	2.9	3.9	2.8	2.9	2.4	2.9	2.8	2.7	4.0	3.9	3.9	3.4	3.4	-0.1
MDMA (Ecstasy)[e]	—	—	—	—	—	—	—	—	—	—	—	—	—	—	—	—	—	—	—	—	—	6.1	6.9	5.8	8.0	11.0	+3.0s
Cocaine	9.0	9.7	10.8	12.9	15.4	15.7	16.5	16.0	16.2	16.1	17.3	16.9	15.2	12.1	10.3	9.4	7.8	6.1	6.1	5.9	6.0	7.1	8.7	9.3	9.8	8.6	-1.2
Crack[h]	—	—	—	—	—	—	—	—	—	—	—	—	5.4	4.8	4.7	3.5	3.1	2.6	2.6	3.0	3.0	3.3	3.9	4.4	4.6	3.9	-0.7s
Other Cocaine[i]	—	—	—	—	—	—	—	—	—	—	—	—	14.0	12.1	8.5	8.6	7.0	5.3	5.4	5.2	5.1	6.4	8.2	8.4	8.8	7.7	-1.1
Heroin[j]	2.2	1.8	1.8	1.6	1.1	1.1	1.1	1.2	1.2	1.3	1.2	1.1	1.2	1.1	1.3	1.3	0.9	1.2	1.1	1.2	1.6	1.8	2.1	2.0	2.0	2.4	+0.4
With a needle[k]	—	—	—	—	—	—	—	—	—	—	—	—	—	—	—	—	—	—	—	—	0.7	0.8	0.9	0.8	0.9	0.8	-0.1
Without a needle[k]	—	—	—	—	—	—	—	—	—	—	—	—	—	—	—	—	—	—	—	—	1.4	1.7	2.1	1.6	1.8	2.4	+0.6
Other Narcotics[l]	9.0	9.6	10.3	9.9	10.1	9.8	10.1	9.6	9.4	9.7	10.2	9.0	9.2	8.6	8.3	8.3	6.6	6.1	6.4	6.6	7.2	8.2	9.7	9.8	10.2	10.6	+0.4
Amphetamines[b,l]	22.3	22.6	23.0	22.9	24.2	26.4	32.2	27.9	26.9	27.9	26.2	23.4	21.6	19.8	19.1	17.5	15.4	13.9	15.1	15.7	15.3	15.3	16.5	16.4	16.3	15.6	-0.7
Methamphetamine[m]	—	—	—	—	—	—	—	—	—	—	—	—	—	—	—	—	—	—	—	—	—	—	—	—	8.2	7.9	-0.3
Crystal Meth. (Ice)[m]	—	—	—	—	—	—	—	—	—	—	—	—	—	—	—	2.7	3.3	2.9	3.1	3.4	3.9	4.4	4.4	5.3	4.8	4.0	-0.8
Sedatives[l,n]	18.2	17.7	17.4	16.0	14.6	14.9	16.0	15.2	14.4	13.3	11.8	10.4	8.7	7.8	7.4	7.5	6.7	6.1	6.4	7.3	7.6	8.2	8.7	9.2	9.5	9.3	-0.2
Barbiturates[l]	16.9	16.2	15.6	13.7	11.8	11.0	11.3	10.3	9.9	9.9	9.2	8.4	7.4	6.7	6.5	6.8	6.2	5.5	6.3	7.0	7.4	7.6	8.1	8.7	8.9	9.2	+0.2
Methaqualone[l,n]	8.1	7.8	8.5	7.9	8.3	9.5	10.6	10.7	10.1	8.3	6.7	5.2	4.0	3.3	2.7	2.3	1.3	1.6	0.8	1.4	1.2	2.0	1.7	1.6	1.8	0.8	-1.0s
Tranquilizers[l]	17.0	16.8	18.0	17.0	16.3	15.2	14.7	14.0	13.3	12.4	11.9	10.9	10.9	9.4	7.6	7.2	7.2	6.0	6.4	6.6	7.1	7.2	7.8	8.5	9.3	8.9	-0.5
Rohypnol[e]	—	—	—	—	—	—	—	—	—	—	—	—	—	—	—	—	—	—	—	—	—	1.2	1.8	3.0	2.0	1.5	-0.6
Alcohol[o]	90.4	91.9	92.5	93.1	93.0	93.2	92.6	92.8	92.6	92.6	92.2	91.3	92.2	92.0	90.7	89.5	88.0	87.5	87.0	80.4	80.7	79.2	81.7	81.4	80.0	80.3	+0.2
Been Drunk[m]	—	—	—	—	—	—	—	—	—	—	—	—	—	—	—	—	65.4	63.4	62.5	62.9	63.2	61.8	64.2	62.4	62.3	62.3	0.0

TABLE 4.10

Long-term trends in lifetime prevalence of use of various drugs for twelfth graders [CONTINUED]

Percent ever used

	Class of 1975	Class of 1976	Class of 1977	Class of 1978	Class of 1979	Class of 1980	Class of 1981	Class of 1982	Class of 1983	Class of 1984	Class of 1985	Class of 1986	Class of 1987	Class of 1988	Class of 1989	Class of 1990	Class of 1991	Class of 1992	Class of 1993	Class of 1994	Class of 1995	Class of 1996	Class of 1997	Class of 1998	Class of 1999	Class of 2000	'99–'00 change
Cigarettes	73.6	75.4	75.7	75.3	74.0	71.0	71.0	70.1	70.6	69.7	68.8	67.6	67.2	66.4	65.7	64.4	63.1	61.8	61.9	62.0	64.2	63.5	65.4	65.3	64.6	62.5	-2.1
Smokeless Tobacco[e,p]	—	—	—	—	—	—	—	—	—	—	—	31.4	32.2	30.4	29.2	—	—	32.4	31.0	30.7	30.9	29.8	25.3	26.2	23.4	23.1	-0.4
Steroids[m]	—	—	—	—	—	—	—	—	—	—	—	—	—	—	3.0	2.9	2.1	2.1	2.0	2.4	2.3	1.9	2.4	2.7	2.9	2.5	-0.4

NOTES: Level of significance of difference between the two most recent classes: s = .05, ss = .01, sss = .001. '—' indicates data not available. Any apparent inconsistency between the change estimate and the prevalence of use estimates for the two most recent classes is due to rounding error.

a Use of "any illicit drug" includes any use of marijuana, LSD, other hallucinogens, crack, other cocaine, or heroin, or any use of other narcotics, amphetamines, barbiturates, methaqualone (excluded since 1990), or tranquilizers not under a doctor's orders.

b Beginning in 1982 the question about amphetamine use was revised to get respondents to exclude the inappropriate reporting of nonprescription amphetamines. The prevalence of use rate dropped slightly as a result of this methodological change.

c Data based on four of five forms in 1976–88; N is four-fifths of N indicated. Beginning in 1999, data based on three of six forms; N is three-sixths of N indicated.

d Adjusted for underreporting of amyl and butyl nitrites.

e Data based on one form; N is one-fifth of N indicated in 1979–88 and one-sixth of N indicated in 1989–2000.

f Question text changed slightly in 1987.

g Adjusted for underreporting of PCP.

h Data based on one of five forms in 1986; N is one-fifth of N indicated. Data based on two forms in 1987–89; N is two-fifths of N indicated in 1987–88 and two-sixths of N indicated in 1989. Data based on six forms in 1990–2000.

i Data based on one form in 1987–89; N is one-fifth of N indicated in 1987–88 and one-sixth of N indicated in 1989. Data based on four of six forms in 1990–2000; N is four-sixths of N indicated.

j In 1995 the heroin question was changed in half of the questionnaire forms. Separate questions were asked for use with injection and without injection. Data presented here represent the combined data from all forms.

k Data based on three of six forms; N is three-sixths of N indicated.

l Only drug use which was not under a doctor's orders is included here.

m Data based on two of six forms; N is two-sixths of N indicated. Steroid data based on one of six forms in 1989–90; N is one-sixth of N indicated in 1989–90. Steroid data based on two of six forms since 1991; N is two-sixths of N indicated since 1991.

n Sedatives: Data based on five forms in 1975–88, six forms in 1989, one form in 1990 (N is one-sixth of N indicated in 1990), and six forms in 1975–88, six forms in 1989, and one of six forms beginning in 1990; N is one-sixth of N indicated beginning in 1990.

o Data based on five forms in 1975–88 and on six forms in 1989–92. In 1993, the question text was changed slightly in three of six forms to indicate that a "drink" meant "more than a few sips." The data in the upper line for alcohol came from the three forms using the original wording (N is three-sixths of N indicated), while the data in the lower line came from the three forms containing the revised wording (N is three-sixths of N indicated). Beginning in 1994, data based on all six forms.

p The prevalence of use of smokeless tobacco was not asked of twelfth graders in 1990 and 1991. Prior to 1990 the prevalence of use question on smokeless tobacco was located near the end of one twelfth-grade questionnaire form, whereas after 1991 the question was placed earlier and in a different form. This shift could explain the discontinuities between the corresponding data.

SOURCE: Lloyd D. Johnston, Patrick M. O'Malley, and Jerald G. Bachman, "Table 4: Long-Term Trends in Lifetime Prevalence of Use of Various Drugs for Twelfth Graders," in *Monitoring the Future: National Results on Adolescent Drug Use—Overview of Key Findings, 2000,* Institute for Social Research, University of Michigan, and the National Institute on Drug Abuse, U.S. Department of Health and Human Services, 2001

TABLE 4.11

Long-term trends in annual prevalence of use of various drugs for twelfth graders

Percent who used in last twelve months

	Class of 1975	Class of 1976	Class of 1977	Class of 1978	Class of 1979	Class of 1980	Class of 1981	Class of 1982	Class of 1983	Class of 1984	Class of 1985	Class of 1986	Class of 1987	Class of 1988	Class of 1989	Class of 1990	Class of 1991	Class of 1992	Class of 1993	Class of 1994	Class of 1995	Class of 1996	Class of 1997	Class of 1998	Class of 1999	Class of 2000	'99–'00 change
Approx. N (in thousands) =	*9.4*	*15.4*	*17.1*	*17.8*	*15.5*	*15.9*	*17.5*	*17.7*	*16.3*	*15.9*	*16.0*	*15.2*	*16.3*	*16.3*	*16.7*	*15.2*	*15.0*	*15.8*	*16.3*	*15.4*	*15.4*	*14.3*	*15.4*	*15.2*	*13.6*	*12.8*	
Any Illicit Drug[a,b]	45.0	48.1	51.1	53.8	54.2	53.1	52.1	49.4	47.4	45.8	46.3	44.3	41.7	38.5	35.4	32.5	29.4	27.1	31.0	35.8	39.0	40.2	42.4	41.4	42.1	40.9	-1.2
Any Illicit Drug Other Than Marijuana[a,b]	26.2	25.4	26.0	27.1	28.2	30.4	34.0	30.1	28.4	28.0	27.4	25.9	24.1	21.1	20.0	17.9	16.2	14.9	17.1	18.0	19.4	19.8	20.7	20.2	20.7	20.4	-0.3
Marijuana/Hashish	40.0	44.5	47.6	50.2	50.8	48.8	46.1	44.3	42.3	40.0	40.6	38.8	36.3	33.1	29.6	27.0	23.9	21.9	26.0	30.7	34.7	35.8	38.5	37.5	37.8	36.5	-1.3
Inhalants[c]	—	3.0	3.7	4.1	5.4	4.6	4.1	4.5	4.3	5.1	5.7	6.1	6.9	6.5	5.9	6.9	6.6	6.2	7.0	7.7	8.0	7.6	6.7	6.2	5.6	5.9	+0.3
Inhalants, Adjusted[c,d]	—	—	—	—	8.9	7.9	6.1	6.6	6.2	7.5	8.4	8.9	8.1	7.1	7.5	7.5	6.9	6.4	7.4	8.2	8.4	8.5	7.3	7.1	6.0	6.2	+0.2
Amyl/Butyl Nitrites[e,f]	—	—	—	—	6.5	5.7	3.7	3.6	3.6	4.0	4.0	4.7	2.6	1.7	1.7	1.4	0.9	0.5	0.9	1.1	1.1	1.6	1.2	0.8	0.9	0.6	-0.3
Hallucinogens	11.2	9.4	8.8	9.6	9.9	9.3	9.0	8.1	7.3	6.5	6.3	6.0	6.4	5.5	5.6	5.9	5.8	5.9	7.4	7.6	9.3	10.1	9.8	9.0	9.4	8.1	-1.3s
Hallucinogens, Adjusted[g]	—	—	—	—	11.8	10.4	10.1	9.0	8.3	7.3	7.6	7.6	8.4	5.8	6.2	6.0	6.1	6.2	7.8	7.8	9.7	10.7	10.0	9.2	9.8	8.7	-1.1
LSD	7.2	6.4	5.5	6.3	6.6	6.5	6.5	6.1	5.4	4.7	4.4	4.5	5.2	4.8	4.9	5.4	5.2	5.6	6.8	6.9	8.4	8.8	8.4	7.6	8.1	6.6	-1.5s
Hallucinogens Other Than LSD	—	—	—	—	6.8	6.2	5.6	4.7	4.1	3.8	3.6	3.0	3.2	2.1	2.2	2.1	2.0	1.7	2.2	3.1	3.8	4.4	4.6	4.6	4.3	4.4	+0.1
PCP[e,f]	—	—	—	—	7.0	4.4	3.2	2.2	2.6	2.3	2.9	2.4	1.3	1.2	2.4	1.2	1.4	1.4	1.4	1.6	1.8	2.6	2.3	2.1	1.8	2.3	+0.5
MDMA (Ecstasy)[e]	—	—	—	—	—	—	—	—	—	—	—	—	—	—	—	—	—	—	—	—	—	4.6	4.0	3.6	5.6	8.2	+2.6ss
Cocaine	5.6	6.0	7.2	9.0	12.0	12.3	12.4	11.5	11.4	11.6	13.1	12.7	10.3	7.9	6.5	5.3	3.5	3.1	3.3	3.6	4.0	4.9	5.5	5.7	6.2	5.0	-1.3s
Crack[h]	—	—	—	—	—	—	—	—	—	—	—	4.1	3.9	3.1	3.1	1.9	1.5	1.5	1.5	1.9	2.1	2.1	2.4	2.5	2.7	2.2	-0.5s
Other Cocaine[i]	—	—	—	—	—	—	—	—	—	—	—	—	9.8	7.4	5.2	4.6	3.2	2.6	2.9	3.0	3.4	4.2	5.0	4.9	5.8	4.5	-1.4s
Heroin[j]	1.0	0.8	0.8	0.8	0.5	0.5	0.5	0.6	0.6	0.5	0.6	0.5	0.5	0.5	0.6	0.5	0.4	0.6	0.5	0.6	1.1	1.0	1.2	1.0	1.1	1.5	+0.4s
With a needle[k]	—	—	—	—	—	—	—	—	—	—	—	—	—	—	—	—	—	—	—	—	0.5	0.5	0.5	0.4	0.4	0.4	0.0
Without a needle[k]	—	—	—	—	—	—	—	—	—	—	—	—	—	—	—	—	—	—	—	—	1.0	1.0	1.2	0.8	1.0	1.6	+0.6ss
Other Narcotics[l]	5.7	5.7	6.4	6.0	6.2	6.3	5.9	5.3	5.1	5.2	5.9	5.2	5.3	4.6	4.4	4.5	3.5	3.3	3.6	3.8	4.7	5.4	6.2	6.3	6.7	7.0	+0.3
Amphetamines[b,j]	16.2	15.8	16.3	17.1	18.3	20.8	26.0	20.3	17.9	17.7	15.8	13.4	12.2	10.9	10.8	9.1	8.2	7.1	8.4	9.4	9.3	9.5	10.2	10.1	10.2	10.5	+0.3
Methamphetamine[m]	—	—	—	—	—	—	—	—	—	—	—	—	—	—	—	—	—	—	—	—	—	—	—	—	4.7	4.3	-0.3
Crystal Meth. (Ice)[m]	—	—	—	—	—	—	—	—	—	—	—	—	—	—	—	1.3	1.4	1.3	1.7	1.8	2.4	2.8	2.3	3.0	1.9	2.2	+0.3
Sedatives[l,n]	11.7	10.8	10.8	9.9	9.9	10.3	10.5	9.1	7.9	6.6	5.8	5.2	4.1	3.7	3.7	3.6	3.6	2.9	3.4	4.2	4.9	5.3	5.4	6.0	6.3	6.3	
Barbiturates[l]	10.7	9.6	9.3	8.1	7.5	6.8	6.6	5.5	5.2	4.9	4.6	4.2	3.6	3.2	3.3	3.4	3.4	2.8	3.4	4.1	4.7	4.9	5.1	5.5	5.8	6.2	+0.4
Methaqualone[l,n]	5.1	4.7	5.2	4.9	5.9	7.2	7.6	6.8	5.4	3.8	2.8	2.1	1.5	1.3	1.3	0.7	0.5	0.6	0.2	0.8	0.7	1.1	1.0	1.1	1.1	0.3	-0.8ss
Tranquilizers[l]	10.6	10.3	10.8	9.9	9.6	8.7	8.0	7.0	6.9	6.1	6.1	5.8	5.5	4.8	3.8	3.5	3.6	2.8	3.5	3.7	4.4	4.6	4.7	5.5	5.8	5.7	-0.1
Rohypnol[e]	—	—	—	—	—	—	—	—	—	—	—	—	—	—	—	—	—	—	—	—	—	1.1	1.2	1.4	1.0	0.8	-0.2
Alcohol[o]	84.8	85.7	87.0	87.7	88.1	87.9	87.0	86.8	87.3	86.0	85.6	84.5	85.7	85.3	82.7	80.6	77.7	76.8	76.0	73.0	73.7	72.5	74.8	74.3	73.8	73.2	-0.6
Been Drunk[m]	—	—	—	—	—	—	—	—	—	—	—	—	—	—	—	—	52.7	50.3	49.6	51.7	52.5	51.9	53.2	52.0	53.2	51.8	-1.4
Cigarettes	—	—	—	—	—	—	—	—	—	—	—	—	—	—	—	—	—	—	—	—	—	—	—	—	—	—	
Smokeless Tobacco[e,p]	—	—	—	—	—	—	—	—	—	—	—	—	—	—	—	—	—	—	—	—	—	—	—	—	—	—	
Steroids[m]	—	—	—	—	—	—	—	—	—	—	—	—	—	—	1.9	1.7	1.4	1.1	1.2	1.3	1.5	1.4	1.4	1.7	1.8	1.7	-0.1

NOTES: Level of significance of difference between the two most recent classes: s = .05, ss = .01, sss = .001. '—' indicates data not available.

Any apparent inconsistency between the change estimate and the prevalence of use estimates for the two most recent classes is due to rounding error.

a Use of "any illicit drug" includes any use of marijuana, LSD, other hallucinogens, crack, other cocaine, or heroin, or any use of other narcotics, amphetamines, barbiturates, methaqualone (excluded since 1990), or tranquilizers not under a doctor's orders.

b Beginning in 1982 the question about amphetamine use was revised to get respondents to exclude the inappropriate reporting of nonprescription amphetamines. The prevalence of use rate dropped slightly as a result of this methodological change.

c Beginning in 1989, data based on five of six forms in 1989–98; N is five-sixths of N indicated. Beginning in 1999, data based on three of six forms; N is three-sixths of N indicated.

d Data based on four of five forms in 1976–88; N is four-fifths of N indicated. Data based on five of six forms in 1989–98; N is five-sixths of N indicated.

TABLE 4.11

Long-term trends in annual prevalence of use of various drugs for twelfth graders [CONTINUED]

^dAdjusted for underreporting of amyl and butyl nitrites.

^eData based on one form; N is one-fifth of N indicated in 1979–88 and one-sixth of N indicated in 1989–2000.

^fQuestion text changed slightly in 1987.

^gAdjusted for underreporting of PCP.

^hData based on one of five forms in 1986; N is one-fifth of N indicated. Data based on two forms in 1987–89; N is two-fifths of N indicated in 1987–88 and two-sixths of N indicated in 1989. Data based on six forms in 1990–2000.

ⁱData based on one form in 1987–89; N is one-fifth of N indicated in 1987–88 and one-sixth of N indicated in 1989. Data based on four of six forms in 1990–2000; N is four-sixths of N indicated.

^jIn 1995 the heroin question was changed in half of the questionnaire forms. Separate questions were asked for use with injection and without injection. Data presented here represent the combined data from all forms.

^kData based on three of six forms; N is three-sixths of N indicated.

^lOnly drug use which was not under a doctor's orders is included here.

^mData based on two of six forms; N is two-sixths of N indicated. Steroid data based on one of six forms in 1989–90; N is one-sixth of N indicated in 1989–90. Steroid data based on two of six forms since 1991; N is two-sixths of N indicated since 1991.

ⁿSedatives: Data based on five forms in 1975–88, six forms in 1989, one form in 1990 (N is one-sixth of N indicated in 1990), and six forms of data adjusted by one-form data beginning in 1991. Methaqualone: Data based on five forms in 1975–88, six forms in 1989, and one of six forms beginning in 1990; N is one-sixth of N indicated beginning in 1990.

^oData based on five forms in 1975–88 and on six forms in 1989–92. In 1993, the question text was changed slightly in three of six forms to indicate that a "drink" meant "more than a few sips." The data in the upper line for alcohol came from the three forms using the original wording (N is three-sixths of N indicated), while the data in the lower line came from the three forms containing the revised wording (N is three-sixths of N indicated). Beginning in 1994, data based on all six forms.

^pThe prevalence of use of smokeless tobacco was not asked of twelfth graders in 1990 and 1991. Prior to 1990 the prevalence of use question on smokeless tobacco was located near the end of one twelfth-grade questionnaire form, whereas after 1991 the question was placed earlier and in a different form. This shift could explain the discontinuities between the corresponding data.

SOURCE: Lloyd D. Johnston, Patrick M. O'Malley, and Jerald G. Bachman, "Table 5: Long-Term Trends in Annual Prevalence of Use of Various Drugs for Twelfth Graders,'" in *Monitoring the Future: National Results on Adolescent Drug Use—Overview of Key Findings, 2000*, Institute for Social Research, University of Michigan, and the National Institute on Drug Abuse, U.S. Department of Health and Human Services, 2001

TABLE 4.12

Long-term trends in 30-day prevalence of use of various drugs for twelfth graders

Percent who used in last thirty days

	Class of 1975	Class of 1976	Class of 1977	Class of 1978	Class of 1979	Class of 1980	Class of 1981	Class of 1982	Class of 1983	Class of 1984	Class of 1985	Class of 1986	Class of 1987	Class of 1988	Class of 1989	Class of 1990	Class of 1991	Class of 1992	Class of 1993	Class of 1994	Class of 1995	Class of 1996	Class of 1997	Class of 1998	Class of 1999	Class of 2000	'99–'00 change
Approx. N (in thousands) =	9.4	15.4	17.1	17.8	15.5	15.9	17.5	17.7	16.3	15.9	16.0	15.2	16.3	16.3	16.7	15.2	15.0	15.8	16.3	15.4	15.4	14.3	15.4	15.2	13.6	12.8	
Any Illicit Drug[a,b]	30.7	34.2	37.6	38.9	38.9	37.2	36.9	32.5	30.5	29.2	29.7	27.1	24.7	21.3	19.7	17.2	16.4	14.4	18.3	21.9	23.8	24.6	26.2	25.6	25.9	24.9	-1.0
Any Illicit Drug Other Than Marijuana[a,b]	15.4	13.9	15.2	15.1	16.8	18.4	21.7	17.0	15.4	15.1	14.9	13.2	11.6	10.0	9.1	8.0	7.1	6.3	7.9	8.8	10.0	9.5	10.7	10.7	10.4	10.4	0.0
Marijuana/Hashish	27.1	32.2	35.4	37.1	36.5	33.7	31.6	28.5	27.0	25.2	25.7	23.4	21.0	18.0	16.7	14.0	13.8	11.9	15.5	19.0	21.2	21.9	23.7	22.8	23.1	21.6	-1.6
Inhalants[c]	—	0.9	1.3	1.5	1.7	1.4	1.5	1.5	1.7	1.9	2.2	2.5	3.5	2.6	2.3	2.7	2.4	2.3	2.5	2.7	3.2	3.2	2.5	2.3	2.0	2.2	+0.2
Inhalants, Adjusted[c,d]	—	—	—	—	3.2	2.7	2.3	2.5	2.5	2.6	2.3	2.7	3.5	2.6	2.3	2.7	2.4	2.3	2.5	2.9	3.0	2.9	2.5	2.9	2.4	2.4	0.0
Amyl/Butyl Nitrites[e,f]	—	—	—	—	6.5	1.8	1.4	1.1	1.4	1.4	1.6	1.3	1.3	0.6	1.4	0.8	0.4	0.4	0.6	0.4	0.4	0.4	0.6	0.4	0.4	0.3	-0.1
Hallucinogens	4.7	3.4	4.1	3.9	4.0	3.7	3.7	3.4	2.8	2.6	2.5	2.5	2.5	2.2	2.2	2.2	2.2	2.1	2.7	3.1	4.4	3.5	3.9	3.8	3.5	2.6	-0.9ss
Hallucinogens, Adjusted[g]	—	—	—	—	5.3	4.4	4.5	3.4	3.5	3.2	3.8	3.5	2.8	2.3	2.9	2.3	2.4	2.1	2.7	3.1	4.4	3.5	3.9	3.8	3.9	3.0	-0.9s
LSD	2.3	1.9	2.1	2.1	2.4	2.3	2.5	2.4	1.9	1.5	1.6	1.7	1.8	1.8	1.8	1.9	1.9	2.0	2.4	2.6	4.0	2.5	3.1	3.2	2.7	1.6	-1.2sss
Hallucinogens Other Than LSD	3.7	2.3	3.0	2.7	2.4	1.4	1.4	1.0	1.3	1.0	1.6	1.3	1.1	0.7	1.4	0.4	0.5	0.6	1.0	0.7	0.6	1.3	0.7	1.0	0.8	0.9	+0.1
PCP[e,j]	—	—	—	—	2.4	1.4	1.4	1.0	1.3	1.0	1.6	1.3	0.6	0.3	1.4	0.4	0.5	0.6	1.0	0.7	0.6	1.3	0.7	1.0	0.8	0.9	+0.1
MDMA (Ecstasy)[e]	—	—	—	—	—	—	—	—	—	—	—	—	—	—	—	—	—	—	—	—	—	2.0	1.6	1.5	2.5	3.6	+1.1
Cocaine	1.9	2.0	2.9	3.9	5.7	5.2	5.8	5.0	4.9	5.8	6.7	6.2	4.3	3.4	2.8	1.9	1.4	1.3	1.3	1.5	1.8	2.0	2.3	2.4	2.6	2.1	-0.5
Crack[h]	—	—	—	—	—	—	—	—	—	—	—	—	1.3	1.6	1.4	0.7	0.7	0.6	0.7	0.8	1.0	1.0	0.9	1.0	1.1	1.0	-0.1
Other Cocaine[i]	—	—	—	—	—	—	—	—	—	—	—	—	4.1	3.2	1.9	1.7	1.2	1.0	1.2	1.3	1.3	1.6	2.0	2.0	2.5	1.7	-0.7s
Heroin[l]	0.4	0.2	0.3	0.3	0.2	0.2	0.2	0.2	0.2	0.3	0.3	0.2	0.2	0.2	0.3	0.2	0.2	0.3	0.2	0.3	0.6	0.5	0.5	0.5	0.5	0.7	+0.2
With a needle[k]	—	—	—	—	—	—	—	—	—	—	—	—	—	—	—	—	—	—	—	—	0.3	0.4	0.3	0.2	0.2	0.2	0.0
Without a needle[k]	—	—	—	—	—	—	—	—	—	—	—	—	—	—	—	—	—	—	—	—	0.6	0.4	0.6	0.4	0.4	0.7	+0.3
Other Narcotics[l]	2.1	2.0	2.8	2.1	2.4	2.4	2.1	1.8	1.8	1.8	2.3	2.0	1.8	1.6	1.6	1.5	1.1	1.2	1.3	1.5	1.8	2.0	2.3	2.4	2.6	2.9	+0.3
Amphetamines[b,l]	8.5	7.7	8.8	8.7	9.9	12.1	15.8	10.7	8.9	8.3	6.8	5.5	5.2	4.6	4.2	3.7	3.2	2.8	3.7	4.0	4.0	4.1	4.8	4.6	4.5	5.0	+0.5
Methamphetamine	—	—	—	—	—	—	—	—	—	—	—	—	—	—	—	—	—	—	—	—	—	—	—	—	1.7	1.9	+0.2
Crystal Meth. (Ice)[m]	—	—	—	—	—	—	—	—	—	—	—	—	—	—	—	1.3	0.6	0.5	0.6	0.7	1.1	1.1	0.8	1.2	0.8	1.0	+0.2
Sedatives[l,n]	5.4	4.5	5.1	4.2	4.4	4.8	4.6	3.4	3.0	2.3	2.4	2.2	1.7	1.4	1.6	1.4	1.5	1.2	1.3	1.8	2.3	2.3	2.1	2.8	2.8	3.1	+0.3
Barbiturates[l]	4.7	3.9	4.3	3.2	3.2	2.9	2.6	2.0	2.1	1.7	2.0	1.8	1.4	1.2	1.4	1.3	1.4	1.1	1.3	1.7	2.2	2.1	2.1	2.6	2.6	3.0	+0.4
Methaqualone[l,n]	2.1	1.6	2.3	1.9	2.3	3.3	3.1	2.4	1.8	1.1	1.0	0.8	0.6	0.5	0.6	0.2	—	—	—	—	—	—	—	—	—	—	
Tranquilizers[l]	4.1	4.0	4.6	3.4	3.7	3.1	2.7	2.4	2.5	2.1	2.1	2.1	2.0	1.5	1.3	1.2	1.4	1.0	1.2	1.4	1.8	2.0	1.8	2.4	2.9	2.6	-0.3
Rohypnol[e]	—	—	—	—	—	—	—	—	—	—	—	—	—	—	—	—	—	—	—	—	—	0.5	0.6	0.3	0.3	0.4	+0.1
Alcohol[o]	68.2	68.3	71.2	72.1	71.8	72.0	70.7	69.7	69.4	67.2	65.9	65.3	66.4	63.9	60.0	57.1	54.0	51.3	51.0	50.1	51.3	50.8	52.7	52.0	51.0	50.0	-1.0
Been Drunk[m]	—	—	—	—	—	—	—	—	—	—	—	—	—	—	—	—	31.6	29.9	28.9	30.8	33.2	31.3	34.2	32.9	32.9	32.3	-0.6
Cigarettes	36.7	38.8	38.4	36.7	34.4	30.5	29.4	30.0	30.3	29.3	30.1	29.6	29.4	28.7	28.6	29.4	28.3	27.8	29.9	31.2	33.5	34.0	36.5	35.1	34.6	31.4	-3.2ss
Smokeless Tobacco[e,p]	—	—	—	—	—	—	—	—	—	—	—	11.5	11.3	10.3	8.4	—	—	11.4	10.7	11.1	12.2	9.8	9.7	8.8	8.4	7.6	-0.7
Steroids[m]	—	—	—	—	—	—	—	—	—	—	—	—	—	—	0.8	1.0	0.8	0.6	0.7	0.9	0.7	0.7	1.0	1.1	0.9	0.8	-0.1

NOTES: Level of significance of difference between the two most recent classes: s = .05, ss = .01, sss = .001. '—' indicates data not available.

Any apparent inconsistency between the change estimate and the prevalence of use estimates for the two most recent classes is due to rounding error.

[a] Use of "any illicit drug" includes any use of marijuana, LSD, other hallucinogens, crack, other cocaine, or heroin, or any use of other narcotics, amphetamines, barbiturates, methaqualone (excluded since 1990), or tranquilizers not under a doctor's orders.

[b] Beginning in 1982 the question about amphetamine use was revised to get respondents to exclude the inappropriate reporting of nonprescription amphetamines. The prevalence of use rate dropped slightly as a result of this methodological change.

[c] Data based on four of five forms in 1976–88; N is four-fifths of N indicated. Data based on five of six forms in 1989–98; N is five-sixths of N indicated. Beginning in 1999, data based on three of six forms; N is three-sixths of N indicated.

[d] Adjusted for underreporting of amyl and butyl nitrites.

[e] Data based on one form; N is one-fifth of N indicated in 1979–88 and one-sixth of N indicated in 1989–2000.

TABLE 4.12

Long-term trends in 30-day prevalence of use of various drugs for twelfth graders [CONTINUED]

[f]Question text changed slightly in 1987.

[g]Adjusted for underreporting of PCP.

[h]Data based on one of five forms in 1986; N is one-fifth of N indicated. Data based on two forms in 1987–89; N is two-fifths of N indicated in 1987–88 and two-sixths of N indicated in 1989. Data based on six forms in 1990–2000.

[i]Data based on one form in 1987–89; N is one-fifth of N indicated in 1987–88 and one-sixth of N indicated in 1989. Data based on four of six forms in 1990–2000; N is four-sixths of N indicated.

[j]In 1995 the heroin question was changed in half of the questionnaire forms. Separate questions were asked for use with injection and without injection. Data presented here represent the combined data from all forms.

[k]Data based on three of six forms; N is three-sixths of N indicated.

[l]Only drug use which was not under a doctor's orders is included here.

[m]Data based on two of six forms; N is two-sixths of N indicated. Steroid data based on one of six forms in 1989–90; N is one-sixth of N indicated in 1989–90. Steroid data based on two of six forms since 1991; N is two-sixths of N indicated since 1991.

[n]Sedatives: Data based on five forms in 1975–88, six forms in 1989, one form in 1990 (N is one-sixth of N indicated in 1990), and six forms of data beginning in 1991. Methaqualone: Data based on five forms in 1975–88, six forms in 1989, and one of six forms beginning in 1990; N is one-sixth of N indicated beginning in 1990.

[o]Data based on five forms in 1975–88 and on six forms in 1989–92. In 1993, the question text was changed slightly in three of six forms to indicate that a "drink" meant "more than a few sips." The data in the upper line for alcohol came from the three forms using the original wording (N is three-sixths of N indicated), while the data in the lower line came from the three forms containing the revised wording (N is three-sixths of N indicated). Beginning in 1994, data based on all six forms.

[p]The prevalence of use of smokeless tobacco was not asked of twelfth graders in 1990 and 1991. Prior to 1990 the prevalence of use question on smokeless tobacco was located near the end of one twelfth-grade questionnaire form, whereas after 1991 the question was placed earlier and in a different form. This shift could explain the discontinuities between the corresponding data.

SOURCE: Lloyd D. Johnston, Patrick M. O'Malley, and Jerald G. Bachman, "Table 6: Long-Term Trends in Thirty-Day Prevalence of Use of Various Drugs for Twelfth Graders," in *Monitoring the Future: National Results on Adolescent Drug Use—Overview of Key Findings, 2000*, Institute for Social Research, University of Michigan, and the National Institute on Drug Abuse, U.S. Department of Health and Human Services, 2001

TABLE 4.13

Long-term trends in 30-day prevalence of daily use of various drugs for twelfth graders

Percent who used in last thirty days

	Class of 1975	Class of 1976	Class of 1977	Class of 1978	Class of 1979	Class of 1980	Class of 1981	Class of 1982	Class of 1983	Class of 1984	Class of 1985	Class of 1986	Class of 1987	Class of 1988	Class of 1989	Class of 1990	Class of 1991	Class of 1992	Class of 1993	Class of 1994	Class of 1995	Class of 1996	Class of 1997	Class of 1998	Class of 1999	Class of 2000	'99–'00 change
Approx. N (in thousands) =	*9.4*	*15.4*	*17.1*	*17.8*	*15.5*	*15.9*	*17.5*	*17.7*	*16.3*	*15.9*	*16.0*	*15.2*	*16.3*	*16.3*	*16.7*	*15.2*	*15.0*	*15.8*	*16.3*	*15.4*	*15.4*	*14.3*	*15.4*	*15.2*	*13.6*	*12.8*	
Marijuana/Hashish	6.0	8.2	9.1	10.7	10.3	9.1	7.0	6.3	5.5	5.0	4.9	4.0	3.3	2.7	2.9	2.2	2.0	1.9	2.4	3.6	4.6	4.9	5.8	5.6	6.0	6.0	0.0
Inhalants[a]	—	*	—	0.1	—	0.1	0.1	0.1	0.1	0.1	0.2	0.2	0.1	0.2	0.2	0.3	0.2	0.1	0.1	0.1	0.1	0.2	0.1	0.2	0.2	0.2	0.0
Inhalants, Adjusted[a,b]	—	—	—	—	0.1	0.1	0.1	0.1	0.1	0.1	0.2	0.2	0.3	0.3	0.3	0.3	0.2	0.1	0.2	0.2	0.2	0.4	0.2	0.3	0.3	0.3	-0.1
Amyl/Butyl Nitrites[c,d]	—	—	—	0.1	—	0.1	0.1	0.1	0.1	0.1	0.3	0.5	0.3	0.1	0.3	0.1	0.5	0.1	0.2	0.1	0.2	0.4	0.3	0.9	0.3	0.3	-0.2
Hallucinogens	0.1	*	*	0.1	0.1	0.1	0.1	0.1	0.1	0.1	0.1	0.1	0.1	*	0.1	0.1	0.1	0.1	0.1	0.1	0.1	0.1	0.1	0.1	0.1	0.2	+0.1
Hallucinogens, Adjusted[e]	*	*	*	*	0.2	0.2	0.1	0.2	0.1	0.2	0.3	0.3	0.2	*	0.3	0.3	0.1	0.1	0.1	*	0.1	0.2	0.2	0.2	0.2	0.2	0.0
LSD	*	0.1	*	*	*	*	0.1	*	*	0.1	*	*	*	*	*	0.1	*	*	0.1	*	0.1	*	0.1	*	*	0.1	+0.1
Hallucinogens Other Than LSD	—	—	—	—	—	—	0.1	*	*	*	0.3	0.2	0.3	0.1	0.2	0.1	0.1	0.1	0.1	0.1	0.1	0.2	0.1	0.3	0.2	0.2	+0.1s
PCP[c,d]	—	—	—	—	0.1	0.1	0.1	0.1	0.1	0.1	0.3	0.2	0.3	0.3	0.2	0.1	0.2	*	0.1	0.2	0.3	0.3	0.1	0.2	0.1	0.2	+0.1s
MDMA (Ecstasy)[c]	—	—	—	—	—	—	—	—	—	—	—	—	—	—	0.2	0.1	*	*	*	*	*	0.0	0.1	0.2	0.1	*	-0.1
Cocaine	0.1	0.1	0.1	0.1	0.2	0.2	0.3	0.2	0.2	0.2	0.4	0.4	0.3	0.2	0.3	0.1	0.1	0.1	0.1	0.1	0.2	0.2	0.2	0.2	0.2	0.1	-0.1
Crack[f]	—	—	—	—	—	—	—	—	—	—	—	0.4	0.1	0.1	0.2	0.1	0.1	*	0.1	0.1	0.1	0.1	0.1	0.1	0.1	0.1	0.0
Other Cocaine[g]	—	—	—	—	—	—	—	—	—	—	—	0.3	0.3	0.2	0.3	0.2	0.2	0.1	0.1	0.2	0.3	0.3	0.2	0.3	0.2	0.1	0.0
Heroin[h]	0.1	*	*	*	*	*	*	*	0.1	*	*	*	0.2	*	0.1	*	*	*	0.1	*	0.1	0.2	0.1	0.1	0.1	0.1	0.0
With a needle[i]	—	—	—	—	—	—	—	—	—	—	—	—	—	—	—	—	—	—	—	—	0.1	0.1	0.1	0.1	0.1	0.1	0.0
Without a needle[i]	—	—	—	—	—	—	—	—	—	—	—	—	—	0.1	—	*	0.1	0.1	*	0.1	*	0.1	0.1	0.1	*	*	0.0
Other Narcotics[j]	0.1	0.2	0.2	0.1	0.1	0.1	0.1	0.1	0.1	0.1	0.1	0.1	0.1	0.1	0.2	0.1	0.1	0.1	0.1	0.1	0.1	0.1	0.1	0.1	0.2	0.5	+0.2s
Amphetamines[j,k]	0.5	0.4	0.5	0.5	0.6	0.7	1.2	0.7	0.8	0.6	0.4	0.3	0.3	0.3	0.3	0.2	0.2	0.2	0.2	0.2	0.3	0.3	0.3	0.3	0.6	0.5	-0.1s
Methamphetamine[l]	—	—	—	—	—	—	—	—	—	—	—	—	—	—	—	—	—	—	—	—	—	—	—	—	0.2	0.1	-0.1s
Crystal Meth. (Ice)[l]	—	—	—	—	—	—	—	—	—	—	—	—	—	—	—	0.1	0.1	0.1	0.1	*	0.1	0.1	0.1	*	0.1	0.1	0.0
Sedatives[l,m]	0.3	0.2	0.2	0.2	0.1	0.2	0.2	0.2	0.2	0.1	0.1	0.1	0.1	0.1	0.1	0.1	0.1	0.1	0.1	*	0.1	0.1	0.1	0.1	0.2	0.1	-0.1s
Barbiturates[j]	0.1	0.1	0.2	0.1	*	0.1	0.1	0.1	0.1	*	0.1	0.1	0.1	*	0.1	0.1	0.1	*	0.1	*	0.1	0.1	0.1	0.1	0.2	0.1	-0.1s
Methaqualone[j,m]	*	*	*	*	*	0.1	0.1	0.1	*	*	*	*	*	0.1	*	*	*	0.1	*	0.1	*	0.0	0.1	0.0	0.0	0.0	0.0
Tranquilizers[j]	0.1	0.2	0.3	0.1	0.1	0.1	0.1	0.1	0.1	0.1	*	*	0.1	0.1	0.1	0.1	0.1	0.1	*	0.1	*	0.2	0.1	0.1	0.1	0.1	-0.1
Rohypnol[c]	—	—	—	—	—	—	—	—	—	—	—	—	—	—	—	—	—	—	—	—	—	0.1	0.0	0.1	0.1	0.1	+0.1
Alcohol																											
Daily[n]	5.7	5.6	6.1	5.7	6.9	6.0	6.0	5.7	5.5	4.8	5.0	4.8	4.8	4.2	4.2	3.7	3.6	3.4	2.5	3.9	3.4	2.9	—	1.5	1.9	1.7	—
Been drunk daily[l]	—	—	—	—	—	—	—	—	—	—	—	—	—	—	3.4	2.9	3.5	3.7	3.9	3.9	3.4	2.9	2.0	1.5	1.9	1.7	-0.2
5+ drinks in a row in last 2 weeks	36.8	37.1	39.4	40.3	41.2	41.2	41.4	40.5	40.8	38.7	36.7	36.8	37.5	34.7	33.0	32.2	29.8	27.9	27.5	28.2	29.8	30.2	31.3	31.5	30.8	30.0	-0.8
Cigarettes																											
Daily	26.9	28.8	28.8	27.5	25.4	21.3	20.3	21.1	21.2	18.7	19.5	18.7	18.7	18.1	18.9	19.1	18.5	17.2	19.0	19.4	21.6	22.2	24.6	22.4	23.1	20.6	-2.5s
Half-pack or more per day	17.9	19.2	19.4	18.8	16.5	14.3	13.5	14.2	13.8	12.3	12.5	11.4	11.4	10.6	11.2	11.3	10.7	10.0	10.9	11.2	12.4	13.0	14.3	12.6	13.2	11.3	-1.9ss
Smokeless Tobacco[c,o]	—	—	—	—	—	—	—	—	—	—	—	4.7	5.1	4.3	3.3	—	—	4.3	3.3	3.9	3.6	3.3	4.4	3.2	2.9	3.2	+0.3
Steroids[l]	—	—	—	—	—	—	—	—	—	—	—	—	—	—	0.1	0.2	0.1	0.1	0.1	0.4	0.2	0.3	0.3	0.3	0.2	0.2	0.0

TABLE 4.13

Long-term trends in 30-day prevalence of daily use of various drugs for twelfth graders [CONTINUED]

NOTES: Level of significance of difference between the two most recent classes: s = .05, ss = .01, sss = .001. '—' indicates data not available. '*' indicates less than .05 percent but greater than 0 percent.

Any apparent inconsistency between the change estimate and the prevalence of use estimates for the two most recent classes is due to rounding error. Daily use is defined as use on 20 or more occasions in the past 30 days except for 5+ drinks, cigarettes, and smokeless tobacco, for which actual daily use is measured.

aData based on four of five forms in 1976–88; N is four-fifths of N indicated. Beginning in 1999, data based on five of six forms in 1989–98; N is five-sixths of N indicated.

bAdjusted for underreporting of amyl and butyl nitrites.

cData based on one form; N is one-fifth of N indicated in 1979–88 and one-sixth of N indicated in 1989–2000.

dQuestion text changed slightly in 1987.

eAdjusted for underreporting of PCP.

fData based on one of five forms in 1986; N is one-fifth of N indicated. Data based on two forms in 1987–89; N is two-fifths of N indicated.

gData based on one form in 1987–89; N is one-fifth of N indicated in 1987–88 and one-sixth of N indicated in 1989. Data based on four of six forms in 1990–2000; N is four-sixths of N indicated.

hIn 1995 the heroin question was changed in half of the questionnaire forms. Separate questions were asked for use with injection and without injection. Data presented here represent the combined data from all forms.

iData based on three of six forms; N is three-sixths of N indicated.

jOnly drug use which was not under a doctor's orders is included here.

kBeginning in 1982 the question about amphetamine use was revised to get respondents to exclude the inappropriate reporting of nonprescription amphetamines. The prevalence of use rate dropped slightly as a result of this methodological change.

lData based on two of six forms; N is two-sixths of N indicated. Steroid data based on one of six forms in 1989–90; N is one-sixth of N indicated in 1989–90. Steroid data based on two of six forms since 1991; N is two-sixths of N indicated since 1991.

mSedatives: Data based on five forms in 1975–88, six forms in 1989, one form in 1990 (N is one-sixth of N indicated in 1990), a nd six forms of data adjusted by one-form data beginning in 1991. Methaqualone: Data based on five forms in 1975–88, six forms in 1989, and one of six forms beginning in 1990; N is one-sixth of N indicated beginning in 1990.

nData based on five forms in 1975–88 and on six forms in 1989–92. In 1993, the question text was changed slightly in three of six forms to indicate that a "drink" meant "more than a few sips." The data in the upper line for alcohol came from the three forms using the original wording (N is three-sixths of N indicated), while the data in the lower line came from the three forms containing the revised wording (N is three-sixths of N indicated). Beginning in 1994, data based on all six forms.

oThe prevalence of use of smokeless tobacco was not asked of twelfth graders in 1990 and 1991. Prior to 1990 the prevalence of use question on smokeless tobacco was located near the end of one twelfth-grade questionnaire form, whereas after 1991 the question was placed earlier and in a different form. This shift could explain the discontinuities between the corresponding data.

SOURCE: Lloyd D. Johnston, Patrick M. O'Malley, and Jerald G. Bachman, "Table 7: Long-Term Trends in Thirty-Day Prevalence of Daily Use of Various Drugs for Twelfth Graders," in *Monitoring the Future: National Results on Adolescent Drug Use—Overview of Key Findings, 2000,* Institute for Social Research, University of Michigan, and the National Institute on Drug Abuse, U.S. Department of Health and Human Services, 2001

in 1992 and 1993, before rising to 3.9 percent in 2000. (See Table 4.10.) Annual prevalence fell from 4.1 percent in 1986 to 1.5 percent in 1991, 1992, and 1993, and increased to 2.2 percent in 2000. (See Table 4.11.) Thirty-day prevalence fell from 1.6 percent in 1988 to 0.6 percent in 1992, but nearly doubled, to 1.1 percent, in 2000. (See Table 4.12.) Annual prevalence among eighth- and tenth-graders more than doubled between 1991 and 2000.

SEDATIVES AND TRANQUILIZERS

During the 1990s the illegal use of sedatives and tranquilizers continued to increase among high school seniors as well as tenth-graders, though the use of tranquilizers among eighth-graders declined somewhat between 1995 and 2000. (See Table 4.1 and Table 4.2.)

STEROIDS

Steroid use decreased somewhat among high school seniors in 2000. Lifetime use was 2.5 percent; annual use, 1.7 percent; and 30-day use, 0.8 percent. (See Table 4.1 and Table 4.2.) Eighth- and tenth-graders were more likely than seniors to have used steroids at some time in their lives. (See Table 4.1.)

ATTITUDES TOWARD DRUG USE

Harmfulness

MARIJUANA. How a student feels about the risk of using a particular drug, and how much he or she disapproves of the use of that drug, generally influences how likely that student, or his or her peer group, is to try the drug. In the 1990s the percentage of students who considered drug use harmful dropped to the lowest levels since the early 1980s. In 1991, 40.4 percent of eighth-graders thought that using marijuana once or twice was harmful, while 57.9 percent considered occasional use harmful. In 2000 only 29 percent of eighth-graders thought that trying marijuana once or twice was harmful, while 47.4 percent considered occasional use dangerous. (See Table 4.14.)

The proportion of tenth-graders who thought that trying marijuana once or twice was harmful fell from 30 percent in 1991 to 18.5 percent in 2000. Over the same period, the percentage of those concerned about the dangers of occasional use fell from 48.6 percent to about 32 percent. (See Table 4.14.)

In 1978 only 8 percent of seniors thought that trying marijuana once or twice was dangerous. This proportion rose to 27.1 percent in 1991, but fell by about half, to 13.7 percent, in 2000. Similarly, the proportion of those concerned about occasional use was just 12 percent in 1978, rose to 40.6 percent in 1991, and fell by nearly half, to 23.4 percent, in 2000. (See Table 4.15.)

In 2000 most students did not consider using marijuana once or twice, or even occasionally, dangerous. However, most did consider regular marijuana use to be dangerous—although 42 percent of seniors did not. (See Table 4.14 and Table 4.15.)

INHALANTS. In 2000, 41.2 percent of eighth-graders and 46.6 percent of tenth-graders thought that trying inhalants once or twice was harmful. More than two-thirds of eighth-graders and three-quarters of tenth-graders considered regular use dangerous. Overall, recognition of the dangers of inhalant use grew slightly among eighth-graders but fell somewhat among tenth-graders—although not enough to be statistically significant. (See Table 4.14.)

LSD. In 2000, 34 percent of eighth-graders, 43 percent of tenth-graders, and 34 percent of twelfth-graders considered using LSD once or twice dangerous, while 57.5 percent of eighth-graders, 72 percent of tenth-graders, and 76 percent of twelfth-graders thought that regular use was dangerous. (See Table 4.14 and Table 4.15.)

COCAINE. Approximately half of eighth-graders (43.3 percent), tenth-graders (48.8 percent), and twelfth-graders (51.1 percent) believed it dangerous to use cocaine powder once or twice. A significantly higher percentage of eighth-graders (65.5 percent), tenth-graders (70.9 percent), and twelfth-graders (69.5 percent) thought it harmful to use it occasionally. A somewhat higher percentage from each grade thought that crack cocaine was dangerous. (See Table 4.14 and Table 4.15.)

It should be noted that a significant percentage of students did not consider it a "great risk" to take cocaine once, twice, or even occasionally. The perceived risk of crack use also continued to decline in all grades, although more slowly at the eighth-grade level.

Disapproval

MARIJUANA. Eighth-graders' disapproval of marijuana use declined from 1991 to 1997, but increased significantly in 2000. The proportion of eight-graders who disapproved of people using marijuana once or twice declined from 84.6 in 1991 to 67.5 percent in 1996, but rose to 72.5 percent in 2000. Among tenth-graders, disapproval of an individual's using marijuana once or twice fell from 74.6 percent in 1991 to 54.9 percent in 2000. Disapproval of those who occasionally use marijuana dropped from 83.7 percent to 67.2 percent over the same period. (See Table 4.16.)

The percentage of twelfth-graders who disapproved of people using marijuana once or twice rose from just 33 percent in 1977 and 1978 to 69.9 percent in 1992, but later fell dramatically, to 52.5 percent in 2000. Similarly, disapproval of occasional use rose from 43.5 percent in 1978 to 79.7 percent in 1992, before falling to 63–66 percent from 1996 through 2000. (See Table 4.17.) In 2000 a higher percentage of students disapproved of regular use:

TABLE 4.14

Trends in harmfulness of drugs as perceived by eighth, tenth, and twelfth grade students, 1991–2000

Percentage saying "great risk"[a]

How much do you think people risk harming themselves (physically or in other ways), if they . . .	8th Grade											10th Grade										
	1991	1992	1993	1994	1995	1996	1997	1998	1999	2000	'99–'00 change	1991	1992	1993	1994	1995	1996	1997	1998	1999	2000	'99–'00 change
Try marijuana once or twice	40.4	39.1	36.2	31.6	28.9	27.9	25.3	28.1	28.0	29.0	+0.9	30.0	31.9	29.7	24.4	21.5	20.0	18.8	19.6	19.2	18.5	-0.7
Smoke marijuana occasionally	57.9	56.3	53.8	48.6	45.9	44.3	43.1	45.0	45.7	47.4	+1.8	48.6	48.9	46.1	38.9	35.4	32.8	31.9	32.5	33.5	32.4	-1.1
Smoke marijuana regularly	83.8	82.0	79.6	74.3	73.0	70.9	72.7	73.0	73.3	74.8	+1.4	82.1	81.1	78.5	71.3	67.9	65.9	65.9	65.8	65.9	64.7	-1.2
Try inhalants once or twice[b]	35.9	37.0	36.5	37.9	36.4	40.8	40.1	38.9	40.8	41.2	+0.3	37.8	38.7	40.9	42.7	41.6	47.2	47.5	45.8	48.2	46.6	-1.6
Try inhalants regularly[b]	65.6	64.4	64.6	65.5	64.8	68.2	68.7	67.2	68.8	69.9	+1.1	69.8	67.9	69.6	71.5	71.8	75.8	74.5	73.3	76.3	75.0	-1.3
Take LSD once or twice[c]	—	—	42.1	38.3	36.7	36.5	37.0	34.9	34.1	34.0	-0.2	—	—	48.7	46.5	44.7	45.1	44.5	43.5	45.0	43.0	-2.1
Take LSD regularly[c]	—	—	68.3	65.8	64.4	63.6	64.1	59.6	58.8	57.5	-1.3	—	—	78.9	75.9	75.5	75.3	73.8	72.3	73.9	72.0	-1.9
Try crack once or twice[b]	62.8	61.2	57.2	54.4	50.8	51.0	49.9	49.3	48.7	48.5	-0.2	70.4	69.6	66.6	64.7	60.9	60.9	59.2	58.0	57.8	56.1	-1.7
Take crack occasionally[b]	82.2	79.6	76.8	74.4	72.1	71.6	71.2	70.6	70.6	70.1	-0.5	87.4	86.4	84.4	83.1	81.2	80.3	78.7	77.5	79.1	76.9	-2.2s
Try cocaine powder once or twice[b]	55.5	54.1	50.7	48.4	44.9	45.2	45.0	44.0	43.3	43.3	0.0	59.1	59.2	57.5	56.4	53.5	53.6	52.2	50.9	51.6	48.8	-2.8ss
Take cocaine powder occasionally[b]	77.0	74.3	71.8	69.1	66.4	65.7	65.8	65.2	65.4	65.5	+0.1	82.2	80.1	79.1	77.8	75.6	75.0	73.9	71.8	73.6	70.9	-2.7ss
Try heroin once or twice without using a needle[c]	—	—	—	—	60.1	61.3	63.0	62.8	63.0	62.0	-1.0	—	—	—	—	70.7	72.1	73.1	71.7	73.7	71.7	-1.9
Take heroin occasionally without using a needle[c]	—	—	—	—	76.8	76.6	79.2	79.0	78.9	78.6	-0.3	—	—	—	—	85.1	85.8	86.5	84.9	86.5	85.2	-1.3
Try one or two drinks of an alcoholic beverage (beer, wine, liquor)	11.0	12.1	12.4	11.6	11.6	11.8	10.4	12.1	11.6	11.9	+0.3	9.0	10.1	10.9	9.4	9.3	8.9	9.0	10.1	10.5	9.6	-1.0
Take one or two drinks nearly every day	31.8	32.4	32.6	29.9	30.5	28.6	29.1	30.3	29.7	30.4	+0.7	36.1	36.8	35.9	32.5	31.7	31.2	31.8	31.9	32.9	32.3	-0.6
Have five or more drinks once or twice each weekend	59.1	58.0	57.7	54.7	54.1	51.8	55.6	56.0	55.3	55.9	+0.6	54.7	55.9	54.9	52.9	52.0	50.9	51.8	52.5	51.9	51.0	-0.9
Smoke one or more packs of cigarettes per day[d]	51.6	50.8	52.7	50.8	49.8	50.4	52.6	54.3	54.8	58.8	+4.0ss	60.3	59.3	60.7	59.0	57.0	57.9	59.9	61.9	62.7	65.9	+3.3s
Use smokeless tobacco regularly[e]	35.1	35.1	36.9	35.5	33.5	34.0	35.2	36.5	37.1	39.0	+1.9	40.3	39.6	44.2	42.2	38.2	41.0	42.2	42.8	44.2	46.7	+2.5s
Take steroids[e]	64.2	69.5	70.2	67.6	—	—	—	—	—	—	—	67.1	72.7	73.4	72.5	—	—	—	—	—	—	—
Approx. N (in thousands) =	*17.4*	*18.7*	*18.4*	*17.4*	*17.5*	*17.9*	*18.8*	*18.1*	*16.7*	*16.7*		*14.7*	*14.8*	*15.3*	*15.9*	*17.0*	*15.7*	*15.6*	*15.0*	*13.6*	*14.3*	

Notes: Level of significance of difference between the two most recent classes: s = .05, ss = .01, sss = .001. '—' indicates data not available. Any apparent inconsistency between the change estimate and the prevalence of use estimates for the two most recent classes is due to rounding error.

[a] Answer alternatives were: (1) No risk, (2) Slight risk, (3) Moderate risk, (4) Great risk, and (5) Can't say, drug unfamiliar.
[b] Beginning in 1997, data based on two-thirds of N indicated due to changes in questionnaire forms.
[c] Data based on one of two forms in 1993–96; N is one-half of N indicated. Beginning in 1997, data based on one-third of N indicated due to changes in questionnaire forms.
[d] Beginning in 1999, data based on two-thirds of N indicated due to changes in questionnaire forms.
[e] Data based on one of two forms in 1991 and 1992. Data based on one of two forms in 1993 and 1994; N is one-half of N indicated.

SOURCE: Lloyd D. Johnston, Patrick M. O'Malley, and Jerald G. Bachman, "Table 8: Trends in Harmfulness of Drugs as Perceived by Eighth, Tenth, and Twelfth Graders, 1991–2000," in *Monitoring the Future: National Results on Adolescent Drug Use—Overview of Key Findings, 2000,* Institute for Social Research, University of Michigan, and the National Institute on Drug Abuse, U.S. Department of Health and Human Services, 2001

TABLE 4.15

Long-term trends in harmfulness of drugs as perceived by twelfth graders

How much do you think people risk harming themselves (physically or in other ways), if they . . .	Class of 1975	Class of 1976	Class of 1977	Class of 1978	Class of 1979	Class of 1980	Class of 1981	Class of 1982	Class of 1983	Class of 1984	Class of 1985	Class of 1986	Class of 1987	Class of 1988	Class of 1989	Class of 1990	Class of 1991	Class of 1992	Class of 1993	Class of 1994	Class of 1995	Class of 1996	Class of 1997	Class of 1998	Class of 1999	Class of 2000	'99–'00 change
													Percentage saying "great risk"														
Try marijuana once or twice	15.1	11.4	9.5	8.1	9.4	10.0	13.0	11.5	12.7	14.7	14.8	15.1	18.4	19.0	23.6	23.1	27.1	24.5	21.9	19.5	16.3	15.6	14.9	16.7	15.7	13.7	-1.9
Smoke marijuana occasionally	18.1	15.0	13.4	12.4	13.5	14.7	19.1	18.3	20.6	22.6	24.5	25.0	30.4	31.7	36.5	36.9	40.6	39.6	35.6	30.1	25.6	25.9	24.7	24.4	23.9	23.4	-0.4
Smoke marijuana regularly	43.3	38.6	36.4	34.9	42.0	50.4	57.6	60.4	62.8	66.9	70.4	71.3	73.5	77.0	77.5	77.8	78.6	76.5	72.5	65.0	60.8	59.9	58.1	58.5	57.4	58.3	+0.9
Try LSD once or twice	49.4	45.7	43.2	42.7	41.6	43.9	45.5	44.9	44.7	45.4	43.5	42.0	44.9	45.7	46.0	44.7	46.6	42.3	39.5	38.8	36.4	36.2	34.7	37.4	34.9	34.3	-0.7
Take LSD regularly	81.4	80.8	79.1	81.1	82.4	83.0	83.5	83.5	83.2	83.8	82.9	82.6	83.8	84.2	84.3	84.5	84.3	81.8	79.4	79.1	78.1	77.8	76.6	76.5	76.1	75.9	-0.2
Try PCP once or twice	—	—	—	—	—	—	—	—	—	—	—	—	55.6	58.8	56.6	55.2	51.7	54.8	50.8	51.5	49.1	51.0	48.8	48.8	44.8	45.0	+0.1
Try MDMA once or twice	—	—	—	—	—	—	—	—	—	—	—	—	—	—	—	—	—	—	—	—	—	—	33.8	34.5	35.0	37.9	+2.9
Try cocaine once or twice	42.6	39.1	35.6	33.2	31.5	31.3	32.1	32.8	33.0	35.7	34.0	33.5	47.9	51.2	54.9	59.4	59.4	56.8	57.6	57.2	53.7	54.2	53.6	54.6	52.1	51.1	-1.0
Take cocaine occasionally	—	—	—	—	—	—	—	—	—	—	—	54.2	66.8	69.2	71.8	73.9	75.5	75.1	73.3	73.7	70.8	72.1	72.4	70.1	70.1	69.5	-0.6
Take cocaine regularly	73.1	72.3	68.2	68.2	69.5	69.2	71.2	73.0	74.3	78.8	79.0	82.2	88.5	89.2	90.2	91.1	90.4	90.2	90.1	89.3	87.9	88.3	87.1	86.3	85.8	86.2	+0.4
Try crack once or twice	—	—	—	—	—	—	—	—	—	—	—	—	57.0	62.1	62.9	64.3	60.6	62.4	57.6	58.4	54.6	56.0	54.0	52.2	48.2	48.4	+0.2
Take crack occasionally	—	—	—	—	—	—	—	—	—	—	—	—	70.4	73.2	75.3	80.4	76.5	76.3	73.9	73.8	72.8	71.4	70.3	68.7	67.3	65.8	-1.5
Take crack regularly	—	—	—	—	—	—	—	—	—	—	—	—	84.6	84.8	85.6	91.6	90.1	89.3	87.5	89.6	88.6	88.0	86.2	85.3	85.4	85.3	0.0
Try cocaine powder once or twice	—	—	—	—	—	—	—	—	—	—	—	—	45.3	51.7	53.8	53.9	53.6	57.1	53.2	55.4	52.0	53.2	51.4	48.5	46.1	47.0	+0.9
Take cocaine powder occasionally	—	—	—	—	—	—	—	—	—	—	—	—	56.8	61.9	65.8	71.1	69.8	70.8	68.6	70.6	69.1	68.8	67.7	65.4	64.2	64.7	+0.5
Take cocaine powder regularly	—	—	—	—	—	—	—	—	—	—	—	—	81.4	82.9	83.9	90.2	88.9	88.4	87.0	88.6	87.8	86.8	86.0	84.1	84.6	85.5	+0.9
Try heroin once or twice	60.1	58.9	55.8	52.9	50.4	52.1	52.9	51.1	50.8	49.8	47.3	45.8	53.6	54.0	53.8	55.6	55.2	50.9	50.7	52.8	50.9	52.5	56.7	57.8	56.0	54.2	-1.7
Take heroin occasionally	75.6	75.6	71.9	71.4	70.9	70.9	72.2	69.8	71.8	70.7	69.8	68.2	74.6	73.8	75.5	76.6	74.9	74.2	72.0	72.1	71.0	74.8	76.3	76.9	77.3	74.6	-2.8
Take heroin regularly	87.2	88.6	86.1	86.6	87.5	86.2	87.5	86.0	86.1	87.2	86.0	87.1	88.7	88.8	89.5	90.2	89.6	89.2	88.3	88.0	87.2	89.5	88.9	89.1	89.9	89.2	-0.7
Try amphetamines once or twice	35.4	33.4	30.8	29.9	29.7	29.7	26.4	25.3	24.7	25.4	25.2	25.1	29.1	29.6	32.8	32.2	36.3	32.6	31.3	31.4	28.8	30.8	31.0	35.3	32.2	32.6	+0.4
Take amphetamines regularly	69.0	67.3	66.6	67.1	69.9	69.1	66.1	64.7	64.8	67.1	67.2	67.3	69.4	69.8	71.2	71.2	74.1	72.4	69.9	67.0	65.9	66.8	66.0	67.7	66.4	66.3	-0.1
Try crystal meth. (ice) once or twice	—	—	—	—	—	—	—	—	—	—	—	—	—	—	—	—	61.6	61.9	57.5	58.3	54.4	55.3	54.4	52.7	51.2	51.3	+0.1
Try barbiturates once or twice	34.8	32.5	31.2	31.3	30.7	30.9	28.4	27.5	27.0	27.4	26.1	25.4	30.9	29.7	32.2	32.4	35.1	32.2	29.2	29.9	26.3	29.1	26.9	29.0	26.1	25.0	-1.1
Take barbiturates regularly	69.1	67.7	68.6	68.4	71.6	72.2	69.9	67.6	67.7	68.5	68.3	67.2	69.4	69.6	70.5	70.2	70.5	70.2	66.1	63.3	61.6	60.4	56.8	56.3	54.1	52.3	-1.7
Try one or two drinks of an alcoholic beverage (beer, wine, liquor)	5.3	4.8	4.1	3.4	4.1	3.8	4.6	3.5	4.2	4.6	5.0	4.6	6.2	6.0	6.0	8.3	9.1	8.6	8.2	7.6	5.9	7.3	6.7	8.0	8.3	6.4	-1.9s
Take one or two drinks nearly every day	21.5	21.2	18.5	19.6	22.6	20.3	21.6	21.6	21.6	23.0	24.4	25.1	26.2	27.3	28.5	31.3	32.7	30.6	28.2	27.0	24.8	25.1	24.8	24.3	21.8	21.7	-0.1
Take four or five drinks nearly every day	63.5	61.0	62.9	63.1	66.2	65.7	64.5	65.5	66.8	68.4	69.8	66.5	69.7	68.5	69.8	70.9	69.5	70.5	67.8	66.2	62.8	65.6	63.0	62.1	61.1	59.9	-1.2
Have five or more drinks once or twice each weekend	37.8	37.0	34.7	34.5	34.9	35.9	36.3	36.0	38.6	41.7	43.0	39.1	41.9	42.6	44.0	47.1	48.6	49.0	48.3	46.5	45.2	49.5	43.0	42.8	43.1	42.7	-0.4
Smoke one or more packs of cigarettes per day	51.3	56.4	58.4	59.0	63.0	63.7	63.3	60.5	61.2	63.8	66.5	66.0	68.6	68.0	67.2	68.2	69.4	69.2	69.5	67.6	65.6	68.2	68.7	70.8	70.8	73.1	+2.3
Use smokeless tobacco regularly	—	—	—	—	—	—	—	—	—	—	—	25.8	30.0	33.2	32.9	34.2	37.4	35.5	38.9	36.6	33.2	37.4	38.6	40.9	41.1	42.2	+1.1
Take steroids	—	—	—	—	—	—	—	—	—	—	—	—	—	—	63.8	69.9	65.6	70.7	69.1	66.1	66.4	67.6	67.2	68.1	62.1	57.9	-4.3s
Approx. N =	2804	2918	3052	3770	3250	3234	3604	3557	3305	3262	3250	3020	3315	3276	2796	2553	2549	2684	2759	2591	2603	2449	2579	2564	2306	2130	

NOTES: Level of significance of difference between the two most recent classes: s = .05. '—' indicates data not available. Any apparent inconsistency between the change estimate and the prevalence of use estimates for the two most recent classes is due to rounding error.

*Answer alternatives were: (1) No risk, (2) Slight risk, (3) Moderate risk, (4) Great risk, and (5) Can't say, drug unfamiliar.

SOURCE: L. Johnston, P. O'Malley, and J. Bachman, "Table 9: Long-Term Trends in Harmfulness of Drugs as Perceived by Twelfth Graders," in *Monitoring the Future National Survey Results on Adolescent Drug Use 2000*, University of Michigan, Institute for Social Research, 2001

TABLE 4.16

Trends in disapproval of drug use by eighth, tenth, and twelfth grade students, 1991–2000

Percentage who "disapprove" or "strongly disapprove"[a]

Do you disapprove of people who . . .	8th Grade 1991	1992	1993	1994	1995	1996	1997	1998	1999	2000	'99–'00 change	10th Grade 1991	1992	1993	1994	1995	1996	1997	1998	1999	2000	'99–'00 change
Try marijuana once or twice	84.6	82.1	79.2	72.9	70.7	67.5	67.6	69.0	70.7	72.5	+1.8s	75.1	74.8	70.3	62.4	59.8	55.5	54.1	56.0	56.2	54.9	-1.3
Smoke marijuana occasionally	89.5	88.1	85.7	80.9	79.7	76.5	78.1	78.4	79.3	80.6	+1.3	83.7	83.6	79.4	72.3	70.0	66.9	66.2	67.3	68.2	67.2	-1.0
Smoke marijuana regularly	92.1	90.8	88.9	85.3	85.1	82.8	84.6	84.5	84.5	85.3	+0.8	90.4	90.0	87.4	82.2	81.1	79.7	79.7	80.1	79.8	79.1	-0.8
Try inhalants once or twice[b]	84.9	84.0	82.5	81.6	81.8	82.9	84.1	83.0	85.2	85.4	+0.2	85.2	85.6	84.8	84.9	84.5	86.0	86.9	85.6	88.4	87.5	-0.9
Take inhalants regularly[c]	90.6	90.0	88.9	88.1	88.8	89.3	90.3	89.5	90.3	90.2	-0.1	91.0	91.5	90.9	91.0	90.9	91.7	91.7	91.1	92.4	91.8	-0.6
Try LSD once or twice[c]	—	—	77.1	75.2	71.6	70.9	72.1	69.1	69.4	66.7	-2.8	—	—	82.1	79.3	77.9	76.8	76.6	76.7	77.8	77.0	-0.8
Take LSD regularly[d]	—	—	79.8	78.4	75.8	75.3	76.3	72.5	72.5	69.3	-3.2s	—	—	86.8	85.6	84.8	84.5	83.4	82.9	84.3	82.1	-2.3
Try crack once or twice[c]	91.7	90.7	89.1	86.9	85.9	85.0	85.7	85.4	86.0	85.4	-0.6	92.5	92.5	91.4	89.9	88.7	88.2	87.4	87.1	87.8	87.1	-0.7
Take crack occasionally[c]	93.3	92.5	91.7	89.9	89.8	89.3	90.3	89.5	89.9	88.8	-1.1	94.3	94.4	93.6	92.5	91.7	91.9	91.0	90.6	91.5	90.9	-0.6
Try cocaine powder once or twice[c]	91.2	89.6	88.5	86.1	85.3	83.9	85.1	84.5	85.2	84.8	-0.4	90.8	91.1	90.0	88.1	86.8	86.1	85.1	84.9	86.0	84.8	-1.2
Take cocaine powder occasionally[c]	93.1	92.4	91.6	89.7	89.7	88.7	90.1	89.3	89.9	88.8	-1.0	94.0	94.0	93.2	92.1	91.4	91.1	90.4	89.7	90.7	89.9	-0.8
Try heroin once or twice without using a needle[d]	—	—	—	—	85.8	85.0	87.7	87.3	88.0	87.2	-0.8	—	—	—	—	89.7	89.5	89.1	88.6	90.1	90.1	+0.1
Take heroin occasionally without using a needle[d]	—	—	—	—	88.5	87.7	90.1	89.7	90.2	88.9	-1.2	—	—	—	—	91.6	91.7	91.4	90.5	91.8	92.3	+0.5
Try one or two drinks of an alcoholic beverage (beer, wine, liquor)	51.7	52.2	50.9	47.8	48.0	45.5	45.7	47.5	48.3	48.7	+0.4	37.6	39.9	38.5	36.5	36.1	34.2	33.7	34.7	35.1	33.4	-1.7
Take one or two drinks nearly every day	82.2	81.0	79.6	76.7	75.9	74.1	76.6	76.9	77.0	77.8	+0.8	81.7	81.7	78.6	75.2	75.4	73.8	75.4	74.6	75.4	73.8	-1.6
Have five or more drinks once or twice each weekend	85.2	83.9	83.3	80.7	80.7	79.1	81.3	81.0	80.3	81.2	+0.9	76.7	77.6	74.7	72.3	72.2	70.7	70.2	70.5	69.9	68.2	-1.7
Smoke one or more packs of cigarettes per day[c]	82.8	82.3	80.6	78.4	78.6	77.3	80.3	80.0	81.4	81.9	+0.5	79.4	77.8	76.5	73.9	73.2	71.6	73.8	75.3	76.1	76.7	+0.6
Use smokeless tobacco regularly	79.1	77.2	77.1	75.1	74.0	74.1	76.5	76.3	78.0	79.2	+1.1	75.4	74.6	73.8	71.2	71.0	71.0	72.3	73.2	75.1	75.8	+0.7
Take steroids[e]	89.8	90.3	89.9	87.9	—	—	—	—	—	—	—	90.0	91.0	91.2	90.8	—	—	—	—	—	—	—
Approx. N (in thousands) =	17.4	18.5	18.4	17.4	17.6	18.0	18.8	18.1	16.7	16.7	—	14.8	14.8	15.3	15.9	17.0	15.7	15.6	15.0	13.6	14.3	—

NOTES: Level of significance of difference between the two most recent classes: s = .05, ss = .01, sss = .001. '—' indicates data not available. Any apparent inconsistency between the change estimate and the prevalence of use estimates for the two years is due to rounding error.

[a] Answer alternatives were: (1) Don't disapprove, (2) Disapprove, and (3) Strongly disapprove. For 8th and 10th grades, there was another category—"Can't say, drug unfamiliar"—which was included in the calculation of these percentages. Percentages are shown for categories (2) and (3) combined.

[b] Beginning in 1997, data based on two-thirds of N indicated due to changes in questionnaire forms.

[c] Data based on one of two forms in 1993–96; N is one-half of N indicated. Beginning in 1997, data based on one-third of N indicated. Beginning in 1999, data based on two-thirds of N indicated due to changes in questionnaire forms.

[d] Data based on two-thirds of N indicated due to changes in questionnaire forms.

[e] Data based on two forms in 1991 and 1992 and on one of two forms in 1993 and 1994; N is one-half of N indicated.

SOURCE: Lloyd D. Johnston, Patrick M. O'Malley, and Jerald G. Bachman, "Table 10: Trends in Disapproval of Drug Use by Eighth, Tenth, and Twelfth Graders, 1991–2000," in *Monitoring the Future: National Results on Adolescent Drug Use—Overview of Key Findings, 2000*, Institute for Social Research, University of Michigan, and the National Institute on Drug Abuse, U.S. Department of Health and Human Services, 2001

TABLE 4.17

Long-term trends in disapproval of drug use by twelfth graders

Do you disapprove of people (who are 18 or older) doing each of the following?[1]	Percentage "disapproving"[2]																										'99–'00 change
	Class of 1975	Class of 1976	Class of 1977	Class of 1978	Class of 1979	Class of 1980	Class of 1981	Class of 1982	Class of 1983	Class of 1984	Class of 1985	Class of 1986	Class of 1987	Class of 1988	Class of 1989	Class of 1990	Class of 1991	Class of 1992	Class of 1993	Class of 1994	Class of 1995	Class of 1996	Class of 1997	Class of 1998	Class of 1999	Class of 2000	
Try marijuana once or twice	47.0	38.4	33.4	33.4	34.2	39.0	40.0	45.5	46.3	49.3	51.4	54.6	56.6	60.8	64.6	67.8	68.7	69.9	63.3	57.6	56.7	52.5	51.0	51.6	48.8	52.5	+3.8s
Smoke marijuana occasionally	54.8	47.8	44.3	43.5	45.3	49.7	52.6	59.1	60.7	63.5	65.8	69.0	71.6	74.0	77.2	80.5	79.4	79.7	75.5	68.9	66.7	62.9	63.2	64.4	62.5	65.8	+3.4
Smoke marijuana regularly	71.9	69.5	65.5	67.5	69.2	74.6	77.4	80.6	82.5	84.7	85.5	86.6	89.2	89.3	89.8	91.0	89.3	90.1	87.6	82.3	81.9	80.0	78.8	81.2	78.6	79.7	+1.1
Try LSD once or twice	82.8	84.6	83.9	85.4	86.6	87.3	86.4	88.8	89.1	88.9	89.5	89.2	91.6	89.3	89.7	89.8	90.1	88.1	85.9	82.5	81.1	79.6	80.5	82.1	83.0	82.4	-0.5
Take LSD regularly	94.1	95.3	95.8	96.4	96.9	96.7	96.8	96.7	97.0	96.8	97.0	96.6	97.8	96.4	96.4	96.3	96.4	95.5	95.8	94.3	92.5	93.2	92.9	93.5	94.3	94.2	-0.1
Try MDMA once or twice	—	—	—	—	—	—	—	—	—	—	—	—	—	—	—	—	—	—	—	—	—	—	82.2	82.5	82.1	81.0	-1.2
Try cocaine once or twice	81.3	82.4	79.1	77.0	74.7	76.3	74.6	76.6	77.0	79.7	79.3	80.2	87.3	89.1	90.5	91.5	93.6	93.0	92.7	91.6	90.3	90.0	88.0	89.5	89.1	88.2	-0.9
Take cocaine regularly	93.3	93.9	92.1	91.9	90.8	91.1	90.7	91.5	93.2	94.5	93.8	94.3	96.7	96.2	96.4	96.7	97.3	96.9	97.5	96.6	96.1	95.6	96.0	95.6	94.9	95.5	+0.5
Try crack once or twice	—	—	—	—	—	—	—	—	—	—	—	—	89.9	89.7	90.1	92.3	92.1	93.1	89.9	89.5	90.2	87.4	86.7	87.0	87.6	87.5	-0.1
Take crack occasionally	—	—	—	—	—	—	—	—	—	—	—	—	92.6	91.6	92.1	94.1	94.0	94.9	92.9	92.3	93.6	91.2	91.5	91.1	92.3	91.9	-0.4
Take crack regularly	—	—	—	—	—	—	—	—	—	—	—	—	94.3	94.2	94.2	94.3	94.2	95.0	93.4	93.1	94.0	91.2	92.3	91.9	93.2	92.8	-0.4
Try cocaine powder once or twice	—	—	—	—	—	—	—	—	—	—	—	—	—	—	—	87.9	88.0	89.4	86.6	87.1	88.3	83.1	83.0	83.1	84.3	84.1	-0.2
Take cocaine powder occasionally	—	—	—	—	—	—	—	—	—	—	—	—	—	—	—	92.1	93.0	94.0	91.6	92.1	93.2	89.4	89.3	90.2	90.0	90.3	+0.3
Take cocaine powder regularly	—	—	—	—	—	—	—	—	—	—	—	—	—	—	—	94.9	95.0	94.3	93.1	93.1	94.1	92.0	91.5	91.9	92.3	92.6	+0.3
Try heroin once or twice	91.5	92.6	92.5	92.0	93.4	93.5	93.5	94.6	94.3	94.0	94.0	93.3	96.2	95.0	95.4	95.1	96.0	96.8	94.4	93.2	92.8	92.1	92.3	93.7	93.5	93.0	-0.5
Take heroin occasionally	—	—	—	—	—	—	—	—	—	—	—	—	—	—	—	—	—	—	—	—	95.7	95.0	95.4	96.1	95.7	96.0	+0.3
Take heroin regularly	96.7	96.0	97.2	97.8	97.9	97.6	97.8	97.5	97.7	98.0	97.6	97.6	98.1	96.9	97.4	97.5	97.8	97.2	97.5	97.1	96.4	95.0	95.4	96.1	96.4	96.6	+0.2
Try amphetamines once or twice	74.8	75.1	74.2	74.8	75.1	75.4	71.1	72.6	72.3	72.8	74.9	76.5	80.7	82.5	83.3	85.3	86.5	86.9	84.2	81.3	82.2	79.9	81.3	82.5	81.9	82.1	+0.2
Take amphetamines regularly	92.1	92.8	92.5	93.5	94.4	93.0	91.7	92.0	92.6	93.6	93.3	93.5	95.4	94.2	94.2	95.5	96.0	95.6	96.0	94.1	94.3	93.5	94.3	94.0	93.7	94.1	+0.4
Try barbiturates once or twice	77.7	81.3	81.1	82.4	84.0	83.9	82.4	84.4	83.1	84.1	84.9	86.8	89.6	89.4	89.3	90.5	90.6	90.3	89.7	87.5	87.3	84.9	86.4	86.0	86.6	85.9	-0.7
Take barbiturates regularly	93.3	93.6	93.0	94.3	95.2	95.4	94.2	94.4	95.1	95.1	95.5	94.9	96.4	95.3	95.3	96.4	97.1	96.5	97.0	96.1	95.2	94.8	95.3	94.6	94.7	95.2	+0.6
Try one or two drinks of an alcoholic beverage (beer, wine, liquor)	21.6	18.2	15.6	15.6	15.8	16.0	17.2	18.2	18.4	17.4	20.3	20.9	21.4	22.6	27.3	29.4	29.8	33.0	30.1	28.4	27.3	26.5	26.1	24.5	24.6	25.2	+0.6
Take one or two drinks nearly every day	67.6	68.9	66.8	67.7	68.3	69.0	69.1	69.9	68.9	72.9	70.9	72.8	74.2	75.0	76.5	77.9	76.5	75.9	77.8	73.1	73.3	70.8	70.0	69.4	67.2	70.0	+2.8
Take four or five drinks nearly every day	88.7	90.7	88.4	90.2	91.7	90.8	91.8	90.9	90.0	91.0	92.0	91.4	92.2	92.8	91.6	91.9	90.6	90.8	90.6	89.8	88.8	89.4	88.6	86.7	86.9	88.4	+1.5
Have five or more drinks once or twice each weekend	60.3	58.6	57.4	56.2	56.7	55.6	55.5	58.8	56.6	59.6	60.4	62.4	62.0	65.3	66.5	68.9	67.4	70.7	70.1	65.1	66.7	64.7	65.0	63.8	62.7	65.2	+2.5
Smoke one or more packs of cigarettes per day	67.5	65.9	66.4	67.0	70.3	70.8	69.9	69.4	70.8	73.0	72.3	75.4	74.3	73.1	72.4	72.8	71.4	73.5	70.6	69.9	68.2	67.2	67.1	68.8	69.5	70.1	+0.6
Take steroids	—	—	—	—	—	—	—	—	—	—	—	—	—	—	—	90.8	90.5	92.1	92.1	91.9	91.0	91.7	91.4	90.8	88.9	88.8	-0.1
Approx. N =	2677	2957	3085	3686	3221	3261	3610	3651	3341	3254	3265	3113	3302	3311	2799	2566	2547	2645	2723	2588	2603	2399	2601	2545	2310	2150	

NOTES: Level of significance of difference between the two most recent classes: s = .05. '—' indicates data not available. Any apparent inconsistency between the change estimate and the prevalence of use estimates for the two most recent classes is due to rounding error.

[1]The 1975 question asked about people who are "20 or older."

[2]Answer alternatives were: (1) Don't disapprove, (2) Disapprove, and (3) Strongly disapprove. Percentages are shown for categories (2) and (3) combined.

SOURCE: L. Johnston, P. O'Malley, and J. Bachman, "Table 11: Long-Term Trends in Disapproval of Drug Use by Twelfth Graders," in Monitoring the Future National Survey Results on Adolescent Drug Use 2000, University of Michigan, Institute for Social Research, 2001

TABLE 4.18

Trends in perceived availability of drugs by eighth, tenth, and twelfth grade students, 1992–2000

How difficult do you think it would be for you to get each of the following types of drugs, if you wanted some?

Percent saying "fairly easy" or "very easy" to get[a]

How difficult...	8th Grade										10th Grade								
	1992	1993	1994	1995	1996	1997	1998	1999	2000	'99–'00 change	1993	1994	1995	1996	1997	1998	1999	2000	'99–'00 change
Marijuana	42.3	43.8	49.9	52.4	54.8	54.2	50.6	48.4	47.0	-1.5	68.4	75.0	78.1	81.1	80.5	77.9	78.2	77.7	-0.6
LSD	21.5	21.8	21.8	23.5	23.6	22.7	19.3	18.3	17.0	-1.3	35.8	36.1	39.8	41.0	38.3	34.0	34.3	32.9	-1.3
PCP[b]	18.0	18.5	17.7	19.0	19.6	19.2	17.5	17.1	16.0	-1.2	23.4	23.8	24.7	26.8	24.8	23.9	24.5	25.0	+0.5
Crack	25.6	25.9	26.9	28.7	27.9	27.5	26.5	25.9	24.9	-1.0	33.0	34.2	34.6	36.4	36.0	36.3	36.5	34.0	-2.4s
Cocaine powder	25.7	25.9	26.4	27.8	27.2	26.9	25.7	25.0	23.9	-1.1	34.1	34.5	35.3	36.9	37.1	36.8	36.7	34.5	-2.2s
Heroin	19.7	19.8	19.4	21.1	20.6	19.8	18.0	17.5	16.5	-1.0	24.3	24.7	24.6	24.8	24.4	23.0	23.7	22.3	-1.5
Other narcotics[b]	19.8	19.0	18.3	20.3	20.0	20.6	17.1	16.2	15.6	-0.6	24.9	26.9	27.8	29.4	29.0	26.1	26.6	27.2	+0.6
Amphetamines	32.2	31.4	31.0	33.4	32.6	30.6	27.3	25.9	25.5	-0.4	46.4	46.6	47.7	47.2	44.6	41.0	41.3	40.9	-0.5
Crystal meth. (ice)[b]	16.0	15.1	14.1	16.0	16.3	15.7	16.0	14.7	14.9	+0.2	16.4	17.8	20.7	22.6	22.9	22.1	21.8	22.8	+0.9
Barbiturates	27.4	26.1	25.3	26.5	25.6	24.4	21.1	20.8	19.7	-1.0	38.8	38.3	38.8	38.1	35.6	32.7	33.2	32.4	-0.8
Tranquilizers	22.9	21.4	20.4	21.3	20.4	19.6	18.1	17.3	16.2	-1.1	30.5	29.8	30.6	30.3	28.7	26.5	26.8	27.6	+0.8
Alcohol	76.2	73.9	74.5	74.9	75.3	74.9	73.1	72.3	70.6	-1.8s	88.9	89.8	89.7	90.4	89.0	88.0	88.2	87.7	-0.5
Cigarettes	77.8	75.5	76.1	76.4	76.9	76.0	73.6	71.5	68.7	-2.8sss	89.4	90.3	90.7	91.3	89.6	88.1	88.3	86.8	-1.5s
Steroids	24.0	22.7	23.1	23.8	24.1	23.6	22.3	22.6	22.3	-0.3	33.6	33.6	34.8	34.8	34.2	33.0	35.9	35.4	-0.5
Approx. N =	8355	16775	16119	15496	16318	16482	16208	15397	15180		14652	15192	16209	14887	14856	14423	13112	13690	

Notes: Level of significance of difference between the two most recent classes: s = .05, ss = .01, sss = .001. '—' indicates data not available.
Any apparent inconsistency between the change estimate and the prevalence of use estimates for the two most recent classes is due to rounding error.

[a] Answer alternatives were: (1) Probably impossible, (2) Very difficult, (3) Fairly difficult, (4) Fairly easy, and (5) Very easy. For 8th and 10th grades, there was another category—"Can't say, drug unfamiliar"—which was included in the calculation of these percentages.

[b] Beginning in 1993, data based on half of forms; N is one-half of N indicated.

SOURCE: Lloyd D. Johnston, Patrick M. O'Malley, and Jerald G. Bachman, "Table 12: Trends in Perceived Availability of Drugs by Eighth, Tenth, and Twelfth Graders, 1992–2000," in *Monitoring the Future: National Results on Adolescent Drug Use—Overview of Key Findings, 2000*, Institute for Social Research, University of Michigan, and the National Institute on Drug Abuse, U.S. Department of Health and Human Services, 2001

TABLE 4.19

Long-term trends in perceived availability of drugs by twelfth graders

Percentage saying "fairly easy" or "very easy" to get*

How difficult do you think it would be for you to get each of the following types of drugs, if you wanted some?	Class of 1975	Class of 1976	Class of 1977	Class of 1978	Class of 1979	Class of 1980	Class of 1981	Class of 1982	Class of 1983	Class of 1984	Class of 1985	Class of 1986	Class of 1987	Class of 1988	Class of 1989	Class of 1990	Class of 1991	Class of 1992	Class of 1993	Class of 1994	Class of 1995	Class of 1996	Class of 1997	Class of 1998	Class of 1999	Class of 2000	'99–'00 change
Marijuana	87.8	87.4	87.9	87.8	90.1	89.0	89.2	88.5	86.2	84.6	85.5	85.2	84.8	85.0	84.3	84.4	83.3	82.7	83.0	85.5	88.5	88.7	89.6	90.4	88.9	88.5	-0.4
Amyl/butyl nitrites	—	—	—	—	—	—	—	—	—	—	—	—	23.9	25.9	26.8	24.4	22.7	25.9	25.9	26.7	26.0	23.9	23.8	25.1	21.4	23.3	+1.9
LSD	46.2	37.4	34.5	32.2	34.2	35.3	35.0	34.2	30.9	30.6	30.5	28.5	31.4	33.3	38.3	40.7	39.5	44.5	49.2	50.8	53.8	51.3	50.7	48.8	44.7	46.9	+2.2
Some other psychedelic	47.8	35.7	33.8	33.8	34.6	35.0	32.7	30.6	26.6	26.6	26.1	24.9	25.0	26.2	28.2	28.3	28.0	29.9	33.5	33.8	35.8	33.9	33.9	35.1	29.5	34.5	+5.0ss
PCP	—	—	—	—	—	—	—	—	—	—	—	—	22.8	24.9	28.9	27.7	27.6	31.7	31.7	31.4	31.0	30.5	30.0	30.7	26.7	28.8	+2.1
MDMA (Ecstasy)	—	—	—	—	—	—	—	—	—	—	—	—	—	—	21.7	22.0	22.1	24.2	28.1	31.2	34.2	36.9	38.8	38.2	40.1	51.4	+11.3sss
Cocaine	37.0	34.0	33.0	37.8	45.5	47.9	47.5	47.4	43.1	45.0	48.9	51.5	54.2	55.0	58.7	54.5	51.0	52.7	48.5	46.6	47.7	48.1	48.5	51.3	47.6	47.8	+0.3
Crack	—	—	—	—	—	—	—	—	—	—	—	—	41.1	42.1	47.0	42.4	39.9	43.5	43.6	40.5	41.9	40.7	40.6	43.8	41.1	42.6	+1.5
Cocaine powder	—	—	—	—	—	—	—	—	—	—	—	—	52.9	50.3	53.7	49.0	46.0	48.0	45.4	43.7	43.8	44.4	43.3	45.7	43.7	44.6	+0.9
Heroin	24.2	18.4	17.9	16.4	18.9	21.2	19.2	20.8	19.3	19.9	21.0	22.0	23.7	28.0	31.4	31.9	30.6	34.9	33.7	34.1	35.1	32.2	33.8	35.6	32.1	33.5	+1.4
Some other narcotic (including methadone)	34.5	26.9	27.8	26.1	28.7	29.4	29.6	30.4	30.0	32.1	33.1	32.2	33.0	35.8	38.3	38.1	34.6	37.1	37.5	38.0	39.8	40.0	38.9	42.8	40.8	43.9	+3.1
Amphetamines	67.8	61.8	58.1	58.5	59.9	61.3	69.5	70.8	68.5	68.2	66.4	64.3	64.5	63.9	64.3	59.7	57.3	58.8	61.5	62.0	62.8	59.4	59.8	60.8	58.1	57.1	-1.0
Crystal meth. (ice)	—	—	—	—	—	—	—	—	—	—	—	—	—	—	—	24.1	24.3	26.0	26.6	25.6	27.0	26.9	27.6	29.8	27.6	27.8	+0.1
Barbiturates	60.0	54.4	52.4	50.6	49.8	49.1	54.9	55.2	52.5	51.9	51.3	48.3	48.2	47.8	48.4	45.9	42.4	44.0	44.5	43.3	42.3	41.4	40.0	40.7	37.9	37.4	-0.5
Tranquilizers	71.8	65.5	64.9	64.3	61.4	59.1	60.8	58.9	55.3	54.5	54.7	51.2	48.6	49.1	45.3	44.7	40.8	40.9	41.1	39.2	37.8	36.0	35.4	36.2	32.7	33.8	+1.1
Alcohol	—	—	—	—	—	—	—	—	—	—	—	—	—	—	—	—	—	—	—	—	—	—	—	—	95.0	94.8	-0.2
Steroids	—	—	—	—	—	—	—	—	—	—	—	—	—	—	—	—	46.7	46.8	44.8	42.9	45.5	40.3	41.7	44.5	44.6	44.8	+0.2
Approx. N =	2627	2865	3065	3598	3172	3240	3578	3602	3385	3269	3274	3077	3271	3231	2806	2549	2476	2586	2670	2526	2552	2340	2517	2520	2215	2095	

NOTES: Level of significance of difference between the two most recent classes: s = .05, ss = .01, sss = .001. '—' indicates data not available.

Any apparent inconsistency between the change estimate and the prevalence of use estimates for the two most recent classes is due to rounding error.

*Answer alternatives were: (1) Probably impossible, (2) Very difficult, (3) Fairly difficult, (4) Fairly easy, and (5) Very easy.

SOURCE: L. Johnston, P. O'Malley, and J. Bachman, "Table 13: Long-Term Trends in Perceived Availability of Drugs by Twelfth Graders," in *Monitoring the Future National Survey Results on Adolescent Drug Use 2000*, University of Michigan, Institute for Social Research, 2001

85.3 percent of eighth-graders, 79.1 percent of tenth-graders, and 79.7 percent of twelfth-graders. (See Table 4.16 and Table 4.17.)

OTHER DRUGS. Disapproval of inhalant use remained virtually unchanged among eighth- and tenth-graders in the 1990s, but students were less disapproving of LSD use in 2000 than they were in 1993. An overwhelming majority of students continued to disapprove of cocaine (including crack), although the percentage dropped slightly. (See Table 4.16 and Table 4.17.)

AVAILABILITY OF DRUGS

Drugs are easily available to those young people who wish to use them. In 2000, 47 percent of eighth-graders, 77.7 percent of tenth-graders, and 88.5 percent of twelfth-graders thought marijuana was "fairly easy" or "very easy" to get. About 17 percent of eighth-graders, 33 percent of tenth-graders, and 47 percent of twelfth-graders thought LSD was easy to get. Nearly all of these percentages, however, were lower than in 1999. (See Table 4.18 and Table 4.19.)

It should be noted that these figures do not distinguish between users and nonusers. Users generally find it easier to get drugs, while nonusers, who are often less familiar with the drug trade, are much more likely to consider it harder to get drugs. Nonetheless, given that almost 9 out of 10 twelfth-graders thought marijuana was easy to get, availability seems to extend beyond just drug-using circles.

YOUTH RISK BEHAVIOR SURVEILLANCE

The biennial *Youth Risk Behavior Surveillance System* (YRBSS), prepared for the U.S. Centers for Disease Control and Prevention (CDC), monitors six categories of high-risk behavior among youths and young adults: alcohol use; tobacco use; drug use; sexual behavior; dietary habits; and physical activity. The surveillance is based on a national survey, and 35 state and 17 local surveys.

Marijuana Use

The 1999 YRBSS found that 47.2 percent of high school students had used marijuana at least once in their lives and that 22.6 percent were "current users" (one or more times during the 30 days before the survey). Twelfth-graders reported the highest percentage of current marijuana use (31.5 percent). The survey found that males (51.0 percent) were significantly more likely than females (43.4 percent) to have ever used marijuana, while blacks and Hispanics were somewhat more likely than whites to have used the drug. (See Table 4.20.)

Cocaine Use

The YRBSS found that 9.5 percent of high school students had used some form of cocaine in their lives and that 4 percent were current users. Overall, males (10.7 percent) were more likely than females (9.5) to have used cocaine.

Hispanics (15.3 percent) were more likely than whites (9.9) to have used the drug, while blacks (2.2 percent) were by far the least likely to have used it. (See Table 4.21.)

Other Drugs

According to the YRBSS 3.7 percent of high school students reported having used steroids during their lives. Males (5.2 percent) were two-and-a-half times as likely as females (2.2 percent) to have used steroids. Hispanics and whites (4.1 percent) were nearly twice as likely as blacks (2.2 percent) to have used steroids. (See Table 4.22.)

Approximately 2 percent of the students surveyed had injected an illegal drug. Males (2.3 percent) were twice as likely as females (1.2 percent) to have injected a drug. Hispanics (1.8 percent) and whites (1.6 percent) were about twice as likely as blacks (0.9 percent) to have done so. Twelfth- (2.3 percent) and eleventh-graders (2.0 percent) were more likely to have injected drugs than tenth- (1.2 percent) and ninth-graders (1.6 percent). (See Table 4.22.)

About 16 percent of the students reported having sniffed or inhaled intoxicating substances—usually glue or paint. Whites and Hispanics (about 16 percent) were three-and-a-half times as likely as blacks (4.5 percent) to have used inhalants. Inhalant use was much more common among younger students. (See Table 4.21.)

How Many Started Before They Reached High School?

The YRBSS found that 11.3 percent of the students tried marijuana before they were 13 years old. Boys (19.1 percent) were more than twice as likely as girls (8.9 percent) to have tried marijuana at a young age. Ninth- (12.7 percent) and tenth-graders (12.6 percent) were more likely than eleventh- and twelfth-graders (9.5 percent) to have used marijuana before age 13—a sign of increased drug use among younger children. Hispanics (13.9 percent) and blacks (14.8 percent) were more likely than whites (9.4 percent) to have tried marijuana at a young age. (See Table 4.23.)

Drug Activity on School Property

About 7 percent of high school students claimed they had used marijuana on school property, while about one-third (30.2 percent) had been offered, sold, or given an illegal drug on school premises. (See Table 4.24.)

THE *PRIDE SURVEY*

Over the past several years, the *PRIDE* (Parents' Resource Institute for Drug Education) *Survey* has become a generally accepted resource for monitoring drug use among the nation's school population. The 13th annual survey, taken during the 1999–2000 school year, involved over 114,000 students in grades 6–12. Survey findings have generally been consistent with other national studies, including the *Monitoring the Future* survey.

TABLE 4.20

Percentage of high school students who drank and used marijuana, by sex, race/ethnicity, and grade, 1999

Category	Lifetime alcohol use* Female	Male	Total	Current alcohol use† Female	Male	Total	Episodic heavy drinking§ Female	Male	Total	Lifetime marijuana use¶ Female	Male	Total	Current marijuana use** Female	Male	Total
Race/Ethnicity															
White††	82.3 (±3.0)§§	81.8 (±3.3)	82.0 (±3.0)	49.8 (±4.8)	54.9 (±4.0)	52.5 (±3.1)	32.2 (±3.1)	39.1 (±3.4)	35.8 (±2.0)	42.3 (±3.1)	49.2 (±5.8)	45.9 (±3.7)	22.9 (±2.6)	29.6 (±4.8)	26.4 (±3.1)
Black††	75.8 (±6.4)	73.8 (±4.3)	74.8 (±4.7)	40.7 (±7.6)	39.1 (±9.2)	39.9 (±8.0)	14.7 (±5.4)	17.4 (±3.4)	16.0 (±2.0)	42.7 (±5.3)	54.8 (±11.5)	48.6 (±7.2)	21.9 (±5.6)	31.2 (±9.3)	26.4 (±6.9)
Hispanic	84.8 (±3.2)	82.2 (±4.2)	83.4 (±2.6)	49.3 (±5.4)	56.3 (±5.7)	52.8 (±4.5)	26.8 (±4.5)	37.5 (±4.9)	32.1 (±4.2)	46.4 (±5.7)	55.8 (±6.1)	51.0 (±5.0)	21.8 (±3.9)	34.8 (±6.8)	28.2 (±4.4)
Grade															
9	74.5 (±5.9)	72.3 (±5.0)	73.4 (±4.6)	41.0 (±5.9)	40.2 (±4.5)	40.6 (±4.4)	20.2 (±3.2)	21.7 (±3.8)	21.1 (±2.3)	28.7 (±5.4)	40.7 (±6.6)	34.8 (±5.0)	18.6 (±3.9)	24.7 (±5.1)	21.7 (±3.7)
10	84.0 (±3.5)	82.4 (±4.5)	83.2 (±3.6)	46.8 (±3.4)	52.7 (±5.8)	49.7 (±3.7)	31.1 (±3.7)	33.4 (±5.5)	32.2 (±3.1)	46.7 (±4.2)	51.6 (±8.3)	49.1 (±4.1)	24.3 (±4.4)	31.4 (±6.4)	27.8 (±4.1)
11	82.2 (±4.2)	79.5 (±4.5)	80.8 (±3.8)	48.3 (±5.1)	53.5 (±5.9)	50.9 (±3.8)	29.0 (±4.8)	38.8 (±5.8)	34.0 (±2.9)	48.5 (±4.2)	51.0 (±6.2)	49.7 (±4.5)	22.1 (±4.5)	31.1 (±6.4)	26.7 (±4.8)
12	87.0 (±2.9)	89.6 (±3.2)	88.3 (±2.2)	56.9 (±5.8)	66.6 (±4.6)	61.7 (±4.4)	33.9 (±5.7)	49.5 (±5.6)	41.6 (±5.3)	53.2 (±6.7)	63.8 (±4.7)	58.4 (±4.6)	26.3 (±5.7)	36.9 (±7.1)	31.5 (±5.6)
Total	81.7 (±2.2)	80.4 (±2.5)	81.0 (±2.0)	47.7 (±2.8)	52.3 (±2.9)	50.0 (±2.5)	28.1 (±2.1)	34.9 (±2.7)	31.5 (±1.9)	43.4 (±2.3)	51.0 (±4.2)	47.2 (±2.6)	22.6 (±1.8)	30.8 (±3.8)	26.7 (±2.5)

* Ever had ≥1 drinks of alcohol.
† Drank alcohol on ≥1 of the 30 days preceding the survey.
§ Drank ≥5 drinks of alcohol on ≥1 occasions on ≥1 of the 30 days preceding the survey.
¶ Ever used marijuana.
** Used marijuana ≥1 times during the 30 days preceding the survey.
†† Non-Hispanic.
§§ Ninety-five percent confidence interval.

SOURCE: "Table 20. Percentage of high school students who drank alcohol and used marijuana, by sex, race/ethnicity, and grade—United States, 1999" in *Youth Risk Behavior Surveillance—United States, 1999*, Centers for Disease Control and Prevention, 2000

TABLE 4.21

Percentage of high school students who used cocaine and inhaled intoxicating substances, by sex, race/ethnicity, and grade, 1999

Category	Lifetime cocaine use*			Current cocaine use†			Lifetime inhalant use§			Current inhalant use¶		
	Female	Male	Total	Female	Male	Total	Female	Male	Total	Female	Male	Total
Race/Ethnicity												
White**	8.7	11.0	9.9	2.8	5.3	4.1	16.5	16.2	16.4	4.3	4.4	4.4
	(±2.0)††	(±1.7)	(±1.5)	(±1.0)	(±1.5)	(±0.6)	(±2.7)	(±2.6)	(±2.4)	(±1.4)	(±1.6)	(±0.8)
Black**	1.5	2.8	2.2	1.1	1.0	1.1	5.5	3.4	4.5	3.1	1.4	2.3
	(±1.0)	(±1.8)	(±1.2)	(±0.9)		(±0.8)	(±1.8)	(±2.1)	(±1.7)	(±1.3)	(±0.9)	(±0.9)
Hispanic	12.3	18.3	15.3	5.4	8.0	6.7	16.6	15.6	16.1	5.0	4.7	4.9
	(±2.8)	(±4.4)	(±3.1)	(±2.1)	(±2.7)	(±2.0)	(±3.4)	(±3.0)	(±2.3)	(±1.6)	(±1.5)	(±1.4)
Grade												
9	4.7	6.8	5.8	2.4	4.3	3.4	18.2	14.6	16.5	7.2	5.4	6.4
	(±1.8)	(±2.3)	(±1.4)	(±1.2)	(±2.0)	(±1.3)	(±3.4)	(±2.5)	(±2.4)	(±2.8)	(±2.2)	(±2.1)
10	9.1	10.7	9.9	2.9	4.5	3.7	16.9	15.1	16.0	3.4	4.0	3.7
	(±2.8)	(±3.1)	(±2.0)	(±1.6)	(±2.2)	(±1.2)	(±4.1)	(±3.0)	(±2.7)	(±1.5)	(±1.8)	(±1.0)
11	9.0	10.9	9.9	3.4	5.6	4.5	12.8	14.0	13.4	2.4	4.1	3.3
	(±2.6)	(±3.9)	(±2.9)	(±1.8)	(±3.3)	(±2.0)	(±4.4)	(±4.0)	(±3.5)	(±1.0)	(±2.0)	(±1.0)
12	11.7	15.7	13.7	2.9	6.6	4.8	8.7	13.9	11.3	1.6	2.8	2.2
	(±3.0)	(±3.5)	(±2.9)	(±1.6)	(±2.7)	(±1.8)	(±2.4)	(±4.6)	(±2.3)	(±0.9)	(±1.2)	(±0.6)
Total	8.4	10.7	9.5	2.9	5.2	4.0	14.6	14.7	14.6	3.9	4.4	4.2
	(±1.6)	(±1.5)	(±1.3)	(±0.8)	(±1.1)	(±0.7)	(±2.0)	(±2.1)	(±1.7)	(±1.0)	(±1.2)	(±0.8)

* Ever tried any form of cocaine (e.g., powder, "crack," or "freebase").
† Used cocaine ≥1 times during the 30 days preceding the survey.
§ Ever sniffed glue or breathed the contents of aerosol spray cans or inhaled any paints or sprays to become intoxicated.
¶ Sniffed glue or breathed the contents of aerosol spray cans or inhaled any paints or sprays to become intoxicated ≥1 times during the 30 days preceding the survey.
** Non-Hispanic.
†† Ninety-five percent confidence interval.

SOURCE: "Table 22. Percentage of high school students who used cocaine and inhaled intoxicating substances, by sex, race/ethnicity, and grade—United States, Youth Risk Behavior Surveillance—United States, 1999, Centers for Disease Control and Prevention, 2000

TABLE 4.22

Percentage of high school students who used, heroin, methamphetamines, illegal steroids, and who injected illegal drugs, by sex, race/ethnicity, and grade, 1999

Category	Lifetime heroin use*			Lifetime methamphetamine use†			Lifetime illegal steroid use§			Lifetime injecting illegal drug use¶		
	Female	Male	Total	Female	Male	Total	Female	Male	Total	Female	Male	Total
Race/Ethnicity												
White**	1.3 (±0.5)††	3.4 (±1.2)	2.4 (±0.7)	9.6 (±1.2)	10.9 (±2.2)	10.3 (±1.4)	2.6 (±1.0)	5.5 (±1.4)	4.1 (±1.0)	0.7 (±0.3)	2.4 (±0.9)	1.6 (±0.4)
Black**	0.8 (±0.7)	1.6 (±1.1)	1.2 (±0.8)	1.3 (±0.9)	2.2 (±1.2)	1.7 (±0.8)	0.9 (±0.8)	3.6 (±1.2)	2.2 (±0.8)	0.5 (±0.5)	1.3 (±0.7)	0.9 (±0.5)
Hispanic	2.0 (±1.1)	3.1 (±1.4)	2.5 (±0.9)	11.6 (±4.4)	11.0 (±4.2)	11.3 (±4.1)	3.4 (±1.4)	4.9 (±2.1)	4.1 (±1.4)	1.2 (±0.9)	2.3 (±1.0)	1.8 (±0.8)
Grade												
9	0.8 (±0.5)	3.1 (±1.8)	2.0 (±1.0)	6.4 (±1.5)	6.2 (±2.0)	6.3 (±1.4)	3.1 (±1.3)	6.2 (±2.2)	4.7 (±1.4)	0.7 (±0.6)	2.5 (±1.3)	1.6 (±0.6)
10	1.4 (±0.8)	2.3 (±1.1)	1.8 (±0.7)	8.1 (±2.1)	10.5 (±3.3)	9.3 (±1.8)	2.3 (±1.5)	4.8 (±2.0)	3.6 (±1.5)	0.6 (±0.3)	1.9 (±1.0)	1.2 (±0.5)
11	1.3 (±0.7)	3.8 (±2.4)	2.6 (±1.3)	9.0 (±2.8)	11.3 (±3.3)	10.1 (±2.4)	1.7 (±1.0)	4.3 (±1.3)	3.0 (±0.8)	0.6 (±0.4)	3.3 (±2.4)	2.0 (±1.2)
12	1.8 (±0.8)	4.8 (±1.5)	3.3 (±0.8)	10.6 (±2.9)	12.4 (±3.1)	11.5 (±2.6)	1.2 (±0.8)	5.3 (±1.6)	3.3 (±0.9)	0.9 (±0.7)	3.7 (±1.5)	2.3 (±0.9)
Total	**1.3 (±0.4)**	**3.5 (±1.0)**	**2.4 (±0.6)**	**8.4 (±1.3)**	**9.9 (±1.6)**	**9.1 (±1.1)**	**2.2 (±0.7)**	**5.2 (±1.0)**	**3.7 (±0.7)**	**0.7 (±0.3)**	**2.8 (±0.8)**	**1.8 (±0.4)**

* Ever used heroin (also called "smack," "junk," or "China White").

† Ever used methamphetamines (also called "speed," "crystal," "crank," or "ice").

§ Ever used illegal steroids.

¶ Ever injected illegal drugs. Students were classified as injecting-drug users only if they a) reported injecting-drug use not prescribed by a physician and b) answered "one or more times" to any of the following questions: "During your life, how many times have you used any form of cocaine including powder, crack, or freebase?" "During your life, how many times have you used heroin (also called smack, junk, or China White)?" "During your life, how many times have you used methamphetamines (also called speed, crystal, crank, or ice)?" or, "During your life, how many times have you taken steroid pills or shots without a doctors prescription?"

** Non-Hispanic.

†† Ninety-five percent confidence interval.

SOURCE: "Table 24. Percentage of high school students who used heroin, methamphetamines, illegal steroids, and who injected illegal drugs, by sex, race/ethnicity, and grade—United States, Youth Risk Behavior Survey, 1999," in *Youth Risk Behavior Surveillance—United States, 1999*, Centers for Disease Control and Prevention, 2000

TABLE 4.23

Percentage of high school students who initiated drug-related behaviors before age 13 years, by sex, race/ethnicity, and grade, 1999

Category	Smoked a whole cigarette before age 13 years			Drank alcohol before age 13 years*			Tried marijuana before age 13 years		
	Female	Male	Total	Female	Male	Total	Female	Male	Total
Race/Ethnicity									
White†	22.6 (±3.0)§	29.5 (±3.1)	26.2 (±2.3)	25.2 (±2.5)	34.1 (±3.8)	29.9 (±2.8)	6.8 (±1.7)	11.9 (±2.1)	9.4 (±1.4)
Black†	12.9 (±3.9)	16.1 (±3.5)	14.4 (±2.9)	26.5 (±5.9)	44.3 (±9.6)	35.2 (±6.6)	7.7 (±3.2)	22.2 (±11.4)	14.8 (±6.4)
Hispanic	21.0 (±3.6)	29.5 (±3.9)	25.1 (±2.5)	30.7 (±3.3)	39.7 (±4.6)	35.1 (±2.8)	8.9 (±2.5)	19.1 (±4.1)	13.9 (±2.6)
Grade									
9	22.8 (±4.7)	31.1 (±6.0)	27.0 (±3.8)	37.7 (±4.0)	42.8 (±7.0)	40.4 (±4.2)	8.9 (±3.3)	16.4 (±2.9)	12.7 (±2.5)
10	27.6 (±4.2)	29.5 (±5.2)	28.5 (±3.6)	30.9 (±4.1)	40.3 (±5.4)	35.6 (±4.0)	10.2 (±2.4)	15.2 (±5.3)	12.6 (±3.1)
11	20.1 (±4.1)	22.2 (±4.0)	21.1 (±2.9)	20.0 (±2.7)	32.2 (±4.5)	26.2 (±3.1)	6.0 (±1.9)	12.9 (±4.5)	9.5 (±2.8)
12	16.7 (±4.2)	24.8 (±5.4)	20.7 (±3.7)	16.0 (±3.6)	32.3 (±7.2)	24.3 (±4.5)	6.0 (±2.5)	13.1 (±5.5)	9.5 (±3.4)
Total	22.1 (±2.2)	27.3 (±2.4)	24.7 (±1.9)	26.8 (±2.1)	37.4 (±3.7)	32.2 (±2.4)	8.0 (±1.6)	14.5 (±2.7)	11.3 (±1.8)

*More than a few sips.

†Non-Hispanic.

§Ninety-five percent confidence interval.

SOURCE: "Table 26. Percentage of high school students who initiated drug-related behaviors before age 13 years, by sex, race/ethnicity, and grade—United States, Youth Risk Behavior Survey, 1999," in *Youth Risk Behavior Surveillance—United States, 1999*, Centers for Disease Control and Prevention, 2000

TABLE 4.24

Percentage of high school students who engaged in drug-related behaviors on school property, by sex, race/ethnicity, and grade, 1999

Category	Cigarette use on school property*			Smokeless tobacco use on school property†			Alcohol use on school property§			Marijuana use on school property¶			Offered, sold, or given an illegal drug on school property**		
	Female	Male	Total	Female	Male	Total	Female	Male	Total	Female	Male	Total	Female	Male	Total
Race/Ethnicity															
White††	14.7 (±2.5)§§	16.5 (±2.9)	15.6 (±2.4)	0.1 (±0.1)	11.4 (±5.3)	5.9 (±2.8)	3.4 (±0.8)	6.1 (±1.7)	4.8 (±1.1)	3.6 (±0.9)	9.2 (±3.0)	6.5 (±1.7)	24.1 (±3.3)	33.2 (±4.0)	28.8 (±2.9)
Black††	5.8 (±4.2)	7.7 (±2.7)	6.7 (±3.2)	0.1 (±0.2)	0.9 (±0.7)	0.5 (±0.4)	2.6 (±1.4)	6.2 (±1.9)	4.3 (±1.0)	4.9 (±1.8)	9.8 (±3.2)	7.2 (±2.2)	20.9 (±5.6)	30.1 (±3.8)	25.3 (±4.0)
Hispanic	10.6 (±2.5)	15.3 (±3.9)	12.9 (±2.6)	1.5 (±1.5)	3.5 (±2.4)	2.5 (±1.4)	6.7 (±1.9)	7.3 (±2.4)	7.0 (±1.6)	6.9 (±2.2)	14.7 (±3.4)	10.7 (±2.4)	29.5 (±3.4)	44.4 (±5.5)	36.9 (±3.7)
Grade															
9	11.7 (±2.4)	11.9 (±3.4)	11.8 (±1.9)	0.3 (±0.3)	6.6 (±4.6)	3.5 (±2.4)	4.5 (±1.5)	4.1 (±1.7)	4.4 (±1.1)	4.4 (±1.6)	8.7 (±3.2)	6.6 (±2.0)	23.5 (±5.8)	31.6 (±4.5)	27.6 (±5.0)
10	15.4 (±4.0)	14.4 (±4.3)	14.9 (±3.7)	0.3 (±0.3)	8.1 (±3.8)	4.2 (±2.0)	4.1 (±1.1)	6.0 (±2.1)	5.0 (±1.3)	3.8 (±1.7)	11.4 (±4.0)	7.6 (±2.1)	26.9 (±4.3)	37.5 (±5.6)	32.1 (±3.9)
11	13.7 (±3.1)	14.8 (±4.1)	14.2 (±2.2)	0.2 (±0.2)	7.8 (±2.9)	4.0 (±1.5)	2.9 (±1.1)	6.5 (±1.6)	4.7 (±1.0)	4.9 (±1.8)	9.2 (±2.5)	7.0 (±1.5)	28.4 (±4.7)	33.9 (±6.8)	31.1 (±4.2)
12	11.7 (±5.0)	18.2 (±5.2)	14.9 (±4.6)	0.2 (±0.3)	9.5 (±5.8)	4.9 (±3.0)	2.4 (±1.3)	7.6 (±2.9)	5.0 (±1.7)	4.2 (±2.0)	10.4 (±3.8)	7.3 (±2.3)	24.4 (±4.1)	36.7 (±4.6)	30.5 (±2.3)
Total	13.2 (±2.0)	14.8 (±2.0)	14.0 (±1.9)	0.3 (±0.2)	8.1 (±3.5)	4.2 (±1.8)	3.6 (±0.7)	6.1 (±1.1)	4.9 (±0.7)	4.4 (±0.8)	10.1 (±2.6)	7.2 (±1.4)	25.7 (±2.4)	34.7 (±3.3)	30.2 (±2.4)

* Smoked cigarettes on ≥1 of the 30 days preceding the survey.

† Used chewing tobacco or snuff on ≥1 of the 30 days preceding the survey.

§ Drank alcohol on ≥1 of the 30 days preceding the survey.

¶ Used marijuana ≥1 times during the 30 days preceding the survey.

** During the 12 months preceding the survey.

†† Non-Hispanic.

§§ Ninety-five percent confidence interval.

SOURCE: "Table 28. Percentage of high school students who engaged in drug-related behaviors on school property, by sex, race/ethnicity, and grade—United States, Youth Risk Behavior Survey, 1999," in *Youth Risk Behavior Surveillance—United States, 1999*, Centers for Disease Control and Prevention, 2000

FIGURE 4.1

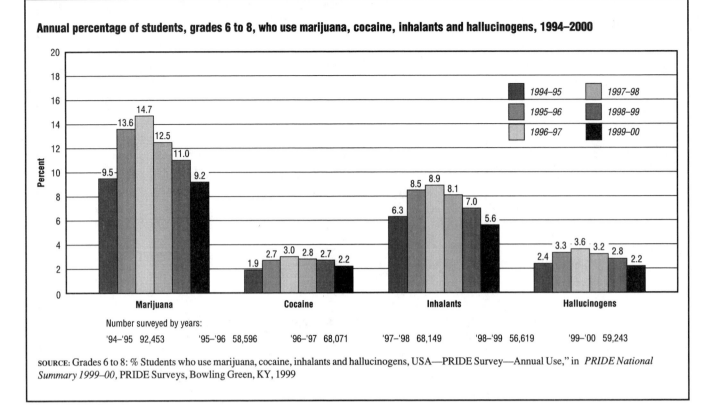

Annual percentage of students, grades 6 to 8, who use marijuana, cocaine, inhalants and hallucinogens, 1994–2000

SOURCE: Grades 6 to 8: % Students who use marijuana, cocaine, inhalants and hallucinogens, USA—PRIDE Survey—Annual Use," in *PRIDE National Summary 1999–00*, PRIDE Surveys, Bowling Green, KY, 1999

One novel feature of the *PRIDE Survey* is that it collects data on junior high school students.

Figure 4.1 and Figure 4.2 summarize trends in the use of various drugs by junior high school students between the 1994–95 and 1999–2000 school years. The use of illicit drugs peaked during 1996–97. That school year, more than one in five (20.7 percent) junior high school students said they had used an illicit drug in the past year. By the 1999–2000 school year, this figure had fallen by about one-third, to 13.6 percent. Despite the drop, nearly one in seven sixth- to eighth-graders had used some illicit drug in the past year. (See Figure 4.2.)

Marijuana and Inhalants

Marijuana is the most commonly used drug among junior high school students. However, its use slipped at the turn of the century. In the 1999–2000 school year, about 1 in 11 (9.2 percent) junior-high students reported using marijuana in the past year—down dramatically from more than 1 in 7 (14.7 percent) during the 1996–1997 school year. The second most commonly used drug was inhalants, which slightly more than 1 in 18 (5.6 percent) students had used in the past year. (See Figure 4.1.)

The use of most drugs increases with grade level. (See Figure 4.3 and Figure 4.4). Inhalants were most commonly used by seventh- to ninth-grade students—which may reflect the ease with which these substances can be obtained. As these young users age, they may begin purchasing illegal drugs rather than using inhalants.

When Do Students Use Drugs?

Figure 4.5 and Figure 4.6 show results from the *PRIDE Survey*'s questions "When do you use marijuana?" and "When do you use cocaine?" The vast majority of cocaine and marijuana users in all grade levels used these drugs during the weekend, when they were generally off from school and given a little more freedom by their parents.

Many students, however, reported that they also used marijuana during the week. About one in seven twelfth-graders (14 percent) smoked on weeknights, and one in nine (11.0) after school. One in 14 (7.2 percent) reported using marijuana before school, and 1 in 22 (4.6 percent) reported using it during school.

NEW TRENDS: ECSTASY AND OTHER "CLUB DRUGS"

The past few years have seen growing concern over a group of substances popularly known as "club drugs." The term usually includes "ecstasy" (MDMA), GHB, Rohypnol, and Ketamine. On July 25, 2000, Alan Leishner, director of the National Institute of Drug Abuse, testified about ecstasy before the U.S. Senate Caucus on International Narcotics Control. Leishner noted that, although it is not a new drug, ecstasy has grown in popularity in recent years, even as the use of cocaine and other drugs fell. Originally confined to teen dance "raves," ecstasy has now spread well outside the club scene, Leishner noted.

FIGURE 4.2

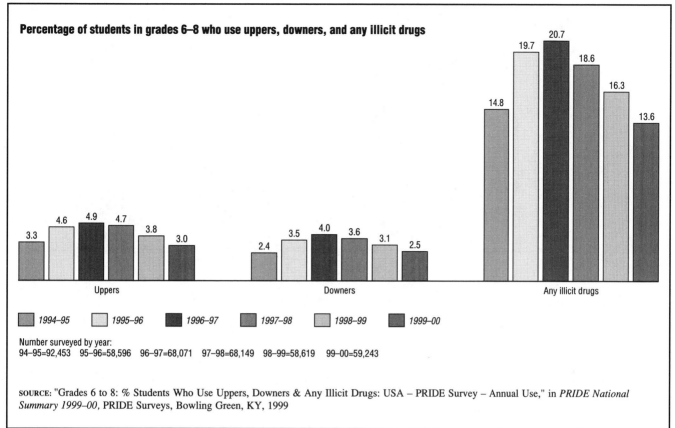

Percentage of students in grades 6–8 who use uppers, downers, and any illicit drugs

| | | | 1994–95 | 1995–96 | 1996–97 | 1997–98 | 1998–99 | 1999–00 |

Number surveyed by year:
94–95=92,453   95–96=58,596   96–97=68,071   97–98=68,149   98–99=58,619   99–00=59,243

SOURCE: "Grades 6 to 8: % Students Who Use Uppers, Downers & Any Illicit Drugs: USA – PRIDE Survey – Annual Use," in *PRIDE National Summary 1999–00,* PRIDE Surveys, Bowling Green, KY, 1999

The 2000 *Monitoring the Future* study revealed that MDMA use was rising sharply among high school and junior high school students. In fact, estimates for 2000 were the highest since the study began asking questions about the drug, in 1996. (See Table 4.1, Table 4.2, Table 4.10, Table 4.11, and Table 4.12.) Lifetime use by seniors reached 11 percent in 2000, up from 6.1 percent in 1996 and up 3 percent from 1999. (See Table 4.10.)

Drugs and Clubs

The use of club drugs is closely tied to "raves"—dance parties usually held late at night in clubs, or sometimes organized as large, outdoor events. In the 1990s raves attracted large numbers of young people, including college and high school students. Although not all, or even a majority of, people who attended raves actually consumed club drugs, the two became inextricably linked.

Many of the fashion trends seen at raves were closely linked to the drugs used at these events. Pacifiers, for example, were used to relieve the jaw tension that sometimes results from using ecstasy. Likewise, hallucinogen use may have inspired the trend of carrying glowing light sticks. The club environment was also a major factor in the use of these drugs: Many users say they consume ecstasy to increase sociability, physical endurance, and the ability to stay up late.

A special section on club drugs was included by the Office of National Drug Control Policy (ONDCP) in its

Pulse Check: Trends in Drug Abuse, Mid-Year 2000 (Washington, D.C., 2000). The report used local researchers, law-enforcement agencies, and treatment professionals to monitor recent changes in drug-use trends in 20 cities across the United States. The report looked at drugs commonly associated with clubs—ecstasy, GHB, Ketamine, and Rohypnol—as well as drugs that have been traditionally noted outside clubs, such as methamphetamine, nitrous oxide, and LSD. In 18 of the 20 sites, local sources listed club drugs, particularly ecstasy, as the most important emerging trend in drug use.

Hospitalizations

In 2000 growing public concern about the use of club drugs prompted the Drug Abuse Warning Network (DAWN) to issue a special report, *The DAWN Report: Club Drugs* (Substance Abuse and Mental Health Services Administration, Washington, D.C., December 2000). While the report showed dramatic increases in some indicators of drug use, the report's conclusions were reserved about the magnitude of the problem.

Club drug-related admissions to hospital emergency departments (EDs) usually involved white users. In 1999 there were 2,106 MDMA mentions for white users, but only 204 for blacks and 126 for Hispanics; in 414 of the MDMA cases, the race was "other/unknown." (See Figure 4.7.) In addition, most admissions involved younger patients. There

FIGURE 4.3

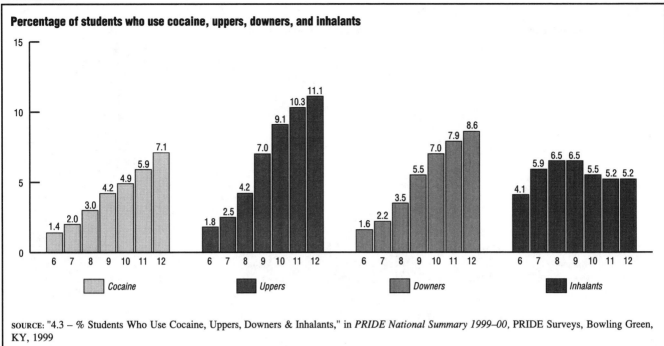

Percentage of students who use cocaine, uppers, downers, and inhalants

SOURCE: "4.3 – % Students Who Use Cocaine, Uppers, Downers & Inhalants," in *PRIDE National Summary 1999–00,* PRIDE Surveys, Bowling Green, KY, 1999

FIGURE 4.4

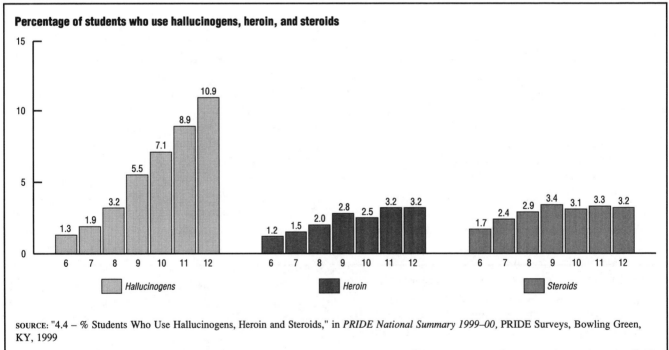

Percentage of students who use hallucinogens, heroin, and steroids

SOURCE: "4.4 – % Students Who Use Hallucinogens, Heroin and Steroids," in *PRIDE National Summary 1999–00,* PRIDE Surveys, Bowling Green, KY, 1999

were 1,923 MDMA mentions for 18- to 25-year-olds, but only 347 for 6- to 17-year-olds, 490 for 26- to 34-year-olds, and 88 for those 35 and older. This general pattern held true for GHB- and LSD-related admissions, but for methamphetamine-related visits, the most frequently mentioned age group was the 35-and-older group. (See Figure 4.8.)

Of the drugs most commonly identified as "club drugs," methamphetamine and LSD were mentioned in the greatest numbers of ED visits in the late 1990s. (See Figure 4.9.) The trend over time, though, did not show an increase. In fact, methamphetamine mentions dropped from 17,696 in 1994 to 10,447 in 1999. (It should be noted that, although methamphetamine and LSD are often used at raves, these drugs have a long history of widespread use in the United States, and therefore it may not be entirely accurate to call them "club drugs.")

FIGURE 4.5

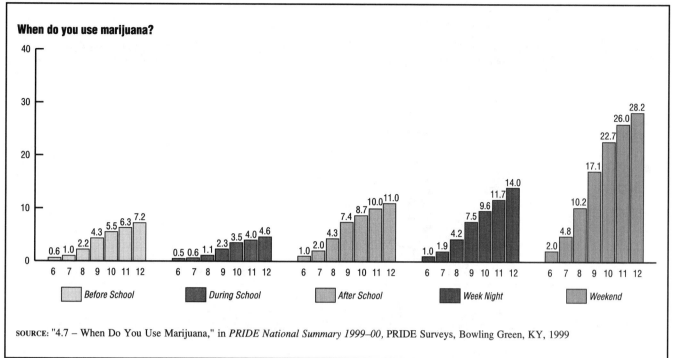

When do you use marijuana?

SOURCE: "4.7 – When Do You Use Marijuana," in *PRIDE National Summary 1999–00,* PRIDE Surveys, Bowling Green, KY, 1999

FIGURE 4.6

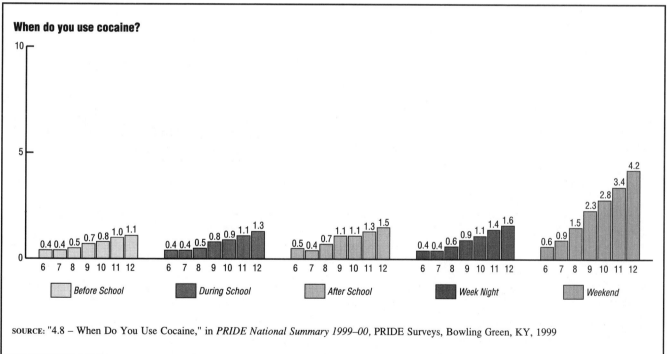

When do you use cocaine?

SOURCE: "4.8 – When Do You Use Cocaine," in *PRIDE National Summary 1999–00,* PRIDE Surveys, Bowling Green, KY, 1999

MDMA and GHB had the strongest upward trends, and the highest numbers of ED mentions, of any club drug besides LSD and methamphetamine. In 1999 there were 2,850 MDMA mentions, compared with 250 in 1994. The rise in GHB mentions was even more dramatic, jumping from 55 in 1994 to 2,973 in 1999. (See Figure 4.9.)

The report suggests caution, though, in interpreting these data. MDMA was involved in only about 1 in 250 drug-relat-ed ED visits in 1999. Although MDMA use is the most rapidly growing trend in youth drug abuse, the problem is not of the magnitude of many other drugs, such as cocaine, methamphetamine, and heroin. (See Table 3.14, Chapter 3.)

ATTITUDES AND INVOLVEMENT OF PARENTS

The *1998 Partnership Attitude Tracking Study* (PATS), a national study released in April 1999 by the

FIGURE 4.7

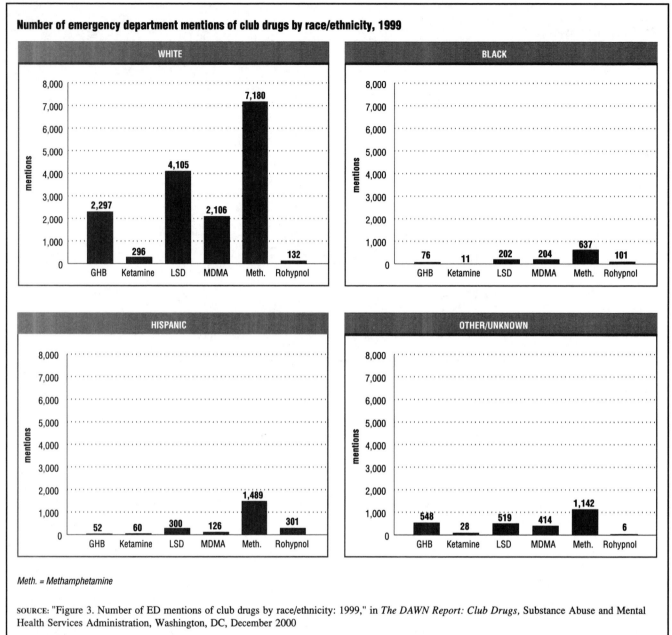

Number of emergency department mentions of club drugs by race/ethnicity, 1999

Meth. = Methamphetamine

SOURCE: "Figure 3. Number of ED mentions of club drugs by race/ethnicity: 1999," in *The DAWN Report: Club Drugs,* Substance Abuse and Mental Health Services Administration, Washington, DC, December 2000

Partnership for a Drug-Free America (PDFA), found that teen drug use was significantly lower in families who talked frequently about the risks of drug use. For instance, 26 percent of teens who learned "a lot" about the dangers of drug use from their parents reported past-year marijuana use, compared with 45 percent who said they learned nothing from their parents about the risks. (See Figure 4.10.)

However, as shown in Figure 4.11, only 27 percent of teens said they learned "a lot" at home about the dangers of drug use, while nearly all parents (98 percent) reported talking with their children about the subject at least once. According to PDFA Chairman James E. Burke, "Some parents may be covering the issue with their children in a

one-time conversation. [They] believe they're doing their job in this area, but the data suggest otherwise."

PATS surveyed preteens (ages 9–12), teenagers, and parents. It found that as children pass from the fourth to the eighth grade, the percentage who claim they want more parental guidance about drugs declines significantly, from 74 percent to 19 percent. And it is during these years that the number of children using marijuana increases significantly, from 3 percent to 31 percent.

Black parents (57 percent) were more likely to say they had talked regularly with their children about drugs than were Hispanic (45 percent) or white (44 percent) parents. Black (31 percent) and Hispanic (29 percent) teens

FIGURE 4.8

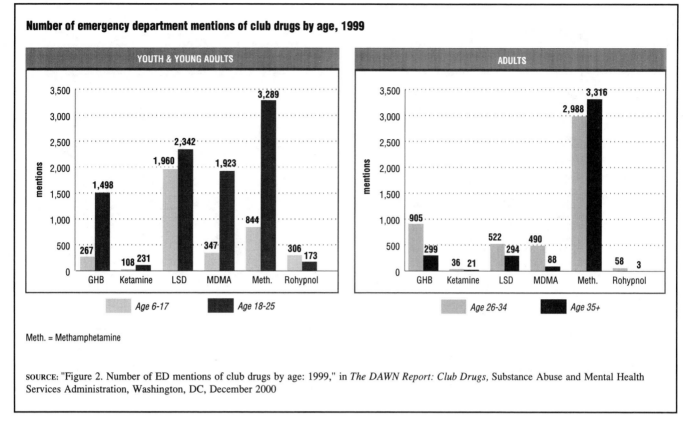

Number of emergency department mentions of club drugs by age, 1999

YOUTH & YOUNG ADULTS

	GHB	Ketamine	LSD	MDMA	Meth.	Rohypnol
Age 6-17	267	108	1,960	347	844	306
Age 18-25	1,498	231	2,342	1,923	3,289	173

ADULTS

	GHB	Ketamine	LSD	MDMA	Meth.	Rohypnol
Age 26-34	905	36	522	490	2,988	58
Age 35+	299	21	294	88	3,316	3

Meth. = Methamphetamine

SOURCE: "Figure 2. Number of ED mentions of club drugs by age: 1999," in *The DAWN Report: Club Drugs,* Substance Abuse and Mental Health Services Administration, Washington, DC, December 2000

were more likely to remember such conversations than were white teens (19 percent).

Many parents find it hard to believe that their own children are at risk. According to the survey, 14 percent of parents thought it possible that their teenager might have used marijuana, but 42 percent of teens indicated that they had tried the drug. Similarly, 37 percent of parents felt it was likely that their teen had been offered marijuana, while 53 percent of teens said they had been offered the drug.

The 1998 CASA survey, discussed below, found that teens less likely to use drugs have parents who are deeply involved in their daily lives. The survey found a correlation between low drug use and the following:

- A parent at home after school.
- Families who eat dinner together.
- Frequency of attendance at religious services.
- More time spent studying and reading than watching television.
- Less time listening to music.

ATTITUDES AND INVOLVEMENT OF TEACHERS AND PRINCIPALS

The *National Survey of American Attitudes on Substance Abuse IV: Teens, Teachers and Principals,* commissioned by the National Center on Addiction and Substance Abuse (CASA) at Columbia University, surveyed teens ages 12–17, as well as teachers and principals of middle schools and high schools. According to the 1998 survey, teens ranked drugs as the most important problem facing them today. Meanwhile, teachers and principals considered bad parents and family problems the biggest issues. The students, though, did not seem as concerned about the job their parents were doing. (See Table 4.25.) In fact, teens ranked "bad parents" and "getting along with parents" tenth in importance—near the bottom of the CASA list. (The complete list is not shown in Table 4.25.) The majority of high school students (51 percent) said that the nation's drug problem is getting worse, compared with 41 percent of teachers and 10 percent of principals.

The 1998 CASA survey found that many principals did not consider drug use a widespread problem—a feeling that most students and teachers did not share. About 58 percent of principals believed that only 1 in 10 students used illegal drugs at least once a month, while only 10 percent thought that the majority of students were at least monthly users. Nearly one-third (31 percent) of the teens said that half or more of their peers used drugs at least once a month. (See Table 4.26.) In addition, only 18 percent of principals thought their schools were not drug-free, compared with 35 percent of teachers and 66 percent of high school students. However, all three groups agree on measures to help alleviate the problem of drugs in schools,

FIGURE 4.9

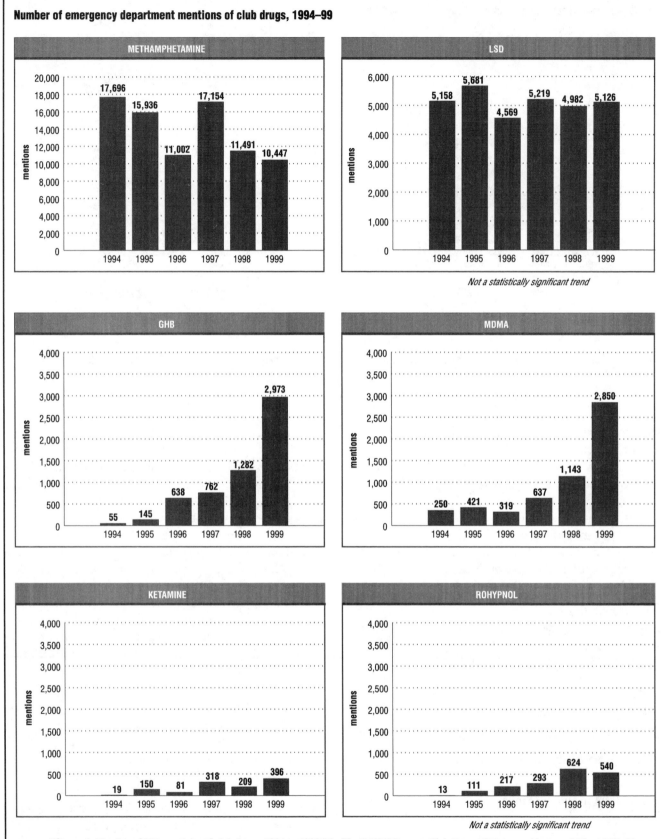

Number of emergency department mentions of club drugs, 1994–99

SOURCE: "Figure 1. Number of ED mentions of club drugs: 1994 to 1999," in *The DAWN Report: Club Drugs*, Substance Abuse and Mental Health Services Administration, Washington, DC, December 2000

FIGURE 4.10

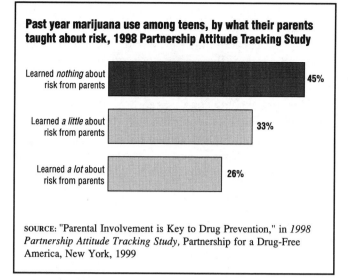

Past year marijuana use among teens, by what their parents taught about risk, 1998 Partnership Attitude Tracking Study

Learned *nothing* about risk from parents — 45%

Learned *a little* about risk from parents — 33%

Learned *a lot* about risk from parents — 26%

SOURCE: "Parental Involvement is Key to Drug Prevention," in *1998 Partnership Attitude Tracking Study,* Partnership for a Drug-Free America, New York, 1999

FIGURE 4.11

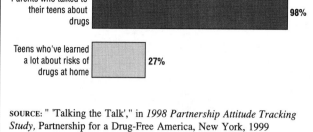

Parents' discussions about drugs with teens, 1998 Partnership Attitude Tracking Study

Parents who talked to their teens about drugs — 98%

Teens who've learned a lot about risks of drugs at home — 27%

SOURCE: " 'Talking the Talk'," in *1998 Partnership Attitude Tracking Study,* Partnership for a Drug-Free America, New York, 1999

TABLE 4.25

The most important problems of teens, according to teens, teachers, and principals

What is the most important problem facing people your age—that is, the thing which concerns you the most? What do you think is the most important problem facing young people today who are the age of your students?

	Teens 12–14	Teens 15–17	Teachers	Principals
Drugs	29%	28%	18%	18%
Social pressures	18%	14%	20%	20%
Bad parents/ Family problems	1%	2%	24%	27%

SOURCE: "What is the most important problem facing people your age—that is, the thing which concerns you the most? What do you think is the most important problem facing young people today who are the age of your students?" in *Back to School—National Survey of American Attitudes on Substance Abuse IV: Teens, Teachers and Principals,* The National Center on Addiction and Substance Abuse at Columbia University, New York, 1998.

TABLE 4.26

Percentage of students who use illegal drugs at least once a month, as perceived by youth, principals, and teachers

In your opinion, what percentage of the students in your school use illegal drugs at least once a month?

	Youth	Principals	Teachers
0	11%		
1–9	16%	(0–10) 58%	(0–5) 26%
10–24	17%	13%	(6–15) 18%
25–49	17%	5%	(16–50) 27%
50–100	31%	10%	6%
Don't Know	9%	14%	23%

SOURCE: "In your opinion, what percentage of the students in your school use illegal drugs at least once a month?" in *Back to School—National Survey of American Attitudes on Substance Abuse IV: Teens, Teachers and Principals,* The National Center on Addiction and Substance Abuse at Columbia University, New York, 1998.

including establishing zero-tolerance policies (students are expelled after their first drug offense); drug testing of students, especially athletes; and locker searches.

SUBSTANCE ABUSE IN MOVIES AND MUSIC

Because teenagers are major consumers of movies and music, many people are concerned about media depictions of tobacco, alcohol, and illicit drug use. A government study, sponsored by the Office of National Drug Control Policy and the Department of Health and Human Services, examined the frequency and nature of substance-use depictions in movies and songs during 1996 and 1997. Released in April 1999, the report, *Substance Use in Popular Movies and Music,* found that characters were shown doing drugs, drinking, or smoking in 98 percent of the two hundred top-grossing movies. (See Figure 4.12.) Fewer than half of the movie scenes depicted any negative consequences of these activities. The movies

studied were rated from "G" (for all ages) to "NC-17" (no one under 17 admitted).

Illicit drugs appeared in about one-fifth (22 percent) of the movies and were fairly evenly distributed across genres: drama (18 percent), comedy (13 percent), and action-adventure (10 percent). (See Figure 4.12.) Of the movies that portrayed illicit drug use, 15 percent contained an "anti-use" statement, and 21 percent depicted a character refusing an offer of illegal drugs. Marijuana appeared most frequently (51 percent), followed by powder cocaine (33 percent).

Of the 18 percent of songs that contained references to illicit drugs, the vast majority were rap songs (63 percent), followed by alternative rock (11 percent), Top 40 (11 percent), heavy metal (9 percent), and country-western (1 percent). Six percent of these songs contained an anti-use statement, and 2 percent depicted a refusal to use drugs. Marijuana was the most frequently mentioned drug (63 percent), followed by crack cocaine (15 percent) and powder cocaine (10 percent).

The study pointed out that individual songs are only a few minutes long, while many movies may last two hours or more, raising the question of whether a single drug reference in a brief song should be compared with a single drug reference in an extended film. Taking this time difference into account, the study determined that illicit drugs appeared nine times more frequently in song lyrics (18 percent) than in five-minute movie segments (2 percent).

Though the study stopped short of saying that music and movies cause young people to use drugs, alcohol, and tobacco, determining the frequency and nature of substance-use depictions in entertainment media is the first step toward understanding whether they influence young people's decisions.

DRUG USE ON COLLEGE CAMPUSES

Alcohol and Drugs on American College Campuses—A Report to College Presidents: 1995, 1996, and 1997 (Core Institute, Carbondale, IL, 1998) is based on the *Core Alcohol and Drug Survey* and was produced under a grant from the U.S. Department of Education. The findings are based on survey responses from 93,679 students at 197 colleges and universities across the country.

The researchers found that the use of alcohol and other drugs on college campuses was generally increasing. Though most (67.7 percent) of the students surveyed in 1997 had not smoked marijuana during the past year, 15.1 percent reported infrequent use (1–6 times a year); 10.1 percent, moderate use (once a month to once a week); and 7.1 percent, frequent use (three times a week to every day).

FIGURE 4.12

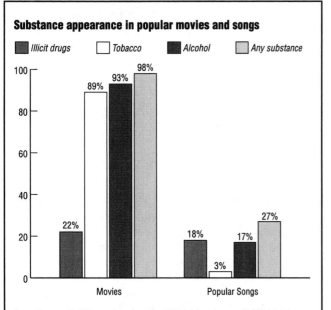

Percentages reflect the number of movies (200 total) and songs (1,000 total) in which substances appeared, whether or not they were used.

SOURCE: Donald F. Roberts, Lisa Henriksen, and Peter G. Christenson, "Substance Appearance in Popular Movies and Songs," in *Substance Use in Popular Movies and Music,* Office of National Drug Control Policy and Substance Abuse and Mental Health Services Administration, Washington, DC, 1999

TABLE 4.27

Percent of students reporting consequences resulting from drug or alcohol use

| | | Frequency of consequence within last year | | | | | | | | | | |
| | Never | | | 1–2 times | | | 3–5 times | | | 6 or more times | | |
Consequence	'95	'96	'97	'95	'96	'97	'95	'96	'97	'95	'96	'97
Had a hangover	40.5	41.2	38.3	25.6	26.1	25.2	13.9	13.6	14.8	20.0	19.2	21.7
Performed poorly on a test or project	79.4	79.2	77.9	13.7	14.1	15.0	4.5	4.2	4.6	2.4	2.5	2.5
Trouble with police/campus authorities	87.2	88.3	85.9	10.4	9.6	11.6	1.5	1.4	1.8	0.8	0.7	0.7
Damaged property, etc.	92.0	93.2	92.1	5.4	4.5	5.1	1.5	1.3	1.6	1.0	1.0	1.1
Argument or fight	69.6	72.1	69.5	20.0	18.4	20.0	6.5	6.0	6.4	3.8	3.5	4.0
Nauseated or vomited	51.3	52.0	47.5	30.8	30.5	32.3	10.8	10.3	12.1	7.1	7.1	8.1
Driven a car while under the influence	66.4	67.5	67.4	17.2	17.2	17.0	7.1	6.5	6.6	9.3	8.8	9.0
Missed a class	70.5	70.6	67.5	14.3	15.1	16.4	7.9	7.5	8.5	7.4	6.9	7.6
Been criticized by someone I know	71.4	72.9	70.1	17.7	17.1	18.6	5.9	5.5	6.3	4.9	4.4	5.0
Thought I might have a drinking problem	88.9	88.8	89.1	6.6	6.6	6.5	1.8	1.8	2.0	2.6	2.7	2.4
Had a memory loss	71.9	72.9	69.0	16.7	16.2	18.4	5.8	5.3	6.2	5.6	5.6	6.4
Done something I later regretted	64.2	65.4	61.9	23.5	23.0	24.7	7.3	6.9	7.6	5.0	4.7	5.8
Arrested for DWI, DUI	98.7	98.5	98.5	1.0	1.3	1.2	0.1	0.1	0.1	0.2	0.1	0.2
Tried unsuccessfully to stop using	94.0	93.8	94.1	3.7	3.9	3.9	1.1	1.1	1.0	1.1	1.2	1.0
Been hurt or injured	86.6	87.7	86.1	10.2	9.4	10.6	2.0	1.8	2.1	1.2	1.1	1.1
Have been taken advantage of sexually	88.2	89.3	87.2	9.1	8.5	10.2	1.3	1.1	1.4	1.3	1.2	1.2
Have taken advantage of someone sexually	94.4	95.3	94.6	3.9	3.3	3.9	0.8	0.6	0.7	0.9	0.8	0.8
Tried to commit suicide	98.5	98.6	98.7	1.1	1.0	0.9	0.1	0.1	0.1	0.3	0.2	0.2
Thought about committing suicide	94.8	95.0	95.2	3.4	3.3	3.1	0.8	0.7	0.7	1.0	1.0	0.9

SOURCE: C. A. Presley, J. S. Leichliter, and P. W. Meilman, "Percent of students reporting consequences resulting from drug or alcohol use," in *Alcohol and Drugs on American College Campuses — A Report to College Presidents: Findings from 1995, 1996, and 1997,* Southern Illinois University, Core Institute, Carbondale, IL, 1998

Almost all (96.3 percent) of the students said they had not used cocaine during the past year, and most of those who had (2.5 percent) said they had used it infrequently. About 6.5 percent indicated that they had used amphetamines, and 7.5 percent said they had used hallucinogens, during the past year—in most cases, only infrequently. Only a very small percentage of students used other drugs. The authors of the study considered alcohol abuse and the increase in marijuana use, especially in combination with alcohol, as the most serious problems on campus.

Consequences of Drug or Alcohol Use

Table 4.27 describes the frequency of various negative consequences of past-year substance abuse. The findings confirm that substantial numbers of students suffered ill effects, both academic- and health-related. About one-third (32.6 percent) of the students reported driving while under the influence. Many educators are especially concerned about the rise in marijuana use, because it is associated with short-term memory loss, impairment of brain-cell functioning, and problems with sequencing ability, time sense, and depth perception—all of which have a significant impact on the learning process.

DRUG CONVICTIONS AND FINANCIAL AID

A provision in the Higher Education Act Amendments of 1998 (PL 105-244), which went into effect in fall 2000, denies federal financial aid—grants, loans, and work assistance—to students convicted of selling or possessing drugs. These students can, however, become re-eligible for aid if they complete a drug rehabilitation program. Table 4.28 shows the different ineligibility periods for substance-abuse convictions.

During the Clinton administration, the law was not strictly enforced. According to a March 3, 2001, *New York Times* article ("Students Find Drug Law Has Big Price: College Aid") 9,200 students were denied financial aid in 2000 because of a drug conviction. However, 279,000 other students with drug convictions managed to receive aid by simply not answering the drug-conviction question on their financial-aid applications. President George W. Bush's administration stated that it would begin enforcing the law strictly. In 2001 the Department of Education made it mandatory that students answer the drug-conviction question on their applications.

Opponents of the bill say that it unfairly denies aid to black and poor students. Because these students are more dependent on aid, they may miss out on a college education altogether if ever convicted on a drug charge. Another objection is that the bill denies a college education to highly troubled students, who may benefit from it most. Representative Barney Frank of Massachusetts introduced legislation to repeal the law, though as of mid-2001 it had not been voted on yet.

TABLE 4.28

Student ineligibility for grants, loans, or work assistance

For possession of a controlled substance, ineligibility period is		For sale of a controlled substance, ineligibility period is	
First conviction	1 year	First conviction	2 years
Second conviction	2 years	Second conviction	Indefinite
Third conviction	Indefinite		

SOURCE: Joel Epstein, "Student Ineligibility for Grants, Loans, or Work Assistance," in *The Higher Education Amendments,* The Higher Education Center for Alcohol and Other Drug Prevention, Newton, MA, 1999

TESTING SCHOOL ATHLETES FOR DRUGS— LANDMARK CASES

By the early 1990s Vernonia (Oregon) School District 47J was facing what it considered a major crisis. According to the school district,

Between 1988 and 1989 the number of disciplinary referrals . . . rose to more than twice the number reported in the early 1980s, and several students were suspended. Students became increasingly rude during class; outbursts of profane language became common.

According to the U.S. District Court for the District of Oregon,

. . . the [school] administration was at its wit's end and . . . a large segment of the student body, particularly those involved in interscholastic athletics, was in a state of rebellion. . . . the staff's direct observations of students using drugs or glamorizing drug and alcohol use led the administration to the inescapable conclusion that the rebellion was being fueled by alcohol and drug abuse as well as the students' misperceptions about the drug culture.

Athletic coaches were also claiming that drug use was contributing to an increased risk of injury on the playing field. As a result, the school system introduced mandatory drug tests for students who wanted to participate in interscholastic sports. The students would be tested at the start of the sports season. Each week during the season, 10 percent of the athletes—their names drawn randomly—would be tested.

In the fall of 1991 James Acton, then a seventh-grader, signed up to play football. His parents refused to grant consent for the testing, and the student was denied permission to play football. The Actons sued the school district. A federal district court dismissed their case. The U.S. Ninth Circuit Court of Appeals, however, agreed that the policy violated both the Fourth and Fourteenth Amendments of the U.S. Constitution. The U.S. Supreme Court, on the other hand, in a 6–3 decision (*Vernonia School District 47J v. Wayne Acton,* 515 U.S. 646), agreed with the school district and upheld the drug testing of athletes.

Writing for the majority, Justice Antonin Scalia observed that the policy was a reasonable application of school authority. Schools have an *in loco parentis* ("in place of a parent") responsibility over students, and they may use this power for the students' "own good and that of their classmates." The students were out of control, and the drug testing was a "legitimate" attempt by school authorities to regain control of the school. In such situations the privacy considerations of students may be overridden.

After the 1995 decision, school districts across the country began testing athletes, and even entire student bodies. In 1998 the Tecumseh School District in Oklahoma began requiring drug tests for all students who participated in extracurricular activities. In March 2001 the U.S. Court of Appeals for the 10th Circuit in Denver ruled that the drug testing of athletes violated students' constitutional rights. In *Lindsay Earls v. Tecumseh School District* (242 F.3d 1264), the justices dealt directly with the *Vernonia* case, disagreeing with a number of points from that ruling. The majority decision, written by Justice Anderson, was that participation in voluntary school activities should not necessarily

> . . . reduce a student's expectation of privacy in his or her body. Members of our society voluntarily engage in a variety of activities every day, and do not thereby suffer a reduction in their constitutional rights.

The dissenting opinion, written by Justice Ebel, agreed with the *Vernonia* ruling that a public school has a

> . . . responsibility to protect the children entrusted to its care from numerous social ills, including the use of illegal drugs. In this regard, a school district has an almost *in loco parentis* relationship with its students, which vests in the school district special responsibilities for, and concomitant authority over, those children.

A number of cases went before U.S. circuit courts of appeal in 2000 and 2001. Mandatory testing was overruled in several cases, although it was upheld in one case. Although the tide seemed to be turning away from allowing mandatory testing, enough decisions upheld the constitutionality of mandatory testing that a final consensus was not reached in 2001.

CHAPTER 5

THE RELATIONSHIP BETWEEN DRUGS AND CRIME

It is widely accepted that there is a strong relationship between drug use and criminal behavior. Regardless of whether drugs turn users into criminals or criminal careers begin before the onset of drug use, one thing is clear: Controlling drug-related crime is likely to remain a major challenge for years to come. This chapter deals with two types of drug offenders: (*a*) those who pass through the judicial system because they have violated drug laws; and (*b*) those who enter the system because they have committed a crime while under the influence of drugs or in order to get money to pay for drugs. These two themes frequently overlap.

In *Drug Use and Crime* (Washington, D.C., 1988) the Bureau of Justice Statistics (BJS) cites three reasons for the strong relationship between drugs and crime:

[Drugs] reduce inhibitions or stimulate aggression and interfere with the ability to earn legitimate income. Further, laws to control drugs and the subsequent emergence of illegal trafficking may directly increase crime because persons who develop a dependence on an illegal drug need a substantial income to pay the higher black market prices for them. In addition, crimes such as extortion, aggravated assault, and homicide are frequent byproducts of illegal drug trafficking.

The BJS points out that social factors—such as childhood abuse, how a person has become socialized, or lack of economic opportunity—may also contribute to drug use and violence:

Drug use does not directly cause criminal behavior, but the same circumstances that might lead a person to begin committing crimes may also contribute to the development of drug habits. For example, social conditions, including poverty and discrimination, may limit opportunity and reduce an individual's investment in society, leading to both drug abuse and criminal behavior. Also, some people enjoy taking risks and are willing, for whatever reason, to violate laws or norms, or they seek possessions or experiences that

are not available by legitimate means. The use of drugs, especially on a regular basis, may not occur among such persons until after they have begun a career of criminal activity. Drug use may thus be only part of a more general lifestyle that also includes other types of criminal activity.

In *Adult Patterns of Criminal Behavior* (National Institute of Justice, Washington, D.C., 1996), University of Nebraska researchers Julie Horney, D. Wayne Osgood, and Ineke Haen Marshall studied 658 newly convicted male prisoners sentenced to the Nebraska Department of Correctional Services during 1989–90. The researchers wanted to determine if changes in life circumstances, such as being unemployed or living with a wife or girlfriend, influenced their criminal behavior. Among their conclusions, they found that

Use of illegal drugs was related to all four measures of offending (any crime, property crime, assault, and drug crime). For example, during months of drug use, the odds of committing a property crime increased by 54 percent; the odds of committing an assault increased by over 100 percent. Overall, illegal drug use increased the odds of committing any crime sixfold.

DRUGS AND ALCOHOL PLAY A MAJOR ROLE IN ARRESTS

The Federal Bureau of Investigation, in its *Crime in the United States, 1999* (Washington, D.C., 2000), estimated that there were 14.4 million arrests in 1999. Drug-abuse violations accounted for 1.6 million (11 percent of all arrests); driving under the influence, 1.5 million (10 percent); drunkenness, 673,400; and liquor-law violations, 683,600. These 4.4 million arrests for drug and alcohol violations accounted for 31 percent of all arrests. In addition, arrests for disorderly conduct (655,600), vagrancy (30,800), and vandalism (285,000) often involved drug and alcohol abuse. (See Table 5.1.)

TABLE 5.1

Estimated arrests, 1999

Arrest totals are based on all reporting agencies and estimates for unreported areas.

Total[1,2]	14,355,600
Murder and nonnegligent manslaughter	14,920
Forcible rape	29,220
Robbery	109,840
Aggravated assault	490,790
Burglary	301,500
Larceny-theft	1,213,300
Motor vehicle theft	144,200
Arson	17,100
Forgery and counterfeiting	109,300
Fraud	371,800
Embezzlement	17,300
Stolen property; buying, receiving, possessing	124,100
Vandalism	285,000
Weapons; carrying, possessing, etc.	175,500
Prostitution and commercialized vice	92,200
Sex offenses (except forcible rape and prostitution)	93,800
Drug abuse violations	1,557,100
Gambling	10,400
Offenses against the family and children	153,500
Driving under the influence	1,549,500
Liquor laws	683,600
Drunkenness	673,400
Disorderly conduct	655,600
Vagrancy	30,800
All other offenses	3,809,000
Suspicion	8,000
Curfew and loitering law violations	170,000
Runaways	150,700
Violent crime[3]	644,770
Property crime[4]	1,676,100
Crime Index total[5]	2,320,900

[1] Does not include suspicion.
[2] Because of rounding, figures may not add to total.
[3] Violent crimes are offenses of murder, forcible rape, robbery, and aggravated assault.
[4] Property crimes are offenses of burglary, larceny-theft, motor vehicle theft, and arson.
[5] Includes arson.

SOURCE: "Table 29. Estimated arrests: United States, 1999", in *Crime in the United States, 1999*, Federal Bureau of Investigation, Washington D.C., 2000

In 1999 more people were arrested for drug and alcohol violations than were arrested for murder, rape, robbery, aggravated assault, burglary, theft, car theft, arson, forgery, fraud, embezzlement, prostitution and vice, gambling, offenses against family and children (usually domestic violence), and curfew/loitering-law violations *combined*. (See Table 5.1.)

ARRESTEE DRUG USE

The *Arrestee Drug Abuse Monitoring Program* (ADAM), prepared by the National Institute of Justice, is based on voluntary urine specimens and anonymous interviews with adult males and females arrested for a variety of serious crimes. (Data from the 1998 and 2000 ADAM reports are presented here.) In 1998, 35 urban sites across the United States participated, contacting about 40,000 adult participants. ADAM tested for 10 drugs but reported on only six categories: cocaine, marijuana, opiates, methamphetamine, phencyclidine (PCP), and "any drug," which could include these other five drugs.

More than 80 percent of the arrestees who were asked to participate agreed to be interviewed, and more than 80 percent of those interviewed provided urine specimens. (The ADAM estimates are likely somewhat low, since it is presumed that many of those who chose not to participate would have tested positive for illegal drugs.) Because drug offenders are more likely to test positive for drugs than those arrested for non-drug-related offenses, ADAM limited participation by drug offenders to 20 percent of the total sample. Twelve sites collected data from juvenile male arrestees.

The 1998 and 2000 ADAM reports noted that, in most sites, approximately two-thirds of adult arrestees tested positive for at least one drug. Among adult males, marijuana was the most frequently detected drug, followed by cocaine. Among adult females, cocaine was the most commonly detected, while among juveniles, marijuana was by far the most frequently detected drug. Multiple-drug use was also common.

Cocaine Use

According to the 1998 ADAM report, older arrestees (36 and above) and females were the most likely to use cocaine. Based on self-reports, female arrestees were more likely than male arrestees to use crack cocaine. (See Figure 5.1 for sites historically showing the highest cocaine-positive rates for both males and females.) Drug testing cannot yet distinguish crack from powder cocaine, so researchers must rely on self-reported data to track trends in crack use.

In 1998 the percentage of adult male arrestees who tested positive for recent cocaine use ranged from a high of 51.3 percent in Atlanta to a low of 8.0 percent in San Jose, California. (See Table 5.2.) Male cocaine users reported recent crack use twice as frequently as they reported recent powder-cocaine use.

The percentage of adult female arrestees who tested positive for recent cocaine use ranged from a high of 67.0 percent in New York City to a low of 9.5 percent in San Jose. (See Table 5.3.) Crack use was reported more than three times as frequently as powder-cocaine use. ADAM data suggest significant crack use among female arrestees in urban areas.

GENDER DIFFERENCES AND REPORTED COCAINE USE. Table 5.4 shows that in 1998 females were often more likely than males to be arrested for drug and alcohol offenses—particularly in large cities. Not surprisingly, those arrested on drug charges were more likely to test positive for cocaine than those arrested for personal, property, and "other" offenses. (See Table 5.5.) Females arrested on "other" charges were also likely to be cocaine-positive.

FIGURE 5.1

Female and male arrestees' cocaine use self-reports, select cities, 1990–98

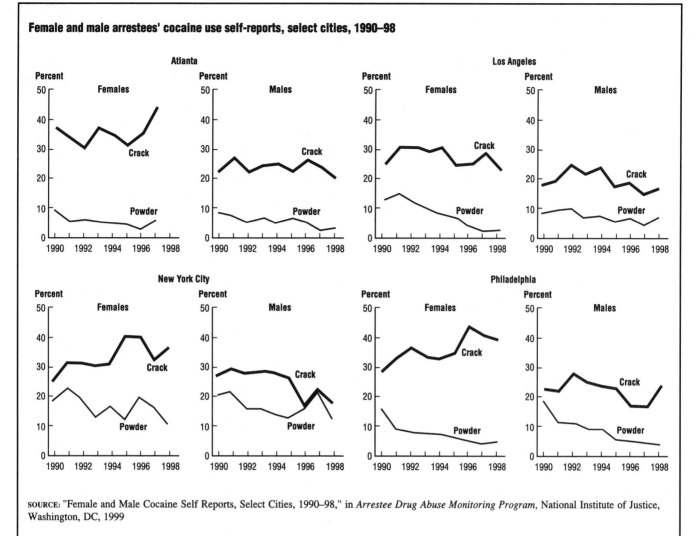

SOURCE: "Female and Male Cocaine Self Reports, Select Cities, 1990–98," in *Arrestee Drug Abuse Monitoring Program,* National Institute of Justice, Washington, DC, 1999

Opiate Use

The use of opiates—including heroin, codeine, and morphine—is relatively low compared with that of cocaine and marijuana use. Though current screening methods cannot distinguish heroin from other opiates, preliminary results from another project indicate that more than 97 percent of ADAM arrestees who tested positive for opiates were heroin users. Older arrestees used opiates at higher rates than did younger arrestees. In a few sites, however, the youngest groups were more likely to test positive. There has been recent concern that opiate use may increase among the young as the price of heroin decreases and purity increases.

Female arrestees were more likely than male arrestees to test positive for opiate use. Opiate-positive rates of adult male arrestees ranged from a high of 18.4 percent in Philadelphia to a low of 1.3 percent in Atlanta (Table 5.2), while among adult female respondents, opiate-positive rates ranged from 27 percent in Chicago to 0 percent in Laredo, Texas (Table 5.3). Two factors may explain these

higher rates: Fewer females are arrested, which may raise the rates; and females are more likely than males to be arrested for offenses that carry a high likelihood of drug use, such as prostitution.

Opiate users tend to be multidrug users, with cocaine being the other drug they most frequently use. (See Table 5.2.) New York City and Washington, D.C., reported levels of cocaine use among opiate-using arrestees of over 70 percent for nearly every year between 1990 and 1998. During those years, the proportion of opiate users who reported using powder cocaine declined, while the proportion who reported using crack increased.

The proportion of opiate-using arrestees who tested positive for marijuana rose from 15 percent in 1990 to about 30 percent in 1998. Benzodiazepines (a class of depressants) were found in opiate-positive arrestees at lower levels than were cocaine or marijuana, with an average rate of about 18 percent for the eight-year period. Methamphetamine use among opiate users was generally quite low, though in three sites—San Diego

TABLE 5.2

Percentage of adult male arrestee positives by drug and site, 1998

	Cocaine %	Opiates %	Marijuana %	Methamphetamine %
Northeast				
New York City	47.1	16.2	38.7	0.0
Philadelphia	44.5	18.4	44.9	0.6
Washington, D.C.	33.3	9.7	38.0	0.0
South				
Atlanta	51.3	1.3	26.0	0.0
Birmingham	41.2	3.7	39.2	0.0
Dallas	29.0	2.3	43.1	3.3
Ft. Lauderdale	50.2	2.0	43.5	0.0
Houston	35.8	7.5	35.8	0.2
Miami	47.3	2.4	29.2	0.2
New Orleans	46.0	12.9	38.3	0.2
Oklahoma City*	27.3	1.9	53.1	8.0
Midwest				
Chicago	44.9	18.3	41.5	0.2
Cleveland	36.8	6.0	36.8	0.0
Des Moines*	18.1	2.8	41.8	10.2
Detroit	28.2	6.8	46.5	0.2
Indianapolis	34.2	1.8	45.1	0.8
Minneapolis*	26.7	4.7	45.4	0.8
Omaha	25.1	2.0	43.9	10.2
St. Louis	34.8	10.9	50.2	0.3
West/Southwest				
Albuquerque*	38.7	8.2	35.9	3.4
Denver	39.6	4.2	41.3	5.2
Laredo*	37.1	11.2	39.3	0.0
Las Vegas*	24.2	2.6	25.8	13.8
Los Angeles	42.7	5.6	27.3	8.0
Phoenix	31.1	5.7	32.2	16.4
Sacramento*	18.2	3.2	44.1	24.6
Salt Lake City*	20.3	8.2	36.8	20.3
San Antonio	27.0	9.6	41.1	2.0
San Diego	19.1	9.3	36.4	33.2
San Jose	8.0	4.4	24.8	19.7
Tucson*	39.4	6.8	39.2	4.0
Northwest				
Anchorage*	19.5	2.3	33.3	0.0
Portland	29.2	15.5	36.9	18.1
Seattle*	35.9	17.4	35.4	6.4
Spokane*	18.3	8.5	42.9	15.8

* New site in 1998.

SOURCE: "Percentage of Adult Male Positives By Drug and Site, 1998," in *Arrestee Drug Abuse Monitoring Program,* National Institute of Justice, Washington, DC, 1999

TABLE 5.3

Percentage of adult female arrestee positives by drug and site, 1998

	Cocaine %	Opiates %	Marijuana %	Methamphetamine %
Northeast				
New York City	67.0	21.8	23.4	0.0
Philadelphia	60.9	14.9	23.7	0.3
Washington, D.C.	40.4	9.8	28.5	0.5
South				
Atlanta	—	—	—	—
Birmingham	56.8	17.6	17.6	0.0
Dallas	29.5	4.8	24.2	4.0
Ft. Lauderdale	53.4	4.7	24.5	0.0
Houston	37.3	7.0	20.1	0.0
Miami	—	—	—	—
New Orleans	38.7	3.4	22.1	0.3
Oklahoma City*	—	—	—	—
Midwest				
Chicago	55.5	27.0	19.7	0.0
Cleveland	40.5	1.4	27.0	0.0
Des Moines*	24.2	6.1	15.2	24.2
Detroit	46.2	21.5	21.5	0.0
Indianapolis	43.2	4.5	31.2	0.0
Minneapolis*	28.6	6.0	22.6	0.0
Omaha	35.5	4.5	28.2	13.6
St. Louis	43.6	4.9	31.9	2.5
West/Southwest				
Albuquerque*	59.1	15.4	24.0	2.4
Denver	49.9	3.4	29.9	4.6
Laredo*	33.3	0.0	13.3	0.0
Las Vegas*	35.1	13.5	21.6	24.3
Los Angeles	44.7	8.8	21.8	11.8
Phoenix	39.6	7.3	24.9	22.4
Sacramento*	30.7	8.4	28.2	29.2
Salt Lake City*	19.6	13.7	29.4	31.4
San Antonio	20.0	8.6	17.5	1.7
San Diego	20.4	6.7	26.7	33.3
San Jose	9.5	4.8	13.6	21.1
Tucson*	41.3	7.4	21.5	2.5
Northwest				
Anchorage*	50.0	3.8	23.1	0.0
Portland	36.7	25.1	23.2	22.3
Seattle*	56.9	17.2	37.9	5.2
Spokane*	31.7	17.1	26.8	22.0

* New site in 1998.

SOURCE: "Percentage of Adult Female Positives By Drug and Site, 1998," in *Arrestee Drug Abuse Monitoring Program,* National Institute of Justice, Washington, DC, 1999

(males and females), San Jose (females), and Spokane, Washington (males and females)—opiate users tested positive for methamphetamine 30 percent of the time or more.

Marijuana Use

Marijuana use among arrestees is high; often, one-third or more reported using the drug within days of their arrest. In general, men were more likely than women to test positive for marijuana, and younger arrestees (15–25 years of age) were much more likely to test positive than older respondents. (See Figure 5.2.)

Alcohol was the substance most frequently used with marijuana. However, respondents also reported using marijuana with powder cocaine, crack, methamphetamine, and PCP.

The proportion of adult male respondents who tested positive for marijuana use ranged from a high of 53.1 percent in Oklahoma City to a low of 24.8 percent in San Jose. (See Table 5.2.) The proportion of female arrestees with marijuana-positive tests ranged from 37.9 percent in Seattle to 13.3 percent in Laredo. (See Table 5.3.)

Methamphetamine Use

Methamphetamine prevalence varied wildly by geographical site. In more than half the 35 sites, prevalence rates were less than 2 percent, while they exceeded 20

TABLE 5.4

Distribution of primary offense charge for female and male arrestees in selected sites, 1998

Site	Personal %	Drugs/Alcohol %	Property %	Other %
Atlanta				
Females	—	—	—	—
Males	26.9	14.6	35.6	22.9
Los Angeles				
Females	14.2	23.3	31.5	31.0
Males	31.6	16.4	36.5	15.4
New York City				
Females	14.7	37.6	22.1	25.7
Males	31.5	14.2	35.1	19.2
Philadelphia				
Females	21.6	18.5	30.2	29.7
Males	32.5	18.3	36.0	13.2
Washington, D.C.				
Females	29.7	23.0	17.5	29.8
Males	36.4	18.9	27.6	17.1

SOURCE: "Distribution of Primary Offense Charge for Female and Male Arrestees in Selected Sites, 1998," in *Arrestee Drug Abuse Monitoring Program,* National Institute of Justice, Washington, DC, 1999

TABLE 5.5

Percent positive for cocaine by primary offense charge for female and male arrestees in selected sites, 1998

Site	Personal %	Drugs/Alcohol %	Property %	Other %
Atlanta				
Females	—	—	—	—
Males	48.4	33.3	60.2	49.7
Los Angeles				
Females	44.0	60.3	57.6	41.0
Males	26.4	59.0	38.8	50.9
New York City				
Females	43.3	81.0	71.2	49.3
Males	37.5	51.1	56.1	42.0
Philadelphia				
Females	36.1	66.7	28.8	90.3
Males	28.8	48.4	50.0	55.3
Washington, D.C.				
Females	23.8	57.6	38.2	61.9
Males	25.8	35.0	43.4	36.9

SOURCE: "Percent Positive for Cocaine by Primary Offense Charge for Female and Male Arrestees in Selected Sites, 1998," in *Arrestee Drug Abuse Monitoring Program,* National Institute of Justice, Washington, DC, 1999

percent in 9 sites. Sites in the West and Northwest had considerably higher rates of methamphetamine use than those in the Northeast, South, or Midwest. Surprisingly, despite reports of active methamphetamine production in, and trafficking from, Mexico, most sites along the southwest border and in Texas showed considerably lower levels of methamphetamine use than sites in the West and Northwest.

Methamphetamine use appeared to be higher among white arrestees, though the proportion of Hispanic arrestees testing positive for the drug increased dramatically in later years. A greater proportion of female arrestees than male arrestees tested positive for methamphetamine in most sites.

Methamphetamine-positive rates for male arrestees ranged from 0 percent at several sites to 33.2 percent in San Diego. (See Table 5.2.) The same pattern applied to female arrestees, ranging from 0 percent to 33.3 percent in San Diego. (See Table 5.3.)

Some Specific Examples

The 2000 ADAM report provided graphic overviews for the individual sites studied. Graphic findings for three cities have been randomly selected and included here—Portland, Oregon (Table 5.6); Omaha, Nebraska (Table 5.7); and New York City (Table 5.8). These findings indicate that drug use among arrestees is high all across the United States, regardless of the size or location of the city.

SENTENCING FOR DRUG VIOLATIONS

Between 1990 and 1997 the state prison population increased 57 percent, from 684,544 to 1,075,167. Violent

FIGURE 5.2

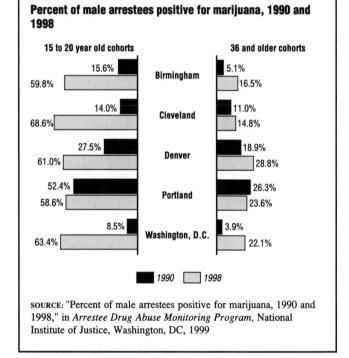

Percent of male arrestees positive for marijuana, 1990 and 1998

SOURCE: "Percent of male arrestees positive for marijuana, 1990 and 1998," in *Arrestee Drug Abuse Monitoring Program,* National Institute of Justice, Washington, DC, 1999

offenders accounted for 51 percent of the increase, while drug offenders comprised about 19 percent of the increase. (See Table 5.9.) But this increase appears to be part of a longer trend. Since 1980 the number of prisoners has been growing steadily, especially the number of prisoners sentenced for drug offenses. (See Figure 5.3.)

The number of offenders entering prison cannot totally explain this growth, however; admissions have

TABLE 5.6

Drug use among arrestees in Portland, Oregon, 1999

CATCHMENT AREA: MULTNOMAH COUNTY		Age of Booked Arrestees (%)					Race of Booked Arrestees (%)			
	Sample Size	15-20	21-25	26-30	31-35	36+	Black	White	Hispanic	Other
Males	652	12.0	18.6	19.2	15.8	34.5	23.0	65.1	7.8	4.0
Females	286	14.0	15.8	19.6	14.7	35.8	23.5	67.7	3.2	5.6

PERCENT POSITIVE FOR DRUGS, BY SEX, AGE, AND RACE

MALE / FEMALE

	Percent Positive	Percent Positive by Age					Percent Positive by Race			
		15-20	21-25	26-30	31-35	36+	Black	White	Hispanic	Other
ANY DRUG	63.8	73.1	66.1	58.4	66.0	61.3	76.0	64.2	39.2	34.6
	68.2	65.0	53.3	76.8	83.3	65.7	71.6	68.4	77.8	50.0
COCAINE	22.7	10.3	14.9	12.8	28.2	34.2	48.0	13.7	25.5	19.2
	33.2	10.0	22.2	41.1	33.3	43.1	55.2	25.4	44.4	31.3
MARIJUANA	34.5	59.0	47.9	35.2	30.1	20.4	40.4	35.4	21.6	15.4
	23.4	52.5	26.7	25.0	21.4	10.8	23.9	24.4	22.2	12.5
OPIATES	12.9	10.3	10.7	11.2	9.7	17.3	8.0	14.2	19.6	3.8
	18.9	15.0	8.9	26.8	26.2	17.6	9.0	21.8	55.6	6.3
METHAM-PHETAMINE	19.8	19.2	17.4	22.4	30.1	15.1	5.3	27.1	3.9	11.5
	24.8	17.5	17.8	32.1	40.5	20.6	4.5	33.2	22.2	12.5
PCP	0.0	0.0	0.0	0.0	0.0	0.0	0.0	0.0	0.0	0.0
	0.7	0.0	0.0	0.0	2.4	1.0	1.5	0.5	0.0	0.0
MULTIPLE DRUGS	22.9	24.4	22.3	20.8	25.2	22.7	24.0	22.6	23.5	15.4
	26.2	22.5	17.8	39.3	28.6	23.5	16.4	30.1	44.4	12.5
Total Males (N)		78	121	125	103	225	150	424	51	26
Total Females (N)		40	45	56	42	102	67	193	9	16

PERCENT POSITIVE FOR DRUGS, BY OFFENSE CATEGORY

Offense	N by Sex		Cocaine		Marijuana		Methamphetamine		PCP		Any Drug	
	M	F	M	F	M	F	M	F	M	F	M	F
VIOLENT OFFENSE	114	41	4.4	14.6	31.6	19.5	17.5	12.2	0.0	0.0	47.4	36.6
Robbery	17	3	5.9	33.3	35.3	0.0	0.0	0.0	0.0	0.0	52.9	66.7
Assault	72	31	4.2	12.9	29.2	16.1	18.1	16.1	0.0	0.0	41.7	32.3
Weapons	5	1	0.0	12.9	60.0	100.0	40.0	0.0	0.0	0.0	80.0	100.0
Other Violent	25	6	4.0	100.0	28.1	33.3	28.0	0.0	0.0	0.0	52.0	33.3
PROPERTY OFFENSE	126	77	34.9	53.2	39.7	22.1	25.4	22.1	0.0	1.3	75.4	80.5
Larceny/Theft	43	30	25.6	33.3	39.5	40.0	23.3	23.3	0.0	0.0	67.4	70.0
Burglary	11	4	18.2	50.0	18.2	25.0	9.1	25.0	0.0	0.0	45.5	75.0
Stolen Vehicle	15	5	13.3	40.0	46.7	40.0	53.3	60.0	0.0	0.0	80.0	100.0
Other Property	65	46	49.2	65.2	38.5	15.2	23.1	19.6	0.0	2.2	83.1	87.0
DRUG OFFENSE	118	73	49.2	50.7	35.6	30.1	33.1	39.7	0.0	1.4	92.4	90.4
Drug Sales	31	11	35.5	27.3	41.9	36.4	25.8	36.4	0.0	0.0	87.1	81.8
Drug Possession	108	73	50.9	50.7	34.3	30.1	33.3	39.7	0.0	1.4	93.5	90.4
PROSTITUTION	0	2	—	50.0	—	0.0	—	50.0	0.0	0.0	—	100.0
OTHER OFFENSE	401	158	20.0	30.4	36.9	22.2	17.0	22.8	0.0	0.6	61.3	65.8

remained fairly constant in recent years, increasing by about 17 percent since 1990. Instead, much of the growth can be traced to an increasing amount of time served by offenders.

Paula M. Ditton and Doris James Wilson, in *Truth in Sentencing in State Prisons* (Bureau of Justice Statistics, Washington, D.C., 1999), defined state sentencing guidelines, which have become more restrictive in recent years:

• Indeterminate sentencing—Parole boards have the authority to release offenders from prison.

• Determinate sentencing—States introduced fixed prison terms, which could be reduced by good-time or earned-time credits.

• Mandatory minimum sentences—States added statutes requiring offenders to be sentenced to a specified amount of prison time.

• Sentencing guidelines—States established sentencing commissions and created ranges of sentences for given offenses and offender characteristics.

• Truth-in-sentencing—First enacted in 1984, truth-in-sentencing laws require offenders to serve a substantial portion of their prison sentence. Parole eligibility and good-time credits are restricted or eliminated.

The definition of truth-in-sentencing varies by state, as do the percentage of sentence that must be served and the crimes covered by the laws. In order to qualify for Truth-in-

TABLE 5.6

Drug use among arrestees in Portland, Oregon, 1999 [CONTINUED]

HISTORIC TRENDS IN PERCENT POSITIVE, BY DRUG

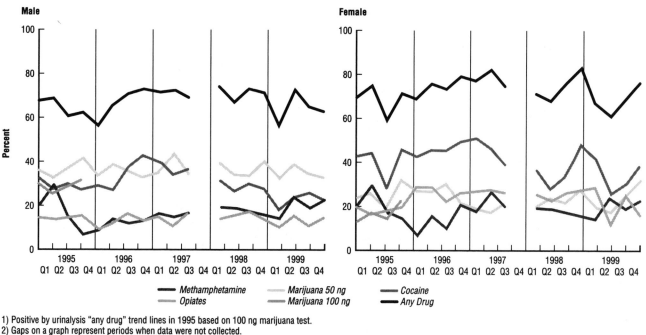

1) Positive by urinalysis "any drug" trend lines in 1995 based on 100 ng marijuana test.
2) Gaps on a graph represent periods when data were not collected.
3) Data collection for 3Q99 and 4Q99 may be influenced by the initiation of the probability based sampling plan.
4) Dramatic fluctuations in trend lines are a result of low sample sizes.

SOURCE: "1999, Adult Program Findings, Portland, Oregon," in *Arrestee Drug Abuse Monitoring Program,* National Institute of Justice, Washington, D.C., 2000

Sentencing Incentive Grants, authorized by the 1994 Crime Act (PL 103-322) to build or expand prison facilities, states must require persons convicted of a violent crime to serve no less than 85 percent of their prison sentence. Since the passage of the Crime Act, virtually every state has passed a truth-in-sentencing law. Fourteen states have passed laws abolishing parole-board release for all offenders sentenced for crimes committed after the effective date of that law.

Though arrests for most offenses declined between 1990 and 1996—with the exception of aggravated assault, fraud, and drug offenses—the number of admissions to state prison relative to the number of arrests increased in many instances. The likelihood of going to prison following arrest for a drug offense increased sharply between 1980 and 1990, from 19 commitments per 1,000 arrests to 103 per 1,000. The rate dropped in 1996, to 77 commitments per 1,000 arrests. More than one-third of prison admissions in 1997 were parole violators, and nearly one-third of these parole violators were drug offenders.

In 1996 drug offenders admitted to prison were sentenced to an average of 57 months; they were expected to serve a minimum of 32 months. For those states that have truth-in-sentencing laws requiring that 85 percent of a sentence be served, drug offenders sentenced to 57 months would serve a minimum of 48 months.

CHARACTERISTICS OF INCARCERATED DRUG OFFENDERS

Every five years, the Bureau of Justice Statistics (BJS) of the U.S. Department of Justice prepares a complete study of prisoners. The prisoners answer dozens of questions on, among other things, their education, age, employment, what type of crime they committed, and their drug and alcohol use. The latest results were reported in *Correctional Populations in the United States, 1997* (Department of Justice, Washington, D.C., 2000) and *Prisoners in 1999* (Department of Justice, Washington, D.C., 2000).

State Drug Offenders

Correctional Populations 1997 reported that drug offenders accounted for over 222,000 prisoners in 1997—including 21 percent of state prisoners. *Prisoners in 1999* found that between 1990 and 1998 the number of drug offenders in state prisons increased by 87,000. Both reports showed that this increase in drug offenses paralleled increases for other crimes. Throughout the 1990s drug offenders comprised about 20 percent of state prisoners. (See Table 5.9 and Table 5.10.)

RACIAL MAKEUP OF STATE OFFENDERS. Despite representing only 12.5 percent of the U.S. population,

TABLE 5.7

Drug use among arrestees in Omaha, Nebraska, 1999

CATCHMENT AREA: DOUGLAS COUNTY	Sample Size	Age of Booked Arrestees (%)					Race of Booked Arrestees (%)			
		15-20	21-25	26-30	31-35	36+	Black	White	Hispanic	Other
Males	449	15.7	19.5	18.3	14.1	32.4	47.5	44.8	5.4	2.2
Females	90	16.7	25.6	15.6	8.9	33.3	51.7	42.5	1.1	4.6

PERCENT POSITIVE FOR DRUGS, BY SEX, AGE, AND RACE

MALE ▬
FEMALE ▬

	Percent Positive	Percent Positive by Age					Percent Positive by Race			
	0 20 40 60 80 100	15-20	21-25	26-30	31-35	36+	Black	White	Hispanic	Other
ANY DRUG	61.5	75.7	73.6	63.4	63.5	44.8	71.7	53.0	58.3	40.0
	62.2	53.3	52.2	64.3	75.0	70.0	71.1	56.8	0.0	50.0
COCAINE	21.6	8.6	14.9	24.4	36.5	23.4	29.2	13.0	33.3	10.0
	32.2	0.0	21.7	28.6	62.5	50.0	33.3	32.4	0.0	25.0
MARIJUANA	51.2	74.3	71.3	50.0	41.3	32.4	63.2	42.0	37.5	30.0
	35.6	53.3	34.8	42.9	25.0	26.7	42.2	32.4	0.0	25.0
OPIATES	0.4	0.0	0.0	1.2	1.6	0.0	0.5	0.5	0.0	0.0
	0.0	0.0	0.0	0.0	0.0	0.0	0.0	0.0	0.0	0.0
METHAM-PHETAMINE	7.8	4.3	5.7	11.0	15.9	5.5	0.0	16.5	4.2	10.0
	11.1	0.0	4.3	7.1	37.5	16.7	2.2	24.3	0.0	0.0
PCP	0.0	0.0	0.0	0.0	0.0	0.0	0.0	0.0	0.0	0.0
	0.0	0.0	0.0	0.0	0.0	0.0	0.0	0.0	0.0	0.0
MULTIPLE DRUGS	18.5	11.4	17.2	23.2	28.6	15.2	21.2	16.5	16.7	10.0
	15.6	0.0	8.7	14.3	37.5	23.3	6.7	29.7	0.0	0.0
Total Males	(N)	70	87	82	63	145	212	200	24	10
Total Females	(N)	15	23	14	8	30	45	37	1	4

PERCENT POSITIVE FOR DRUGS, BY OFFENSE CATEGORY

Offense	N by Sex		Cocaine		Marijuana		Methamphetamine		PCP		Any Drug	
	M	F	M	F	M	F	M	F	M	F	M	F
VIOLENT OFFENSE	159	15	20.8	13.3	50.9	46.7	6.9	0.0	0.0	0.0	57.9	60.0
Robbery	5	1	40.0	0.0	80.0	100.0	0.0	0.0	0.0	0.0	80.0	100.0
Assault	125	13	18.4	15.4	47.2	46.2	5.6	0.0	0.0	0.0	53.6	61.5
Weapons	30	1	23.3	0.0	56.7	0.0	13.3	0.0	0.0	0.0	66.7	0.0
Other Violent	21	0	19.0	—	66.7	—	4.8	—	0.0	—	66.7	—
PROPERTY OFFENSE	65	22	27.7	40.9	49.2	40.9	6.2	9.1	0.0	0.0	63.1	68.2
Larceny/Theft	24	14	37.5	35.7	50.0	42.9	0.0	7.1	0.0	0.0	62.5	64.3
Burglary	11	0	27.3	—	63.6	—	0.0	—	0.0	—	72.7	—
Stolen Vehicle	0	0	—	—	—	—	—	—	—	—	—	—
Other Property	33	8	21.2	50.0	48.5	37.5	12.1	12.5	0.0	0.0	63.6	75.0
DRUG OFFENSE	55	19	38.2	57.9	61.8	52.6	18.2	31.6	0.0	0.0	78.2	94.7
Drug Sales	7	0	42.9	—	85.7	—	28.2	—	0.0	—	85.7	—
Drug Possession	51	19	39.2	57.9	60.8	52.6	17.6	31.6	0.0	0.0	78.4	94.7
PROSTITUTION	0	0	—	—	—	—	—	—	—	—	—	—
OTHER OFFENSE	247	42	18.6	28.6	53.0	23.8	7.7	7.1	0.0	0.0	62.3	50.0

in 1998 blacks made up 47 percent of state prisoners, about the same as in 1990 (46 percent). However, they accounted for 57 percent of drug offenders in these institutions. Between 1990 and 1998 the number of drug offenders in state prisons increased by 87,100—55,000 (63 percent) of whom were black. (See Table 5.11 and Table 5.12.)

Hispanics represent about 12 percent of the U.S. population. In 1998 they represented 17 percent of all state prisoners and 22 percent of drug offenders. (See Table 5.11.) Whites accounted for about 33 percent of state prisoners and 20 percent of drug offenders, though they comprise more than two-thirds of the American population.

Federal Drug Offenders

In 1998 federal prisoners comprised about 9 percent of all U.S. inmates. That is, only about 1 in 11 prisoners in America is in a federal prison; the rest are incarcerated in state prisons. However, between 1990 and 1998, while the state prison population grew about 66 percent, the population of federal prisons grew from 56,989 to 108,925—an increase of more than 91 percent. (See Table 5.13.)

Most of the total growth in the federal prison population is due to an increasing number of incarcerated drug offenders. The number of federal drug offenders increased 107 percent between 1990 and 1998, from 30,470 to 63,011. This accounted for nearly two-thirds (62.7

TABLE 5.7

Drug use among arrestees in Omaha, Nebraska, 1999 [CONTINUED]

HISTORIC TRENDS IN PERCENT POSITIVE, BY DRUG

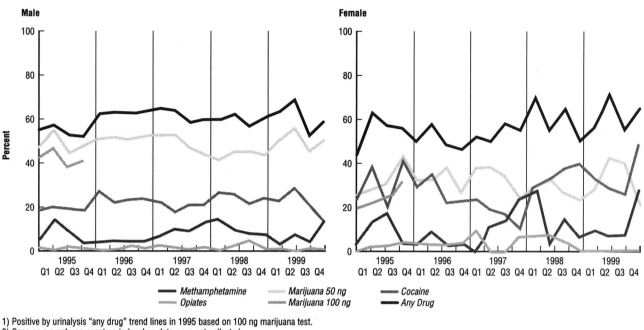

1) Positive by urinalysis "any drug" trend lines in 1995 based on 100 ng marijuana test.
2) Gaps on a graph represent periods when data were not collected.
3) Data collection for 3Q99 and 4Q99 may be influenced by the initiation of the probability based sampling plan.
4) Dramatic fluctuations in trend lines are a result of low sample sizes.

SOURCE: "1999, Adult Program Findings, Omaha, Nebraska," in *Arrestee Drug Abuse Monitoring Program,* National Institute of Justice, Washington, D.C., 2000

percent) of the increase in the federal prison population during the same period. (See Table 5.13.)

RACIAL MAKEUP OF FEDERAL OFFENDERS. In 1997 the Bureau of Justice Statistics estimated there were about 84,000 inmates in federal prisons. Of these, more than 53,000 (64 percent) were sentenced for drug violations.

The majority of federal drug offenders are black or Hispanic. According to *Correctional Populations 1997,* only 24 percent of federal drug offenders were white, while 34 percent were Hispanic and 42 percent were black. About half of white inmates (49.4 percent) were sentenced for drug offenses, compared with more than two-thirds (67.2 percent) of Hispanic inmates and nearly three-quarters (74 percent) of black inmates.

Prior Offenses

Most drug offenders (70.1 percent, state; 85.8 percent, federal) were incarcerated for drug trafficking. More than one-fourth (27.1 percent) of state drug offenders, but only 5.3 percent of federal drug offenders, were in prison for possession. (See Table 5.14.)

In 1997 drug offenders in state prisons reported extensive criminal histories: 53.8 percent were on parole or probation, or had escaped from custody; 82.6 percent had a prior probation or incarceration sentence; and 45 percent had three or more prior sentences. Drug offenders in federal prisons reported less severe criminal histories. (See Table 5.14.)

Cocaine/crack was by far the most common drug involved in current offenses—reported by 72.1 percent of state drug offenders and 65.5 percent of federal drug offenders. Marijuana, heroin/other opiates, and stimulants were each involved in 10 percent or more of current drug offenses. (See Table 5.14.)

GANGS, CRACK, AND CRIME

Drug-related crime is an especially cruel fact of life in many American inner cities, as well as in a growing number of rural and suburban communities. It is commonly thought that crack cocaine, which was introduced to the United States around 1985, was spread through gang organizations.

The stereotype of a gang, as presented in the media, emphasizes the violent behavior, the gang's group identity as opposed to individual behavior, and the connection between gang activity and drug dealing. Social scientists who have looked closely at gang activity are beginning to question this overly simplistic view.

TABLE 5.8

Drug use among arrestees in New York City, New York, 1999

CATCHMENT AREA: BRONX, QUEENS, STATEN ISLAND, MANHATTAN, BROOKLYN	Sample Size	Age of Booked Arrestees (%)					Race of Booked Arrestees (%)			
		15-20	21-25	26-30	31-35	36+	Black	White	Hispanic	Other
Males	2190	19.1	13.2	13.0	16.0	38.7	55.7	12.1	30.5	1.8
Females	1200	12.5	11.3	13.3	22.0	40.9	62.1	12.9	24.3	0.7

Catchment Area: Five Boroughs – Bronx Co., Queens Co., Richmond Co., New York Co., King Co.

PERCENT POSITIVE FOR DRUGS, BY SEX, AGE, AND RACE

MALE ▇▇▇ FEMALE ▒▒▒

	Percent Positive	Percent Positive by Age					Percent Positive by Race			
		15-20	21-25	26-30	31-35	36+	Black	White	Hispanic	Other
ANY DRUG	74.7	67.5	73.6	71.8	80.3	77.1	77.2	69.3	73.7	51.3
	81.3	66.0	73.3	84.4	83.7	85.7	81.9	85.1	79.3	37.5
COCAINE	44.2	8.9	25.3	44.7	57.5	62.5	48.0	44.7	39.0	20.5
	65.1	16.0	34.1	73.1	78.0	79.0	65.9	66.9	63.1	25.0
MARIJUANA	40.8	64.4	64.9	39.8	37.0	22.8	40.4	37.0	43.3	38.5
	26.2	54.0	43.0	28.1	18.9	16.3	26.8	19.5	29.0	0.0
OPIATES	15.2	2.6	7.6	12.7	19.7	22.8	11.3	17.5	22.5	0.0
	21.1	4.7	14.1	30.6	22.3	24.1	14.9	37.7	27.9	25.0
METHAM-PHETAMINE	0.0	0.0	0.0	0.0	0.0	0.0	0.0	0.0	0.0	0.0
	0.0	0.0	0.0	0.0	0.0	0.0	0.0	0.0	0.0	0.0
PCP	0.9	1.0	0.7	0.7	0.6	1.1	0.6	1.6	1.1	0.0
	1.1	1.3	1.5	0.6	2.7	0.2	1.2	1.9	0.3	0.0
MULTIPLE DRUGS	23.5	7.9	22.9	23.6	30.2	28.6	20.7	28.4	28.2	7.7
	28.7	9.3	18.5	40.0	33.7	30.8	23.5	35.7	37.9	12.5
Total Males	(N)	418	288	284	351	847	1186	257	649	39
Total Females	(N)	150	135	160	264	490	740	154	290	8

PERCENT POSITIVE FOR DRUGS, BY OFFENSE CATEGORY

Offense	N by Sex		Cocaine		Marijuana		Methamphetamine		PCP		Any Drug	
	M	F	M	F	M	F	M	F	M	F	M	F
VIOLENT OFFENSE	456	206	30.7	39.3	40.6	33.5	0.0	0.0	0.4	2.4	60.7	65.5
Robbery	81	37	25.9	51.4	61.7	27.0	0.0	0.0	0.0	5.4	76.5	81.1
Assault	271	133	32.5	37.6	37.3	36.1	0.0	0.0	0.7	3.0	58.3	64.7
Weapons	76	39	28.9	33.3	46.1	33.3	0.0	0.0	1.3	2.6	64.5	64.1
Other Violent	169	71	33.1	31.0	33.1	29.6	0.0	0.0	0.0	1.4	57.4	53.5
PROPERTY OFFENSE	602	311	48.3	65.9	33.6	19.3	0.0	0.0	1.0	1.3	72.8	78.8
Larceny/Theft	176	120	47.2	52.5	32.4	10.8	0.0	0.0	1.7	0.8	72.7	63.3
Burglary	45	14	44.4	57.1	24.4	28.6	0.0	0.0	2.2	0.0	66.7	85.7
Stolen Vehicle	24	8	50.0	37.5	41.7	37.5	0.0	0.0	0.0	0.0	83.3	75.0
Other Property	493	262	48.5	64.9	33.5	19.8	0.0	0.0	0.8	1.5	73.2	77.9
DRUG OFFENSE	848	505	52.6	80.8	48.8	25.0	0.0	0.0	1.2	1.0	88.8	92.9
Drug Sales	272	161	55.9	81.4	42.3	21.7	0.0	0.0	1.8	1.2	87.9	88.2
Drug Possession	684	410	53.7	80.0	49.4	26.1	0.0	0.0	0.9	1.0	89.6	93.9
PROSTITUTION	39	185	43.6	66.5	35.9	31.9	0.0	0.0	0.0	0.5	61.5	88.6
OTHER OFFENSE	608	208	38.0	51.4	35.9	24.5	0.0	0.0	0.5	0.0	66.1	67.8

James C. Howell and Scott H. Decker, in *The Youth Gangs, Drugs, and Violence Connection* (Office of Juvenile Justice and Delinquency Prevention, Washington, D.C., 1999), explored the relationship between drugs and gang violence. They questioned the stereotypical interpretation that gang violence was linked to the increasingly violent drug business. Instead, they proposed that in most cases street gangs are not dealing drugs, but that individuals within the gang become involved in drugs, drawing friends and partners into the business. Gang involvement may promote individual participation in violence, drug use, and drug trafficking, and perhaps prolong gang-member involvement in drug sales.

Howell and Decker quote Ira Reiner, Los Angeles County district attorney, who in 1992 concluded, after a comprehensive assessment of Los Angeles youth gangs:

Gang members are heavy drug users and even heavier drug sellers [than nongang youth], yet drugs and gangs are not two halves of the same phenomenon. Though they threaten many of the same neighborhoods and involve some of the same people, gangs and drugs must be treated as separate evils.

Reiner also concluded that, although many individual gang members (and former members) are involved in drugs, "drugs remain peripheral to the purposes and activities of the gang."

TABLE 5.8

Drug use among arrestees in New York City, New York, 1999 [CONTINUED]

HISTORIC TRENDS IN PERCENT POSITIVE, BY DRUG

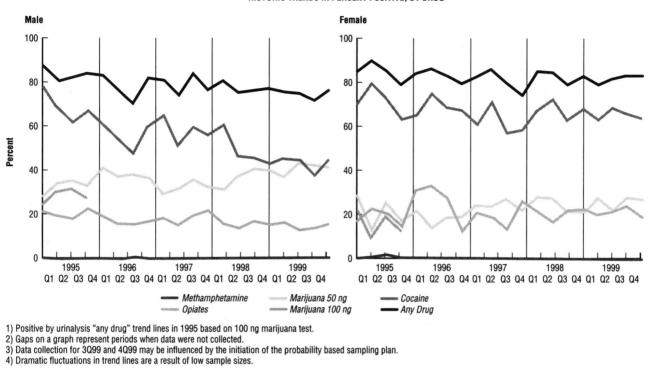

Legend:
— Methamphetamine — Marijuana 50 ng — Cocaine
— Opiates — Marijuana 100 ng — Any Drug

1) Positive by urinalysis "any drug" trend lines in 1995 based on 100 ng marijuana test.
2) Gaps on a graph represent periods when data were not collected.
3) Data collection for 3Q99 and 4Q99 may be influenced by the initiation of the probability based sampling plan.
4) Dramatic fluctuations in trend lines are a result of low sample sizes.

SOURCE: "1999, Adult Program Findings, New York City, New York," in *Arrestee Drug Abuse Monitoring Program,* National Institute of Justice, Washington, D.C., 2000

Studies of gangs in different cities have found that the "gangs" most heavily involved in dealing drugs are not actually youth gangs but criminal organizations calling themselves gangs. Because the rapid increase in gang activity coincided with the rise of crack, authorities assume that the two are linked. But Howell and Decker think that the lack of economic opportunity, rather than the desire to deal drugs, may drive many inner-city youths into gang participation. Crack dealing does lead to violence, both among dealers and within the community, but the connection to youth gangs, according to Howell and Decker, is still poorly understood and has been oversimplified by the media.

Sociologists and law enforcement officials maintain that juveniles join gangs for a variety of reasons, including a sense of belonging and identity—something that many who come from broken homes lack. Children are recruited to participate in a wide range of illegal activities because they will not be criminally prosecuted. This protects the older gang members from arrest.

Experts assume that youths are drawn to the drug trade because of the potentially large profits to be made as lookouts and runners for crack houses, as well as for couriers and sellers. The promise of financial reward is especially tempting in areas where employment opportunities are nearly nonexistent.

John P. Moore and Craig P. Terrett, in *Highlights of the 1997 National Youth Gang Survey* (Office of Juvenile Justice and Delinquency Prevention, Washington, D.C., 1999), reported on survey responses from over three thousand local law enforcement agencies across the country. Respondents estimated that 42 percent of the youth gangs in their area were involved in the street sale of drugs, while 33 percent were involved in drug distribution. According to the responses, gang members were responsible for 33 percent of crack cocaine sales, 32 percent of marijuana sales, 16 percent of powder cocaine sales, 12 percent of methamphetamine sales, and 9 percent of heroin sales. The respondents also reported a high degree of gang-member involvement in aggravated assault and larceny/theft (28 percent), burglary (26 percent), and robbery (13 percent). These percentages have decreased since 1994—consistent with the national decline in both adult and juvenile violent-crime arrests.

LEGACY OF THE CRACK COCAINE SCARE

In the 1980s crack cocaine cast a frightening pall over the United States. Authorities warned of instant addiction

TABLE 5.9

Estimated number of prisoners in custody of state correctional authorities, by the most serious offense, 1990–97

Most serious offense	Number of inmates in state prison							
	1990	1991	1992	1993	1994	1995	1996	1997
Total	684,544	728,605	778,245	828,400	904,647	989,005	1,032,676	1,075,167
Violent offenses	313,600	339,500	369,100	393,500	425,700	459,600	484,800	507,800
Murder[1]	72,000	77,200	85,900	92,800	100,700	110,600	118,200	125,800
Manslaughter	13,200	13,100	14,000	14,600	15,200	16,300	16,800	17,000
Rape	24,500	25,500	27,300	27,100	27,700	28,500	28,200	27,500
Other sexual assault	39,100	43,000	46,200	49,000	53,300	57,000	60,700	64,200
Robbery	99,200	107,800	113,600	122,100	131,700	139,600	146,100	152,000
Assault	53,300	59,000	67,600	72,200	80,100	89,000	95,200	100,500
Other violent[2]	12,400	13,100	14,500	15,600	17,000	18,600	19,600	20,700
Property offenses	173,700	180,700	181,600	189,600	207,000	226,600	231,700	236,400
Burglary	87,200	90,300	90,500	94,300	101,800	108,900	111,700	114,900
Larceny	34,800	35,700	33,500	35,300	39,600	44,500	45,000	45,100
Motor vehicle theft	14,400	16,000	18,100	18,900	19,700	21,300	20,200	19,800
Fraud	20,200	20,400	20,200	21,300	23,600	26,300	27,600	28,900
Other property[3]	17,100	18,200	19,400	19,800	22,300	25,600	27,200	27,700
Drug offenses	148,600	155,200	168,100	177,000	193,500	212,800	216,900	222,100
Public-order offenses[4]	45,500	49,500	56,300	64,000	74,400	86,500	96,000	106,200
Other/unspecified[5]	3,100	2,900	3,200	4,300	3,900	3,500	3,200	2,700

Note: Previously published estimates for 1992-96 have been revised based on data from the 1997 Survey of Inmates in State Correctional Facilities. The offense distributions for year-end 1991 and 1997 are based on survey data. The offense distributions for other years are estimated using forward and backward stock-flow methods. All estimates are based on the total number of prisoners in physical custody, including those with sentences of 1 year or less and those who were unsentenced. Due to rounding, detail may not sum to total.
[1]Includes nonnegligent manslaughter.
[2]Includes extortion, intimidation, criminal endangerment, and other violent offenses.
[3]Includes possession and selling of stolen property, destruction of property, trespassing, vandalism, criminal tampering, and other property offenses.
[4]Includes weapons, drunk driving, escape, court offenses, obstruction, commercialized vice, morals and decency charges, liquor law violations, and other public-order offenses.
[5]Includes juvenile offenses and unspecified felonies.

SOURCE: "Table 1.13. Estimated number of prisoners in custody of State correctional authorities, by the most serious offense, 1990–97," in *Correctional Populations in the United States, 1997,* Department of Justice, Washington, DC, 2000

and predicted a generation of crack-addicted babies. Dealers turned neighborhoods into drug markets. Heavily armed gangs fought over turf, and murder rates shot up.

However, a decade later it appeared that the worst fears were unfounded. Crack did not spread as rapidly as some expected, since it appealed mainly to hardcore drug users. Nor did it prove instantly addictive; many crack users, once considered virtually untreatable, have been quite successfully treated. The number of crack users began to fall dramatically in the 1990s. In the latest *National Household Survey on Drug Abuse* only 2 percent of the American population reported ever having used crack.

In 1998, for the seventh straight year, serious crime in the United States declined. Robbery fell 11 percent, and murder rates dropped 8 percent. According to Alfred Blumstein, a criminologist at Carnegie Mellon University, the decline in robbery is particularly significant. He believes it reflects a diminished demand for crack cocaine, since "robbery is a favorite way to get drugs." He also credits the strength of the economy, which provides jobs to unskilled young people who had previously turned to selling drugs when they were shut out of the job market.

However, the aftershocks of the crack scare can still be felt today. In the first 10 years after Congress tough-

ened drug laws in response to the crack "epidemic," the number of people imprisoned for drug offenses increased more than 400 percent.

Though crack has a relatively limited appeal, the drug accounts for a high percentage of prisoners serving time for drug violations. Crack was the drug involved for 40.7 percent of state prisoners convicted of a drug offense. The most frequently involved drug among federal drug offenders was powder cocaine (42.2 percent), but crack was second, at 26.6 percent.

Sentencing Disparity

Crack cocaine has been the focus of harsh penalties under mandatory minimum sentencing laws. Table 5.15 shows the disparity in federal sentencing for powder-cocaine and crack offenses. Federal courts treat quantities of crack cocaine 100 times more seriously than the same quantities of powder cocaine. So, for example, 5 grams of crack carries the same five-year minimum sentence as 500 grams of powder cocaine. This is often referred to as the "100:1 sentencing disparity."

Mandatory minimum sentences also vary considerably from state to state. Georgia, for instance, mandates a life sentence for the sale of any amount of cocaine—even a few grams—if the seller has previously been convicted of a felony. Nevada, on the other hand, mandates a one-year sentence for the sale of any amount of cocaine by a first-time offender.

According to Jonathan P. Caulkin, C. Peter Rydell, William L. Schwabe, and James Chiesa, in *Mandatory* *Minimum Drug Sentences: Throwing Away the Key or the Taxpayers' Money?* (Drug Policy Research Center, RAND Corporation, Santa Monica, CA, 1997), basing sentences on quantity of mixture in possession, type of mixture (crack or powder), and number of prior drug felony convictions omits several important factors. It does not consider intent to break the law, importance of the offender's role in the drug-dealing operation, and position in the overall drug-commerce hierarchy.

Therefore, a cocaine wholesaler who deals in one-pound quantities of powder cocaine (454 grams) is not

FIGURE 5.3

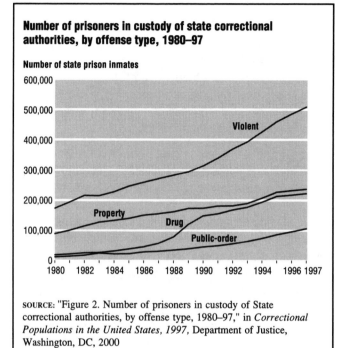

Number of prisoners in custody of state correctional authorities, by offense type, 1980–97

SOURCE: "Figure 2. Number of prisoners in custody of State correctional authorities, by offense type, 1980–97," in *Correctional Populations in the United States, 1997*, Department of Justice, Washington, DC, 2000

TABLE 5.10

Growth of sentenced prisoners under state jurisdiction, by offense and gender, 1990–98

	Total		Male		Female	
	Increase, 1990–98	Percent of total	Increase, 1990–98	Percent of total	Increase, 1990–98	Percent of total
Total	**452,100**	**100%**	**418,600**	**100%**	**33,600**	**100%**
Violent	229,300	51	220,300	53	9,000	27
Property	67,900	15	61,200	15	6,800	20
Drug	87,100	19	75,000	18	12,100	36
Public-order	68,100	15	62,600	15	5,600	17

SOURCE: A. Beck, "Partitioning the total growth of sentenced prisoners under state jurisdiction, by offense and gender, 1990–98," in *Prisoners in 1999*, Bureau of Justice Statistics, Washington, DC, 2000

TABLE 5.11

Estimated number of sentenced prisoners under state jurisdiction, by offense, gender, race, and Hispanic origin, 1998

Offenses	All	Male	Female	White	Black	Hispanic
Total	**1,141,700**	**1,071,400**	**70,300**	**380,400**	**531,100**	**194,000**
Violent offenses	**545,200**	**525,100**	**20,100**	**180,300**	**257,700**	**87,600**
Murder[a]	134,600	128,500	6,100	42,400	67,100	21,500
Manslaughter	17,600	15,800	1,800	6,200	7,100	3,400
Rape	29,600	29,300	300	13,500	12,100	2,400
Other sexual assault	71,200	70,500	700	41,400	17,500	9,300
Robbery	159,600	154,600	5,000	33,000	96,700	25,400
Assault	109,500	104,500	5,000	33,800	48,800	22,000
Other violent	23,100	21,800	1,300	10,000	8,400	3,800
Property offenses	**242,900**	**224,500**	**18,500**	**104,200**	**97,700**	**34,000**
Burglary	118,000	114,400	3,600	49,900	48,100	16,600
Larceny	45,500	39,600	5,900	17,200	20,500	6,100
Motor vehicle theft	20,100	19,400	800	8,000	7,300	4,400
Fraud	30,200	23,300	6,900	15,700	11,100	2,800
Other property	29,100	27,800	1,300	13,300	10,700	4,100
Drug offenses	**236,800**	**212,900**	**23,900**	**46,300**	**134,800**	**51,700**
Public-order offenses[b]	**113,900**	**106,500**	**7,500**	**49,200**	**39,400**	**20,100**
Other/unspecified[c]	**2,800**	**2,500**	**200**	**400**	**1,500**	**700**

Note: Data are for inmates with a sentence of more than 1 year under the jurisdiction of State correctional authorities. The number of inmates by offense were estimated using 1997 Survey of Inmates in State Correctional Facilities and rounded to the nearest 100.

[a] Includes nonnegligent manslaughter.
[b] Includes weapons, drunk driving, court offenses, commercialized vice, morals and decency charges, liquor law violations, and other public-order offenses.
[c] Includes juvenile offenses and unspecified felonies.

SOURCE: A. Beck, "Estimated number of sentenced prisoners under state jurisdiction, by offense, gender, race, and Hispanic origin, 1998," in *Prisoners in 1999*, Bureau of Justice Statistics, Washington, D.C., 2000

subject to a mandatory minimum sentence under federal law, but the street-level dealer, who turns a small amount of cocaine into a like quantity of crack, is.

COCAINE SENTENCING AND RACE. The cocaine/ crack sentencing disparity has changed the racial make-up of America's prisons. Because of the federal government's increased emphasis on stiffer crack penalties, law enforcement began concentrating much of its attention on the highly visible, often violent crack trade in inner cities instead of on the larger traffic in cocaine going on across the country. As a result, nearly 90 percent of the prisoners convicted of a crack offense under federal law are black.

TABLE 5.12

Growth of sentenced prisoners under state jurisdiction, by offense, race, and Hispanic origin, 1990–98

	White		Black		Hispanic	
	Increase, 1990–98	Percent of total	Increase, 1990–98	Percent of total	Increase, 1990–98	Percent of total
Total	**137,000**	**100%**	**216,400**	**100%**	**78,700**	**102%**
Violent	62,700	45	111,600	52	43,900	56
Property	29,000	21	26,800	12	9,800	12
Drug	16,700	12	55,000	25	13,000	18
Public-order	29,500	21	22,800	11	11,800	15

SOURCE: A. Beck, "Partitioning the total growth of sentenced prisoners under state jurisdiction, by offense, race, and Hispanic origin, 1990–98," in *Prisoners in 1999,* Bureau of Justice Statistics, Washington, DC, 2000

Reasons for the Policy

Congress has justified the 100:1 sentencing disparity based on the belief that crack is far more dangerous than powdered cocaine to both the user and the community. Compared with powder cocaine, crack provides a faster, more intense high—which increases the risk of addiction. Furthermore, because crack is so cheap, it is available to many more people.

Although approximately half of all crack users are white, most images of crack users tend to be of minorities in central cities. Supporters of harsher penalties for crack use point to the breakdown of families in these areas. They further note the violent drug trade that has developed to market crack—a trade, they believe, that has contributed to the decay of the inner city.

Opponents of the sentencing policy believe that many people find the harsher penalties acceptable because they are generally levied against blacks, not whites. They observe that cocaine is cocaine and that the huge disparity in sentencing is not fair. They further note that many of the problems associated with crack use have as much to do with poverty, unemployment, and homelessness as the drug itself.

The Supreme Court Decides

The case of *Johnson v. U.S.* (Fourth Circuit Court of Appeals, August 31, 1995, unpublished) was appealed to the U.S. Supreme Court to determine whether the "existence of widely disparate sentencing schemes for the same offense present important issues of federal law." The

TABLE 5.13

Number of sentenced inmates in federal prisons, by most serious offense, 1990, 1995, and 1998

Offenses	Number of sentenced inmates in Federal prisons			Percent change, 1990–98	Percent of total growth, 1990–98
	1990	1995	1998		
Total	56,989	88,101	108,925	91.1%	100.0%
Violent offenses	9,557	11,321	12,656	32.4%	6.0%
Homicide[a]	1,233	966	1,344	9.0	0.2
Robbery	5,158	6,341	8,773	70.1	7.0
Other violent	3,166	4,014	2,539	-19.8	-1.2
Property offenses	7,935	7,524	8,627	8.7%	1.3%
Burglary	442	164	249	-43.7	-0.4
Fraud	5,113	5,629	6,465	26.4	2.6
Other property	2,380	1,731	1,913	-19.6	-0.9
Drug offenses	30,470	51,737	63,011	106.8%	62.7%
Public-order offenses	8,585	15,762	22,273	159.4%	26.4
Immigration	1,728	3,612	7,430	330.0	11.0
Weapons	3,073	7,519	8.742	184.5	10.9
Other public-order	3,784	4,631	6,101	61.2	5.0
Other/unspecified[b]	442	1,757	2,358	433.5%	3.7%

Note: All data are from the BJS Federal justice database. Data for 1990 and 1995 are for December 31. Data for 1998 are for September 30. Numbers may differ from the Federal Bureau of Prisons' count because the Federal Justice Statistics Program includes prisoners in transit. Data are based on all sentenced inmates, regardless of sentence length.

[a] Includes murder, nonnegligent manslaughter, and negligent manslaughter.
[b] Includes offenses not classifiable or not a violation of the United States Code.

SOURCE: A. Beck, "Number of sentenced inmates in federal prisons, by most serious offense, 1990, 1995, and 1998," in *Prisoners in 1999,* Bureau of Justice Statistics, Washington, D.C., 2000

TABLE 5.14

Percentage of drug offenders in state and federal prisons

	Percent of drug offenders	
	State	Federal
Type of drug offense		
Possession	27.1%	5.3%
Trafficking[a]	70.1	85.8
Other	2.8	8.9
Status at arrest		
None	46.2%	75.9%
Status	53.8	24.1
On parole[b]	27.4	10.2
On probation	25.9	13.8
Escaped from custody	0.5	0.2
Criminal history		
None	17.4%	40.6%
Priors	82.6	59.4
Violent recidivists	23.6	12.1
Drug recidivists only	14.1	15.9
Other recidivists[c]	44.9	31.4
Number of prior probation/incarceration sentences		
0	17.4%	40.6%
1	20.2	19.5
2	17.5	15.5
3–5	27.2	18.2
6–10	11.5	5.0
11 or more	6.3	1.2
Type of drug involved in current offense[d]		
Marijuana/hashish	12.9%	18.9%
Cocaine/crack	72.1	65.5
Heroin/other opiates	12.8	9.9
Depressants	1.2	0.6
Stimulants	9.9	11.0
Hallucinogens	1.1	1.7

[a]Includes those reporting an intent to distribute.
[b]Includes supervised release.
[c]Includes recidivists with unknown offense types.
[d]More than one type of drug may have been involved in the current offense.

SOURCE: Christopher J. Mumola, "Percent of drug offenders in state and federal prisons," in *Substance Abuse and Treatment, State and Federal Prisoners, 1997*, Bureau of Justice Statistics, Washington, DC, 1999

TABLE 5.15

Federal mandatory minimum sentences for cocaine offenses

	Grams of mixture (prior drug felony convictions)	
Sentence	Powder	Crack
None	> 0 gm (None)	Same
15 days	> 0 gm (One)	Same
90 days	> 0 gm (Two or more)	Same
5 years	≥ 500 gm (None)	≥ 5 gm (None)[a]
10 years	≥ 500 gm (One or more)	≥ 5 gm (One or more)
	≥ 5000 gm (None)	≥ 50 gm (None)
20 years	≥ 5000 gm (One)	≥ 50 gm (One)
Life	≥ 5000 gm (Two or more)	≥ 50 gm (Two or more)

[a]There are also five-year mandatory minimum crack sentences for simple possession of more than 5 grams (no prior convictions), more then 3 grams (one prior), and more than 1 gram (two or more priors).

SOURCE: Jonathan P. Caulkins, C. Peter Rydell, William L. Schwabe, et al., "Federal mandatory minimum sentences for cocaine offenses," in *Mandatory Minimum Drug Sentences: Throwing Away the Key or the Taxpayers' Money?*, MR-827-DPRC, RAND, Santa Monica, CA, 1997

certiorari (that is, it refused to hear) to *Johnson vs. U.S.* (64 LW 3501), which let stand the lower court's ruling.

U.S. Sentencing Commission Considers the Disparity

The U.S. Sentencing Commission, an independent agency in the judicial branch of government, is charged with developing and monitoring sentencing policies and practices for the federal courts. The commission issues sentencing guidelines that, subject to congressional review, prescribe the appropriate form and severity of punishment for offenders convicted of federal crimes.

In 1995 the commission issued a report identifying the 100:1 federal sentencing ratio for crack and powder-cocaine offenses as "a primary cause of the growing disparity between sentences for black and white Federal defendants." The commission recommended that, while a greater penalty for crack was justifiable, the huge differences between the sentences were not. Based on this, they recommended that more flexible sentencing be considered. The recommendation met with a frosty reception in Congress, which, with the agreement of President Clinton, rejected the proposal.

Two years later, in April 1997, the commission submitted new recommendations on cocaine sentencing. Again, the commission found the huge disparity unacceptable. In its unanimous recommendation, the commission said:

> Although research and public support may support somewhat higher penalties for crack than for powder cocaine, a 100-to-1 quantity ratio cannot be justified. . . . The commission is firmly and unanimously in agreement that the current penalty differential for federal powder and crack cocaine cases should be reduced by changing the quantity levels that trigger mandatory minimum penalties for both powder and crack cocaine.

Fourth Circuit had already ruled against Johnson, citing *U.S. v. Fisher* (58 F.3d 96, Fourth Circuit Court of Appeals, 1995). In *U.S. v. Fisher,* the defendants, convicted of selling crack, had appealed on the grounds that the disparity in federal sentencing for crack and powder-cocaine offenses was unconstitutional.

The Fourth Circuit Court of Appeals observed that Congress had intended "to address separately the trafficking of cocaine base and, because of its more destructive nature, to impose a heavier penalty for violations involving that substance." Furthermore, it intended "to carve out a heavier penalty for the particularly harmful form of cocaine known as 'cocaine base' or 'crack.'" The court concluded that since the "legislative history demonstrates that Congress intended . . . to penalize more severely violations involving crack cocaine," it was constitutional.

The U.S. Supreme Court agreed with the lower court's findings. On January 22, 1996, the Court denied

The commission offered a range of possible options. For example:

> For powder cocaine, the commission recommends that the current 500-gram trigger for the five-year mandatory minimum sentence should be reduced to a level between 125 and 375 grams, and for crack cocaine, the current five-gram trigger should be increased to between 25 and 75 grams. . . . The ten-year mandatory minimum penalties should be revised accordingly.

In his concurring opinion, Michael S. Gelacak, vice chairman of the Sentencing Commission, concluded that

> Congress established an unfair mandatory minimum of five years for trafficking in five grams of crack cocaine. . . . The result is extremely severe sentences for those at the lower ends of the drug distribution chain.
>
> I support severe sentences for serious criminal conduct. I oppose a penalty structure that results in unfair sentences, and it is clear to me that the current mandatory minimum sentences for five grams of crack cocaine are unjust and that failing to correct the imbalance with powder cocaine does not serve justice.
>
> I am also troubled by the economics of this penalty structure. Incarceration is expensive. Whether lengthy federal prison sentences for street-level crime is the wisest use of scarce resources deserves far more consideration. I believe the country would be better served by our dealing more directly with these issues.

Although the Sentencing Commission makes recommendations to Congress, it does not have the power to change sentencing policies. Since the commission's recommendations in 1995 and 1997, Congress as of 2001 had not reduced the mandatory minimums. Each year, the commission publishes a manual of sentencing guidelines that federal judges are expected to follow. As of 2001 the latest edition, the *United States Sentencing Commission Supplement to the 2000 Guidelines Manual,* still contained the 100:1 disparity in mandatory minimum sentences between crack and powder-cocaine offenses.

IS THERE REALLY A DIFFERENCE BETWEEN CRACK AND POWDERED COCAINE?

Drs. Dorothy K. Hatsukami and Marian W. Fischman, in "Crack Cocaine and Cocaine Hydrochloride—Are the Differences Myth or Reality?" (*Journal of the American Medical Association,* November 20, 1996), studied cocaine research to determine the differences and similarities between the effects of crack cocaine and cocaine hydrochloride (generally powdered, but can be taken intravenously).

They found that "cocaine in any form produces the same physiological and subjective effects." They also noted, however, that

> . . . the route of administration plays a major role in the rate of onset as well as intensity and duration of a drug's effect. The more immediate and greater the magnitude

of effect, the greater likelihood that the drug will be abused. Orally ingested cocaine achieves maximum concentration most slowly, followed by the intranasal (snorting through the nose) route. Intravenous and smoked cocaine achieve maximal concentration and effect most rapidly.

They further found that "most studies show that cocaine smokers and intravenous users often use more cocaine than intranasal users." In addition,

> Regardless of whether the use of cocaine is in the hydrochloride or crack form, cocaine users are heavy users of other illicit and licit drugs. Crack cocaine users are more likely to use a greater variety of other illicit drugs than users of cocaine hydrochloride. This observation has been made even among adolescents.

The researchers also found crack users more likely to be depressed and to have more sex partners and acts of unprotected sex. As a result, "crack cocaine smokers have been found to have rates of HIV infection as high as those among intravenous drug users." The researchers did not link the violence often surrounding crack use to the pharmacology of the drug but rather to the social and cultural factors surrounding its sale.

Crack users were more frequently involved in drug sales and non-drug-related crime, although many may have been involved in these activities before they started smoking crack. Furthermore, the higher crime rate may well be linked to the social and cultural environment in which crack users live.

Hatsukami and Fischman noted that

> The issue is not the differences between crack cocaine and cocaine hydrochloride because they are essentially the same drug and can cause the same effects and consequences. The primary issues are the speed and intensity of delivery of the drug, the accessibility and cost of the unit price of the drug, and the cultural environment and social context in which the drug is used.

Based on these findings, the researchers recommended a 2:1–3:1 ratio in federal sentencing for crack and cocaine hydrochloride offenses, rather than the current 100:1. They concluded that

> Instead of using the differences between crack cocaine and cocaine hydrochloride to justify enormous differences in prison sentences for those convicted of selling cocaine, focusing on approaches that could lead to better treatment and prevention is a more constructive and ultimately more cost-effective approach to this issue.

ECSTASY ANTI-PROLIFERATION ACT OF 2000

Recognizing that the use of ecstasy (MDMA) is a rapidly growing problem among youths, Congress passed the Ecstasy Anti-Proliferation Act of 2000 (Public Law 106-310). One requirement of the bill was that the United States Sentencing Commission (USSC) "review and append existing sentencing guidelines to provide for increased penalties" reflecting the dangers caused by the rapidly growing use of ecstasy, the increase in illegal traffic, the young age of users, and other factors.

The USSC released its sentencing guidelines for MDMA offenses in May 2001 (*Report to Congress: MDMA Drug Offenses Explanation of Recent Guideline Amendments*). Effective November 1, 2001, the new guidelines require judges to impose much stiffer penalties on offenders convicted of ecstasy-related crimes in federal court. The new guidelines treat ecstasy somewhat more leniently than heroin but more punitively than cocaine.

The USSC cited several reasons why the drug will be treated more harshly than cocaine: (*a*) MDMA can cause more brain damage than cocaine; (*b*) it is marketed aggressively to youth; and (*c*) it is both a hallucinogen and a stimulant. Whereas there is a 100:1 sentencing disparity between crack and powder-cocaine offenses, there is a 2.5:1 disparity between MDMA and powder-cocaine offenses (1 gram of ecstasy carries the same sentence as 2.5 grams of cocaine).

IS INCARCERATION THE SOLUTION?

Harsher laws and penalties have not reduced overall drug use. General Barry McCaffrey, the head of the White House National Drug Control Policy Office, has said, "We can't incarcerate our way out of this problem." He believes that more than a quarter-million Americans in prison for drug offenses could be better dealt with in treatment programs—which, he says, would save up to $5 billion a year. He favors long sentences for dealers and treatment for low-level users.

The RAND Corporation's *Mandatory Minimum Drug Sentences* concluded that mandatory sentences are the least cost-effective way of reducing cocaine consumption. For violent crimes, long sentences keep the offenders off the street, it reported, but for drug crimes, "a jailed suppli-

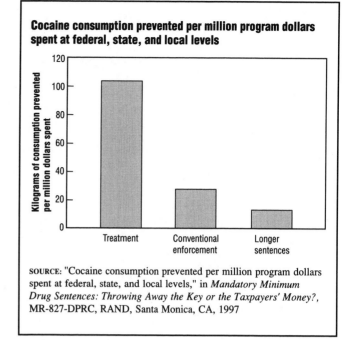

FIGURE 5.4

Cocaine consumption prevented per million program dollars spent at federal, state, and local levels

SOURCE: "Cocaine consumption prevented per million program dollars spent at federal, state, and local levels," in *Mandatory Minimum Drug Sentences: Throwing Away the Key or the Taxpayers' Money?*, MR-827-DPRC, RAND, Santa Monica, CA, 1997

er is often replaced by another supplier." The researchers feel that drug treatment is the most cost-effective way to reduce cocaine use. According to the RAND study, treatment of heavy users is eight to nine times more cost-effective than long mandatory sentences in reducing the market for powder cocaine. (See Figure 5.4.)

In February 2001 the Bush administration announced its drug budget for 2002. Coming after years of reduced federal spending for drug rehabilitation, the budget for drug treatment increased by $111 million. But long mandatory prison terms and locking up small-time dealers remains the strategy for Congress. According to Dr. James Alan Fox, dean of the College of Criminal Justice at Northeastern University, "For politicians, the drug debate is driven by the three R's—retribution, revenge, retaliation—and that leads to the fourth R, re-election."

CHAPTER 6

DRUG TRAFFICKING

In America, all matters relating to public health receive careful attention. No other country gives such careful study to questions that affect it, or makes such determined efforts to improve it and raise it to a higher level. In the last few years our attention has been drawn to a condition which has now become a grave menace to our nation's welfare, something which is extraneous, artificial, and wholly uncalled for, yet which is assuming such proportions that we must recognize it as a threatening danger. This is the great increase of the drug habit. To meet this danger, most drastic laws regulating the sale and distribution of drugs have been in force for a number of years; yet we see these laws, theoretically perfect, totally unable to cope with the situation.

— Ellen N. LaMotte, writing in *The Atlantic Monthly,* June 1922

CRIMINAL PENALTIES FOR DRUG TRAFFICKING

Stiff Federal Penalties

The Controlled Substances Act (PL 91-513, 1970) provides penalties for the unlawful manufacture, distribution, and dispensing, or trafficking, of controlled substances, based on the schedule (rank) of the drug or substance. Generally, the more dangerous the drug and the larger the quantity involved, the stiffer the penalty.

Trafficking of heroin, cocaine, LSD, and PCP—all of them Schedule I or II drugs—carries penalties of not less than 5 years for the first offense to not less than 10 years to life imprisonment for the second offense. (See Table 6.1.) Trafficking of Schedule I and II drugs can also carry fines that reach well into the millions of dollars.

If death or serious injury results from a second offense for cocaine or PCP trafficking, the penalty is always at least a life sentence. (See Table 6.1.) These severe penalties were included in the Narcotics Penalties and Enforcement Act of 1986 (PL 99-570). Since 1988 the president has had the authority to seek the death

penalty in any case in which a drug kingpin (a major drug dealer) commits or orders a murder.

Offenses involving Schedule III, IV, and V drugs carry penalties of not more than 1–5 years for a first offense and not more than 30 years for a second offense. Fines range up to $250,000 for an individual, and up to $1 million for more than one individual, for a first offense; and, for a second offense, up to $2 million for an individual and up to $10 million for more than one individual. (See Table 6.1.)

SPECIAL MARIJUANA PENALTIES. Table 6.2 illustrates the penalties for marijuana, hashish, and hashish oil trafficking. Special penalties exist for marijuana because it has no medical use officially recognized by the federal government and because of the very large quantities in which it is manufactured, transported, and sold. Trafficking of 1,000 kilograms (kg) or more of marijuana can carry life imprisonment and up to a $10 million fine for the first offense. Smaller quantities of less than 50 kg carry a penalty up to 5 years for the first offense and up to 10 years for the second offense. Fines for trafficking in these smaller quantities range from $250,000 to $2 million.

State Laws

The states have the discretionary power to make their own drug laws. Possession of marijuana may be a misdemeanor in one state but a felony in another. Prison sentences can also vary for the same charges in different states—distribution of 500 grams of cocaine as a Class C felony may specify 10–50 years in one state and 24–40 years in another.

Changes in 1990 (PL 101-647) to the Controlled Substances Act led to more than 450 new drug laws in 44 states and the District of Columbia. Most states have followed the model of the Controlled Substances Act and have enacted laws that facilitate seizure of drug-trafficking profits, specify greater penalties for trafficking, and promote "user accountability" by punishing drug users.

TABLE 6.1

Federal trafficking penalties*

CSA	2nd Offense	1st Offense	Quantity	Drug	Quantity	1st Offense	2nd Offense
I and II	Not less than 10 years, Not more than life.	Not less than 5 years, Not more than 40 years.	10-99 gm pure or 100-999 gm mixture	Methamphetamine	100 gm or more pure or 1 kg or more mixture.	Not less than 10 years, Not more than life.	Not less than 20 years, Not more than life.
			100-999 gm mixture	Heroin	1 kg or more mixture		
			500-4,999 gm mixture	Cocaine	5 kg or more mixture	If death or serious injury, not less than 20 years, or more than life.	If death or serious injury, not less than life.
	If death or serious injury, not less than life.	If death or serious injury, not less than 20 years, or more than life.	5-49 gm mixture	Cocaine Base	50 gm or more mixture		
			10-99 gm pure or 100-999 gm mixture	PCP	100 gm or more pure or 1 kg or more mixture		
	Fine of not more than $4 million individual, $10 million other than individual.	Fine of not more than $2 million individual, $5 million other than individual.	1-9 gm mixture	LSD	10 gm or more mixture	Fine of not more than $4 million individual, $10 million other than individual.	Fine of not more than $8 million individual, $20 million other than individual.
			40-399 gm mixture	Fentanyl	400 gm or more mixture		
			10-99 gm mixture	Fentanyl Analogue	100 gm or more mixture		

CSA	Drug	Quantity	1st Offense	2nd Offense
III	Others (Law does not include marijuana, hashish, or hash oil.)	Any	Not more than 20 years. If death or serious injury, not less than 20 years, not more than life. Fine $1 million individual, $5 million not individual.	Not more than 30 years. If death or serious injury, life. Fine $2 million individual, $10 million not individual.
III	All (Includes anabolic steroids as of 2-27-91.)	Any	Not more than 5 years. Fine not more than $250,000 individual, $1 million not individual.	Not more than 30 years. If death or serious injury, life. Fine $2 million individual, $10 million not individual.
IV	All	Any	Not more than 3 years. Fine not more than $250,000 individual, $1 million not individual.	Not more than 30 years. If death or serious injury, life. Fine $2 million individual, $10 million not individual.
V	All	Any	Not more than 1 year. Fine not more than $100,000 individual, $250,000 not individual.	Not more than 30 years. If death or serious injury, life. Fine $2 million individual, $10 million not individual.

*Does not include marijuana, hashish or hash oil.

SOURCE: *Drugs of Abuse*, Drug Enforcement Administration, Arlington, VA, 1996

IS THE PROFIT WORTH THE RISK?

Only in the illicit drug industry can seizures of between 10 and 30 percent of production, the forfeiture of a (small) percentage of financial and other assets and the loss, through death or imprisonment, of a percentage of operatives, impose merely an imperceptible or short-term impact on retail price and still allow large net profits at every stage of the distribution chain.

— *World Drug Report,* United Nations Drug Programme, New York, 1997

Despite the possibility of long prison terms, up to life imprisonment, many drug dealers feel the enormous potential profits are worth the risk. The media often report drug "busts" and indictments of persons involved in multimillion- or billion-dollar operations. Paying fines of hundreds of thousands of dollars, or even millions of dollars, becomes part of doing business when the profits are so high. Exact figures on the amount of money made from drug trafficking and sales are impossible to calculate.

AN ENORMOUS WORLDWIDE TRADE

The United Nations, in its *Economic and Social Consequences of Drug Abuse and Illicit Drug Trafficking* (International Drug Programme, New York, 1998), estimated the total revenue of the world drug trade at about $400 billion. This amounts to about 8 percent of all international trade.

The *World Drug Report 2000* (International Drug Programme, Oxford University Press, 2001) estimates that 180 million people—4.2 percent of the world's population over age 15—were users of illicit drugs in the 1990s. The survey concluded that about 9 million used heroin; 14 million, cocaine; 144 million, cannabis; and 29 million, amphetamine-type stimulants.

OVERALL PRODUCTION OF ILLICIT DRUGS

Tables 6.3 and 6.4 show estimates of how much opium, cocaine, and marijuana are cultivated and produced. Cannabis production increased slightly between 1999 and 2000 but remained near its lowest level in 15 years. The total number of hectares of coca cultivated in 1999 and 2000 was at the lowest level in more than 10 years, in spite of the sharp rise in cultivation in Colombia. Even so, the total number of metric tons of coca leaf produced in 1999 and 2000 was at the highest level in more than 10 years, and more than double the amounts estimated for 1993 and 1994.

Despite a dramatic decline in Mexican opium cultivation between 1998 and 2000, the world total rose to 201,965 hectares of opium cultivated in 2000. (See Table 6.3.) Much of this can be attributed to a rise in Burmese opium production. Eighty-six percent of the world's opium poppy, which yields more than 90 percent of the world's opium gum, is cultivated in Burma and Afghanistan. (Note: The figures in Tables 6.3 and 6.4 are estimates and may vary considerably from year to year.)

COCAINE

According to the Bureau for International Narcotics and Law Enforcement of the U.S. Department of State, in its *International Narcotics Control Strategy Report, 2000* (Washington, D.C., 2001):

> Though cocaine use has fallen sharply in the last decade and half, cocaine remains our greatest illicit drug threat. Despite successes in limiting the Andean coca crop, cocaine still flows to the U.S. in enormous quantities. The 300 or so metric tons of cocaine that typically flow to the U.S. in any given year are enough to supply the consuming public with high purity drugs at stable prices.

Similarly, *The NNICC Report 1997: The Supply of Illicit Drugs to the United States* (Washington, D.C., 1998), prepared by the National Narcotics Intelligence Consumers Committee (NNICC), found cocaine "readily available in all major U.S. metropolitan areas." The General Accounting Office, in *Drug Control—Observations on Elements of the Federal Drug Control Strategy* (Washington, D.C., 1997), noted that "the amount of cocaine and heroin seized between 1990 and 1995 had little impact on the availability of illegal drugs in the United States in satisfying estimated U.S. demand."

TABLE 6.2

Federal drug trafficking penalties—Marijuana, 1996

Description	Quantity	1st Offense	2nd Offense
Marijuana	1,000 kg or more mixture; or 1,000 or more plants	• Not less than 10 years, not more than life • If death or serious injury, not less than 20 years, not more than life • Fine not more than $4 million individual, $10 million other than individual	• Not less than 20 years, not more than life • If death or serious injury, not more than life • Fine not more than $8 million individual, $20 million other than individual
Marijuana	100 kg to 999 kg mixture; or 100-999 plants	• Not less than 5 years, not more than 40 years • If death or serious injury, not less than 20 years, not more than life • Fine not more than $2 million individual, $5 million other than individual	• Not less than 10 years, not more than life • If death or serious injury, not more than life • Fine not more than $4 million individual, $10 million other than individual
Marijuana	50 to 99 kg mixture; or 50 to 99 plants	• Not more than 20 years • If death or serious injury, not less than 20 years, not more than life • Fine $1 million individual, $5 million other than individual	•Not more than 30 years •If death or serious injury, not more than life •Fine $2 million individual, $10 million other than individual
Marijuana Hashish Hashish Oil	Less than 50 kg mixture 10 kg or more 1 kg or more	• Not more than 5 years • Fine not more than $250,000, $1 million other than individual	• Not more than 10 years • Fine $500,000 individual, $2 million other than individual

(Marijuana is a Schedule I Controlled Substance)

SOURCE: "Federal drug trafficking penalties—Marijuana, 1996," in *Drugs of Abuse*, Drug Enforcement Administration, Arlington, VA, 1996

Generally, this easy availability of cocaine was reflected in the stability in cocaine prices. In 1997 cocaine prices ranged from $10,000 to $42,000 per kilogram (2.2 pounds), a figure more or less unchanged from the previous four years. (See Table 6.5.) Cocaine prices ranged from $200 to $2,800 per ounce and $20 to $200 per gram. Crack prices varied from as little as $2 to as much as $50 per rock (single crystallized dose).

The purity of cocaine remained relatively high and stable between 1993 and 1997—at around 64 percent in one-gram amounts, and at somewhat higher levels in larger quantities. (See Table 6.6.) With the relatively low price of powdered cocaine, a growing number of crack users are buying powdered cocaine and making their own crack.

The Process of Making and Distributing Cocaine

The coca plant, from which cocaine is prepared, is grown primarily in Colombia, Peru, and Bolivia. In 1998 the Drug Enforcement Administration (DEA) estimated that 555 metric tons of cocaine base were produced in the Andean region. Of these 555 metric tons, an estimated 240 came from Peru, 165 from Colombia, and 150 from Bolivia. (See Table 6.7.)

Once the cocaine is converted into base, it is then transported from the jungles of Bolivia and Peru to southern

TABLE 6.3

Illicit drug cultivation worldwide, 1987–2000

All figures in hectares

	2000	1999	1998	1997	1996	1995	1994	1993	1992	1991	1990	1989	1988	1987
Opium														
Afghanistan	64,510	51,500	41,720	39,150	37,950	38,740	29,180	21,080	19,470	17,190	12,370	18,650	23,000	18,500
India[1]	-	-	-	2,050	3,100	4,750	5,500	4,400	-	-	-	-	-	-
Iran[1]	-	-	-	-	-	-	-	-	-	-	-	-	-	-
Pakistan	515	1,570	3,030	4,100	3,400	6,950	7,270	6,280	8,170	8,205	8,220	6,050	11,588	9,970
Total SW Asia	**65,025**	**53,070**	**44,750**	**45,300**	**44,450**	**50,440**	**41,950**	**31,760**	**27,640**	**25,395**	**20,590**	**24,700**	**34,588**	**28,470**
Burma	108,700	89,500	130,300	155,150	163,100	154,070	154,070	146,600	153,700	160,000	150,100	143,000	104,200	76,021
China	-	-	-	-	-	1,275	1,965	-	-	-	-	-	-	-
Laos	23,150	21,800	26,100	28,150	25,250	19,650	19,650	18,520	25,610	29,625	30,580	42,130	40,400	-
Thailand	890	835	1,350	1,650	2,170	1,750	2,110	2,110	2,050	3,000	3,435	4,075	2,843	2,934
Vietnam	2,300	2,100	3,000	6,150	3,150	-	-	-	-	192,625	184,185	189,205	147,443	78,955
Total SE Asia	**135,040**	**114,235**	**160,750**	**191,100**	**193,670**	**176,745**	**177,795**	**167,230**	**181,360**	**1,160**				
Colombia	-	7,500	6,100	6,600	6,300	6,540	20,000	20,000	20,000	3,400	3,200	4,500	na	na
Lebanon	-	-	-	-	90	150	-	440	na	1,145	845	1,220	710	-
Guatemala	-	-	-	-	-	39	50	438	730	3,765	5,450	6,600	5,001	5,160
Mexico	1,900	3,600	5,500	4,000	5,100	5,050	5,795	3,960	3,310					
Total Other	**1,900**	**11,100**	**11,600**	**10,600**	**11,490**	**11,779**	**25,845**	**24,838**	**24,040**	**9,470**	**9,495**	**12,320**	**5,711**	**5,160**
Total Opium	**201,965**	**178,405**	**217,100**	**247,000**	**249,610**	**238,964**	**245,590**	**223,828**	**233,040**	**227,490**	**214,200**	**226,225**	**187,742**	**112,585**
Coca														
Bolivia	14,600	21,800	38,000	45,800	48,100	48,600	48,100	47,200	45,500	47,900	50,300	52,900	48,900	41,300
Colombia	136,200	122,500	101,800	79,500	67,200	50,900	45,000	39,700	37,100	37,500	40,100	42,400	34,000	25,600
Peru	34,200	38,700	51,000	68,800	94,400	115,300	108,600	108,800	129,100	120,800	121,300	120,400	110,400	108,800
Ecuador	-	-	-	-	-	-	-	-	-	40	120	150	240	300
Total Coca	**185,000**	**183,000**	**190,800**	**194,100**	**209,700**	**214,800**	**201,700**	**195,700**	**211,700**	**206,240**	**211,820**	**215,850**	**193,540**	**176,000**
Cannabis														
Mexico	3,900	3,700	4,600	4,800	6,500	6,900	10,550	11,220	16,420	17,915	35,050	53,900	5,003	5,250
Colombia	5,000	5,000	5,000	5,000	5,000	5,000	4,986	5,000	2,000	2,000	1,500	2,270	4,188	5,005
Jamaica	-	-	-	317	527	305	308	744	389	950	1,220	280	607	680
Total Cannabis	**8,900**	**8,700**	**9,600**	**10,117**	**12,027**	**12,205**	**15,844**	**16,964**	**18,809**	**20,865**	**37,770**	**56,450**	**9,798**	**10,935**

[1]USG surveys in 1998 revealed no cultivation of opium in Iran's traditional growing areas.

SOURCE: "Worldwide Illicit Drug Cultivation, 1987–2000 (All Figures in Hectares)" in *International Narcotics Control Strategy Report,* U.S. Department of State, Washington, D.C., 2001

Colombia, where it is processed into cocaine hydrochloride (white powder) at clandestine drug laboratories. Recently, small, independent Bolivian and Peruvian trafficking groups have also been processing cocaine. After processing, it is shipped to the United States and Europe.

Caribbean and Central American countries serve as transit countries for the shipment of drugs into the United States. Drug traffickers shift routes according to law enforcement and interdiction pressures. Recently, drug flow has been steadily increasing through the Central American countries. In 1998 Central American governments stepped up antidrug operations in response.

The Colombian government has disrupted the activities of two major drug-trafficking organizations, the Medellin and Cali cartels, by either capturing or killing their key leaders. Nonetheless, this disruption has not reduced drug-trafficking activities. Independent traffickers, as well as splinter groups from the Cali cartel, have increasingly moved into the market, and huge volumes of cocaine are still being shipped to the United States through the Caribbean.

MOST COCAINE ENTERS THE U.S. THROUGH MEXICO. Much South American cocaine is sent to Mexican traffickers, who then smuggle it into the United States. As Mexi-can traffickers have become more sophisticated, it is suspected that many are bypassing their Colombian contacts and dealing directly with Peruvian and Bolivian producers.

Until only a decade ago, almost all drugs, especially cocaine, entered the United States through Florida. Florida was a major entry point mainly because of its thousands of miles of coastline, where boats could secretly dock, and the millions of acres in the Everglades, where planes could covertly land.

Today, after intensive law enforcement efforts to make it more difficult to land drugs in Florida, nearly 70 percent of the cocaine sold in the United States passes through Mexico and across the Mexico–U.S. border. The 2,000-mile border is patrolled by a relatively small number of Immigration and Naturalization Service (INS) officers, who must divide their limited time between illegal aliens trying to cross the border and drug traffickers trying to smuggle drugs into the United States. The United States has introduced soldiers into the area to assist the INS, although some observers question whether soldiers trained to fight wars have the correct preparation to patrol a border populated by farmers and ranchers.

Mexico, the main transit and distribution hub for drugs moving to the United States, now rivals Colombia

TABLE 6.4

Potential illicit drug production worldwide, 1987–2000

(All figures in metric tons)

	2000	1999	1998	1997	1996	1995	1994	1993	1992	1991	1990	1989	1988	1987
Opium Gum														
Afghanistan	3,656	2,861	2,340	2,184	2,174	1,250	950	685	640	570	415	585	750	600
India	-	-	-	30	47	77	90	-	-	-	-	-	-	-
Iran	-	-	-	-	-	-	-	-	-	-	-	-	-	300
Pakistan	11	37	66	85	75	155	160	140	175	180	165	130	205	205
Total SW Asia	*3,667*	*2,898*	*2,406*	*2,299*	*2,296*	*1,482*	*1,200*	*825*	*815*	*750*	*580*	*715*	*955*	*1,105*
Burma	1,085	1,090	1,750	2,365	2,560	2,340	2,030	2,575	2,280	2,350	2,255	2,430	1,280	835
China	-	-	-	-	-	19	25	-	-	-	-	-	-	-
Laos	210	140	140	210	200	180	85	180	230	265	275	380	255	225
Thailand	6	6	16	25	30	25	17	42	24	35	40	50	25	24
Vietnam	15	11	20	45	25	-	-	-	-	-	-	-	-	-
Total SE Asia	*1,316*	*1,247*	*1,926*	*2,645*	*2,815*	*2,564*	*2,157*	*2,797*	*2,534*	*2,650*	*2,570*	*2,860*	*1,560*	*1,084*
Colombia	-	75	61	66	63	65	-	-	-	-	-	-	-	-
Lebanon	-	-	-	-	1	1	-	4	-	34	32	45	-	-
Guatemala	-	-	-	-	-	-	-	-	-	11	13	12	8	3
Mexico	21	43	60	46	54	53	60	49	40	41	62	66	67	50
Total Other	*21*	*118*	*121*	*112*	*118*	*119*	*60*	*53*	*40*	*86*	*107*	*123*	*75*	*53*
Total Opium	*5,004*	*4,263*	*4,453*	*5,056*	*4,285*	*4,165*	*3,417*	*3,675*	*3,389*	*3,486*	*3,257*	*3,698*	*2,590*	*2,242*
Coca Leaf														
Bolivia	13,400	22,800	52,900	70,100	75,100	85,000	89,800	84,400	80,300	78,000	77,000	78,200	79,500	79,200
Colombia[1]	583,000	521,400	437,600	347,000	302,900	229,300	35,800	31,700	29,600	30,000	32,100	33,900	27,200	20,500
Peru	54,400	69,200	95,600	130,200	174,700	183,600	165,300	155,500	223,900	222,700	196,900	186,300	187,700	191,000
Ecuador	-	-	-	-	-	-	-	100	100	40	170	270	400	400
Total Coca	*650,800*	*613,400*	*586,100*	*547,300*	*552,700*	*497,900*	*290,900*	*271,700*	*333,900*	*330,740*	*306,170*	*298,670*	*294,800*	*291,100*
Cannabis														
Mexico[2]	7,000	3,700	8,300	8,600	11,700	12,400	5,540	6,280	7,795	7,775	19,715	30,200	5,655	5,933
Colombia	4,000	4,000	4,000	4,133	4,133	4,133	4,138	4,125	1,650	1,650	1,500	2,800	7,775	5,600
Jamaica	-	-	-	214	356	206	208	502	263	641	825	190	405	460
Belize	-	-	-	-	-	-	-	-	-	49	60	65	120	200
Others	3,500	3,500	3,500	3,500	3,500	3,500	3,500	3,500	3,500	3,500	3,500	3,500	3,500	1,500
Total Cannabis	*14,500*	*11,200*	*15,800*	*16,447*	*19,689*	*20,239*	*13,386*	*14,407*	*13,208*	*13,615*	*25,600*	*36,755*	*17,455*	*13,693*

[1] Coca and Cocaine yield figures for 1995-1999 were revised upward in 1999, based on USG studies.

[2] Cannabis yield figures updated in November 1999, based on information provided by the Mexican Attorney General's Office.

SOURCE: "Worldwide Potential Illicit Drug Production: 1987–2000 (All Figures in Metric Tons)," in *International Narcotics Control Strategy Report*, U.S. Department of State, Washington, D.C., 2001

TABLE 6.5

Cocaine price ranges, 1993–97
in dollars per kilogram

Location	1993	1994	1995	1996	1997
National	10,500–40,000	10,500–40,000	10,500–36,000	10,500–36,000	10,000–42,000
Miami	16,000–24,000	16,000–22,000	15,000–25,000	14,000–25,000	12,500–28,000
New York City	17,000–25,000	16,000–23,000	17,000–27,000	16,000–25,000	17,000–42,000
Chicago	20,000–30,000	21,000–25,000	21,000–25,000	18,000–25,000	18,000–32,000
Los Angeles	14,000–20,000	15,000–20,000	15,000–20,000	12,500–20,000	12,000–17,500

SOURCE: "Cocaine price ranges (per kilogram)," in *The NNICC Report 1997: The Supply of Illicit Drugs to the United States,* National Narcotics Intelligence Consumers Committee, Washington, DC, 1998

TABLE 6.7

Coca cultivation and leaf production, Andean region, 1994–98

	1994	1995	1996	1997	1998
Net cultivation	**201,700**	**214,800**	**209,700**	**194,100**	**190,800**
Hectares					
Peru	108,600	115,300	94,400	68,800	51,000
Bolivia	48,100	48,600	48,100	45,800	38,000
Colombia	45,000	50,900	67,200	79,500	101,800
Potential leaf production	**291,200**	**309,400**	**303,600**	**263,900**	**229,900**
Metric tons					
Peru	165,400	183,600	174,700	130,200	95,600
Bolivia	89,800	85,000	75,100	70,100	52,900
Colombia	36,000	40,800	53,800	63,600	81,400
Potential cocaine	**760**	**780**	**760**	**650**	**555**
Metric tons					
Peru	435	460	435	325	240
Bolivia	255	240	215	200	150
Colombia	70	80	110	125	165

SOURCE: "Andean region," in *Major Coca & Opium Producing Nations: Cultivation and Production Estimates, 1994–98,* Drug Enforcement Administration, Arlington, VA, n.d.

TABLE 6.6

Cocaine purity, 1993–97
Annual national average—percent

	1993	1994	1995	1996	1997
Kilogram	82	83	83	82	80
Ounce	70	74	65	67	64
Gram	63	63	61	61	64

SOURCE: "Cocaine purity (annual national average—percent)," in *The NNICC Report 1997: The Supply of Illicit Drugs to the United States,* National Narcotics Intelligence Consumers Committee, Washington, DC, 1998

ifornia regions. In addition, more drugs are moving overland into Mexico, primarily through Guatemala.

After the drugs have been unloaded, the cocaine is transported, usually by truck, to warehouses in cities such as Guadalajara or Juarez, which are operating bases for the major drug organizations. Mexican smugglers, often with experience smuggling illegal workers, and who frequently have family or friends in the United States, are paid to carry the drugs across the border. Sometimes the drugs are carried across the border in backpacks; sometimes they are hidden in cars and trucks; and, occasionally, they are flown into the United States.

In Mexico, where unemployment is common and the value of the peso dropped sharply in the mid-1990s, the hundreds or thousands of dollars to be earned from drug smuggling can be very attractive. Few of the smugglers know any more about the makeup of the drug ring than the identity of the individual who gives them the drugs, and capturing them does not significantly restrict the flow of drugs.

Drug syndicates have become very powerful in Mexico, and Mexican traffickers use their vast wealth to corrupt and influence public officials. For example, it is estimated that the Arelleno-Felix organization pays $1 million per week to Mexican federal, state, and local officials to ensure the continued flow of drugs to U.S.–Mexico border cities. In 1997 the head of Mexico's National Institute to Combat Drugs, General Jesus Gutierrez Rebello, was arrested for taking money and gifts from drug dealers. General Barry McCaffrey, the U.S. drug coordinator, had recently praised the general for his integrity and commitment to the drug war.

Mexican drug organizations have been implicated in dozens of political assassinations in Tijuana since the mid-1990s. In 1994 a presidential candidate and Tijuana's police chief were assassinated, and a second police chief, Alfredo de la Torre Marquez, was assassinated in 1999. In 2000 the murders of two federal prosecutors and an army captain were among the many that American officials suspect were ordered by drug cartels. Other high-profile

for dominance of the Western Hemisphere drug trade. Powerful Mexican drug syndicates have become dominant in the cocaine trade and the U.S. wholesale market. The Mexican government has intensified its investigations of the four largest drug-trafficking organizations—the Juarez cartel, the Tijuana cartel, the Gulf cartel, and the Caro Quintero organization.

Most cocaine destined for the United States is transported from South American countries to northern Mexico. In the early 1990s traffickers used aircraft to deliver cocaine, but over the past few years they have shifted to the maritime movement of drugs. According to U.S. law enforcement officials, most drugs enter Mexico via ship or small boat through the Yucatan Peninsula and Baja Cal-

victims have included lawyers, police officers, judges, and prosecutors—anyone who might stand in the way of the high-stakes trafficking enterprise.

A major obstacle to joint law enforcement and prosecution efforts is the widespread corruption of Mexican officials, especially police. According to the *International Narcotics Control Strategy Report, 2000,* "Pervasive corruption in Mexican government institutions remains the greatest challenge facing the GOM [government of Mexico] in its efforts to fight drug trafficking and organized crime." Police in Mexico are paid very little, and many feel they have a right to supplement their salaries with bribes.

SMUGGLERS WILL USE ANY METHOD. In 1993 Mexican police discovered an elaborate cocaine-smuggling tunnel that extended 1,400 feet from Tijuana, Mexico, to the outskirts of San Diego, California. Short tunnels have been found in the past, but nothing like this air-conditioned, well-lighted tunnel that would have provided a secret, comfortable route for transporting tons of cocaine. Those involved in smuggling find innumerable ways to get cocaine into the United States, because the profits from even relatively small amounts of the drug are worth the risk of being caught.

Drug couriers will go to extreme lengths, including swallowing packets of drugs and excreting them after they have entered the United States. One courier had half a pound of cocaine surgically implanted under the skin of each of his thighs. Panamanian cocaine smugglers have developed a new technology that combines cocaine with vinyl, which is then incorporated into luggage and sneakers. The cocaine is separated after it reaches its destination.

The U.S. Customs Service and the U.S. Fish and Wildlife Service seized several kilograms of cocaine within a shipment of boa constrictors. The smugglers had wrapped the cocaine in rubber containers and forced them down the snakes' throats. Cocaine was found implanted in dogs' stomachs, and liquid cocaine was discovered in a shipment of tropical fish.

Cocaine may be hidden in the walls and support beams of cargo containers or mixed in with legal cargo such as coffee. Fishing vessels with hidden compartments often conceal cocaine. Cocaine is hidden in the walls of planes flying regularly scheduled flights. Other smugglers drop the cocaine by parachute to waiting accomplices below. Some traffickers have bought old, propeller-driven airplanes to fly in cocaine. Today, with the price of aging jet aircraft dropping sharply, some smugglers have even bought Boeing 727 jets to haul in large amounts of drugs. Once, 65 pounds of cocaine was found hidden inside the cockpit of an American Airlines Boeing 757 jetliner.

AFTER COCAINE REACHES THE U.S. The primary entry ports into the United States are southern Florida, southern California, Arizona, and Texas. Colombia-based traffickers continue to control wholesale-level distribution throughout the northeastern United States and along the eastern seaboard in cities such as Boston, Miami, Newark, New York City, and Philadelphia, often employing Dominican criminals as subordinates. Mexico-based traffickers operate out of Chicago and control the western and midwestern United States, in such cities as Chicago, Dallas, Denver, Houston, Los Angeles, Phoenix, San Diego, San Francisco, and Seattle.

From these distribution cities, drug carriers transport cocaine throughout the country in commercial and private vehicles, including trains, buses, airplanes, and even postal trucks. U.S. law enforcement officials have encountered smuggling operations that use concealed compartments within campers, recreational vehicles, tractor trailers, and vans. Modern communications have made it very difficult to catch these drug dealers. They keep in touch with each other by using beepers and pay phones in their efforts to avoid getting caught.

Many observers note that drug traffickers have little difficulty funneling drugs north through Mexico, because of Mexico's weak political and law enforcement institutions. These observers often forget that traffickers have little trouble making their way across the United States as well, and that they threaten the integrity of U.S. law enforcement institutions.

Between 1992 and 1997, 28 INS (Immigration and Naturalization Service) and customs employees on the southwest border were convicted for drug-related crimes. The crimes are attractive for some law enforcement officials because they can earn thousands of dollars by simply looking the other way as a car or truck carrying hidden cocaine passes across the border.

HOW MUCH COCAINE IS SEIZED? To give an idea of how enormous the challenge is to find smuggled drugs, the U.S. Customs Service reported that, during 2000, 67 million people entered the country on commercial and private flights. Another 11 million came by sea and 375 million by land through 301 ports of entry.

The Customs Service estimates that two-thirds of all cocaine entering the United States crosses through a border facility manned by a government agent. Most of it is hidden in some way in the huge number of tractor trailers and passenger vehicles. Customs estimates that it seizes only 10 percent of smuggled drugs. Many experts believe it seizes much less.

For the United States, interdiction, or stopping drugs at the border, has been a high-priority, high-visibility effort in the war against drugs. In 1997 cocaine seizures in the Americas declined, just as cocaine production in South American source countries declined. According to the Federal-wide Drug Seizure System (FDSS), U.S. government agencies seized 95.5 metric tons of cocaine in 1997, compared with 128.7 metric tones in 1996—a 26 percent decrease. Cocaine seizures on the high seas represented a more significant proportion of total seizures in 1997 than in the year before. (See Table 6.8.) Most of the maritime interdiction occurred in the South Atlantic and Caribbean. About six metric tons were seized in the Pacific, mainly from one vessel off Colombia's west coast.

In 1997 cocaine seizures by U.S. authorities at the southwest border declined by half from 1996. In Mexico, however, cocaine seizures increased considerably, from 23.6 metric tons in 1996 to 34.4 metric tons in 1997. (See Table 6.8.) Mexico still remained the major entry point to the U.S. drug market.

The *United States Customs Service Fiscal Accountability Report FY 2000* (Department of the Treasury, Washington, D.C., 2001) reports that Customs made thousands of drug seizures in 2000, spending more than half of its law enforcement time investigating narcotics smuggling. Customs seized more than 150,000 pounds of cocaine in 2,489 seizures, 2,555 pounds of heroin in 859 seizures, and 1.3 million pounds of marijuana in 14,861 seizures.

A growing proportion of drugs shipped into the United States is intended for further shipment to Canada and Europe. Over the past few years, cocaine dealers have begun developing Europe as a lucrative market for sales. As a result, cocaine seizures in Europe have increased.

HEROIN

Growing Popularity, Higher Purity, and Increasing Profits

HEROIN USE ON THE RISE. Recent developments in the heroin trade have raised serious concern in the United States. The *International Narcotics Control Strategy Report* (Washington, D.C., 1999), prepared by the Bureau for International Narcotics and Law Enforcement Affairs of the U.S. Department of State, observes that

> Though cocaine dominates the U.S. drug scene, heroin is lurking conspicuously in the wings. . . . [H]eroin has a special property that appeals to the drug trade's long range planners: as an opiate, it allows many addicts to develop a long-term tolerance to the drug. Where constant cocaine or crack use may kill a regular user in five years, a heroin addiction can last for a decade or more, as long as the addict has access to a regular maintenance "fix." This pernicious property of tolerance potentially assures the heroin trade of a long-term customer base of hard-core addicts.

Unfortunately, the U.S. customer base may be on the rise. Estimates of the U.S. heroin addict population, which for two decades had remained steady at 500,000 individuals, have been revised upward. Evidence of combined drug use suggests that more of the nation's two-million-plus hard-core cocaine addicts are using heroin to cushion the "crash" that follows the euphoria of using crack.

The *NNICC Report 1997* (Washington, D.C., 1998) noted that "heroin remained readily available to addicts in all major [U.S.] metropolitan areas throughout 1997." The Office of National Drug Control Policy (ONDCP) estimates that Americans now consume about 10 metric tons

TABLE 6.8

Cocaine seizures, 1996 and 1997

Federal-wide Drug Seizure System (FDSS) cocaine seizures (metric tons)

Location	1996		1997	
State	105.5	82%	64.4	67%
High seas	23.2	18%	31.1	33%
Total cocaine seized	128.7 metric tons		95.5 metric tons	

Cocaine seizures at the SW border and Mexico (metric tons)

Location	1996	1997	Percent change
U.S. southwest border*	35.5	17.4	–51%
Mexico**	23.6	34.4	+46%
Total U.S. SWB/Mexico	59.1	51.7	–12%

* Data provided by EPIC Border Land Interdiction Seizure System
** Data provided by Mexican government

SOURCE: "FDSS cocaine seizures (metric tons)," in *The NNICC Report 1997: The Supply of Illicit Drugs to the United States,* National Narcotics Intelligence Consumers Committee, Washington, DC, 1998

TABLE 6.9

Heroin purity, 1995–98
National average (percent)

Quantity	1995		1996		1997		1998	
	Purchases	Seizures	Purchases	Seizures	Purchases	Seizures	Purchases	Seizures
Kilogram	71	83	51	71	58	72	58	72
Ounce	62	69	52	57	57	67	57	68
Gram	59	59	52	52	56	58	57	57

SOURCE: "Heroin: annual purity data," in *Illegal Drug Price/Purity Report,* Drug Enforcement Administration, Arlington, VA, 1999

TABLE 6.10

Heroin price ranges, 1995–98
National range (dollars)

Quantity	Source	1995	1996	1997	1998
Kilogram	Mexico	50,000–175,000	45,000–175,000	50,000–175,000	16,000–190,000
	South America	80,000–185,000	85,000–185,000	60,000–180,000	50,000–200,000
	Southeast Asia	70,000–260,000	95,000–210,000	50,000–250,000	80,000–180,000
	Southwest Asia	70,000–260,000	80,000–260,000	70,000–200,000	55,000–190,000
Ounce	Powder	800–18,000	1,500–10,000	2,000–12,000	2,500–15,000
	Black tar	700–12,000	600–11,000	400–11,000	400–6,500
Gram	Powder	70–800	75–600	80–600	70–400
	Black tar	80–500	60–600	60–600	80–600

SOURCE: "Heroin: annual price range," in *Illegal Drug Price/Purity Report,* Drug Enforcement Administration, Arlington, VA, 1999

of heroin a year, up dramatically from the estimated 5 tons consumed annually during the mid-1980s.

INCREASING PURITY. Like cocaine, heroin is now being produced with much higher purity than before. In 1998, according to the Drug Enforcement Administration (DEA), the average purity for a gram of heroin was 57 percent (Table 6.9), which was much higher than the 27 percent purity in 1991, and far higher than the average of 7 percent in 1987. In 1998 the street-level purity of heroin was highest in the Northeast. High-purity heroin can prove deadly to a user who does not realize that the drug he or she is taking is so unadulterated.

This rise in purity has been tied to the increased availability of high-purity South American heroin. Colombian drug traffickers have been trying to break into the heroin market by producing a very high-quality drug. This has forced heroin producers from other areas to improve the purity of their product.

The increasing purity of heroin has led to a change in the way many people take the drug. Injecting heroin into a blood vein is the most practical and efficient way to take low-purity heroin. However, the growing availability of higher-purity heroin has made it easier to smoke or snort the drug. Being able to snort heroin makes it more attractive to potential users who feel uncomfortable sticking needles into their bodies. Furthermore, it removes the fear of getting AIDS, which often occurs among intravenous drug users who share needles. Nonetheless, about three in five heroin users inject the drug, while only one in eight snorts it.

BIGGER PROFITS. Heroin is more lucrative for dealers than most other drugs. While a kilogram of cocaine might fetch between $10,000 and $42,000, a kilo of heroin could be worth as much as $200,000. (See Table 6.10.) According to the ONDCP, in 1998 the price of a gram of heroin ranged from less than $100 on the coasts to over $300 in midwestern cities. On the street, heroin is usually sold in a $10 or $20 bag, enough for one person to shoot up or snort. *The NNICC Report 1997* noted that "stable whole-sale prices per kilogram and high retail-level purity indicated steady supplies of the drug."

Heroin Production and Distribution

Opium poppies, from which heroin is made, are mainly grown in three regions of the world—Southeast Asia, Southwest Asia, and Mexico and South America. According to the DEA, worldwide opium production dropped significantly in 1998 to 3,460 metric tons, 19 percent below the record level reached in 1996. (See Figure 6.1.) A regional drought in Southeast Asia caused most of the decline.

In 1998 Southeast Asia was responsible for approximately 75 percent of the world's opium poppy cultivation and 55 percent of the world's estimated opium production. (See Figure 6.2.) Of this, about 83 percent of the opium poppy cultivation and 92 percent of the opium production occurred in Burma, the world's leading opium producer. Most of the remaining poppy cultivation and production took place in Southwest Asia (mainly Afghanistan, the second-highest producer), which accounted for about 21 percent of worldwide opium poppy cultivation and 41 percent of opium production. (See Figure 6.2.)

MEXICO, SOUTH AMERICA, AND CENTRAL AMERICA. Although poppy farming in Mexico and South America accounted for only about 5 percent of worldwide opium poppy cultivation, and less than 4 percent of opium production, the DEA believes that South America has become the major source of heroin seized in the United States. Much Asian heroin is used in the country in which it was produced, in nearby countries, or in Europe. Virtually all Colombian and Mexican heroin, however, ends up in the United States.

In the northeastern United States, South American heroin—primarily high-purity, white powdered heroin—is widely available. In 1997 close to 85 percent of all identifiable heroin bought in the eastern half of the United

FIGURE 6.1

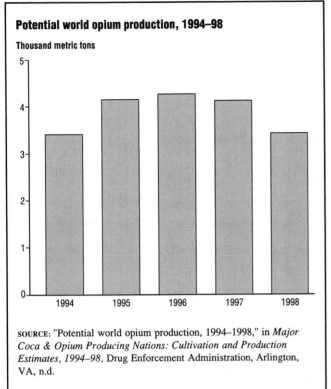

Potential world opium production, 1994–98

Thousand metric tons

SOURCE: "Potential world opium production, 1994–1998," in *Major Coca & Opium Producing Nations: Cultivation and Production Estimates, 1994–98,* Drug Enforcement Administration, Arlington, VA, n.d.

FIGURE 6.2

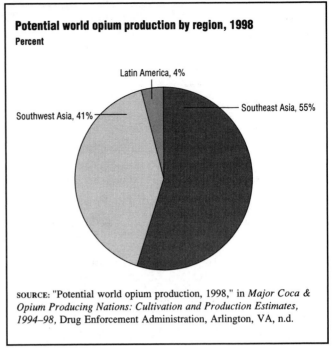

Potential world opium production by region, 1998
Percent

Latin America, 4%

Southwest Asia, 41%

Southeast Asia, 55%

SOURCE: "Potential world opium production, 1998," in *Major Coca & Opium Producing Nations: Cultivation and Production Estimates, 1994–98,* Drug Enforcement Administration, Arlington, VA, n.d.

States was of South American origin. Although Southeast Asian heroin accounted for more than two-thirds of the total samples sold in the eastern half of the United States in 1991, by 1997 very few heroin purchases were determined to be of either Southeast or Southwest Asian origin.

Many Colombian coca traffickers have been requiring their dealers to accept a small amount of heroin along with their normal deliveries of coca. This has allowed the Colombian producers to use an already existing network to introduce their very pure heroin into the U.S. market. Much of the growing Colombian heroin production is sent through Central America and Mexico by smugglers traveling on commercial airline flights into the United States. These smugglers hide the drugs in false-sided luggage, clothing, hollowed-out shoe soles, or inside their bodies. The Colombia-based heroin traffickers have established distribution outlets throughout the eastern half of the United States. (See Figure 6.3.)

Just about all the heroin samples purchased at the retail level in the western half of the United States were of Mexican origin. "Black tar" and brown powdered heroin were predominant. Black tar heroin is so named because it looks like roofing tar. Once considered inferior to Colombian and Asian heroin, black tar is now so pure it can be smoked or snorted.

Mexican heroin is targeted almost exclusively to the American market. The long Mexico–U.S. land border provides many opportunities for drug smugglers to sneak across. Females are used more frequently than males as couriers for

transporting heroin across the border. Mexican heroin is smuggled in cars, trucks, and buses, and may also be hidden on or in the body of the smuggler. Many smugglers send their drugs via overnight-package express services.

SOUTHWEST ASIA (THE GOLDEN CRESCENT). At one time, perhaps half the heroin shipped into the United States came from Iran, Afghanistan, and Pakistan—the Golden Crescent. Currently, however, only a small percentage is thought to come to the United States from this area; most of its production is shipped to Europe.

Afghanistan, which has undergone a protracted civil war, can do little to control opium production or heroin trafficking. An estimated 95 percent of the country's opium poppy cultivation, and most of Southwest Asia's morphine base and heroin processing labs, are located in Taliban-controlled territory. In late 1997 the Taliban, the Islamic fundamentalist group and ruling political faction in Afghanistan, agreed to eliminate some of the poppy cultivation. However, in 1998 the Afghan crop was at an all-time high. Opium is the country's largest cash crop.

By 2000, after strong pressure from the United States, the Pakistani government had nearly eliminated opium cultivation. Iran also grows very few opium poppies, perhaps as a result of an Iranian government crackdown on heroin users. It is generally believed that Iran's opium production provides barely enough for native drug abusers, and that Iran imports heroin from neighboring Afghanistan.

Drug abusers in Southwest and Central Asia use some of the opium grown in the Southwest Asian region, but most of its opium is shipped to Turkey, where it is made into heroin in secret laboratories.

About 80 percent of the heroin from Southwest Asia is shipped to the European market from Turkey along the "Balkan Route." This supply line originates in Afghanistan and Pakistan, passes through Turkey, and splits into branches. The northern route carries heroin to Romania, Hungary, the Czech and Slovak Republics, and points north. The southern branch crosses through Croatia, Slovenia, the former Yugoslav republic of Macedonia, Greece, and Albania to the countries of Western Europe. Every country along the route now faces serious domestic drug problems. Turkish drug syndicates, which control distribution in a large number of European cities, dominate most of the Balkan Route drug business.

The growth of corruption and criminal organizations in Russia has led to a growth of drug trafficking and drug abuse there. Russian drug traffickers transport Southwest Asian heroin through Central Asia to Russia and on to Europe. Russian authorities have noted a huge increase in domestic drug use in Russia and estimate that there are more than two million users in the country, although the figure could well be higher.

SOUTHEAST ASIA (THE GOLDEN TRIANGLE). Burma supplies as much as half of all the opium produced in the world—even after the decrease in cultivation due to unfavorable growing conditions in 1998. The opium produced in Burma, Thailand, and Laos (the Golden Triangle) has traditionally gone by sea from Thailand to Hong Kong or Taiwan, where it is processed into heroin for local use or shipped on to the United States. Trafficking through China is on the increase, and much Golden Triangle opium is being processed into heroin in that country. A growing amount of heroin has been moving through Singapore and Malaysia, despite their strict drug laws.

NIGERIA—A MAJOR TRANSSHIPMENT BASE. According to the U.S. Department of State, "Nigeria remains a worldwide hub of narcotics trafficking and money laundering activity. Nigerian organized criminal groups dominate the African drug trade, and transport narcotics to markets in the United States, Europe, Asia, and Africa" (*International Narcotics Control Strategy Report, 2000*). The nation's continuing political corruption and turbulence have made it easier for criminal organizations to develop and use Nigeria as a transshipment point for Asian heroin.

Before 1997 Nigerian drug traffickers paid couriers between $2,000 and $5,000 (what an average Nigerian would earn in 16 years) to transport a pound or two of heroin into the United States. There is hardly a country in the world that does not report arrests of Nigerians for heroin trafficking.

The only way inspectors can determine that someone is carrying drugs is by intuition. Passengers who are nervous and sweating, or who do not have a legitimate expla-

FIGURE 6.3

Air routes for illicit drug movement from South America to the U.S.

Couriers use international air routes from Colombia through the Caribbean to the East Coast or through Central America to Texas and on to the East Coast markets.

SOURCE: "South America," in *The NNICC Report 1997: The Supply of Illicit Drugs to the United States,* National Narcotics Intelligence Consumers Committee, Washington, DC, 1998

nation for why they have come to the United States, are generally those who draw the attention of customs agents.

Beginning in late 1996, traffickers began using Express Mail Services (EMS) to ship heroin, concealing it in such items as pots and pans, children's books, and decorative figurines. The use of EMS is far cheaper than couriers, and packages can be mailed anonymously, with less chance of tracing them back to the trafficker if the heroin is discovered. Nigerian traffickers often use Thailand as a base of operation for their heroin trafficking. Most parcels seized originate in Thailand.

Government Heroin Seizures

Figure 6.4 shows the origin of heroin seized in the United States in 1997. Three-quarters of the heroin seized originated in South America, while 14 percent came from Mexico. Although the amount seized is an indicator of the locations from which heroin is shipped, it does not necessarily show where all the heroin used in America originated.

MARIJUANA

Marijuana is by far the most frequently used illegal drug. The ONDCP's *Pulse Check: Trends in Drug Abuse Mid-Year 2000* found marijuana "widely available" in more than 90 percent of the country. According to the report, high-quality marijuana is increasingly available because of "improved cultivating techniques by marijuana growers (especially hydroponic growers)."

Marijuana is made from the flowering tops and leaves of the cannabis plant, which are collected, trimmed, dried,

FIGURE 6.4

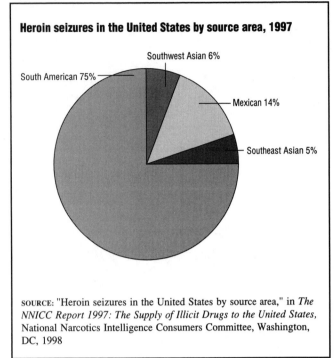

Heroin seizures in the United States by source area, 1997

South American 75%

Southwest Asian 6%

Mexican 14%

Southeast Asian 5%

SOURCE: "Heroin seizures in the United States by source area," in *The NNICC Report 1997: The Supply of Illicit Drugs to the United States,* National Narcotics Intelligence Consumers Committee, Washington, DC, 1998

TABLE 6.11

Marijuana price ranges and potency, 1995–98
National range (dollars)

Type	Quantity	1995	1996	1997	1998
Commercial grade	Pound	300–4,000	100–4,000	100–6,000	250–3,200
	Ounce	40–400	40–400	40–600	30–450
Potency (THC)		3.97%	4.60%	4.95%	5.86%
Sinsemilla	Pound	800–8,000	700–10,000	250–8,000	850–6,000
	Ounce	100–900	60–800	100–800	160–600
Potency (THC)		7.51%	9.22%	12.20%	12.27%

SOURCE: "Marijuana: annual price and potency data," in *Illegal Drug Price/Purity Report,* Drug Enforcement Administration, Arlington, VA, 1999

and then smoked in a pipe or as a cigarette. Many users smoke "blunts," named after the inexpensive blunt cigars from which they are made. Blunt cigars are approximately five inches long and can be purchased at any store that sells tobacco products. A marijuana blunt is made up of the outside blunt cigar casing stuffed with marijuana or a marijuana/tobacco mixture. A blunt may contain as much marijuana as six regular marijuana cigarettes. In some cases, blunt users add crack cocaine or PCP to the mixture to make it more potent. These are sometimes called "turbos," "woolies," or "woolie blunts."

More Potent Marijuana

The flowering tops of the cannabis plant, also known as colas or buds, are highly valued because of their higher THC (tetrahydrocannabinol) content. The higher the THC content, the more effective the drug. An increasing number of marijuana users are choosing to use sinsemilla, the potent flowering tops and buds of the female plant.

During the 1970s and 1980s the THC content of commercial-grade marijuana averaged less than 2 percent. By comparison, the average in 1998 was 5.86 percent, up from 3.97 percent in 1995. The average THC content of sinsemilla in 1998 was 12.27 percent, up from 7.51 percent in 1995. (See Table 6.11.)

Marijuana with even higher potency, called "skunk," "skunkweed," or "nederweed," with a THC content of over 20 percent, has been available in the Netherlands and Latin America. Raids in Alaska have also uncovered marijuana with THC content well above 20 percent. This marijuana is grown by indoor cultivators who focus their efforts on hybridizing, cloning, and growing high-potency marijuana.

In 1998 the price of commercial-grade marijuana ranged from $250 to $3,200 per pound. The cost of sinsemilla ranged from $850 to $6,000 per pound. (See Table 6.11.) Commercial-grade marijuana is usually sold in small $5 and $10 bags on the street.

Foreign Production

Morocco is one of the largest producers of marijuana in the world. Virtually all of its production is exported to other North African nations and Europe. Traffickers in Nigeria and Kenya export large amounts of marijuana to Europe. In 1997 South Africa was one of the world's largest producers of marijuana. Although most of the marijuana produced in South Africa was for domestic or regional use, some was smuggled to Australia, the Netherlands, and the United Kingdom. Brazil is also a major producer of marijuana, most of which is consumed in Brazil itself.

Most foreign marijuana available in the United States comes from Mexico. Significant quantities also come into the American market from Colombia and Jamaica. Some marijuana arrives on the U.S. West Coast from Asia, most notably Thailand and Cambodia.

Mexican marijuana enters the United States mainly by land, although some of it is smuggled in private aircraft. Almost all Colombian marijuana is shipped by noncommercial vessels or is transshipped through northern Mexico. Most Jamaican marijuana arrives by cargo vessel, pleasure boat, or fishing boat. Most marijuana enters the United States through Florida, except the Mexican variety, which usually comes through Texas and California. (See Figure 6.5.)

Between 1990 and 1997 Mexico eradicated about 82,600 hectares of marijuana. Figure 6.6 shows the

FIGURE 6.5

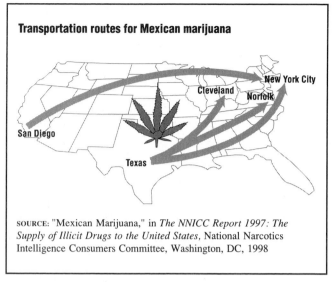

Transportation routes for Mexican marijuana

SOURCE: "Mexican Marijuana," in *The NNICC Report 1997: The Supply of Illicit Drugs to the United States,* National Narcotics Intelligence Consumers Committee, Washington, DC, 1998

FIGURE 6.6

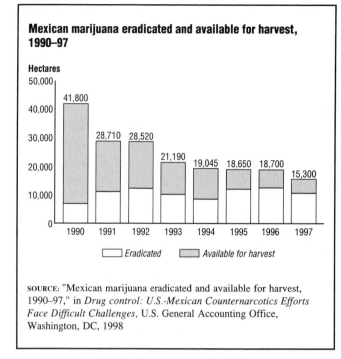

Mexican marijuana eradicated and available for harvest, 1990–97

SOURCE: "Mexican marijuana eradicated and available for harvest, 1990–97," in *Drug control: U.S.-Mexican Counternarcotics Efforts Face Difficult Challenges,* U.S. General Accounting Office, Washington, DC, 1998

substantial decline in the amount of marijuana under cultivation during this period—from a high of 41,800 hectares in 1990 to a low of 15,300 hectares in 1997. Seizures of Mexican marijuana increased from 102 metric tons in 1991 to 742 metric tons in 1998.

Domestic Production

OUTDOOR PRODUCTION. The National Narcotics Intelligence Consumers Committee (NNICC) observes, "It was difficult to estimate the amount of marijuana actually produced in the United States in 1997 as there were no national surveys conducted of cannabis cultivation." It is thought that at least 25–35 percent of the marijuana consumed in the United States is domestically produced.

Domestic growers usually plant cannabis in remote areas, often camouflaging it with surrounding vegetation or crops such as corn or soybeans. Large amounts of cannabis are grown in Tennessee, Kentucky, Hawaii, California, and Idaho. Growers also plant cannabis in suburban and rural gardens, interspersed with legitimate crops.

Preliminary data indicated that four million cultivated plants were eradicated in 1997, destroying a potential 1,822 metric tons of marijuana. In addition, government agents seized about 689 metric tons of marijuana.

INDOOR PRODUCTION. Marijuana can also be grown indoors very successfully. Growing the plant indoors makes it harder for the Drug Enforcement Administration (DEA) to find. Furthermore, indoor growing provides a controlled environment favorable to the production of more valuable, high-potency sinsemilla plants. According to the DEA, a healthy indoor-grown sinsemilla plant can produce up to a pound of high-THC-content marijuana.

Indoor cultivation permits year-round production in a variety of settings, from a handful of plants grown in a closet to elaborate, specially constructed (sometimes

underground) greenhouses containing thousands of plants. Indoor cultivators often use such advanced growing practices as hydroponics (automatic metering of light, water, and fertilizers) and atmospheres enriched with carbon dioxide.

In 1997 federal authorities seized 2,941 indoor-growing operations. The five leading states for indoor operations—California, Florida, Oregon, Kentucky, and Washington—accounted for nearly half of the indoor-grown marijuana eradicated in the United States in 1997.

Domestic Marijuana Eradication

The DEA-sponsored Domestic Cannabis Eradication and Suppression Program cooperates with a number of federal, state, and local organizations to destroy marijuana plants on both private and public lands. Among these are the Civil Air Patrol, the National Guard, the U.S. military, the U.S. Fish and Wildlife Service, the National Park Service, and the Bureau of Indian Affairs. In 1997 the program destroyed 241 million plants, including 3.8 million outdoor-cultivated cannabis plants, 225 million low-potency wild (ditchweed) plants, and 221,000 indoor-grown cannabis plants.

METHAMPHETAMINES

A Growing Problem

Methamphetamine use in the United States is growing rapidly. Traditionally, outlaw motorcycle gangs and independent producers supplied methamphetamines to the United States. Although these groups still contribute to the U.S. supply of the drug, traffickers operating out of

TABLE 6.12

Methamphetamine price ranges, 1995–98
National range (dollars)

Quantity	Division	1995	1996	1997	1998
Pound	National	3,000–20,000	4,000–30,000	3,500–30,000	3,500–30,000
Ounce	National	400–2,700	500–2,700	400–2,800	500–2,500
	San Francisco	400–900	500–900	400–800	450–800
	San Diego	500–1,000	500–1,000	500–800	500–750
	Phoenix	575–1,500	700–1,500	500–800	500–800
Grams	National	40–200	37–200	37–200	25–150
	San Francisco	60–100	45–100	50–75	No Data
	San Diego	50–80	50–75	50–75	50–80
	Phoenix	70–110	45–100	40–100	80–135

SOURCE: "Methamphetamine: annual price data," in *Illegal Drug Price/Purity Report,* Drug Enforcement Administration, Arlington, VA, 1999

Mexico have taken over. Over the past few years, these groups have revolutionized the production of methamphetamines by operating large-scale laboratories, both in Mexico and the United States, capable of producing huge quantities of high-purity methamphetamines.

At first, the drug manufacturers distributed their product throughout the western United States. They have since expanded their distribution channels, sending the drug into the Midwest and South, particularly into Georgia, Kansas, Missouri, Nebraska, and Iowa.

To serve this growing trade, a number of independent, small-scale producers have begun operating in the Midwest. Traditionally, these small-scale operations were located in sparsely populated or isolated rural areas in order to avoid detection, but producers have apparently become more brazen. Nonetheless, large laboratories operating in California and Mexico remain the major suppliers of methamphetamines to the United States.

Methamphetamine Prices

In 1998 wholesale methamphetamine cost between $3,500 and $30,000 a pound, while an ounce ran $500–$2,500. At the street level, a gram of methamphetamine costs $25–$150. (See Table 6.12.)

Clandestine Laboratories

From a trafficker's standpoint, according to the Department of State's Bureau for International Narcotics and Law Enforcement Affairs (*International Narcotics Control Strategy Report, 1999,* Washington, D.C.):

> Methamphetamine's great advantage is its relative ease of manufacture from readily available chemicals. Like other synthetics, methamphetamine appeals to large and small criminal enterprises alike, as it frees them from dependence on vulnerable crops such as coca or opium poppy. Even a small organization can control the whole process, from manufacture to sale on the street. The drugs can be made almost anywhere and generate large profit margins.

Ephedrine is the key ingredient in the making of methamphetamines. In 1989 the DEA was authorized under the Chemical Diversion and Trafficking Act to regulate bulk sales of ephedrine, but over-the-counter sales were not included. As a result, manufacturers simply bought ephedrine at drugstores and then used it to manufacture methamphetamines.

The passage of the Domestic Chemical Diversion Control Act of 1993 (PL 103-200) made it illegal to sell ephedrine over the counter. Pseudoephedrine, a substitute for ephedrine, however, was not included in the ban. Pseudoephedrine is found in more than 100 over-the-counter drugs, including Sudafed and Actifed. Manufacturers have been able to use pseudoephedrine taken from these drugs to make methamphetamines, often for less than they could with ephedrine.

The Comprehensive Methamphetamine Control Act of 1996 (PL 104-237) made it illegal to knowingly possess certain chemicals (known as precursor chemicals) used in the preparation of methamphetamines, and doubled the possible penalty for manufacturing and/or distribution from 10 to 20 years. The Methamphetamine Trafficking Penalty Enhancement Act of 1998 (PL 105-277), signed into law as part of the omnibus spending agreement for 1999, further increased penalties for trafficking methamphetamines. Authorities are targeting companies that knowingly supply chemicals essential to methamphetamine producers, domestically and internationally. The importance of controlling precursor chemicals has been established in international treaties and laws.

Clandestine methamphetamine laboratories in the United States are usually operated as temporary manufacturing facilities. The drug producers make a batch of the finished drug, tear down the laboratory, and then either store it for later use or rebuild it in another place. This constant assembling and disassembling of laboratories is necessary to avoid detection by law enforcement authorities.

Laboratory Seizures

Still, in 1997 federal authorities seized 1,435 clandestine drug laboratories, up significantly from the 218 seized in 1993. (See Table 6.13.) Nearly all (99 percent) of the laboratories raided had been making methamphetamine. In 1997, 92 percent of the "meth lab" seizures in the United States were in the cities of Dallas, Denver, Los Angeles, New Orleans, Phoenix, St. Louis, San Diego, and San Francisco.

TABLE 6.13

Clandestine laboratory seizures reported to the DEA, by selected drug type, 1991–97

Drug Type	1997	1996	1995	1994	1993	1992	1991
Methamphetamine	1,435	879	327	263	218	288	315
Methcathinone	7	10	19	20	22	6	5
Amphetamine	2	5	2	6	12	12	20
PCP	2	1	6	9	6	4	3
MDMA	5	3	2	4	3	9	1
Fentanyl	0	0	0	0	2	0	1
MDA	0	0	0	0	2	2	5
Cocaine	0	0	0	0	1	4	4
P2P	0	3	4	1	1	3	7
Methaqualone	0	0	0	0	0	1	1
Other	0	0	2	3	3	3	13
Total # of Seizures	1,451	901	362	306	270	322	375

SOURCE: "Clandestine laboratory seizures reported to the DEA (by selected drug type)," in *The NNICC Report 1997: The Supply of Illicit Drugs to the United States,* National Narcotics Intelligence Consumers Committee, Washington, DC, 1998

CHAPTER 7
THE WAR ON DRUGS—A DAUNTING CHALLENGE

DRUGS ARE A PART OF THE ECONOMY

The narcotics industry is a boon not only to coca farmers but also to the economies of debt-ridden South American countries. In Peru, where about half the population lives in poverty, drug trafficking annually infuses approximately $1 billion into the economy. In 1995 the United Nations estimated that the drug industry—cultivation, processing, and transporting—accounted for about 11 percent of the gross national product (GNP) of Peru. In 1999 the Colombian government began to include revenues from narcotics in its gross national product, adding as much as 1 percent to the value of its deteriorating economy. The dependence of drug-producing countries on drug revenues is one reason antidrug policies are so hard to effectively implement and sustain.

COOPERATION AND DRUG ERADICATION PROGRAMS

To stem the flow of drugs into the United States, the American government has encouraged governments of countries where cocaine, opium, and marijuana are either grown, manufactured, or transported to try to control the drug trade in their countries. A major part of these campaigns has been crop eradication programs aimed at wiping out the illegal crops. In most cases the United States has supplied personnel and/or considerable financial assistance to these programs.

In many cases cooperation has been reluctant. The *International Narcotics Control Strategy Report, 1999* (Bureau for International Narcotics and Law Affairs, Washington, D.C., 2000) observed that

> At this time, there are only three countries that cultivate coca on a significant scale: Bolivia, Colombia, and Peru. Because alkaloid content is high in Bolivian and Peruvian coca, every two hundred hectares [one hectare equals 2.47 acres] of coca bushes taken out of production deprives drug traffickers of approximately one metric ton of finished cocaine. Thus even manual destruction of the bush can have a lasting impact.

Peru and Bolivia, both of which have a long tradition of coca leaf chewing in the highlands, continue to grow legal coca both for traditional reasons and for commercial export to pharmaceutical companies. Peru only permits eradication of tended coca away from population centers. Bolivia also permits manual eradication of illegal coca, but has legislative restrictions against herbicide spraying. Only Colombia permits and conducts an extensive aerial eradication program.

In 1998 the Colombian government sprayed record amounts of coca plants—over 65,000 hectares. The percentage of plants that died because of the spraying also increased. Traffickers responded by expanding coca cultivation to remote areas beyond the reach of the spray aircraft. Consequently, Colombia showed a net increase in its coca harvest, with 101,800 hectares harvested in 1998.

In nearby Bolivia about 11,621 hectares of coca plants were destroyed, while an estimated 38,000 were harvested. The Peruvian government eradicated 7,825 hectares, nearly doubling its goal of 4,000 hectares, in 1998. Peru harvested 51,000 hectares of coca, a 26 percent decline from the previous year.

Mexico appeared to be quite successful in eradicating poppy fields used to furnish opium to produce heroin. In 1998 Mexico eradicated an estimated 9,500 hectares of poppies, while only 5,500 hectares reached harvest. Colombia sprayed over 3,000 hectares of poppy cultivation, while 6,100 hectares of poppies were harvested.

Arguments for Growing Other Crops

U.S. officials have worked to convince farmers raising illegal drugs in other countries that they should grow other crops instead. For example, the U.S. Agency for International Development (USAID) supports licit

TABLE 7.1

United States bilateral counterdrug agreements, 1997

	Shipboarding	Shiprider	Pursuit	Entry to Investigate	Overflight	Order to land
Antigua & Barbuda	X	X	X	X	X	X
Bahamas		X			X	
Barbados[a]						
Belize	X	X	X	X		
Costa Rica						
Cuba						
Dominica	X	X	X	X		
Dominican Republic	X	X	X	X	b	
Ecuador						
El Salvador						
French West Indies						
Grenada	X	X	X	X	X	X
Guatemala						
Haiti			X	X	X	
Honduras						
Jamaica[a]						
Mexico						
Netherlands Antilles		X	X	X	X	
Nicaragua						
Panama		X				
St. Kitts & Nevis	X	X	X	X	X	X
St. Lucia	X	X	X	X	X	X
St. Vincent/Grenadines	X	X	X	X		
Suriname						
Trinidad & Tobago	X	X	X	X	X	X
Turks & Caicos		X-air only				
U.K. West Indies	X	X				
Venezuela	X		X-air only			

Note: Empty cells indicate no agreement in this area.

[a]Agreement with Barbados and Jamaica have been signed but implementation is pending ratification by host government parliaments and approval of implementation legislation.

[b]The Dominican Republic has granted temporary overflight authority over its territorial waters to dissuade and detect illegal migration and illegal drug trafficking through March 15, 1998.

Shipboarding: = Standing authority for the U.S. Coast Guard to stop, board, and search foreign vessels suspected of illicit traffic located seaward of the territorial sea of any nation.

Shiprider: = Standing authority to embark law enforcement officials on vessel platforms of the parties. These officials may then authorize certain law enforcement actions.

Pursuit: = Standing authority for U.S. law enforcement assets to pursue fleeing vessels or aircraft suspected of illicit drug traffic into foreign waters or airspace. May also include authority to stop, board, and search pursued vessels.

Entry to investigate: = Standing authority for U.S. law enforcement assets to enter foreign waters or airspace to investigate vessels or aircraft located therein suspected of illicit drug traffic. May also include authority to stop, board, and search such vessels.

Overflight:= Standing authority for U.S. law enforcement assets to fly in foreign airspace when in support of counterdrug operations.

Order to land: = Standing authority for U.S. law enforcement assets to order to land in the host nation aircraft suspected of illicit drug traffic.

SOURCE: "U.S. Bilateral Counterdrug Agreements, as of August 1997," in *Drug Control: Update on U.S. Interdiction Efforts in the Caribbean and Eastern Pacific* U.S. General Accounting Office, Washington, D.C., 1997

agricultural production, vital to the eventual elimination of the illicit coca and cocaine industry. In addition, USAID has assisted in improving roads and building bridges for better access to markets. Many of the areas where coca has been cultivated have poor road systems, making it difficult to get alternative crops, often fresh produce, to the marketplace before they rot.

Farmers in Bolivia, one of the poorest countries in the Western Hemisphere, are reluctant to give up planting coca, a sure cash crop, to risk planting an unknown crop. Some Bolivian farmers who agree to plant alternative crops complain that neither financial compensation nor promised agricultural alternatives are delivered. Drug enforcement agents claim that farmers are eradicating worn-out plots of coca and planting new plots elsewhere.

However, efforts focused in the Chapare coca-growing areas, where coca was the principal crop grown prior to 1992, have been successful. Three times as much land is now dedicated to growing alternative crops, such as bananas, pineapples, palm hearts, black pepper, and passion fruit, as to growing coca. Farmers' net income from licit crops increased by 52 percent in 1998.

Peru is also widely claimed by U.S. officials as a major success story in reducing coca production. In 1997 the area devoted to coca leaf cultivation fell by about 27 percent, a reduction of 25,400 hectares.

Nonetheless, even when new farming techniques have apparently been accepted, they can easily backfire. Attempts in Thailand in the 1970s to teach the farmers drip irrigation and terraced rice farming so they would not plant poppies led to their tending drip-irrigated, terraced poppy fields. In South America, improved roads to transport the new fruit crops to market have made it that much easier to get coca to the airport.

COOPERATION IN FIGHTING DRUG TRAFFICKERS

Other countries are frequently reluctant to cooperate with the United States to stop drug traffickers. In the Caribbean Basin, while most of the islands have bilateral agreements with the United States, these agreements are limited to maritime matters that permit American ships to seize traffickers in the territorial waters of particular Caribbean islands. Other problems revolve around the transit zone, the area between the South American continent and the 12-mile contiguous zone offshore the United States within which U.S. interdiction forces can operate. Very few transit-zone countries permit American planes to fly in their airspace to force suspected traffickers to land. Twelve transit-zone countries have no maritime agreements with the United States. (See Table 7.1.)

Bilateral agreements are not the same in each country, and some provide very limited rights to U.S. law enforcement authorities. For example, a U.S.–Belize agreement allows the U.S. Coast Guard to board suspected Belizean vessels on the high seas without prior notification. The agreement with Panama requires U.S. Coast Guard vessels in Panamanian waters to be escorted by a Panamanian government ship.

NEGOTIATION IN FIGHTING DRUG TRAFFICKERS

Counternarcotics efforts are often hindered by foreign-relations tensions between the United States and Latin American countries and by the countries' own political turmoil. For example, the U.S. counternarcotics effort seemed to be in trouble when the United States gave up control of the Panama Canal and the Canal Zone at the end of 1999. Although many Panamanian citizens enjoyed the boost to the economy brought by the American presence, many others were happy to see the Americans leave.

The termination of the treaty required the withdrawal of all U.S. military personnel from Panama. Howard Air Force Base in Panama had been the region's top counternarcotics outpost, with more than two thousand surveillance flights initiated each year. New operating locations in Ecuador, Curacao, and Aruba were negotiated in time to fill the role played by Howard AFB.

Establishing these new locations was not easy, however. The United States failed to negotiate a new contract with Panama, and also failed to negotiate a move to Costa Rica. In January 2000, shortly after agreeing to let the United States set up operations in Ecuador, its then-president, Jamil Mahuad, was overthrown in a military coup, jeopardizing the deal. Although there were ambivalent feelings about the U.S. presence in Ecuador, the deal stuck. Nonetheless, U.S. officials expect some resistance because of the close ties between Ecuadorian political leaders and Colombian drug traffickers.

FIGURE 7.1

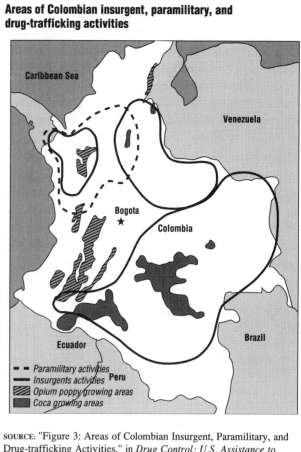

Areas of Colombian insurgent, paramilitary, and drug-trafficking activities

SOURCE: "Figure 3: Areas of Colombian Insurgent, Paramilitary, and Drug-trafficking Activities," in *Drug Control: U.S. Assistance to Colombia Will Take Years to Produce Results,* Government Accounting Office, Washington, DC, 2000

The General Accounting Office, in *Drug Control— Update on U.S. Interdiction Efforts in the Caribbean and Eastern Pacific* (Washington, D.C., 1997), noted that corruption-related problems continue throughout the Caribbean:

> Once the influence of drug trafficking becomes entrenched, corruption inevitably follows and democratic governments may be placed in jeopardy. . . . [L]ow salary levels for law enforcement officers and other public servants . . . make them susceptible to accepting bribes.

Effective law enforcement operations and adequate judicial and legislative tools are essential to the success of efforts to stop the flow of drugs from both source and transit countries. Though the United States can provide assistance, these countries must seize the illegal drugs. They must also arrest and prosecute or extradite the traffickers, when possible, in order to stop the production and movement of drugs internationally.

However, many of these Caribbean countries are poor, and therefore lack the resources and capabilities necessary to combat drug trafficking within their borders.

In addition, lack of equipment and inadequately trained personnel limit the governments' ability to detect and interdict (prohibit) drugs and drug traffickers.

Many countries have tried to control their drug growers and traffickers, but it is often very difficult. The huge amounts of money involved have led to bribes of government officials, border guards, and soldiers. In countries where the military plays a major role in government, many high-ranking officers, including leading generals, have been directly involved in drug trafficking.

In Colombia, insurgent groups (rebels against the government) are becoming more powerful and more actively involved in drug-trafficking activities, making it difficult for Colombian law enforcement to deal with drug trafficking within the country. Figure 7.1 shows Colombia's major coca- and opium poppy–producing areas and the areas of paramilitary and insurgent activity.

According to the *International Narcotics Control Strategy Report, 1999,* "The United States will continue to provide necessary leadership and assistance to our partners in the global antidrug effort. As one of the countries most affected by illegal drugs, we cannot afford to give up any of the ground gained in the last decade."

DRUG CERTIFICATION PROCESS

To promote international cooperation to control drug production and trafficking, the United States uses the drug certification process, which involves the threat of, or application of, sanctions for noncompliance. Sanctions range from suspension of U.S. foreign assistance and preferential trade benefits to curtailment of air transportation. Another major sanction is public criticism for failing the standard.

Sections 489 and 490 of the Foreign Assistance Act of 1961 (PL 87-195), as amended, establish the drug certification process. The president is required to submit to Congress an annual list of major drug-producing and drug-transiting countries, and also to certify the countries that have been fully cooperative with U.S. or United Nations narcotics-reduction goals (and are, therefore, fully eligible to receive U.S. foreign aid). Congress then has 30 days to disapprove the president's certification, in order to stop financial aid and other benefits from going to specific countries.

In 2001 President George W. Bush determined the following countries to be major drug-producing or drug-transiting countries: Afghanistan, Bahamas, Bolivia, Brazil, Burma, Cambodia, China, Colombia, Dominican Republic, Ecuador, Guatemala, Haiti, India, Jamaica, Laos, Mexico, Nigeria, Pakistan, Panama, Paraguay, Peru, Thailand, Venezuela, and Vietnam. On March 1, 2001, President Bush determined all but four of these countries

to be in full compliance with the goals and objectives of the 1988 United Nations Convention Against Illicit Traffic in Narcotic Drugs and Psychotropic Substances. Two countries—Afghanistan and Burma—were not certified. The United States voted not to provide foreign assistance to these countries. Two other countries—Cambodia and Haiti—were certified because of "vital national interests," although they were not found in compliance with the U.S. war on drugs.

Some observers questioned the certification of Mexico and Colombia as fully cooperative in fighting illegal drugs when most hard drugs flooding the United States come from these countries. There were serious questions as to their commitment to stopping the production and delivery of drugs.

Other critics suggested that the process was too unilateral. Some countries, such as Mexico, felt the U.S. wielded its assistance unfairly, since the certification is primarily in American interests. Several senators criticized the process, saying that it did not really foster multilateral cooperation. Partnerships, through bilateral counterdrug agreements, they said, would be a more effective policy.

HAVE INTERDICTION AND ERADICATION HELPED?

Interdiction and eradication, integral elements of U.S. international narcotics-control policy, are intended to stop the flow of foreign drugs into the United States. In 1998 the U. S. government budgeted about $60 million for eradication and alternate development programs—less than one-third of the State Department's narcotics-control budget request. Most of the eradication programs target coca cultivation in the South American Andes (Bolivia, Colombia, and Peru). The Andean countries help to finance and carry out eradication programs.

Eradication programs seem to have encouraged alliances between peasants and guerillas. In Colombia, guerilla groups have widened their areas of control and now represent a significant threat to the government. (See Figure 7.2.) By defending poor coca-growing farmers from what is viewed as U.S. intervention, guerillas gain political and financial strength. Furthermore, some observers suspect that much of the funds and equipment intended for drug eradication is being used to fight the rebel groups.

Some analysts believe that current efforts have essentially failed and that new policies, programs, and priorities are needed. The General Accounting Office, in *Drug Control—Observations on U.S. Counternarcotics Activities* (Washington, D.C., 1998), asserts that

Although U.S. and host-nation counter-narcotics efforts have resulted in the arrest of major drug traffickers and the seizure of large amounts of drugs, they have not materially reduced the availability of drugs in the United States. A key reason for the lack of success of U.S. counternarcotics programs is that international drug-trafficking organizations have become sophisticated, multibillion-dollar industries that quickly adapt to new U.S. drug control efforts. As success is achieved in one area, the drug-trafficking organizations quickly change tactics, thwarting U.S. efforts.

Despite some successes, cocaine, heroin, and other illegal drugs continue to be readily available in the United States.

U.S. officials estimated that, of the 650 metric tons of cocaine produced in 1997, about 430 metric tons were destined for U.S. markets. Even the 100 metric tons or so of cocaine that the U.S. government typically seizes annually have little discernible effect on price or availability. The demand for cocaine in this country is approximately 300 metric tons per year. The current U.S. demand for heroin is estimated to be about 10 metric tons per year, an amount easily supplied by Colombia.

Even the Department of State's *International Narcotics Control Strategy Report, 1999,* after its upbeat opening, "The U.S. and its allies made solid gains at the drug trade's expense in 1998," soon noted that

> . . . in spite of our combined efforts to disrupt supply through a broad spectrum of crop control and interdiction measures, in 1998, the drug syndicates exported hundreds of tons of cocaine and heroin around the world. . . . [T]he drug trade is a formidable enemy. In many cases, the drug trade's organization, power, and wealth are comparable to or surpass those of many of the countries in which it operates.

Eradication programs are intended to decrease coca production to make cocaine scarcer and more expensive, thereby decreasing use. According to Phillip Coffin, a research associate at the Lindesmith Center, a New York–based drug policy think tank, the programs are ineffective ("Foreign Policy in Focus: Coca Eradication," *Foreign Policy in Focus,* October 1998). In his view, "eradication has not succeeded by any measure."

Coffin claims that when coca cultivation is eradicated in one area, farmers who still grow coca earn more for their product. That, in turn, tempts other farmers to move into or expand coca cultivation. Though there may be significant increases in the price that coca leaves bring in South America, cocaine prices in the United States are affected very little. Coffin found evidence that suggests that price is not a crucial variable in predicting overall consumption.

Coffin claims that Peru's success in reducing cultivation is not due to eradication but to a mysterious fungus. According to Peruvian drug trade analysts, there is now a resurgence in growing. Coffin also points out that while coca growing in Peru has declined, cultivation in Colombia has significantly increased, leaving total production in the Andean region largely unchanged.

FIGURE 7.2

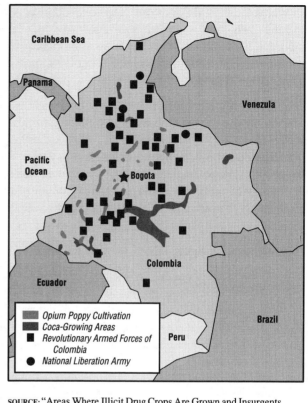

Areas of illicit drug crop growth and insurgent operations in Colombia

SOURCE: "Areas Where Illicit Drug Crops Are Grown and Insurgents Operate," in *Drug Control: U.S. Counternarcotics Efforts in Columbia Face Continuing Challenges,* U.S. General Accounting Office, Washington, D.C., 1998

WHY IS THE "WAR ON DRUGS" SO DIFFICULT?

The goal of the "war on drugs" is to stop the flow of a product that is in high demand, generally cheap to make, offers a huge profit, and is easy to produce and transport. While certain traffickers may dominate for a time, the drug trade is generally characterized by a large number of traffickers. Capturing one or two major figures or hundreds of lesser traffickers does little to slow the drug trade.

Trying to stop the flow of drugs is like trying to slay the hydra, a mythological dragonlike monster with many heads. When one head was cut off, another grew in its place. When one drug policy is put into place, drug traffickers simply change their operations to circumvent it. When one route is blocked or one method of production shut down, they change to another. Production costs are so low and the profit is so great that even if a trafficker loses most of his product, he can still earn a huge amount of money.

Since 90–95 percent of the street price of drugs is directly based on the costs of wholesale and retail distribution within the United States, even if half the cultivated drugs were destroyed and the price of coca leaf doubled, it would hardly affect the final price.

Furthermore, if the United States cannot successfully interdict the flow of drugs through its closest neighbors, upon which the United States can exert some political and economic influence and even introduce advisors and equipment, how successful can it be in attempts to stop the trafficking of drugs from far-off countries such as Afghanistan or Burma?

Finally, foreign countries—the producing nations—are being asked to solve a problem that is in many ways an American dilemma. Americans want drugs, and as long as this demand persists, suppliers will find a way to deliver the product. Many producer nations feel that a "war on drugs" would be more successful if it focused on lowering demand rather than eradicating or interdicting the supply.

MONEY LAUNDERING

The U.S. attorney general defines money laundering as "all activities designed to conceal the existence, nature, and final disposition of funds gained through illicit activities." It is the attempt to make funds earned illegally appear as if they were earned legally. Money laundering can range from things as simple as mailing a packet of money out of the country to complex international bank transactions. Many techniques money launderers use are legitimate—except that the source of the money is illegal.

Before 1986 the main tool against money laundering was the Bank Secrecy Act of 1970 (PL 91-508), which required financial institutions to file a currency transaction report (CTR) on all cash deposits of more than $10,000. Reports also had to be filed for international transactions of more than $10,000. Money launderers avoided these regulations by "smurfing," or making multiple transactions in amounts just under the limit (this is now illegal). Until the early 1980s, bank compliance with the law was lax and penalties were lenient. As a result of the Eduardo Orozco case (Orozco laundered approximately $151 million in drug profits through 18 New York banks), compliance became stricter.

Money laundering became a federal crime with the passage of the Money Laundering Control Act of 1986 (PL 99-570). It prohibits engaging in financial transactions or transfers of funds or property derived from "specified unlawful activity" and engaging in monetary transactions in excess of $10,000 with property derived from proceeds of "specified unlawful activity." In addition, the act prohibits the structuring of currency transactions to evade the CTR reporting requirement.

Increasingly, the government has been monitoring all transactions of those known or suspected of money laundering or drug trafficking. In addition, U.S. banks must have "know your customer" policies. Under these policies, financial institutions must verify the business of a new account holder and monitor the activity of all business customers so that they can report any activity inconsistent with that type of business.

How Laundering Is Done

Drug dealing creates a great amount of cash, which, in order to hide its illegitimate origins, must be funneled into legitimate businesses, into offshore banks, or out of the country to pay foreign drug dealers. Federal law enforcement officials estimate that drug traffickers launder between $100 billion and $300 billion each year, much of it through legal financial institutions.

Generally, drug traffickers need to pay expenses to suppliers and distributors, reinvest in the illegal enterprise, and use their earnings to ensure financial security and an extravagant lifestyle befitting a successful drug trafficker. In addition, some dealers invest in legitimate businesses to help hide illegal funds and to serve as a springboard for political influence and corruption.

Although the stereotype of the drug dealer is a man with bundles of bills of large denominations, most of the drug trade is carried out in fives, tens, and twenties. These small denominations are converted into larger bills by exchanging them at a bank, post office, check cashing service, or other institution. The larger bills are then smuggled out of the country.

The money laundering process usually involves three stages. In the first, the placement stage, the illegal funds enter the financial system, most often going into foreign accounts. The money crosses borders by courier, by smuggling, or through electronic-funds transfers from one bank to another.

Laundered money is most vulnerable to detection at the placement stage. Therefore, government efforts have concentrated on making it difficult to place illegal funds without detection. Many countries have instituted regulations requiring banks and other financial institutions to report currency transactions of over $10,000 (in U.S. dollars) and to report suspicious transactions. Other measures include cross-border monetary declaration requirements and "know your customer" rules for those who accept cash deposits.

After the funds are in the financial system, they are then moved from institution to institution to hide the source and ownership of the funds. This is the layering stage. To circumvent the reporting requirements, numerous deposits just under the $10,000 cash transaction threshold may be made. The high volume of wire transfers and the speed with which they are accomplished make it almost impossible to distinguish an illegal transfer from a legal one. A major bank in New York handles about 40,000 transfers every day, moving about $3 billion.

The third stage, the integration stage, involves the reinvestment of the funds into legitimate businesses. This may be accomplished by creating dummy, or "front," corporations to receive and distribute funds, and by making foreign real estate investments. These "front" companies can be art dealerships, precious metal stores, jewelry shops, real estate investment companies, car and boat dealerships, or banking institutions—any type of business that can easily justify the transfer of large amounts of cash. In his June 1998 testimony before the House Committee on Banking and Financial Services, Jonathan Winer, deputy assistant secretary of the Bureau for International Narcotics and Law Enforcement Affairs, warned, "Ultimately, this laundered money flows into global financial systems where it can undermine national economies and currencies. Money laundering is not only a law enforcement problem but a serious national and international security threat as well."

Money laundering is the most vulnerable point for drug kingpins (the heads of drug organizations). Although they may be well insulated from street-level dealers, the kingpins do not keep the same distance from their money. Money laundering will almost always leave a paper trail of transactions that can be traced, although in many instances a complicated investigative effort is necessary.

In 1998 U.S. law enforcement officials completed Operation Casablanca, the largest, most comprehensive, and most significant drug money-laundering case in U.S. history. The indictment charged Mexican bank officials and Venezuelan bankers. Several American banks, including Citibank and Bank of America, testified or were cited for failure to supervise their own operations. The international ring was linked to the Colombian Cali cartel.

Although 100 people were charged in the operation, the majority remain fugitives. Of the defendants brought up on criminal charges, about 30 pleaded guilty, several were convicted, one reached a civil settlement, one was convicted (but had the conviction overturned), and several were acquitted of criminal charges.

International Crime Control Strategy

President Bill Clinton, in a statement before the UN General Assembly on September 22, 1997, remarked that

In the twenty-first century, our security will be challenged increasingly by interconnected groups that traffic in terror, organized crime and drug smuggling. Already these international crime and drug syndicates drain up to $750 billion a year from legitimate economies. That sum exceeds the combined GNP of more than half the nations in this room.

In 1998 President Clinton released the first International Crime Control Strategy in U.S. history, containing eight goals to fight international crime. One of the goals addresses financial crime, with the following specific objectives:

• Combat money laundering by denying criminals access to financial institutions and by strengthening enforcement efforts to reduce inbound and outbound movement of criminal proceeds.

• Seize the assets of international criminals through aggressive use of forfeiture laws.

• Enhance bilateral and multilateral cooperation against all financial crime by working with foreign governments to establish or update enforcement tools and to implement multilateral anti-money-laundering standards.

• Target offshore centers, where government policies protect the secrecy of financial transactions, for international fraud, counterfeiting, electronic-access schemes, and other financial crimes.

International Cooperation

Money laundering is an international activity that can be fought only with international cooperation. As more countries have tightened controls and shared information, narcotics dealers have become more sophisticated in their techniques. International criminals are not tied to geographic boundaries and can operate in "safe haven" jurisdictions that permit, or even encourage, money laundering in their territories. In addition, cyberbanking and digital cash are two of the latest methods used by money launderers to keep one step ahead of legislation.

The 1988 Vienna Convention made the laundering of drug money an international crime. The Financial Action Task Force (FATF) extended the Vienna Convention proposal to include the laundering of proceeds from all crimes. The United States is a leading member of FATF, which consists of 26 of the world's developed nations and two international organizations, the European Commission and the Gulf Cooperation Council. FATF has established global anti-money-laundering policies designed to coordinate international efforts.

At the United Nations General Assembly Special Session on International Drug Control in 1998, 185 member countries agreed to undertake special efforts against the laundering of drug money and to adopt, if they had not already, national anti-money-laundering legislation and programs by the year 2003. The agreement sets out specific provisions to be implemented and recognizes the Forty Recommendations, the basic framework the FATF set up in 1990 and revised in 1996, as the standard by which measures against money laundering should be judged.

CHAPTER 8

DRUG TREATMENT

What we're doing is simply a holding action. We've arrested more people than the prosecutors can prosecute, than the judges can convict, than the jails can hold. Until there's a demand reduction—and that means education and treatment—you're not going to see any change.

—Captain Harvey Ferguson, former chief of narcotics enforcement, Seattle, Washington

WHAT IS ADDICTION AND WHAT CAUSES IT?

Many people and agencies treat all drug use the same and do not differentiate between use, abuse, and addiction. However, many researchers, public-health officials, and treatment professionals continually debate the definition of addiction.

Differentiating Abuse and Dependence

The 2000 *Diagnostic and Statistical Manual of Mental Disorders-IV Text Revision,* or DSM-IV-TR (American Psychiatric Association, 2000), is the most widely used reference for diagnosing and treating mental illness and substance-related disorders. It distinguishes between "substance abuse" and "substance dependence." The DSM-IV-TR stresses that these terms should not be used interchangeably, and that they are distinct from common terms like "substance use" and "substance misuse."

"Substance abuse" can be diagnosed only when one of the following conditions has been observed in the past year: The patient has (1) repeatedly failed to live up to major obligations, such as on the job, at school, or in the family, because of drug use; (2) used the substance in dangerous situations, such as before driving; (3) had multiple legal problems due to drug use; or (4) continued to use drugs in the face of interpersonal problems, such as arguments or fights caused by substance use.

The DSM-IV-TR requires that at least three of the following conditions be met in the previous year before

a person can be said to be "substance dependent": The patient has (1) experienced increased tolerance; (2) experienced withdrawal; (3) had a loss of control over quantity or duration of use; (4) had a continuing wish or inability to decrease use; (5) spent inordinate amounts of time procuring or consuming drugs, or recovering from substance use; (6) given up important goals or activities because of substance use; or (7) continued to use despite knowledge that he or she has experienced damaging effects.

Applying the Definition

Since the 1960s one tradition in the field of sociology has been to study the "labeling process" by which people are identified and treated as addicts. Rather than formulating a definition of what makes a person an addict, researchers study differences in who is labeled an addict and who is not—the process by which people become known as "addicts." For example, sociologists have pointed out that while doctors use opiates and painkillers more than people in any other profession, often using on the job and in increasing amounts, they are less likely to be called addicts than users in the street who consume the same amount of drugs. Furthermore, when physicians do get caught—and labeled "addicts"—they are more likely to go into treatment and less likely to end up in jail or in prison or lose their jobs than poor addicts with fewer social and economic resources.

The major argument of these researchers is that drug users of different social classes vary in how likely they are to be caught and labeled addicts. Furthermore, how addicts are treated by society—whether they end up in jail or in treatment, for example—is not totally due to whether or not they are addicted. This argument serves to explain part of the reason why white users are found more often in treatment while black users are more often found in jail or prison. (See Figure 8.1.)

FIGURE 8.1

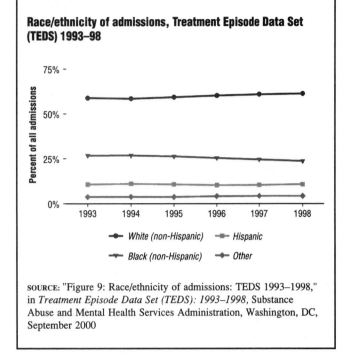

Race/ethnicity of admissions, Treatment Episode Data Set (TEDS) 1993–98

SOURCE: "Figure 9: Race/ethnicity of admissions: TEDS 1993–1998," in *Treatment Episode Data Set (TEDS): 1993–1998,* Substance Abuse and Mental Health Services Administration, Washington, DC, September 2000

The "Disease" Model of Addiction

In the past 20 years advances in neuroscience have led to new understanding of how people become addicted and why they stay that way. The "disease model" of addiction has been proposed by psychiatric and medical researchers. Addicts, they say, respond to drugs differently than people who are not addicted. Much of the difference is associated with differences in brain functioning and can be linked to genetic factors. Current treatment approaches emphasize that addiction must be treated in the same way as other chronic diseases.

The *Journal of the American Medical Association* published an article (A. McLellan, D. Lewis, C. O'Brien, and H. Kleber, "Drug Dependence, a Chronic Medical Illness," October 4, 2000) that likened drug dependence to chronic illnesses such as diabetes, hypertension, and asthma. The article reviewed scientific studies of twins and children of parents who were dependent on alcohol or other drugs. The authors reported high degrees of correlation between parental and sibling dependence, suggesting a strong genetic component in addiction and alcoholism. Moreover, people who used drugs over long periods had different patterns of brain function, which seemed to lead them to continue to use drugs. Findings like this have led the director of the National Institute on Drug Abuse, Alan Leshner, to conclude that changes in the brain are responsible for addiction.

Social and Cultural Explanations of Addiction

Despite these important advances, psychologists and sociologists stress that other factors are involved in addic-

tion. Psychologists have showed links between childhood abuse, other trauma, and life stress in contributing to addiction. Sociologists have pointed out that cross-cultural and social class differences in addiction exist. For example, addiction disproportionately affects the poor.

Although brain changes occur after continued drug use and may cause individuals to continue using drugs, these changes are temporary. Researchers have shown that they do not last more than a few months. Yet addicts are at risk of relapsing months, and even years, after they have quit using drugs—long after their brains have returned to normal functioning. Although brain function is important, sociologists and psychologists argue that it cannot explain why all, or even most, addicts become addicted.

A historical event that fueled this line of research was American involvement in the Vietnam conflict in the 1960s and 1970s. Many American soldiers began using heroin while in Vietnam and came back addicted. Yet most of them stopped using heroin after returning. This phenomenon focused attention on users who either do not become addicted or who cycle between abstinence and relapse.

Norman Zinberg, a Harvard University professor of psychiatry, was the first to study "controlled users" of marijuana, opiates, and hallucinogens in the 1970s and 1980s (*Drug, Set, and Setting,* Yale University Press, 1984). He showed that the social situations in which people use drugs have a profound impact on whether or not they become addicted. So, for example, people who use heroin with intimate groups of friends and do not interact with hard-core addicts often do not become addicted. Conversely, people who use in risky environments—such as "shooting galleries" or "crack houses"—use drugs in ways that make it more likely they will become addicts.

An Integrated Approach to Treatment

Biological, psychological, and social approaches have been incorporated in a variety of treatment settings. Patients are often treated with drugs, such as methadone or naltrexone, that intervene in the chemical causes of addiction. Counselors and patients may discuss problems that trigger drug use. Finally, therapists frequently suggest behavioral modification, such as staying away from people and places that may lead the user to consume drugs.

HOW MANY PEOPLE ARE BEING TREATED?

The *Uniform Facility Data Set* (UFDS), formerly the *National Drug and Alcoholism Treatment Unit Survey* (NDATUS), examines the nation's providers of substance-abuse treatment. These include facilities that treat only substance abuse (called "free-standing") and specialized units within institutions such as hospitals. The survey is administered by the Substance Abuse and Mental Health Services Administration (SAMHSA), in cooperation with state

TABLE 8.1

Number of clients in treatment, aged 12 and over, by substance abuse problem, according to state or jurisdiction, 1998

State or jurisdiction[1]	Substance abuse problem											
	Number of clients[2]				Percent distribution[2]				Clients per 100,000 population aged 12+[2]			
	Total	Both alcohol and drug abuse	Drug abuse only	Alcohol abuse only	Total	Both alcohol and drug abuse	Drug abuse only	Alcohol abuse only	Total	Both alcohol and drug abuse	Drug abuse only	Alcohol abuse only
Total	1,030,028	509,784	275,320	244,924	100.0	49.5	26.7	23.8	462	229	123	110
Alabama	8,933	4,274	2,929	1,730	100.0	47.8	32.8	19.4	245	117	80	47
Alaska	2,915	1,439	215	1,261	100.0	49.4	7.4	43.3	583	288	43	252
Arizona	19,804	8,795	5,883	5,126	100.0	44.4	29.7	25.9	533	237	158	138
Arkansas	7,006	4,096	1,480	1,430	100.0	58.5	21.1	20.4	326	191	69	67
California	126,340	57,515	41,512	27,313	100.0	45.5	32.9	21.6	491	224	161	106
Colorado	24,079	10,890	4,280	8,909	100.0	45.2	17.8	37.0	722	327	128	267
Connecticut	16,037	7,079	6,192	2,766	100.0	44.1	38.6	17.2	585	258	226	101
Delaware	3,767	1,912	1,059	796	100.0	50.8	28.1	21.1	603	306	170	128
Dist. of Columbia	6,499	3,949	1,654	896	100.0	60.8	25.5	13.8	1,448	880	368	200
Florida	45,591	24,867	11,961	8,763	100.0	54.5	26.2	19.2	365	199	96	70
Georgia	15,775	7,231	4,452	4,092	100.0	45.8	28.2	25.9	252	116	71	65
Hawaii	3,012	1,700	663	649	100.0	56.4	22.0	21.5	300	169	66	65
Idaho	2,896	1,858	430	608	100.0	64.2	14.8	21.0	278	179	41	58
Illinois	45,872	22,638	12,088	11,146	100.0	49.4	26.4	24.3	466	230	123	113
Indiana	16,855	7,384	3,695	5,776	100.0	43.8	21.9	34.3	340	149	74	116
Iowa	7,287	3,646	1,028	2,613	100.0	50.0	14.1	35.9	301	151	42	108
Kansas	8,951	5,022	1,557	2,372	100.0	56.1	17.4	26.5	412	231	72	109
Kentucky	14,656	6,597	2,712	5,347	100.0	45.0	18.5	36.5	442	199	82	161
Louisiana	16,991	9,664	4,162	3,165	100.0	56.9	24.5	18.6	473	269	116	88
Maine	8,577	4,306	1,195	3,076	100.0	50.2	13.9	35.9	809	406	113	290
Maryland	23,960	11,001	7,921	5,038	100.0	45.9	33.1	21.0	558	256	184	117
Massachusetts	42,508	23,781	9,871	8,856	100.0	55.9	23.2	20.8	824	461	191	172
Michigan	48,963	19,858	13,266	15,839	100.0	40.6	27.1	32.3	615	249	167	199
Minnesota	10,403	5,532	2,227	2,644	100.0	53.2	21.4	25.4	264	140	57	67
Mississippi	8,877	5,028	1,882	1,967	100.0	56.6	21.2	22.2	391	222	83	87
Missouri	17,596	11,330	2,913	3,353	100.0	64.4	16.6	19.1	387	249	64	74
Montana	2,470	1,326	317	827	100.0	53.7	12.8	33.5	322	173	41	108
Nebraska	5,515	3,065	746	1,704	100.0	55.6	13.5	30.9	396	220	54	122
Nevada	7,962	4,678	1,590	1,694	100.0	58.8	20.0	21.3	548	322	110	117
New Hampshire	3,374	1,741	312	1,321	100.0	51.6	9.2	39.2	338	175	31	133
New Jersey	24,666	11,999	8,882	3,785	100.0	48.6	36.0	15.3	367	179	132	56
New Mexico	10,304	4,280	2,051	3,973	100.0	41.5	19.9	38.6	714	297	142	275
New York	115,870	49,495	49,257	17,118	100.0	42.7	42.5	14.8	773	330	329	114
North Carolina	25,358	13,535	4,538	7,285	100.0	53.4	17.9	28.7	402	215	72	115
North Dakota	3,011	1,418	365	1,228	100.0	47.1	12.1	40.8	549	259	67	224
Ohio	42,490	23,839	7,413	11,238	100.0	56.1	17.4	26.4	453	254	79	120
Oklahoma	8,750	3,480	2,587	2,683	100.0	39.8	29.6	30.7	315	125	93	97
Oregon	18,116	9,644	4,631	3,841	100.0	53.2	25.6	21.2	653	348	167	139
Pennsylvania	36,536	21,460	8,282	6,794	100.0	58.7	22.7	18.6	357	210	81	66
Rhode Island	6,390	2,957	2,143	1,290	100.0	46.3	33.5	20.2	768	355	258	155
South Carolina	9,648	3,661	2,443	3,544	100.0	37.9	25.3	36.7	307	116	78	113
South Dakota	2,785	1,261	205	1,319	100.0	45.3	7.4	47.4	446	202	33	211
Tennessee	12,903	5,111	4,502	3,290	100.0	39.6	34.9	25.5	280	111	98	71
Texas	47,379	28,033	11,108	8,238	100.0	59.2	23.4	17.4	300	177	70	52

TABLE 8.1

Number of clients in treatment, aged 12 and over, by substance abuse problem, according to state or jurisdiction, 1998 [CONTINUED]

State or jurisdiction[1]	Substance abuse problem											
	Number of clients[2]				Percent distribution[2]				Clients per 100,000 population aged 12+[2]			
	Total	Both alcohol and drug abuse	Drug abuse only	Alcohol abuse only	Total	Both alcohol and drug abuse	Drug abuse only	Alcohol abuse only	Total	Both alcohol and drug abuse	Drug abuse only	Alcohol abuse only
Utah	11,650	5,815	3,431	2,404	100.0	49.9	29.5	20.6	705	352	208	145
Vermont	2,577	1,414	317	846	100.0	54.9	12.3	32.8	507	278	62	166
Virginia	20,888	10,595	4,431	5,862	100.0	50.7	21.2	28.1	364	185	77	102
Washington	31,953	18,864	4,438	8,651	100.0	59.0	13.9	27.1	675	398	94	183
West Virginia	4,658	1,630	792	2,236	100.0	35.0	17.0	48.0	296	103	50	142
Wisconsin	18,916	8,279	3,089	7,548	100.0	43.8	16.3	39.9	432	189	71	172
Wyoming	1,709	812	223	674	100.0	47.5	13.0	39.4	406	193	53	160

* Excludes jurisdictions outside the United States and the District of Columbia.

[1] Facilities operated by federal agencies are included in the states in which the facilities are located.

[2] Changes in the distribution and rates from figures reported in earlier publications may be because the questionnaire response order was changed in 1998.

SOURCE: "Table 5.3: Clients in treatment per 100,000 population aged 12 and over by substance abuse problem, according to State of jurisdiction: October 1, 1998," in *Uniform Facility Data Set (UFDS): 1998,* Substance Abuse and Mental Health Services Administration, Rockville, MD, 2000

TABLE 8.2

Substance abuse clients in treatment by sex, race/ethnicity, age group, and type of care, 1991–98

Sex, race/ethnicity, age, and type of care	1991[1]	1992[1]	1993	1995	1996	1997	1998	1991	1992	1993	1995	1996	1997	1998
	Number of clients in treatment							Percent distribution						
Total	811,819	944,880	944,208	1,009,127	940,141	929,086	1,038,378	100.0	100.0	100.0	100.0	100.0	100.0	100.0
Sex														
Male	588,295	671,426	663,968	707,252	640,369	632,113	715,479	72.5	71.1	70.3	70.1	68.1	68.0	68.9
Female	223,524	273,454	280,240	301,875	299,772	296,973	322,899	27.5	28.9	29.7	29.9	31.9	32.0	31.1
Race/ethnicity														
White	498,922	565,038	564,224	621,099	550,496	524,947	605,793	61.5	59.8	59.8	61.5	58.6	56.5	58.3
Black or African-American	172,144	204,286	212,607	219,064	219,409	230,971	247,840	21.2	21.6	22.5	21.7	23.3	24.9	23.9
Hispanic	114,735	138,136	130,460	127,047	130,140	132,459	140,499	14.1	14.6	13.8	12.6	13.8	14.3	13.5
Asian or Pacific Islander	7,118	7,210	8,365	9,143	8,987	7,697	9,300	0.9	0.8	0.9	0.9	1.0	0.8	0.9
American Indian or Alaska Native	14,857	12,408	23,303	24,292	25,011	24,459	26,724	1.8	1.3	2.5	2.4	2.7	2.6	2.6
Other	4,043	17,801	5,249	8,482	6,098	8,553	8,222	0.5	1.9	0.6	0.8	0.6	0.9	0.8
Age group														
Under 18 years	48,045	51,252	59,820	70,050	76,687	81,456	100,322	5.9	5.4	6.3	6.9	8.2	8.8	9.7
18 to 24 years	147,617	155,916	153,053	143,750	122,739	160,376	182,986	18.2	16.5	16.2	14.2	13.1	17.3	17.6
18 to 20 years	42,378	44,554	45,548	46,642	n/c	62,046	68,677	5.2	4.7	4.8	4.6	n/c	6.7	6.6
21 to 24 years	105,239	111,362	107,505	97,108	n/c	98,330	114,309	13.0	11.8	11.4	9.6	n/c	10.6	11.0
25 to 34 years	286,066	332,334	325,332	314,003	283,673	270,286	282,467	35.2	35.2	34.5	31.1	30.2	29.1	27.2
35 to 44 years	216,778	267,153	264,892	299,620	295,780	264,549	293,561	26.7	28.3	28.1	29.7	31.5	28.5	28.3
45 to 64 years	105,107	129,271	131,350	167,757	145,819	135,758	162,795	12.9	13.7	13.9	16.6	15.5	14.6	15.7
65 years & over	8,206	8,954	9,761	13,947	15,443	16,661	16,247	1.0	0.9	1.0	1.4	1.6	1.8	1.6
Type of care														
Outpatient	712,669	822,941	823,147	864,285	825,176	808,956	915,798	87.8	87.1	87.2	85.6	87.8	87.1	88.2
Residential	84,723	97,101	99,343	120,951	97,698	103,750	107,961	10.4	10.3	10.5	12.0	10.4	11.2	10.4
Hospital inpatient	14,427	24,838	21,718	23,891	17,267	16,380	14,619	1.8	2.6	2.3	2.4	1.8	1.8	1.4
Receiving opioid substitutes[2]	99,111	117,508	112,715	117,895	123,906	138,009	149,030	12.2	12.4	11.9	11.7	13.2	14.9	14.4

[1] Numbers published here differ from earlier published numbers because sex, race/ethnicity, and age group were imputed where these numbers were unknown.
[2] Clients receiving opioid substitutes may be in any type of care (outpatient, residential, or hospital inpatient).

n/c Data not collected.

SOURCE: "Table 2.4: Substance abuse treatment clients by sex, race/ethnicity, age group, and type of care: 1991–1998," in *Uniform Facility Data Set (UFDS): 1998, Substance Abuse and Mental Health Services Administration*, Rockville, MD, 2000

FIGURE 8.2

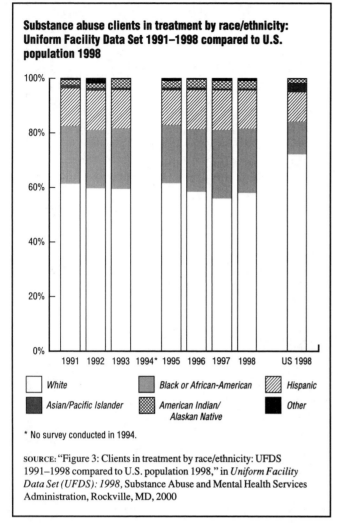

Substance abuse clients in treatment by race/ethnicity: Uniform Facility Data Set 1991–1998 compared to U.S. population 1998

White
Black or African-American
Hispanic
Asian/Pacific Islander
American Indian/Alaskan Native
Other

* No survey conducted in 1994.

SOURCE: "Figure 3: Clients in treatment by race/ethnicity: UFDS 1991–1998 compared to U.S. population 1998," in *Uniform Facility Data Set (UFDS): 1998,* Substance Abuse and Mental Health Services Administration, Rockville, MD, 2000

ed in Massachusetts (824 per 100,000). Treatment rates were lowest in Alabama (245 per 100,000) and Georgia (252 per 100,000). (See Table 8.1.)

Client Characteristics

GENDER AND AGE. In 1998 most substance abusers in treatment were men (68.9 percent). The percentage of women in treatment rose slightly between 1991 and 1998, from 27.5 percent to 31.1 percent. By far, the largest age groups in treatment were those 25–34 and 35–44. (See Table 8.2.)

RACE/ETHNICITY. Most people seeking treatment were white (58.3 percent), but blacks, Hispanics, and American Indian/Alaskan Natives were overrepresented in abuse programs when compared with their proportion in the general population. Blacks (about 12 percent of the general population) made up an estimated 23.9 percent of clients; Hispanics (about 11 percent of the population) accounted for 13.5 percent of clients; and American Indians/Alaskan Natives (less than 1 percent of the population) made up 2.6 percent of those getting treatment. (See Table 8.2 and Figure 8.2.)

The racial and ethnic composition of those getting treatment changed only slightly between 1980 and 1998. The proportion of non-Hispanic whites declined from 62.7 percent in 1980 to 58.3 percent in 1998, while the percentage of non-Hispanic blacks increased from 20.6 to 23.9 percent. The proportion of Hispanics getting treatment stayed about the same.

TYPES OF TREATMENT

According to the 1998 *Uniform Facility Data Set,* most patients (88.2 percent) in treatment were receiving outpatient rehabilitation. (See Table 8.2.) An outpatient is a patient who has been scheduled for an appointment with a counselor at least once within the last month. During that meeting, the patient receives counseling designed to help him or her overcome drug dependency. Counseling might also include participation in group therapy sessions.

About 10.4 percent of substance abusers were receiving 24-hour rehabilitation treatment, usually in a residential facility, a halfway house, or a correctional institution. Another 1.4 percent were receiving 24-hour detoxification in a hospital setting. (See Table 8.2 and Figure 8.3.)

Many feel that including detoxification under "treatment" may be misleading, since it is only the first step toward entering rehabilitation. Its purpose is to eliminate the immediate effects of the drug on the abuser. While it is necessary to detox in order to enter treatment, detoxification alone is not treatment and is most unlikely to succeed in breaking drug addictions.

In 1998, 85.6 percent of clients in treatment were enrolled in drug-free programs, while 14.4 percent were in

agencies and other federal agencies concerned with substance-abuse treatment. About 87 percent of the treatment facilities that received the 1998 survey responded. The results of the survey were released in *Uniform Facility Data Set (UFDS): 1998* (Substance Abuse and Mental Health Services Administration, Rockville, Maryland, 2000).

On October 1, 1998, 1.03 million clients were being treated for substance abuse in the United States. This number is a snapshot of the treatment units on a particular day and does not indicate how many people were being treated over the course of the year. The one-day statistics, however, amount to 462 clients per 100,000 in the general population age 12 and older, or 1 out of 235 U.S. residents, under treatment for substance abuse on that day. About 50 percent of clients were being treated for abuse of both alcohol and drugs, while 27 percent were being treated for abusing only drugs, and 24 percent for abusing only alcohol.

The number of clients in treatment varied considerably by state. The highest rate of treatment was more than three times the national average, in the District of Columbia (1,448 per 100,000). The next-highest rate was report-

narcotic-substitute programs. (See Table 8.2 and Figure 8.3.) Narcotic-substitute programs involve the prescription of a regulated narcotic, such as methadone, as an oral substitute for heroin. Methadone, first approved for use in 1972, is an "agonist" (a chemical substance that can activate a receptor to induce a pharmacological response) that reduces the craving for heroin by binding to the brain receptor. While heroin addiction disrupts many physiological functions, methadone normalizes those functions. Many studies have shown methadone to be effective, and many thousands of people lead normal lives using this heroin substitute.

LAAM (levo-alpha-acetylmethadol), approved in 1993, is another agonist used in treating drug dependency. While methadone must be taken daily, LAAM can be taken three times a week. Clinical experience with both methadone and LAAM indicates that these medications have a much lower potential for abuse than heroin.

Naltrexone is an "antagonist" (a chemical substance that reduces the effect of another chemical substance on the body) that blocks the effect of heroin on the brain's receptors and can reduce involuntary compulsive drug craving. It can be prescribed by physicians and is effective both against alcohol dependency and in detoxification. Buprenorphine, which is currently undergoing approval by the Food and Drug Administration, acts as an agonist at lower doses and as an antagonist at higher doses.

STATISTICS ON ADMITTED PATIENTS

The *Treatment Episode Data Set* (TEDS) gathers data from treatment agencies about admitted patients. Most states require that all facilities that receive public funds must report, and many states also require private facilities to report data on their admissions. One important distinction between TEDS data and data from other sources (such as UFDS) is that TEDS reports "admissions," not persons. When interpreting statistics it must be kept in mind that some people may have been admitted more than once.

Treatment Episode Data Set (TEDS): 1993–1998 (Substance Abuse and Mental Health Services Administration, Washington, D.C., 2000) reports that more than 1.5 million admissions were made in 1998. This number has remained relatively stable since about 1993, though more than 1.6 million admissions were reported in 1994, 1995, and 1996. In 1998 alcohol use was reported in nearly half of admissions (46.5 percent). Slightly less than 1 in 3 admissions (29.8 percent) were for opiate use or cocaine use; more than 1 in 8 (13.3 percent) were for marijuana or hashish use; and less than 1 in 20 (4.5 percent) were for stimulant use. (See Table 8.3.)

Age Differences in Type of Drug Admissions

TEDS data show that there are significant differences in the types of drugs that people of different ages are

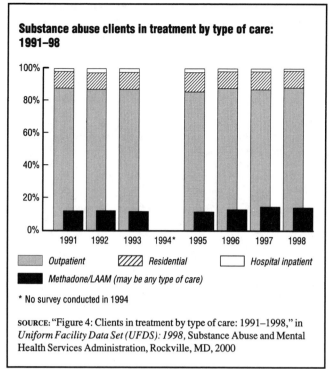

FIGURE 8.3

Substance abuse clients in treatment by type of care: 1991–98

Outpatient   Residential   Hospital inpatient

Methadone/LAAM (may be any type of care)

* No survey conducted in 1994

SOURCE: "Figure 4: Clients in treatment by type of care: 1991–1998," in *Uniform Facility Data Set (UFDS): 1998,* Substance Abuse and Mental Health Services Administration, Rockville, MD, 2000

admitted for using. The average age for all admissions in 1998 was 33 years. Admissions for alcohol involved the oldest clients (38.1 years), followed by admissions for opiates (37.3 years for opiates other than heroin, and 35.6 years for heroin), tranquilizers (37.1 years), and sedatives (36.2 years). Admissions for other types of drugs involved considerably younger clients. Admissions for hallucinogens (21.5 years), inhalants (22.4 years), and marijuana and hashish (22.8 years) involved the youngest clients. (See Table 8.4.) For patients ages 12–17, the primary substance of abuse was marijuana, followed by alcohol. (See Figure 8.4.)

Type of Treatment and Source of Referral by Type of Drug Admissions

The type of treatment and the source of referral to treatment also vary by the type of drug abused. More than four out of five (80.4 percent) admissions for marijuana use were to ambulatory (walk-in) outpatient treatment. Slightly more than one-half of admissions for smoked cocaine—"crack" or "freebase"—were to ambulatory treatment (52.2 percent). More than a quarter of admissions for cocaine, methamphetamine, hallucinogens, PCP, and inhalants were made to residential rehabilitation facilities, though only about one in eight admissions for alcohol and heroin were to such facilities. (See Table 8.5.)

How people end up in treatment is important: They may enter because they feel they have a problem, because they are arrested and sentenced by a criminal court, because they are ordered by their school or employer, or for a number of other reasons. One in three clients come

TABLE 8.3

Admissions by primary substance of abuse, Treatment Episode Data Set (TEDS) 1993–98

[Based on administrative data reported to TEDS by all reporting States and jurisdictions.]

Primary substance	Number						Percent distribution					
	1993	1994	1995	1996	1997	1998	1993	1994	1995	1996	1997	1998
Total	1,584,033	1,635,782	1,635,963	1,601,214	1,537,143	1,564,156	100.0	100.0	100.0	100.0	100.0	100.0
Alcohol	894,523	861,108	826,037	801,538	733,300	726,800	56.5	52.6	50.5	50.1	47.7	46.5
Alcohol only	542,629	506,693	477,814	458,838	413,267	411,575	34.3	31.0	29.2	28.7	26.9	26.3
Alcohol w/secondary drug	351,894	354,415	348,223	342,700	320,033	315,225	22.2	21.7	21.3	21.4	20.8	20.2
Opiates	206,865	231,674	236,613	232,242	236,055	233,507	13.1	14.2	14.5	14.5	15.4	14.9
Heroin	192,840	216,238	220,849	216,204	220,575	216,834	12.2	13.2	13.5	13.5	14.3	13.9
Other	14,025	15,436	15,764	16,038	15,480	16,673	0.9	0.9	1.0	1.0	1.0	1.1
Non-RX methadone	1,279	1,322	1,272	1,256	1,108	1,096	0.1	0.1	0.1	0.1	0.1	0.1
Other	12,746	14,114	14,492	14,782	14,372	15,577	0.8	0.9	0.9	0.9	0.9	1.0
Cocaine	277,076	293,666	272,286	256,920	230,129	233,493	17.5	18.0	16.6	16.0	15.0	14.9
Smoked cocaine	201,216	217,344	202,865	190,143	169,724	170,491	12.7	13.3	12.4	11.9	11.0	10.9
Non-smoked cocaine	75,860	76,322	69,421	66,777	60,405	63,002	4.8	4.7	4.2	4.2	3.9	4.0
Marijuana/hashish	111,265	139,670	170,974	192,103	198,079	208,671	7.0	8.5	10.5	12.0	12.9	13.3
Stimulants	28,907	45,167	63,217	52,893	68,048	70,618	1.8	2.8	3.9	3.3	4.4	4.5
Methamphetamine	20,771	33,440	47,684	40,998	53,560	55,745	1.3	2.0	2.9	2.6	3.5	3.6
Other amphetamines	7,222	10,971	14,684	10,919	13,771	14,114	0.5	0.7	0.9	0.7	0.9	0.9
Other stimulants	914	756	849	976	717	759	0.1	*	0.1	0.1	*	*
Other drugs	21,262	21,497	20,792	18,968	17,571	19,270	1.3	1.3	1.3	1.2	1.1	1.2
Tranquilizers	4,430	4,602	4,302	4,275	4,045	4,056	0.3	0.3	0.3	0.3	0.3	0.3
Benzodiazepine	2,964	3,207	3,138	3,286	3,118	3,291	0.2	0.2	0.2	0.2	0.2	0.2
Other tranquilizers	1,466	1,395	1,164	989	927	765	0.1	0.1	0.1	0.1	0.1	*
Sedatives/hypnotics	3,666	3,444	3,204	3,172	3,086	3,040	0.2	0.2	0.2	0.2	0.2	0.2
Barbiturates	1,582	1,554	1,446	1,379	1,203	1,056	0.1	0.1	0.1	0.1	0.1	0.1
Other sedatives/hypnotics	2,084	1,890	1,758	1,793	1,883	1,984	0.1	0.1	0.1	0.1	0.1	0.1
Hallucinogens	2,856	2,690	3,015	2,771	2,626	2,226	0.2	0.2	0.2	0.2	0.2	0.1
PCP	3,330	3,447	3,504	2,491	1,888	1,771	0.2	0.2	0.2	0.2	0.1	0.1
Inhalants	2,879	2,675	2,308	1,978	1,800	1,516	0.2	0.2	0.1	0.1	0.1	0.1
Over-the-counter	524	583	543	544	496	456	*	*	*	*	*	*
Other	3,577	4,056	3,916	3,737	3,630	6,205	0.2	0.2	0.2	0.2	0.2	0.4
None reported	44,135	43,000	46,044	46,550	53,961	71,797	2.8	2.6	2.8	2.9	3.5	4.6

* Less than 0.05 percent.

SOURCE: "Table 2.1: Admissions by primary substance of abuse: TEDS 1993–1998: Number and percent distribution," in *Treatment Episode Data Set (TEDS): 1993–1998*, Substance Abuse and Mental Health Services Administration, Washington, DC, September 2000

on their own. For heroin the number of admissions made by individual choice is double that for all drugs (65 percent), but for marijuana/hashish admissions, only half the average number of admissions are initiated by the client (17.5 percent). Heroin admissions were the least likely to be referred by the criminal justice system (11.4 percent), while marijuana/hashish admissions were the most likely to be referred by the criminal justice system (53.9 percent). (See Table 8.5.)

HOW EFFECTIVE IS TREATMENT?

The first major study of drug-treatment effectiveness was the *Drug Abuse Reporting Program* (DARP), which studied over 44,000 clients in more than 50 treatment centers from 1969 to 1973. A smaller group of these clients was then studied 6 and 12 years after their treatment. A second principal study was the *Treatment Outcome Prospective Study* (TOPS) taken during the 1980s. Both the DARP and TOPS studies found major reductions in both drug abuse and criminal activity after treatment.

The *Services Research Outcomes Study,* or SROS (Substance Abuse and Mental Health Services Administration, Rockville, Maryland, 1998), confirmed that both drug use and criminal behavior are reduced after drug treatment. With its extended time frame, the SROS provides the best nationally representative data to answer the question, "Does treatment work?"

During 1995 and 1996, the SROS surveyed 1,799 persons, of which nearly three-quarters (71.4 percent) were male. Based on this sample, it is possible to project what is taking place in the overall U.S. population of treatment clients. Interviews focused on clients' behavior and circumstances during the five years before entering treatment and the five years after their 1990 discharges from treatment. Substance-abuse histories on each of the clients were provided by a nationwide sample of 99 drug-treatment facilities in rural, suburban, and urban locations.

Treatment substantially reduced the percentage of respondents who reported the use of any illicit drugs five years after treatment: an overall drop of 21 percent from

TABLE 8.4

Admissions by primary substance of abuse, according to sex, race/ethnicity, and age, Treatment Episode Data Set (TEDS) 1998
Percent distribution and average age at admission
[Based on administrative data reported to TEDS by 48 States and jurisdictions.]

Sex, race/ethnicity, and age at admission	All admissions	Alcohol only	Alcohol With secondary drug	Opiates Heroin	Opiates Other opiates	Cocaine Smoked cocaine	Cocaine Other route	Marijuana/ hashish	Stimulants Methamphetamine/ amphetamine	Stimulants Other stimulants	Tranquilizers	Sedatives	Hallucinogens	PCP	Inhalants	Other/ none specified
Total	1,564,156	411,575	315,225	216,834	16,673	170,491	63,002	208,671	69,859	759	4,056	3,040	2,226	1,771	1,516	78,458
Sex																
Male	69.8	77.0	73.5	66.9	50.0	58.1	65.8	76.7	52.9	61.8	42.4	41.9	76.4	65.5	77.5	57.6
Female	30.2	23.0	26.5	33.1	50.0	41.9	34.2	23.3	47.1	38.2	57.6	58.1	23.6	34.5	22.5	42.4
Total	100.0	100.0	100.0	100.0	100.0	100.0	100.0	100.0	100.0	100.0	100.0	100.0	100.0	100.0	100.0	100.0
No. of admissions	1,558,972	407,393	314,793	216,754	16,661	170,421	62,963	208,557	69,826	759	4,052	3,038	2,219	1,770	1,514	78,252
Race/ethnicity																
White (non-Hispanic)	61.2	73.0	63.4	49.9	84.4	33.1	49.5	59.1	80.4	73.1	89.8	86.2	80.9	29.2	69.0	75.3
Black (non-Hispanic)	23.5	12.0	23.6	22.0	7.3	59.3	34.6	26.4	2.1	14.2	4.1	6.8	7.7	35.5	4.6	16.4
Hispanic origin	10.9	9.8	8.0	24.6	3.7	5.6	13.4	10.1	9.9	8.0	4.2	4.6	6.9	27.9	15.7	4.9
Mexican	4.7	5.6	3.2	8.8	1.4	1.6	4.3	4.3	7.6	3.9	2.0	1.8	3.4	15.9	13.0	0.7
Puerto Rican	3.7	1.4	2.7	13.0	1.3	2.3	5.3	3.2	0.3	2.1	1.0	1.6	1.9	4.3	0.7	0.9
Cuban	0.2	0.2	0.2	0.2	0.2	0.4	0.8	0.2	0.1	0.4	0.2	0.3	0.2	0.3	0.1	0.1
Other Hispanic	2.3	2.6	2.0	2.7	0.8	1.3	3.0	2.4	1.9	1.6	0.9	1.0	1.4	7.4	1.9	3.1
Other	4.4	5.3	5.0	3.5	4.6	1.9	2.5	4.4	7.6	4.7	1.9	2.4	4.5	7.4	10.7	3.4
Alaska Native	0.4	0.7	0.5	0.3	0.2	0.1	0.2	0.2	0.2	0.8	0.2	0.2	0.1	0.3	1.4	0.1
American Indian	2.1	3.2	3.0	0.7	0.9	0.6	1.0	1.9	2.6	1.7	0.8	1.1	1.8	2.1	7.4	1.5
Asian/Pacific Isl.	0.7	0.5	0.6	0.6	2.0	0.5	0.4	1.2	2.9	0.8	0.2	0.8	1.0	1.0	0.8	0.3
Other	1.1	0.9	0.9	2.0	1.5	0.7	0.8	1.2	1.9	1.3	0.7	0.3	1.6	4.0	1.1	1.5
Total	100.0	100.0	100.0	100.0	100.0	100.0	100.0	100.0	100.0	100.0	100.0	100.0	100.0	100.0	100.0	100.0
No. of admissions	1,540,619	401,731	312,899	216,001	16,537	169,736	62,380	206,710	69,415	752	4,020	3,019	2,204	1,762	1,500	71,953
Age at admission																
Under 15 years	2.4	0.5	1.2	*	0.1	0.1	0.4	7.0	0.7	7.5	0.8	0.8	5.2	0.9	23.0	19.3
15 to 19 years	11.2	4.5	10.6	3.4	2.2	2.3	6.0	42.2	10.6	19.6	5.5	4.7	51.2	13.9	33.0	13.2
15 to 17 years	7.1	2.2	6.4	0.8	0.9	0.8	2.7	30.8	5.3	15.3	2.7	2.9	33.0	6.9	26.1	9.2
18 to 19 years	4.1	2.3	4.3	2.6	1.4	1.5	3.3	11.3	5.3	4.2	2.8	1.8	18.2	7.0	6.9	4.0
20 to 24 years	10.6	7.6	11.0	10.0	6.4	6.5	10.7	18.5	16.8	11.5	7.8	8.8	22.8	22.0	12.5	9.7
25 to 29 years	13.4	10.5	14.2	14.2	12.0	16.6	17.4	11.4	21.8	13.2	9.8	9.8	7.0	19.7	6.7	10.7
30 to 34 years	16.8	14.6	18.9	17.7	17.0	25.8	23.2	8.4	21.1	13.5	14.9	17.9	4.4	20.7	7.6	11.8
35 to 39 years	18.1	19.0	20.4	19.5	22.1	25.6	21.7	6.5	16.9	15.1	20.5	22.4	4.1	15.1	7.4	12.4
40 to 44 years	13.3	16.5	13.6	18.0	20.0	14.6	12.8	3.7	8.2	9.4	19.1	17.2	2.5	5.2	6.8	9.5
45 to 49 years	7.6	11.7	6.5	11.2	12.1	5.7	5.2	1.5	2.7	4.8	10.5	9.6	2.0	1.7	2.0	5.8
50 to 54 years	3.5	7.0	2.3	4.0	4.8	1.9	1.7	0.5	0.9	3.4	4.9	4.6	0.5	0.5	0.4	3.3
55 to 59 years	1.7	4.2	0.9	1.3	1.6	0.6	0.6	0.2	0.2	1.2	2.7	2.0	- -	0.3	0.3	1.8
60 to 64 years	0.8	2.1	0.2	0.5	0.8	0.2	0.2	*	0.1	0.5	1.8	1.2	0.1	0.1	0.1	0.9
65 years and over	0.7	1.9	0.2	0.3	0.9	0.1	0.1	0.1	*	0.3	1.7	1.0	0.1	0.1	0.1	1.6
Total	100.0	100.0	100.0	100.0	100.0	100.0	100.0	100.0	100.0	100.0	100.0	100.0	100.0	100.0	100.0	100.0
No. of admissions	1,560,915	410,947	314,666	216,536	16,600	170,104	62,787	208,002	69,756	756	4,034	3,026	2,212	1,765	1,497	78,227
Average age at admission	33.0 yrs	38.1 yrs	32.5 yrs	35.6 yrs	37.3 yrs	34.4 yrs	32.8 yrs	22.8 yrs	29.8 yrs	29.3 yrs	37.1 yrs	36.2 yrs	21.5 yrs	28.3 yrs	22.4 yrs	28.6 yrs

* Less than 0.05 percent.
— Quantity is zero.

SOURCE: "Table 3.1a: Admissions by primary substance of abuse, according to sex, race/ethnicity, and age: TEDS 1998," in *Treatment Episode Data Set (TEDS): 1993–1998*, Substance Abuse and Mental Health Services Administration, Washington, DC, September 2000

the five years before treatment. This decrease was found for almost every individual drug. The most significant drop was in cocaine use (45 percent), followed by marijuana (28 percent), crack (17 percent), and heroin and alcohol use (14 percent). (See Figure 8.5.)

Gender, Age, and Racial/Ethnic Differences

Females showed a greater decrease than males in posttreatment substance abuse for any illicit drug and for each of the most frequently used illicit drugs—marijuana,

cocaine, crack, and heroin. Figure 8.6 shows the difference between (a) the percentage of males and females using five or more times across the five years after treatment; and (b) the percentage of males and females using five or more times across the five years before treatment. For males, the difference in heroin use before and after treatment was not statistically significant.

Among adults, older age groups generally reduced their drug use to a greater degree after treatment than

FIGURE 8.4

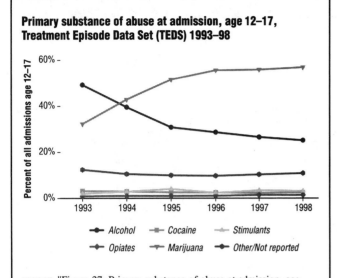

Primary substance of abuse at admission, age 12–17, Treatment Episode Data Set (TEDS) 1993–98

SOURCE: "Figure 27: Primary substance of abuse at admission, age 12–17: TEDS 1993–1998," in *Treatment Episode Data Set (TEDS): 1993–1998,* Substance Abuse and Mental Health Services Administration, Washington, DC, September 2000

FIGURE 8.6

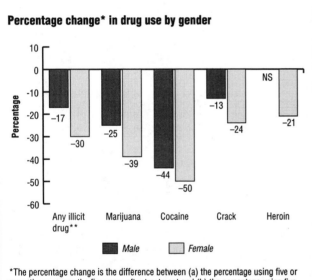

Percentage change* in drug use by gender

*The percentage change is the difference between (a) the percentage using five or more times across the five years after treatment and (b) the percentage using five or more times across the five years before treatment, divided by (b). All percentages shown are significant at the 0.05 level. "NS" means that the difference was not significant.
**"Any illicit drug" includes marijuana, cocaine, crack, heroin, inhalants, PCP, other hallucinogens, illegal methadone, narcotics, methamphetamines, downers, and other illicit drugs.

SOURCE: Percentage change in drug use by sex," in *Services Research Outcomes Study,* Substance Abuse and Mental Health Services Administration, Rockville, MD, 1998

FIGURE 8.5

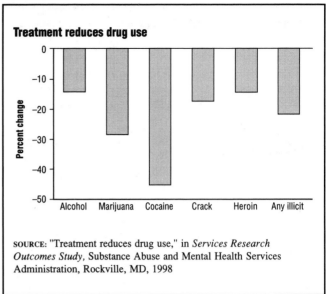

Treatment reduces drug use

SOURCE: "Treatment reduces drug use," in *Services Research Outcomes Study,* Substance Abuse and Mental Health Services Administration, Rockville, MD, 1998

of crack is typically more than 20 years. For other drugs, no statistically significant increases or decreases were detected for those who were adolescents when discharged from treatment. (See Figure 8.7.)

Treatment reduced illicit drug use among black, white, and Hispanic clients, although only black respondents reduced their crack and heroin use to a statistically significant extent (23 percent and 18 percent, respectively). Black clients were more likely to have used crack and heroin before treatment than whites and Hispanics.

Types and Length of Treatment

Figure 8.8 shows changes in drug-use rates by the type of treatment that the client received. Those in methadone-treatment facilities were the only ones who showed a significant decrease in heroin use: a 27 percent drop from pretreatment use. Methadone treatment had little or no effect on crack use; most clients in methadone treatment (79 percent) reported heroin as their main drug. The most significant decreases in crack and cocaine use (32 percent and 55 percent drops, respectively) were among residential clients. Cocaine use also declined considerably in outpatient drug-free settings (a 42 percent drop) and in inpatient treatments (a 47 percent drop).

The length of stay was consistently associated with the extent of change in drug use. In general, the longer the stay, the more likely clients were to reduce or eliminate substance abuse after treatment. (See Figure 8.9.) This may relate to the type of treatment and the time required for completion of the treatment. Clients who completed their treatment plan, whichever type was used, were more likely than noncompleters to reduce their pretreatment drug use for every principal drug except crack.

younger age groups did. Adolescents, however, showed a 13 percent increase in alcohol abuse and a 202 percent increase in crack use after treatment. The increase in crack use by adolescents came from a pretreatment low of 5 percent of adolescents using crack; the age of first use

TABLE 8.5

Admissions by primary substance of abuse, according to treatment characteristics, Treatment Episode Data Set (TEDS) 1998

Percent distribution
[Based on administrative data reported to TEDS by 48 States and jurisdictions.]

Treatment Characteristic	All admissions	Alcohol only	Alcohol With secondary drug	Heroin	Other opiates	Smoked cocaine	Other route	Marijuana/hashish	Methamphetamine/amphetamine	Other stimulants	Tranquilizers	Sedatives	Hallucinogens	PCP	Inhalants	Other/none specified
Total	1,564,156	411,575	315,225	216,834	16,673	170,491	63,002	208,671	69,859	759	4,056	3,040	2,226	1,771	1,516	78,458
Ambulatory	63.9	62.1	60.8	59.5	61.8	52.2	57.1	80.4	61.8	76.8	55.2	62.4	63.7	67.0	60.9	87.4
Outpatient	50.9	52.5	50.3	37.5	42.9	37.8	44.2	65.4	50.5	63.0	42.9	50.1	51.1	58.1	47.8	79.3
Intensive outpatient	9.5	8.7	9.8	3.6	11.4	13.6	12.3	13.6	10.2	13.4	11.0	10.4	11.0	8.6	11.5	6.4
Detoxification	3.4	0.9	0.7	18.4	7.5	0.8	0.5	1.4	1.1	0.4	1.3	1.9	1.7	0.2	1.6	1.6
Residential/rehabilitation	17.9	11.7	22.9	12.9	17.2	29.9	28.0	15.8	26.5	15.9	21.5	19.7	27.7	26.7	25.7	7.1
Short-term (<31 days)	8.6	6.8	13.6	4.8	9.6	12.1	11.3	6.6	10.0	5.9	13.1	9.8	10.0	5.9	9.7	2.4
Long-term (31+ days)	8.3	3.8	8.3	7.4	6.0	17.3	14.4	8.4	15.8	7.0	6.4	8.5	16.1	20.2	13.7	3.1
Hospital (non-detox)	1.0	1.1	1.0	0.6	1.5	0.5	2.2	0.8	0.7	3.0	2.1	1.4	1.6	0.6	2.2	1.6
Detoxification (24-hour service)	18.2	26.3	16.3	27.6	21.0	17.9	14.9	3.8	11.7	7.2	23.2	17.9	8.6	6.3	13.5	5.5
Free-standing residential	16.6	24.1	15.0	23.5	17.8	17.1	13.9	3.6	11.5	6.7	19.9	15.6	7.6	6.2	12.9	4.1
Hospital inpatient	1.7	2.1	1.3	4.1	3.2	0.8	1.0	0.2	0.2	0.5	3.4	2.3	0.9	0.1	0.6	1.5
Total	100.0	100.0	100.0	100.0	100.0	100.0	100.0	100.0	100.0	100.0	100.0	100.0	100.0	100.0	100.0	100.0
No. of admissions	1,564,156	411,575	315,225	216,834	16,673	170,491	63,002	208,671	69,859	759	4,056	3,040	2,226	1,771	1,516	78,458
Source of referral																
Individual	33.0	26.0	27.1	65.0	46.6	36.2	35.3	17.5	27.9	31.3	39.3	34.0	25.7	20.2	25.8	36.4
Criminal justice/DUI	35.3	44.8	36.1	11.4	17.0	25.7	29.3	53.9	42.0	36.1	16.2	22.9	41.3	50.0	32.6	25.1
Substance abuse provider	12.3	11.1	16.3	13.2	15.4	17.9	13.2	6.8	7.2	7.6	16.5	14.2	12.0	12.3	8.8	3.3
Other health care provider	7.6	8.5	8.1	5.0	12.3	7.6	7.7	5.6	6.1	10.4	17.7	17.9	8.8	5.5	14.0	13.2
School (educational)	1.5	0.7	1.0	0.1	0.2	0.1	0.3	4.7	0.6	5.6	0.6	0.8	3.7	0.5	4.6	8.0
Employer/EAP	1.2	1.4	1.3	0.5	1.5	1.0	2.1	1.7	0.7	1.1	0.9	1.6	0.2	0.4	0.4	1.7
Other community referral	9.2	7.5	10.0	4.9	7.1	11.5	12.0	9.7	15.5	7.9	8.8	8.7	8.3	11.0	13.7	12.4
Total	100.0	100.0	100.0	100.0	100.0	100.0	100.0	100.0	100.0	100.0	100.0	100.0	100.0	100.0	100.0	100.0
No. of admissions	1,481,029	389,918	300,052	212,565	15,680	160,368	59,409	195,267	67,341	712	3,882	2,866	2,074	1,735	1,407	67,753
Methadone use planned as part of treatment	5.8	0.1	0.2	37.5	20.6	0.2	0.2	0.2	0.2	0.3	1.1	0.9	0.2	0.2	0.4	0.5
No. of admissions	1,460,134	387,192	290,146	211,804	15,614	162,813	60,414	193,082	61,673	724	3,855	2,829	2,018	1,741	1,424	64,805

SOURCE: "Table 3.4 Admissions by primary substance of abuse, according to treatment characteristics: TEDS 1998," in *Treatment Episode Data Set (TEDS): 1993–1998,* Substance Abuse and Mental Health Services Administration, Washington, DC, September 2000

Criminal Behavior and Lifestyle Changes

The SROS, like previous studies, showed that treatment for substance abuse can significantly reduce crime. Criminal activities such as breaking and entering, drug sales, prostitution, driving under the influence, and theft/larceny decreased between 23 and 38 percent after drug treatment. However, incarceration and parole/probation violations actually increased, by 17 and 26 percent, respectively. (See Figure 8.10.)

According to the researchers, "It is possible that the same circumstances that led clients to seek treatment (35 percent entered treatment because of pressure from the criminal justice system) also placed them under more stringent supervision in the form of probation, parole, and incarceration, and this increase in supervision reduced the commission of primary offenses." Another explanation was that clients were more visible or easily apprehended when they were under supervision.

Older persons were much more likely to reduce criminal activities after treatment than were younger persons. Those over 30 generally decreased their criminal behavior in every area. Like drug use, criminal activity decreased the most with longer stays and with completed treatment.

Lifestyle characteristics also became more positive after treatment. Suicide attempts declined by 43 percent, time spent on the streets by 40 percent, loss of child custody by 30 percent, and being assaulted by 21 percent. (See Figure 8.11.) There was no significant change in the rate of full-time employment for clients discharged from treatment. About three-quarters of clients had been employed full-time for some period before and after treatment. However, clients were less likely to have a full-time job after treatment than before if they

• Were Hispanic or black.

• Were 30 years old or older.

• Had nine or fewer years of education.

FIGURE 8.7

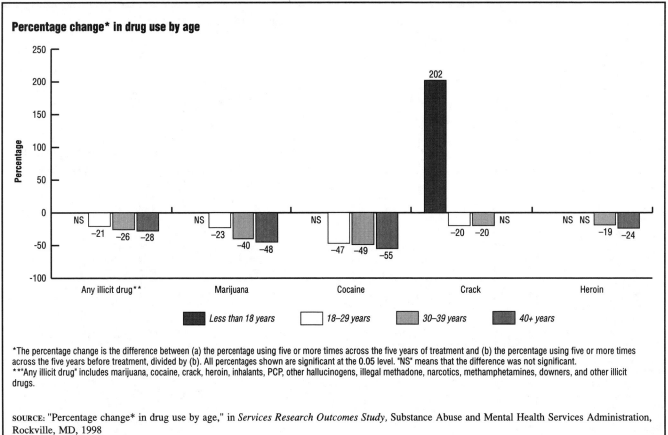

Percentage change* in drug use by age

*The percentage change is the difference between (a) the percentage using five or more times across the five years of treatment and (b) the percentage using five or more times across the five years before treatment, divided by (b). All percentages shown are significant at the 0.05 level. "NS" means that the difference was not significant.
***"Any illicit drug" includes marijuana, cocaine, crack, heroin, inhalants, PCP, other hallucinogens, illegal methadone, narcotics, methamphetamines, downers, and other illicit drugs.

SOURCE: "Percentage change* in drug use by age," in *Services Research Outcomes Study,* Substance Abuse and Mental Health Services Administration, Rockville, MD, 1998

• Were in methadone programs.

• Reported heroin as their main drug at the beginning of treatment.

How Is Success Measured?

Abstinence is usually the measure of success when treatment providers conduct patient follow-up studies. However, Hazelden Foundation, a nonprofit organization that provides chemical-dependency treatment and education, maintains that abstinence is not the only indicator of successful outcome, and suggests that as long as individuals are moving toward abstinence, progress is being made. Other important indicators include the frequency and amount of alcohol/drug use before and after treatment; the patient's quality of life; and decreases in legal, health care, and job problems. Hazelden measures success by using data self-reported by patients and verified by relatives, friends, and/or laboratory tests (e.g., urinalysis).

Hazelden uses the Minnesota Model of treatment, a program that integrates behavioral treatment concepts with traditional Twelve Step treatment based on Alcoholics Anonymous (AA). A 1998 study (Randy Stinchfield and Patricia Owen, "Hazelden's Model of Treatment and Its Outcome," *Addictive Behaviors*) of 1,083 clients using this model found that 53 percent maintained absti-

nence during the year after treatment, and an additional 35 percent reduced their use. Before treatment, 76 percent of Hazelden's patients used alcohol or drugs daily; one year after treatment, less than 1 percent used them daily. Between 70 and 80 percent reported an improved quality of life in such areas as family relationships, job performance, and ability to handle problems. Hazelden considers these findings a treatment success.

Many studies have shown a strong correlation between high abstinence rates and compliance with aftercare and/or participation in Twelve Step programs. These findings confirm that addiction needs to be treated as a chronic illness. In Hazelden's study, 72 percent attended AA or other Twelve Step groups after treatment. Of the 28 percent who did not, only 18 percent remained abstinent, while 57 percent of those who did attend AA stayed abstinent.

A. Thomas McLellan et al. (*Training about Alcohol and Substance Abuse for All Primary Care Physicians,* Josiah Macy, Jr. Foundation, New York, 1995) maintain that "substance abuse is a real medical disorder. It is a recurring disorder much like diabetes, hypertension, or asthma, with profound and expensive public health and safety implications." These are chronic diseases that have serious consequences for the patient, including death. When substance abuse is treated as a chronic disease, they note that success is similar to that of treatment of other chronic illnesses.

FIGURE 8.8

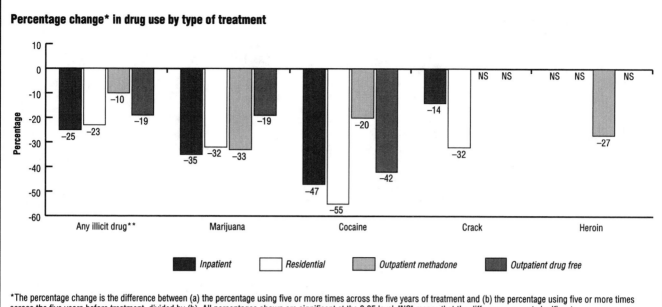

*The percentage change is the difference between (a) the percentage using five or more times across the five years of treatment and (b) the percentage using five or more times across the five years before treatment, divided by (b). All percentages shown are significant at the 0.05 level. "NS" means that the difference was not significant.
***"Any illicit drug" includes marijuana, cocaine, crack, heroin, inhalants, PCP, other hallucinogens, illegal methadone, narcotics, methamphetamines, downers, and other illicit drugs.

SOURCE: "Percentage change* in drug use by type of treatment," in *Services Research Outcomes Study,* Substance Abuse and Mental Health Services Administration, Rockville, MD, 1998

FIGURE 8.9

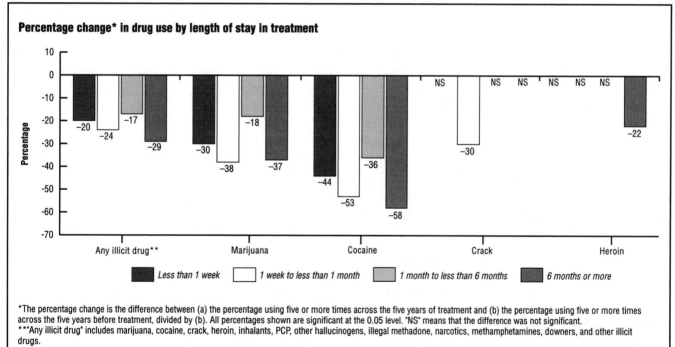

*The percentage change is the difference between (a) the percentage using five or more times across the five years of treatment and (b) the percentage using five or more times across the five years before treatment, divided by (b). All percentages shown are significant at the 0.05 level. "NS" means that the difference was not significant.
***"Any illicit drug" includes marijuana, cocaine, crack, heroin, inhalants, PCP, other hallucinogens, illegal methadone, narcotics, methamphetamines, downers, and other illicit drugs.

SOURCE: "Percentage change* in drug use by length of stay," in *Services Research Outcomes Study,* Substance Abuse and Mental Health Services Administration, Rockville, MD, 1998

For example, despite the real dangers, less than 50 percent of diabetics take their medicine properly, and fewer than 30 percent follow their diet. Within 12 months, 30–50 percent have to be retreated. Similarly, fewer than 30 percent of hypertension patients take their medicine properly, and fewer than 30 percent follow their diet.

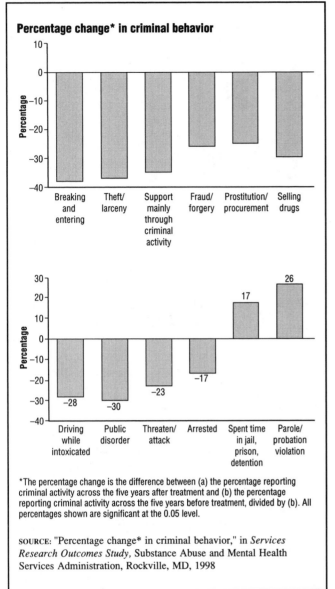

Percentage change* in criminal behavior

*The percentage change is the difference between (a) the percentage reporting criminal activity across the five years after treatment and (b) the percentage reporting criminal activity across the five years before treatment, divided by (b). All percentages shown are significant at the 0.05 level.

SOURCE: "Percentage change* in criminal behavior," in *Services Research Outcomes Study,* Substance Abuse and Mental Health Services Administration, Rockville, MD, 1998

FIGURE 8.11

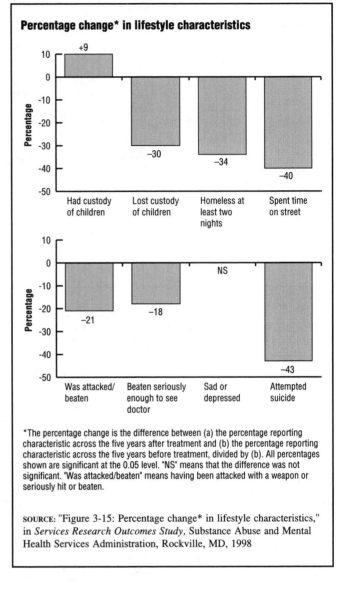

Percentage change* in lifestyle characteristics

*The percentage change is the difference between (a) the percentage reporting characteristic across the five years after treatment and (b) the percentage reporting characteristic across the five years before treatment, divided by (b). All percentages shown are significant at the 0.05 level. "NS" means that the difference was not significant. "Was attacked/beaten" means having been attacked with a weapon or seriously hit or beaten.

SOURCE: "Figure 3-15: Percentage change* in lifestyle characteristics," in *Services Research Outcomes Study,* Substance Abuse and Mental Health Services Administration, Rockville, MD, 1998

Within a year, 50–60 percent must be retreated. Finally, fewer than 30 percent of asthma sufferers take their medicine properly, and 60–80 percent must be retreated within 12 months.

Along the same lines, McLellan et al. note that

Studies of treatment response have shown that patients who comply with the recommended regimen of education, counseling, and medication, which characterizes most contemporary forms of treatment, typically have favorable outcomes during treatment and longer-lasting benefits after treatment. Thus, it is discouraging to those in the treatment field that so many substance-dependent patients fail to comply with the recommended course of treatment and subsequently resume substance use. Factors such as low socioeconomic class, co-morbid psychiatric conditions, and lack of family or social supports for continuing abstinence are among the most important variables associated with lack of treatment compliance,

and ultimately, to reoccurrence of the disorder following treatment.

HOW MUCH DOES THE NATION SPEND ON DRUG TREATMENT?

The U.S. General Accounting Office (GAO), the investigative arm of Congress, in *Drug Abuse—Research Shows Treatment Is Effective, but Benefits May Be Overstated* (Washington, D.C., 1998), reported on the federal government's funding for substance abuse and treatment, as well as treatment approaches, evaluations, and effectiveness. The study focused on the 1998 funding, which included grants to states, direct services, and research. In 1998 federal funding for treatment of drug abuse was about $3.2 billion, or one-fifth of the total drug-control budget. (See Figure 8.12.)

A number of federal entities received treatment-related funding, but the bulk of the money went to the Department of Health and Human Services (HHS) and Veterans

Affairs (VA). (See Table 8.6.) Over half (54 percent) of the $3.2 billion for 1998 was allocated to the HHS. Of this $1.7 billion, the HHS dedicated $944 million to SAMHSA. The other major recipient was the Health Care Financing Administration, which received $360 million to pay for drug-treatment services for Medicaid and Medicare beneficiaries. The National Institutes of Health received about one-sixth of the total HHS drug-treatment funds, to conduct research in the areas of drug abuse and underage alcohol use.

In 1998 about $1.1 billion, or 34 percent of the total drug-treatment budget, was allocated to VA for medical care and drug-treatment services. Other federal agencies that received drug-treatment funds for 1998 include the Departments of Education and Justice, the federal judiciary, and the Office of National Drug Control Policy (ONDCP). (See Table 8.6.) Part of the money allocated to the Department of Justice was for support of its Drug Intervention Program, a new program that supports drug testing, treatment, and graduated sanctions for drug offenders, in an effort to break the cycle of drug abuse and violence.

Cost of Drug Treatment Per Client

The *National Treatment Improvement Evaluation Study* (Substance Abuse and Mental Health Services Administration, Rockville, Maryland, 1997) examines the costs of the various types of treatment. Costs ranged from a low of approximately $1,800 per client to a high of about $6,800 per client. The least expensive type of treatment in 1997 was the outpatient nonmethadone treatment, which cost about $15 a day and had an average treatment period of approximately 120 days. Substance-abuse treatment provided in prisons or jails, while costing more per day ($24), had the same average cost of $1,800 per client, because of a shorter length of treatment. (See Table 8.7.) This cost is over and above all other costs of incarceration.

Outpatient methadone treatment programs cost about $3,900—$13 a day for a treatment period of about 300 days. Short-term residential care was $130 a day for an average stay of 30 days, for a total average cost estimated at $3,900. The most expensive treatment, because the average length of stay was 140 days at $49 per day, was long-term residential. Its total cost was $6,800. (See Table 8.7.)

Who Pays for Drug Treatment?

According to the *National Expenditure for Mental Health, Alcohol, and Other Drug Abuse Treatment* (Substance Abuse and Mental Health Services Administration, Rockville, Maryland, 1998), federal, state, and local government agencies financed nearly half ($3.5 billion) of the $7.6 billion spent in 1996 on treatment for drug abuse and combined drug/alcohol abuse disorders. Medicare and Medicaid spending raised the total public spending by another $1.5 billion. This means that two out of every

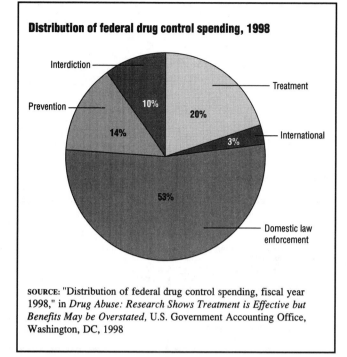

FIGURE 8.12

Distribution of federal drug control spending, 1998

Interdiction — 10%
Prevention — 14%
Treatment — 20%
International — 3%
Domestic law enforcement — 53%

SOURCE: "Distribution of federal drug control spending, fiscal year 1998," in *Drug Abuse: Research Shows Treatment is Effective but Benefits May be Overstated,* U.S. Government Accounting Office, Washington, DC, 1998

three treatment dollars came from taxes and Social Security. Private insurance accounted for another $1.5 billion, or about 20 percent of total drug-treatment costs. Patients (through out-of-pocket expenditures) and other private sources provided the remainder.

For the same year, 1996, the *Uniform Facility Data Set* (Substance Abuse and Mental Health Services Administration, Rockville, Maryland, 1997) reported that 69 percent of total treatment-facility funding was public. About half of total treatment-facility funding (48.1 percent) came from special appropriations from local, state, and federal funds earmarked for substance-abuse treatment. Nearly 21 percent came from Medicaid (16.5 percent) and Medicare (4.1 percent). Client payments funded 10.7 percent of treatment costs, and nearly 16 percent of costs were paid by private health insurance. (See Table 8.8.)

Table 8.8 also shows the source of funding for the types of facility ownership. Private for-profit facilities received more than half (54 percent) of their funds from private sources—client payments and private health insurance. Public funds accounted for 90 percent of the total funding for public facilities.

Private Insurance Coverage

Treatment often depends on coverage offered by a patient's health insurance policy or whether the patient has any health coverage at all. In the 1990s, as health care expenses continued to rise, companies cut back on substance-abuse treatment. According to Dr. Herbert Kleber, medical director of the National Center on Addiction and Substance Abuse (CASA), managed care has made it

TABLE 8.6

Federal budget authority for drug treatment activities, by agency, 1994–99
Dollars in millions

Agency	Fiscal year						1994–98 percent change
	1994 actual	1995 actual	1996 actual	1997 actual	1998 enacted	1999 requested	
Health and Human Services	$1,532.9	$1,559.5	$1,471.1	$1,660.2	$1,717.7	$1,832.4	12.1
Veterans Affairs[a]	853.8	966.1	1,080.9	1,056.4	1,096.9	1,138.7	28.5
Defense	6.2	6.2	5.8	6.4	6.2	6.0	0.0
Education	108.2	115.4	119.2	119.8	125.8	129.9	16.3
Housing and Urban Development	25.0	5.4	0.0	3.0	3.2	3.2	−87.2
The Judiciary	63.0	67.8	59.7	69.6	74.7	83.8	18.6
Justice	61.3	68.3	94.8	126.6	160.9	219.7	162.5
ONDCP	1.9	15.6	5.1	26.9	23.8	32.3	1,152.6
Total[b]	$2,652.3	$2,953.2[c]	$2,836.6	$3,068.9	$3,209.1	$3,446.0	21

[a]Includes 100 percent of medical costs provided to veterans with a diagnosis of drug abuse when treatment is provided in a specialized drug or substance abuse treatment program. For veterans with a secondary or associated diagnosis of drug abuse who receive care in other settings, only a proportion of medical costs are included.
[b]Expenditures have been rounded, affecting percentages and totals.
[c]Includes $148.9 million for the Social Security Administration.
Note: ONDCP = Office of National Drug Control Policy

SOURCE: "Federal budget authority for drug treatment activities, by agency, fiscal years 1994–99," in *Drug Abuse: Research Shows Treatment is Effective but Benefits May be Overstated,* U.S. General Accounting Office, Washington, DC, 1998

harder for addicted people to get access to treatment, particularly inpatient care. Some observers fear that managed-care companies have a financial incentive to shorten treatment and limit residential care, if they cover substance abuse at all. Even in the few states, such as Texas, that consider drug addiction a disability, and therefore covered by health insurance, the health insurance companies are very reluctant to provide coverage.

In 1999 President Bill Clinton ordered health plans that cover federal employees to offer equivalent coverage for physical illness, mental illness, and substance abuse. Senator Paul Wellstone (D-MN) and Representative Jim Ramstad (R-MN) introduced legislation—Fairness in Treatment: The Alcohol and Drug Addiction Recovery Act of 2001—that would force private insurers to cover addictive disorders just as they do other illnesses. They argue not only that drug treatment is cost-effective but also that insurers should be required to treat addiction like other types of chronic illness.

IS DRUG TREATMENT WORTH THE MONEY?

Peter Rydell and Susan Everingham, in *Controlling Cocaine: Supply Versus Demand Programs* (RAND, Santa Monica, California, 1994), studied various drug-control strategies—treatment, domestic enforcement, interdiction, and source country control—used to reduce cocaine use. Rydell and Everingham concluded that to achieve a 1 percent reduction in cocaine consumption in the United States, the country would have to spend either $34 million on treatment, $250 million on domestic enforcement, almost $400 million on interdiction, or around $800 mil-

lion for source control. This means domestic enforcement would be 7.3 times as costly as drug treatment.

Treatment versus Incarceration

The *National Treatment Improvement Evaluation Study,* or NTIES (Substance Abuse and Mental Health Services Administration, Rockville, Rockville, Maryland, 1997) observed that "treatment appears to be cost-effective, particularly when compared to incarceration, which is often the alternative." Although NTIES did not examine the cost of incarceration, it did refer to a study by the American Correctional Association, which gave the estimated 1994 cost of incarceration as $18,330 per prisoner annually. The most expensive treatment in 1997, according to NTIES, was $6,800 per client for long-term residential programs—just over one-third the cost of a year of incarceration.

Arizona is the first state to treat, rather than incarcerate, all its nonviolent drug offenders. An Arizona Supreme Court study of the first year of probation with mandatory drug treatment, released in 1999, estimated that the state's new program saved more than $2.5 million and is likely to show even greater savings in the future. It estimated the cost of treatment, counseling, and probation at $16.06 a day, compared with $50 a day to keep an inmate in prison. The program is largely paid for by a tax on a legal drug: alcohol. Daily financial savings are not the only benefit of treatment versus incarceration, however. Most addicts, untreated, emerge from prison and quickly return to drug use, often committing crimes to get money for the drugs.

Of the 2,622 people treated by the program, 77.5 percent subsequently tested free of drugs. Arizona drug users

TABLE 8.7

Comparative cost of treatment

Type, length, and cost of treatment

Methadone	$13/day	$3,900/client	(about 300 days)
Outpatient nonmethadone	$15/day	$1,800/client	(about 120 days)
Correctional	$24/day	$1,800/client	(about 75 days)
Long-term residential	$49/day	$6,800/client	(about 140 days)
Short-term residential	$130/day	$3,900/client	(about 30 days)

SOURCE: "Comparative cost of treatment," in *The National Treatment Improvement Evaluation Study,* Substance Abuse and Mental Health Services Administration, Rockville, MD, 1997

TABLE 8.8

Drug treatment funding, by funding source and treatment facility type

	Source of Funding (percent)					
Ownership	Client payments	Private health insurance	Medicaid	Medicare	Local/ state/ fed.	Other/ unknown
All facilities	10.7	15.8	16.5	4.1	48.1	4.8
Public	4.6	3.0	9.5	1.2	79.5	2.3
Private non-profit	9.4	15.4	17.9	3.2	48.3	5.9
Private-for-profit	22.4	31.6	19.7	10.6	11.8	3.7

SOURCE: "UFDS Funding Source by Facility Ownership," in *Uniform Facility Data Set (UFDS): Data for 1996 and 1980–1996,* Substance Abuse and Mental Health Services Administration, Rockville, MD, 1997

on probation are expected to help pay for their treatment; 77.1 percent made at least one payment. And what happens to those for whom treatment is unsuccessful? According to Barbara Broderick, Arizona's director of adult probation, "When we can't get someone to change, we send them to prison. You can't continue to waste resources."

Other Measures of Cost-Effectiveness

DRUG TREATMENT FOR EMPLOYEES. In 1998 John Saylor, manager of Employee Assistance Programs for AMR Corporation (which includes American Airlines), testified before the Senate Committee on Labor and Human Resources about the value of treatment for alcohol and drug addiction for AMR and its employees. Saylor was "charged with the task of ensuring that any AMR-insured person will receive the best available treatment for his/her alcoholism or drug addiction, with no limit on days or sessions, and no limit on dollars other than the lifetime maximum for all medical care (currently at $1,000,000)." He was confident that this corporate investment turned out to be both prudent and highly successful.

Saylor reported that follow-up studies of employees who received alcohol or drug treatment showed that 75–80 percent remained completely drug and alcohol free during their year of monitoring. He estimated that the average cost to AMR for complete treatment has been between $5,000 and $6,000 per person. With other serious life-threatening diseases, the first day of treatment alone can cost that much, according to Saylor. He is convinced that the expenditure of this "moderate amount of money" reduced accidents, injuries, and diseases.

DRUG TREATMENT FOR WELFARE RECIPIENTS. According to the National Conference of State Legislatures, federal studies estimate that up to 35 percent of the welfare population is addicted to drugs or alcohol. Welfare recipients who cannot get or keep a job are dropped from the welfare rolls. Therefore, those on the rolls who have substance-abuse problems jeopardize a state's ability

to meet strict federal work participation requirements, which could result in financial penalties.

As a result, many states are using their Temporary Assistance to Needy Families (TANF) money, in addition to Substance Abuse and Mental Health block grants, to expand their substance-abuse treatment for welfare recipients. Senator Martha Yeager Walker, chair of the West Virginia Senate Health and Human Services Committee, noted that

We need to reach these hard-to-serve welfare recipients, those struggling with substance abuse, domestic violence or other impediments to self-sufficiency. Our welfare caseloads are dropping, and those left on the rolls will be parents who need intensive services. It is critical, not only for their individual self-sufficiency, but also for their children.

WHERE TO GO FOR HELP

God grant me the SERENITY to accept the things I cannot change, the COURAGE to change the things I can, and the WISDOM to know the difference.

— Invocation used in most Twelve Step programs

Many organizations provide assistance for addicts, their families, and friends. Most of the self-help groups are based on the Twelve Step program of Alcoholics Anonymous (AA). While AA is a support group for problem drinkers, Al-Anon/Alateen is for friends and families of alcoholics. Families Anonymous provides support for family members and friends concerned about a loved one's problems with drugs and/or alcohol. Other organizations include Adult Children of Alcoholics, Cocaine Anonymous, and Narcotics Anonymous. For an addict, many of these organizations can provide immediate help. For families and friends, they can provide knowledge, understanding, and support. For contact information for some of these organizations, see "Important Names and Addresses."

CHAPTER 9
AIDS AND INTRAVENOUS DRUG USE

WHAT IS AIDS?

AIDS (acquired immunodeficiency syndrome) is an infectious disease caused by the human immunodeficiency virus (HIV), which weakens the victim's immune system. The immune system is a complicated, coordinated system of organs and cells that work together to prevent the invasion of foreign substances, including viruses. Unfortunately, due to the complex nature of HIV, the immune system is unable to produce sufficient antibodies to fight the virus.

Once individuals are infected with HIV, their weakened immune systems leave them more susceptible to opportunistic illnesses, such as tuberculosis and cancer, that a healthy immune system might otherwise be able to fight. (Some research indicates that the virus may actually cause cancer.) For most people, once the protective immune system has been destroyed, other infectious agents (bacteria, protozoa, fungi, and other viruses), as well as cancers, use this opportunity to infect and destroy the entire system.

How Many AIDS Cases?

By June 2000 a total of 753,907 AIDS cases had been reported to the Centers for Disease Control and Prevention (CDC) in Atlanta. (See Table 9.1.) This number represents all cases of AIDS ever reported in the United States. About half of the 753,907 people were still alive at the end of June 2000.

Signs and Symptoms

Only a test given by a qualified health professional can absolutely diagnose AIDS. In addition to having one or more opportunistic infections (bacterial, fungal, protozoal, and viral infections that take advantage of HIV-weakened immune systems), persons with AIDS also have other symptoms. They often experience a general malaise (feeling poorly), weight loss, nausea, fever, night sweats,

swollen lymph glands, persistent cough, unexplained bleeding, watery diarrhea, loss of memory, balance problems, mood changes, blurring or loss of vision, and thrush (a white coating of the tongue and throat). Although many individuals who have AIDS or carry HIV may live for many years with treatment, there is no known cure or vaccine. Usually, it is opportunistic infections that cause the person's death—not the virus.

WAYS AIDS IS TRANSMITTED

While much has been done to educate the American public about how AIDS is transmitted, too many individuals are unaware of, or ignore the facts about, the methods of transmission. Some people are in "high-risk groups," but they are not the only ones who become infected with HIV.

HIV can only be transmitted in the following ways:

- Having oral, anal, or vaginal sex with an infected person.

- Sharing drug needles or syringes with an infected person.

- Passing from an infected mother to her baby, perinatally (at some point around the time of birth) and through breast milk.

- Receiving a transplanted organ or body fluids, such as blood transfusions or blood products, from an infected person.

In this country, the group at greatest risk for HIV infection and AIDS has historically been sexually active homosexual and bisexual males. By mid-2000 among adults and adolescents 13 years of age and older, about half (47 percent) of all AIDS cases had resulted from men who had sex with men. (See Table 9.1.)

The second most common way (25 percent) that AIDS is transmitted is through injecting drugs. Since the reporting of

TABLE 9.1

AIDS cases by age group, exposure category, and sex, July 1999–June 2000

Adult/adolescent exposure category	Males July 1999–June 2000 No.	(%)	Males Cumulative total No.	(%)	Females July 1999–June 2000 No.	(%)	Females Cumulative total No.	(%)	Totals[1] July 1999–June 2000 No.	(%)	Totals[1] Cumulative total[2] No.	(%)
Men who have sex with men	14,393	(44)	348,657	(56)	–	–	–	–	14,393	(33)	348,657	(47)
Injecting drug use	6,595	(20)	137,650	(22)	2,795	(27)	51,592	(41)	9,390	(22)	189,242	(25)
Men who have sex with men and inject drugs	1,668	(5)	47,820	(8)	–	–	–	–	1,668	(4)	47,820	(6)
Hemophilia/coagulation disorder	106	(0)	4,847	(1)	5	(0)	274	(0)	111	(0)	5,121	(1)
Heterosexual contact:	2,659	(8)	27,952	(5)	4,114	(39)	50,257	(40)	6,773	(16)	78,210	(10)
Sex with injecting drug user	586		8,973		1,059		20,093		1,645		29,066	
Sex with bisexual male		–		–	174		3,465		174		3,465	
Sex with person with hemophilia		11		63		14	413		25		476	
Sex with transfusion recipient with HIV infection		24	405			25	585		49		990	
Sex with HIV-infected person, risk not specified	2,038		18,511		2,842		25,701		4,880		44,213	
Receipt of blood transfusion, blood components, or tissue[3]	135	(0)	4,920	(1)	135	(1)	3,746	(3)	270	(1)	8,666	(1)
Other/risk not reported or identified	7,268	(22)	48,343	(8)	3,420	(33)	19,042	(15)	10,688	(25)	67,387	(9)
Adult/adolescent subtotal	32,824	(100)	620,189	(100)	10,469	(100)	124,911	(100)	43,293	(100)	745,103	(100)

Pediatric (<13 years old) exposure category

	No.	(%)	No.	(%)	No.	(%)	No.	(%)	No.	(%)	No.	(%)
Hemophilia/coagulation disorder	3	(3)	229	(5)	–	–	7	(0)	3	(1)	236	(3)
Mother with/at risk for HIV infection:	84	(85)	3,979	(88)	111	(89)	4,048	(95)	195	(87)	8,027	(91)
Injecting drug use		14	1,573			29	1,564		43		3,137	
Sex with an injecting drug user		15	747			15	709		30		1,456	
Sex with a bisexual male		1		86		1		86		2	172	
Sex with person with hemophilia		–		17		3		16		3		33
Sex with transfusion recipient with HIV infection		–		11		–		14		–		25
Sex with HIV-infected person, risk not specified		19	588			22	622		41		1,210	
Receipt of blood transfusion, blood components, or tissue		1		74		2		78		3	152	
Has HIV infection, risk not specified		34	883			39	959		73		1,842	
Receipt of blood transfusion, blood components, or tissue[3]	3	(3)	240	(5)	1	(1)	141	(3)	4	(2)	381	(4)
Risk not reported or identified	9	(9)	77	(2)	13	(10)	83	(2)	22	(10)	160	(2)
Pediatric subtotal	99	(100)	4,525	(100)	125	(100)	4,279	(100)	224	(100)	8,804	(100)
Total	**32,923**		**624,714**		**10,594**		**129,190**		**43,517**		**753,907**	

[1] Includes 3 persons whose sex is unknown.

[2] Includes persons known to be infected with human immunodeficiency virus type 2 (HIV-2).

[3] Thirty-nine adults/adolescents and 2 children developed AIDS after receiving blood screened negative for HIV antibody. Thirteen additional adults developed AIDS after receiving tissue, organs, or artificial insemination from HIV-infected donors. Four of the 13 received tissue, organs, or artificial insemination from a donor who was negative for HIV antibody at the time of donation.

SOURCE: "Table 5. AIDS cases by age group, exposure category, and sex, reported through June 2000, United States," in *HIV/AIDS Surveillance Report*, Centers for Disease Control and Prevention, 2000

AIDS cases began in 1981, usage of intravenous drugs as a cause of AIDS has grown from 11 percent of all reported AIDS cases to 25 percent in 1994, where it has more or less remained. Additionally, 6 percent of men who contracted AIDS both had sex with men and were intravenous (IV) drug users. Four percent of those diagnosed with AIDS contracted HIV through sex with an IV drug user. Overall, IV drug use played a role in 35 percent of AIDS cases. (See Table 9.1.)

Among children under 13 years of age, the overwhelming majority (91 percent) were infected by their HIV-infected mothers. (See Table 9.1.) Most of these mothers became infected from IV drug use (39 percent) or having sex with IV drug users (18 percent).

RACE, ETHNICITY, AND GENDER OF AIDS VICTIMS

Race and Ethnicity

Although blacks constitute less than 13 percent of the U.S. population, they comprise more than one-third (37 percent) of reported AIDS cases in adults and more than

TABLE 9.2

AIDS cases among adult and adolescent men, by race/ethnicity and exposure category, July 1999–June 2000

	White, not Hispanic				Black, not Hispanic				Hispanic			
	July 1999–June 2000		Cumulative total		July 1999–June 2000		Cumulative total		July 1999–June 2000		Cumulative total	
Exposure category	No.	(%)	No.	(%)	No.	(%)	No.	(%)	No.	(%)	No.	(%)
Men who have sex with men	7,586	(63)	220,156	(74)	4,283	(31)	76,637	(37)	2,261	(36)	46,996	(42)
Injecting drug use	1,364	(11)	27,502	(9)	3,426	(25)	70,230	(34)	1,753	(28)	39,228	(35)
Men who have sex with men and inject drugs	817	(7)	24,422	(8)	561	(4)	15,429	(7)	266	(4)	7,473	(7)
Hemophilia/coagulation disorder	84	(1)	3,753	(1)	11	(0)	559	(0)	6	(0)	429	(0)
Heterosexual contact:	423	(4)	5,375	(2)	1,635	(12)	16,027	(8)	567	(9)	6,288	(6)
Sex with an injecting drug user	*123*		*1,913*		*341*		*5,233*		*118*		*1,759*	
Sex with person with hemophilia	*1*		*31*		*8*		*21*		*1*		*10*	
Sex with transfusion recipient with HIV infection	*6*		*153*		*14*		*154*		*3*		*87*	
Sex with HIV-infected person, risk not specified	*293*		*3,278*		*1,272*		*10,619*		*445*		*4,432*	
Receipt of blood transfusion, blood components, or tissue	53	(0)	3,161	(1)	55	(0)	1,056	(1)	19	(0)	574	(1)
Risk not reported or identified	1,663	(14)	11,701	(4)	3,977	(29)	25,883	(13)	1,455	(23)	9,861	(9)
Total	**11,990**	**(100)**	**296,070**	**(100)**	**13,948**	**(100)**	**205,821**	**(100)**	**6,327**	**(100)**	**110,849**	**(100)**

	Asian/Pacific Islander				American Indian/Alaska Native				Cumulative totals[1]			
	July 1999–June 2000		Cumulative total		July 1999–June 2000		Cumulative total		July 1999–June 2000		Cumulative total	
Exposure category	No.	(%)	No.	(%)	No.	(%)	No.	(%)	No.	(%)	No.	(%)
Men who have sex with men	169	(52)	3,474	(72)	59	(47)	1,022	(57)	14,393	(44)	348,657	(56)
Injecting drug use	13	(4)	251	(5)	23	(18)	283	(16)	6,595	(20)	137,650	(22)
Men who have sex with men and inject drugs	7	(2)	177	(4)	16	(13)	302	(17)	1,668	(5)	47,820	(8)
Hemophilia/coagulation disorder	4	(1)	70	(1)	1	(1)	30	(2)	106	(0)	4,847	(1)
Heterosexual contact:	28	(9)	182	(4)	5	(4)	50	(3)	2,659	(8)	27,952	(5)
Sex with an injecting drug user	*4*		*49*		*–*		*14*		*586*		*8,973*	
Sex with person with hemophilia	*1*		*1*		*–*		*–*		*11*		*63*	
Sex with transfusion recipient with HIV infection	*–*		*8*		*1*		*2*		*24*		*405*	
Sex with HIV-infected person, risk not specified	*23*		*124*		*4*		*34*		*2,038*		*18,511*	
Receipt of blood transfusion, blood components, or tissue	6	(2)	112	(2)	2	(2)	9	(0)	135	(0)	4,920	(1)
Risk not reported or identified	97	(30)	561	(12)	19	(15)	107	(6)	7,268	(22)	48,343	(8)
Total	**324**	**(100)**	**4,827**	**(100)**	**125**	**(100)**	**1,803**	**(100)**	**32,824**	**(100)**	**620,189**	**(100)**

[1] Includes 819 men whose race/ethnicity is unknown.

SOURCE: "Table 9. Male adult/adolescent AIDS cases by exposure category and race/ethnicity, reported through June 2000, United States," in *HIV/AIDS Surveillance Report,* Centers for Disease Control and Prevention, 2000

one-half (59 percent) of the cases in children. Similarly, although Hispanics make up only 12 percent of the national population, they make up 18 percent of reported AIDS cases among adults and 23 percent of pediatric AIDS cases. (See Table 9.2, Table 9.3, and Table 9.4.)

Among non-Hispanic black males with AIDS, 34 percent of all cumulative cases were intravenous drug users, and among Hispanics, 35 percent were, compared to only 9 percent of non-Hispanic whites. A smaller percentage of AIDS cases resulting from IV drug use occurred among American Indian (16 percent) and Asian/Pacific Islander (5 percent) males. To these numbers must also be added figures for males who both had sex with men and also injected drugs: 7 percent for blacks, 8 percent for whites,

7 percent for Hispanics, 4 percent for Asians/Pacific Islanders, and 17 percent for American Indians/Alaskan Natives. (See Table 9.2.)

Women

IV drug use has played an ever-growing role in how women contract HIV and AIDS. Nearly half of American Indian (45 percent), black (42 percent), white (42 percent), and Hispanic (40 percent) women diagnosed with AIDS contracted the disease as a result of IV drug use. (See Table 9.3.)

Another 16 percent of all women contracted AIDS through having sex with an injecting drug user. Such high-risk activity played a major role in AIDS contraction

TABLE 9.3

AIDS cases among adult and adolescent women, by race/ethnicity and exposure category, July 1999–June 2000

Exposure category	White, not Hispanic July 1999– June 2000		Cumulative total		Black, not Hispanic July 1999– June 2000		Cumulative total		Hispanic July 1999– June 2000		Cumulative total	
	No.	(%)	No.	(%)	No.	(%)	No.	(%)	No.	(%)	No.	(%)
Injecting drug use	621	(33)	11,403	(42)	1,631	(25)	29,945	(42)	506	(28)	9,895	(40)
Hemophilia/coagulation disorder	–	–	102	(0)	3	(0)	109	(0)	2	(0)	53	(0)
Heterosexual contact:	700	(38)	10,896	(40)	2,536	(38)	27,203	(38)	810	(45)	11,641	(47)
Sex with injecting drug user	232		4,415		604		10,252		210		5,262	
Sex with bisexual male	60		1,475		88		1,364		18		530	
Sex with person with hemophilia	5		286		5		81		3		39	
Sex with transfusion recipient with HIV infection	11		306		11		160		2		96	
Sex with HIV-infected person, risk not specified	392		4,414		1,828		15,346		577		5,714	
Receipt of blood transfusion, blood components, or tissue	38	(2)	1,815	(7)	75	(1)	1,273	(2)	16	(1)	543	(2)
Risk not reported or identified	506	(27)	2,999	(11)	2,380	(36)	13,211	(18)	480	(26)	2,578	(10)
Total	**1,865**	**(100)**	**27,215**	**(100)**	**6,625**	**(100)**	**71,741**	**(100)**	**1,814**	**(100)**	**24,710**	**(100)**

Exposure category	Asian/Pacific Islander July 1999– June 2000		Cumulative total		American Indian/Alaska Native July 1999– June 2000		Cumulative total		Cumulative totals[1] July 1999– June 2000		Cumulative total	
	No.	(%)	No.	(%)	No.	(%)	No.	(%)	No.	(%)	No.	(%)
Injecting drug use	7	(8)	109	(16)	24	(40)	181	(45)	2,795	(27)	51,592	(41)
Hemophilia/coagulation disorder	–	–	6	(1)	–	–	2	(1)	5	(0)	274	(0)
Heterosexual contact:	43	(52)	330	(49)	20	(33)	143	(36)	4,114	(39)	50,257	(40)
Sex with injecting drug user	5		83		7		69		1,059		20,093	
Sex with bisexual male	5		71		3		19		174		3,465	
Sex with person with hemophilia	–		5		1		2		14		413	
Sex with transfusion recipient with HIV infection	–		19		1		3		25		585	
Sex with HIV-infected person, risk not specified	33		152		8		50		2,842		25,701	
Receipt of blood transfusion, blood components, or tissue	5	(6)	98	(15)	1	(2)	14	(4)	135	(1)	3,746	(3)
Risk not reported or identified	28	(34)	127	(19)	15	(25)	59	(15)	3,420	(33)	19,042	(15)
Total	**83**	**(100)**	**670**	**(100)**	**60**	**(100)**	**399**	**(100)**	**10,469**	**(100)**	**124,911**	**(100)**

[1] Includes 176 women whose race/ethnicity is unknown.

SOURCE: "Table 11. Female adult/adolescent AIDS cases by exposure category and race/ethnicity, reported through June 2000, United States," in *HIV/AIDS Surveillance Report,* Centers for Disease Control and Prevention, 2000

for female Hispanics (21 percent), American Indians (17 percent), whites (16 percent), blacks (14 percent), and Asians/Pacific Islanders (12 percent). (See Table 9.3.)

Of the nearly 52,000 women who have contracted AIDS through IV drug use, almost 6 of 10 (58 percent) have been black (Table 9.3).

DRUG USE BEHAVIOR THAT TRANSMITS HIV

Perinatal Transmission

Pregnant mothers infected with HIV risk passing the virus to their infants perinatally (sometime around the time of birth). Researchers estimate that a woman has a 13 to 40 percent chance of passing HIV infection to her infant. Moreover, pregnancy itself may accelerate the course of HIV disease in the mother, most likely as a result of an altered immune system during pregnancy.

Very little is known about female IV drug users' contraceptive practices to avoid transmission of HIV. Although heroin can suppress fertility to some degree in women, New York City officials report that birth rates among addicted women are higher than those among nonaddicted women.

Intravenous drug use, promiscuity, and prostitution are all linked with the lack of contraceptive use. The Centers for Disease Control and Prevention (CDC) reports that the majority of women with AIDS are of childbearing age (20 to 44 years), which indicates the likelihood of an increasing population of children with HIV infection.

While investigators often treat sexual behavior and drug use separately, many times they are linked. Female IV drug users may use sex to obtain drugs from partners who are also IV drug users. Women are much more

TABLE 9.4

Pediatric AIDS cases by race/ethnicity and exposure category, July 1999–June 2000

Exposure category	White, not Hispanic				Black, not Hispanic				Hispanic			
	July 1999–June 2000		Cumulative total		July 1999–June 2000		Cumulative total		July 1999–June 2000		Cumulative total	
	No.	(%)	No.	(%)	NO.	(%)	No.	(%)	No.	(%)	No.	(%)
Hemphilia/coagulation disorder	1	(3)	159	(10)	—	—	34	(1)	—	—	37	(2)
Mother with/at risk for HIV infection:	30	(86)	1,161	(76)	134	(90)	4,936	(96)	30	(88)	1,857	(92)
Injecting drug use	8		480		27		1,893		7		741	
Sex with injecting drug user	7		228		17		725		6		491	
Sex with bisexual male	—		65		1		64		1		40	
Sex with person with hemophilia	1		18		1		7		1		8	
Sex with transfusion recipient with HIV infection	—		8		—		8		—		9	
Sex with HIV–infected person, risk not specified	6		143		30		796		5		256	
Receipt of blood transfusion, blood components, or tissue	2		44		1		75		—		32	
Has HIV infection, risk not specified	6		175		57		1,368		10		280	
Receipt of blood transfusion, blood component, or tissue	1	(3)	189	(12)	1	(1)	89	(2)	1	(3)	92	(5)
Risk not reported or identified	3	(9)	26	(2)	14	(9)	99	(2)	3	(9)	30	(1)
Total	**35**	**(100)**	**1,535**	**(100)**	**149**	**(100)**	**5,158**	**(100)**	**34**	**(100)**	**2,016**	**(100)**

Exposure category	Asian/Pacific Islander				American Indian/Alaska Native				Cumulative totals[1]			
	July 1999–June 2000		Cumulative total		July 1999–June 2000		Cumulative total		July 1999–June 2000		Cumulative total	
	No.	(%)	No.	(%)	No.	(%)	No.	(%)	No.	(%)	No.	(%)
Hemophilia/coagulation disorder	—	—	3	(6)	1	(50)	2	(6)	3	(1)	236	(3)
Mother with/at risk for HIV infection:	—	—	31	(63)	1	(50)	28	(90)	195	(87)	8,027	(91)
Injecting drug use	—		4		1		14		43		3,137	
Sex with injecting drug user	—		5		—		6		30		1,456	
Sex with bisexual male	—		2		—		—		2		172	
Sex with person with hemophilia	—		—		—		—		3		33	
Sex with transfusion recipient with HIV infection	—		—		—		—		—		25	
Sex with HIV-infected person, risk not specified	—		9		—		4		41		1,210	
Receipt of blood transfusion, blood components, or tissue	—		1		—		—		3		152	
Has HIV infection, risk not specified	—		10		—		4		73		1,842	
Receipt of blood transfusion, blood components, or tissue	1	(33)	11	(22)	—	—	—	—	4	(2)	381	(4)
Risk not reported or identified	2	(67)	4	(8)	—	—	1	(3)	22	(10)	160	(2)
Total	**3**	**(100)**	**49**	**(100)**	**2**	**(100)**	**31**	**(100)**	**224**	**(100)**	**8,804**	**(100)**

[1]Includes 15 children whose race/ethnicity is unknown.

SOURCE: "Table 15. Pediatric AIDS cases by exposure category and race/ethnicity, reported through June 2000, United States," in *HIV/AIDS Surveillance Report*, Centers for Disease Control and Prevention, 2000

frequently involved in prostitution to fund drug habits than men. What exacerbates the danger to these women is the powerlessness they experience due to their intense need for drugs and severe poverty. Because many men seek out dangerous sexual services from drug-addicted prostitutes, they are at great risk.

Most children diagnosed with pediatric AIDS (52 percent) received it perinatally from mothers with HIV infection due to IV drug use or having sex with an IV drug user. This is true of 61 percent of Hispanic children with AIDS, 51 percent of black children with AIDS, and 46 percent of white children with AIDS. Significant percentages of American Indian (65 percent) and Asian/Pacific Islander children (18 percent, much lower than other groups) contracted AIDS from such mothers, but the total number of AIDS cases among children of these groups is so small that these percentages must be viewed with caution. (See Table 9.4.)

A 1997 Institute of Medicine report recommended HIV testing as a standard part of the testing women receive during prenatal care. Researchers have found that treating pregnant HIV-infected women with an antiviral drug reduces the transmission rate. In addition, planned cesarean section deliveries may prevent more cases of mother-to-baby HIV infection.

Sharing Equipment

As with other blood-borne infections common to IV drug users, HIV spreads from user to user by the sharing of blood-contaminated equipment. At least five pieces of the IV user's equipment can become contaminated—the syringe, needle, "cooker," cotton, and rinse water.

The syringe and the needle can become contaminated when infected blood is left behind between uses. This can often occur when users draw blood back and forth into a syringe several times while it is still inserted in the vein in an attempt to inject all of the drug. This practice, known as "booting," does not occur when users practice intramuscular or subcutaneous injection, known as "skin popping."

Bleach, hydrogen peroxide, and alcohol have killed HIV in vitro (isolated in a test tube). Bleach, alcohol, liquid detergent, or hydrogen peroxide can be effective methods of cleaning a syringe and needle if the solution is flushed completely into the syringe. However, using disinfected syringes and needles is still not as safe as using new, sterile equipment.

The "cooker" is any small container, usually a spoon or a bottle cap, that is used to dissolve the injectable drug, most often a powder. Contamination may occur when infected blood is pushed out of the needle or syringe into the cooker while a new shot of the drug is being drawn up. If the needle and syringe are effectively sterilized, the cooker will not be contaminated. In the event of cooker contamination, heating the cooker between shots can kill the virus.

A piece of cotton is sometimes used as a strainer to trap any impurities from the cooker solution. The solution is strained through the cotton as it is drawn into the syringe. Instead of disposing of each piece of cotton immediately after use, a user will sometimes "beat the cotton" with a little water in an attempt to extract the tiniest bit of the drug that may be left in it. Thus, the cotton can become infected if the syringe and needle have not been properly sterilized.

Syringes and needles are usually rinsed out before reuse, not necessarily to decontaminate them but to prevent clotting. If the rinse water does not contain bleach adequate for disinfecting, the use and reuse of the same rinse water can be a source of contamination.

HOW AVAILABLE SHOULD HYPODERMIC SYRINGES BE?

Although there has been some regulation of hypodermic syringes in the United States since they were invented in the 19th century, they were widely available until the 1970s. Needles could be purchased without a prescription, and drug users were able to freely acquire as many clean needles as they wanted.

In the 1970s and 1980s, though, almost every state and the District of Columbia criminalized the possession or sale of syringes without a prescription. Syringes had been sold alongside cocaine kits and marijuana paraphernalia at "head shops" in cities across the country. As part of a larger project to get tough on drug use and eliminate head shops, laws were passed to limit the sale of syringes.

As it became recognized that dirty needles were causing HIV transmission in the late 1980s, needle-exchange programs were started in some cities. Since then they have provided the major means of reducing HIV transmission among IV drug users. However, despite the positive impact of needle-exchange programs, it has been noted that they cannot meet the demand for syringes alone. In later years new efforts were under way to decriminalize syringe sale and possession in a number of states.

Needle Exchange Programs

A GROWING NUMBER. The first needle exchange programs (NEPs, or SEPs, for syringe exchange programs), in which sterile needles are exchanged for used, potentially contaminated needles, were opened in San Francisco in 1987 and Tacoma, Washington, in 1988. By September 1, 1993, at least 37 NEPs were operating in 30 cities in 12 states.

Between December 1997 and March 1998, the Beth Israel Medical Center (New York), in collaboration with the North American Syringe Exchange Network (NASEN), surveyed the 113 SEPs in the United States that were members of NASEN. Although the exact number of SEPs in the United States is unknown, most are believed to be members of NASEN. One hundred SEPs participated in the survey. Of these, 54 began operating before 1995; 20, in 1995; 18, in 1996; and 8, in 1997. These 100 SEPs operated in 80 cities in 30 states, the District of Columbia, and Puerto Rico. Over half (52) were located in four states (California, 19; New York, 14; Washington, 11; and Connecticut, 8). Nine cities had two or more SEPs.

In 1997 the reporting SEPs exchanged about 17.5 million syringes. The 10 most active SEPs (those that exchanged 500,000 syringes or more) exchanged approximately 10.3 million syringes, or 59.2 percent of all syringes exchanged. The SEP in San Francisco reported exchanging the largest number of syringes (1.9 million) in 1997. During 1997, 48 SEPs (50 percent) reported exchanging 55,000 or fewer syringes each; of these, 24 (25 percent) exchanged fewer than 10,000 each. (See Table 9.5.)

Virtually all the programs offered information about safer injection methods and referral to substance abuse treatment programs. In 1997, 52 of the SEPs operated in states where it was legal to do so, 16 in states where they were illegal but tolerated, and 32 where they were illegal and had to operate underground.

HELPING INTRAVENOUS DRUG USERS. The Centers for Disease Control and Prevention (CDC), in "Changing Syringe Laws Is Part of Strategy to Help Stem HIV

Spread" (*HIV/AIDS Prevention*, December 1997), pointed out that drug users must have access to clean syringes and drug treatment as part of a complete HIV prevention plan. One way to make this happen is to change the drug paraphernalia laws so that clean needles and syringes are available to intravenous drug users.

Public Health Service policy recommends that IV drug users be counseled and encouraged to stop using and injecting drugs, if possible, through substance abuse treatment, including relapse prevention. Failing this, however, drug users should follow various preventive measures, such as

- Never reusing or sharing syringes, water, or drug preparation equipment.

- Using only syringes obtained from a reliable source (e.g., pharmacies).

- Using a new, sterile syringe to prepare and inject drugs.

- Safely disposing of syringes after one use.

AN INTENSE POLITICAL DEBATE. Needle exchange has led to intense political debate in the United States, particularly in some states (California and New York) and cities (Baltimore, Maryland; New York City; Boston, Massachusetts; and Berkeley, California). However, in many cities (Seattle, Washington; Tacoma, Washington; San Francisco, California; Honolulu, Hawaii; and New Haven, Connecticut), large-scale NEPs were set up with substantial community support.

Those who support NEPs stress the importance of the programs as gateways to counseling, education, and other referral services for addicts. This comprehensive approach is known as "harm reduction." Supporters also say that NEPs facilitate proper disposal of injection equipment and serve as outlets to supply addicts with materials that help to curb the spread of HIV.

Those opposing NEPs fear that needle programs will increase drug use by providing the means (needles and syringes) to inject drugs, although no American or foreign study has shown that NEPs increase drug use. Opponents also believe providing NEPs would appear to condone drug use and therefore undermine the message that using drugs is illegal, unhealthy, and morally wrong. In addition, they maintain that NEPs may draw scarce resources away from other, possibly more effective, programs, such as drug treatment.

Some opponents claim that needle "exchange" programs are not in fact exchanges, but giveaways. They say that participants rarely exchange dirty needles for clean ones, meaning the dirty needles are still on the streets. However, NEPs typically operate on the principle of a one-for-one exchange.

TABLE 9.5

Number and percentage of syringe exchange programs (SEPs) and sterile syringes provided by SEPs, by size of program, 1997

Size of SEP*	SEPs		Total syringes exchanged	
	No.	(%)	No.	(%)
<10,000	24	(25)	82,356	(0.5)
10,000–55,000	24	(25)	700,274	(4.0)
55,001–499,999	38	(40)	6,334,375	(36.3)
≥500,000	10	(10)	10,330,103	(59.2)
Total	**96**	**(100)**	**17,447,108**	**(100.0)**

*Based on the number of syringes exchanged in 1997.

SOURCE: "Number and percentage of syringe exchange programs (SEPs) and sterile syringes provided by SEPs, by size of program—United States, 1997," in "Update: Syringe Exchange Programs—United States, 1997," *Morbidity and Mortality Weekly Report*, vol. 47, no. 31, Centers for Disease Control and Prevention, August 14, 1998

THE EFFECTIVENESS OF NEPS WORLDWIDE. Susan F. Hurley, Damien J. Jolley, and John M. Kaldor, in "Effectiveness of Needle-Exchange Programmes for Prevention of HIV Infection" (*The Lancet*, June 21, 1997), studied cities around the world with and without NEPs. They found that, on average, HIV increased 5.9 percent in cities without NEPs and decreased by 5.8 percent in cities with NEPs.

They also observed that "NEPs led to a reduction in HIV incidence among injecting drug users" and that their findings "strongly support the view that NEPs are effective." The researchers concluded that with their findings "and the interpretation of previous studies by the Panel on Needle Exchange and Bleach Distribution Programs [National Research Council and Institute of Medicine], the view that NEPs are not effective no longer seems tenable."

IMPROVING ACCESS TO STERILE SYRINGES IS WIDELY SUPPORTED. The National Academy of Sciences, American Medical Association, American Public Health Association, National Institutes of Health Consensus Panel, Centers for Disease Control and Prevention, American Bar Association, and President George Herbert Walker Bush's and President Bill Clinton's AIDS Advisory Commissions—virtually every established medical, scientific, and legal body that has studied the issue of needle exchange programs—agree on the validity of improved access to sterile syringes to reduce the spread of infectious diseases, including HIV/AIDS. In July 1997 the U.S. Conference of Mayors endorsed federal and state policy changes to improve access to sterile syringes.

Fifteen of the top 20 most widely circulated U.S. newspapers have editorialized in favor of NEPs or syringe deregulation. Public opinion has been moderately in favor of NEPs. A 2000 Kaiser Family Foundation poll found 58 percent of the population favor NEPs and 61 percent favor allowing users to purchase needles at pharmacies. Hart Research polls found between 54 and 55 percent support for NEPs from 1995 through 1997.

However, only about one-third of the poll respondents supported syringe deregulation.

Two Harris polls, one in September 1997 and one in October 1997, found only 44 percent public support for community programs to dispense clean needles. When told that the American Medical Association and other medical and public health organizations had endorsed these programs, support rose to 50 percent.

Banning Federal Funds for Needle Exchanges

In 1988 Congress passed the Health Omnibus Programs Extension Act (PL 100-607), banning the expenditure of federal funds for needle exchange. At the same time Congress authorized funding for research into needle exchange programs. Under the conditions of the Department of Health and Human Services Appropriations Act of 1997 (PL 105-78), lifting the ban and using federal funds to support NEPs depended on a determination by the secretary of Health and Human Services (HHS) that such programs reduce transmission of HIV without encouraging the use of illegal drugs.

In a February 1997 report to Congress, HHS Secretary Donna E. Shalala announced that a review of the scientific literature indicated that needle exchange programs "can be an effective component of a comprehensive strategy to prevent HIV and other blood-borne infectious diseases in communities that choose to include them." For example, *Preventing HIV Transmission: The Role of Sterile Needles and Bleach* (National Research Council and Institute of Medicine, Washington, D.C., September 1995) concluded that NEPs have beneficial effects on reducing behaviors such as multiperson reuse of syringes. This report estimated a reduction in risk behaviors of 80 percent and a reduction in HIV transmission of 30 percent or greater.

In April 1998 Secretary Shalala reported that a review of research findings indicated that needle exchange programs "do not encourage the use of illegal drugs." In addition, NEPs can reduce drug use through effective referrals to drug treatment and counseling.

RELUCTANCE TO LIFT THE BAN. Both Congress and the president have been very reluctant to lift the ban on federal monies for needle exchange programs. To approve of a needle exchange program might appear to give official sanction to a strategy many voters consider promoting drug use. Many legislators fear that approving such a policy would be the first step along the road to legalization of drugs.

Others fear that approval of needle exchange programs, while perhaps good policy, is only an inadequate first step toward the comprehensive drug treatment program needed to reduce drug addiction. President Bill Clinton, who saw drug abuse increase during his term in office, was very reluctant to approve any program that could be perceived as being weak on drugs.

Therefore, in spite of the scientific evidence that NEPs reduce the spread of AIDS without increasing drug use, the Clinton administration decided that local communities choosing to implement their own programs must use their own dollars to fund needle exchange programs. AIDS researchers and activists criticized the decision for putting politics above saving lives. As of mid-2001 the George W. Bush administration had not yet made any major decisions regarding needle exchanges.

THE AMERICAN BAR ASSOCIATION AND STATE LEGISLATION RELATED TO NEEDLE POSSESSION. A report prepared by the AIDS Coordinating Committee of the American Bar Association (ABA) outlined the ABA's stance on the deregulation of syringes (*Deregulation of Hypodermic Needles and Syringes as a Public Health Measure: A Report on Emerging Policy and Law in the United States*, Washington, D.C., 2001). The ABA supports the deregulation of needle exchange programs and the relaxation of laws concerning the sale and possession of syringes.

The association advocates an approach that extends beyond NEPs. They advocate laws that allow IV users to obtain needles from any pharmacy whenever they are needed. There are several advantages of this approach. One is that it sidesteps the objection that states should not fund NEPs because it sends the "wrong message." Legalizing possession of syringes would allow users to purchase needles directly from pharmacies like any other purchase, thus not involving the government or government funds.

A second benefit is that such policies would allow much greater access to needles than NEPs alone. Because of the stigma attached to IV drug use, many users do not want to enter NEPs and be identified as addicts. Also, it is often inconvenient for users to get to NEPs, since they may be located many miles from where they live. In addition, users may not be able to get as many needles as they need at once, considering that some users inject a dozen or more times a day.

The ABA identifies three types of deregulation that have been passed in state legislatures. In Oregon and Alaska, syringes are "completely deregulated"—that is, they can be bought and sold by anyone, under any circumstances. Next are states that have "unrestricted pharmacy sales," where anyone can buy as many needles as desired without a prescription, so long as it is at a pharmacy. Finally, a number of states have passed "10 and under deregulation," which allows the sale and possession of up to 10 syringes.

As of March 2001, 10 states allow users increased access to syringes. Alaska and Oregon have completely deregulated syringes. Rhode Island, Ohio, and Wisconsin allow unrestricted pharmacy sales. New York, New Hampshire, Connecticut, Maine, and Minnesota have enacted 10 and under deregulation.

CHAPTER 10
THE NATIONAL DRUG CONTROL STRATEGY

Drug dependence is a chronic, relapsing disorder that exacts an enormous cost on individuals, families, businesses, communities, and nations. Addicted individuals frequently engage in self-destructive and criminal behavior. Treatment can help them end dependence on addictive drugs. Treatment programs also reduce the consequences of addiction on the rest of society. Providing treatment for America's chronic drug users is both compassionate public policy and a sound investment.

— *National Drug Control Strategy, 2001,* Office of National Drug Control Policy

THE COST OF DRUG ABUSE

The Levin Group, sponsored by the National Institute on Drug Abuse (NIDA) and the National Institute on Alcohol Abuse and Alcoholism (NIAAA), has calculated the economically measurable costs of illegal drug abuse. The group concluded that in 1995 illegal drugs cost the nation close to $110 billion. Although the study is now several years old, it is a powerful indicator of the magnitude of the cost of drugs to the American economy.

In 1995 total estimated spending for health care services for drug problems was $11.9 billion. This amount included specialized detoxification and rehabilitation services, as well as prevention, training, and research expenditures ($5.3 billion), plus the costs of treatment for drug-related health problems ($6.6 billion). Lost potential productivity due to drug abuse cost an estimated $77.6 billion. Other economic impacts, including motor vehicle crashes, fire destruction, and criminal justice system expenses, accounted for the remaining $20.4 billion.

The Anti-Drug Abuse Act of 1988 (PL 100-690) established the creation of a drug-free America as a U.S. policy goal. To accomplish this goal, the law established the Office of National Drug Control Policy (ONDCP) "to set priorities and objectives for national drug control, promulgate *The National Drug Control Strategy* on an annual

basis, and oversee the strategy's implementation." To stress the importance of the issue, the director of the ONDCP has become a cabinet-level position.

A NEW STRATEGY

The U.S. government has been waging a "war on drugs" ever since President Richard Nixon (1969–1973) introduced the term to focus the nation's growing concerns about drug abuse. The *National Drug Control Strategy, 2001* recommends that the nation look at its drug problem in a new way:

> The metaphor of a "war on drugs" is misleading. Although wars are expected to end, drug education—like all schooling—is a continuous process. The moment we believe ourselves victorious and drop our guard, drug abuse will resurface in the next generation. To reduce the demand for drugs, prevention must be ongoing. Addicted individuals should be held accountable for their actions and offered treatment to help change destructive behavior.

> Cancer is a more appropriate metaphor for the nation's drug problem. Dealing with cancer is a long-term proposition. It requires the mobilization of support mechanisms—medical, educational, social, and financial—to check the spread of the disease and improve the patient's prognosis. Symptoms of the illness must be managed while the root cause is attacked. The key to reducing the incidence of drug abuse and cancer is prevention coupled with treatment and accompanied by research.

The *Strategy* establishes five long-term goals intended to lead to a decline in drug use in the United States. Two major goals are to limit the demand for and the supply of drugs. Though both must be advanced simultaneously, demand must be the priority. People's demand for drugs sets the drug-abuse cycle in motion. Traffickers supply drugs because a profit can be made. Prevention is the key to demand reduction. The *Strategy* focuses particularly on the education of children to enable them to

TABLE 10.1

Goals of the Office of National Drug Control Policy, 2000

Goal 1: Educate and enable America's youth to reject illegal drugs as well as alcohol and tobacco.

Objective 1: Educate parents and other care givers, teachers, coaches, clergy, health professionals, and business and community leaders to help youth reject illegal drugs and underage alcohol and tobacco use.
Objective 2: Pursue a vigorous advertising and public communications program dealing with the dangers of illegal drugs, alcohol, and tobacco use by youth.
Objective 3: Promote zero tolerance policies for youth regarding the use of illegal drugs, alcohol, and tobacco within the family, school, workplace, and community.
Objective 4: Provide students in grades K–12 with alcohol, tobacco, and drug prevention programs and policies that are research based.
Objective 5: Support parents and adult mentors in encouraging youth to engage in positive, healthy lifestyles and modeling behavior to be emulated by young people.
Objective 6: Encourage and assist the development of community coalitions and programs in preventing drug abuse and underage alcohol and tobacco use.
Objective 7: Create partnerships with the media, entertainment industry, and professional sports organizations to avoid the glamorization, condoning, or normalization of illegal drugs and the use of alcohol and tobacco by youth.
Objective 8: Develop and implement a set of research-based principles upon which prevention programming can be based.
Objective 9: Support and highlight research, including the development of scientific information, to inform drug, alcohol, and tobacco prevention programs targeting young Americans.

Goal 2: Increase the safety of America's citizens by substantially reducing drug-related crime and violence.

Objective 1: Strengthen law enforcement—including federal, state, and local drug task forces—to combat drug-related violence, disrupt criminal organizations, and arrest and prosecute the leaders of illegal drug syndicates.
Objective 2: Improve the ability of High Intensity Drug Trafficking Areas (HIDTAs) to counter drug trafficking.
Objective 3: Help law enforcement to disrupt money laundering and seize and forfeit criminal assets.
Objective 4: Break the cycle of drug abuse and crime.
Objective 5: Support and highlight research, including the development of scientific information and data, to inform law enforcement, prosecution, incarceration, and treatment of offenders involved with illegal drugs.

Goal 3: Reduce health and social costs to the public of illegal drug use.

Objective 1: Support and promote effective, efficient, and accessible drug treatment, ensuring the development of a system that is responsive to emerging trends in drug abuse.
Objective 2: Reduce drug-related health problems, with an emphasis on infectious diseases.
Objective 3: Promote national adoption of drug-free workplace programs that emphasize a comprehensive program that includes: drug testing, education, prevention, and intervention.
Objective 4: Support and promote the education, training, and credentialing of professionals who work with substance abusers.
Objective 5: Support research into the development of medications and related protocols to prevent or reduce drug dependence and abuse.
Objective 6: Support and highlight research and technology, including the acquisition and analysis of scientific data, to reduce the health and social costs of illegal drug use.
Objective 7: Support and disseminate scientific research and data on the consequences of legalizing drugs.

Goal 4: Shield America's air, land, and sea frontiers from the drug threat.

Objective 1: Conduct flexible operations to detect, disrupt, deter, and seize illegal drugs in transit to the United States and at U.S. borders.
Objective 2: Improve the coordination and effectiveness of U.S. drug law enforcement programs with particular emphasis on the Southwest Border, Puerto Rico, and the U.S. Virgin Islands.
Objective 3: Improve bilateral and regional cooperation with Mexico as well as other cocaine and heroin transit zone countries in order to reduce the flow of illegal drugs into the United States.
Objective 4: Support and highlight research and technology—including the development of scientific information and data—to detect, disrupt, deter, and seize illegal drugs in transit to the United States and at U.S. borders.

Goal 5: Break foreign and domestic drug sources of supply.

Objective 1: Produce a net reduction in the worldwide cultivation of coca, opium, and marijuana and in the production of other illegal drugs, especially methamphetamine.
Objective 2: Disrupt and dismantle major international drug trafficking organizations and arrest, prosecute, and incarcerate their leaders.
Objective 3: Support and complement source country drug control efforts and strengthen source country political will and drug control capabilities.
Objective 4: Develop and support bilateral, regional, and multilateral initiatives and mobilize international organizational efforts against all aspects of illegal drug production, trafficking, and abuse.
Objective 5: Promote international policies and laws that deter money laundering and facilitate anti-money laundering investigations as well as seizure and forfeiture of associated assets.
Objective 6: Support and highlight research and technology, including the development of scientific data, to reduce the worldwide supply of illegal drugs.

SOURCE: "Strategic Goals and Objectives, National Drug Control Strategy," in *The National Drug Control Strategy, 2000*, Office of National Drug Control Policy, Washington, D.C., April 2001

reject substance abuse. Two of the goals address the harm to society caused by drug abuse.

Goal one calls for educating the nation's young people to reject both legal and illegal drugs, and goal two calls for the reduction of drug-related crime and violence. Goal three suggests methods of lessening the health and social costs of drug abuse. Goal four recommends ways to stop the flow of drugs into the country, and goal five suggests how the United States can, on its own and in cooperation with other countries, reduce or eliminate the international drug trade. Table 10.1 shows the five goals and the objectives that need to be accomplished to reach them.

THE FEDERAL DRUG BUDGET

The amount spent by the federal government to control drugs has risen from $1.5 billion in 1981 to $2.7 billion in 1985, $13.5 billion in 1996, and $18.1 billion for

FIGURE 10.1

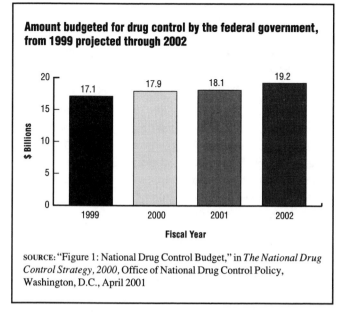

Amount budgeted for drug control by the federal government, from 1999 projected through 2002

SOURCE: "Figure 1: National Drug Control Budget," in *The National Drug Control Strategy, 2000,* Office of National Drug Control Policy, Washington, D.C., April 2001

regular appropriations in 2001. The requested budget for 2002 called for $19.2 billion. (See Figure 10.1.)

The $1.5 billion federal budget for drug control in 1981 split the monies evenly between supply reduction (domestic law enforcement and international/border law enforcement) and demand reduction (research; prevention, which consists of education, community action, and workplace education and control; and treatment). President Ronald Reagan's administration (1981–89) favored a strict approach to drug use and increased law enforcement. Under that administration, two-thirds of the funds were allocated to law enforcement activities.

This proportion remained the case under the administration of President George Bush (1989–93) and continued during the administration of his son, President George W. Bush (2001–). Funding by *Strategy* goal is summarized in Table 10.2. In 2001 total funding, including emergency supplemental funding, included $2.3 billion for resources to reduce drug use by young people, $8.1 billion to reduce drug-related crime, $3.1 billion to make treatment available, $2.6 billion to interdict the flow of drugs across U.S. borders, and $2 billion to reduce sources of supply.

Each year, the Office of the National Drug Control Policy (ONDCP) is required to report its program and budget priorities over a five-year planning period. Through the year 2006, funding for the following major program areas was to be emphasized:

- Support for Plan Colombia and Andean Coca Reduction, or continued efforts to reduce total South American coca.

- National Youth Anti-Drug Media Campaign, or the use of the media to change youth attitudes about drug use and its consequences.

TABLE 10.2

Federal drug funding by goal

Budget Authority (BA) in millions of dollars

Goal	FY 00 Final BA	FY 01 Enacted	FY 02 Request	FY 01-02 Change	% Change
1. Reduce youth drug use	2,131.9	2,296.3	2,222.2	(74.1)	(3.2%)[1]
2. Reduce drug-related crime	7,247.4	8,052.9	8,257.8	204.8	2.5%
3. Reduce consequences	2,854.0	3,101.2	3,303.6	202.4	6.5%
4. Shield air, land, and sea frontiers	2,488.8	2,555.7	2,772.9	217.3	8.5%
5. Reduce sources of supply	3,218.4	2,047.0	2,622.3	575.2	28.1%[2]
Total	**17,940.3**	**18,053.1**	**19,178.8**	**1,125.7**	**6.2%**

[1] This change is principally associated with the proposed termination of HUD's Drug Elimination Grant Program (close to $140 million in Goal 1 resources). This decision is based, in part, on Inspector General reviews, which suggest that this program is an ineffective means of delivering services to public housing residents.

[2] In FY 2000, Goal 5 includes $1.3 billion for Plan Colombia. These resources provide critical support for activities and equipment in both FY 2000 and FY 2001.

SOURCE: "Table 2: Drug Funding by Goal," in *The National Drug Control Strategy, 2000,* Office of National Drug Control Policy, Washington, D.C., April 2001

- Community Coalitions, or assistance to local groups in combating the use of illegal drugs, alcohol, and tobacco by youth.

- Criminal Justice Treatment Programs, or programs for criminal offenders encompassing the integrated application of testing, assessment, referral, supervision, treatment, and rehabilitation; routine progress reports to maintain judicial oversight; graduated sanctions for noncompliance; relapse prevention and skill building; and structured transition back into the mainstream community.

- Drug Courts, or criminal justice measures to intervene and provide sanctions and services for drug-using juvenile and adult offenders.

- Close the Public System Treatment Gap, or measures designed to close the gap between the number of persons in need of drug treatment and the number receiving it.

- School Drug-Prevention Coordinators, or an initiative to help school districts recruit, hire, and train drug-prevention coordinators in middle schools.

- High Intensity Drug Trafficking Area Programs, or programs that use shared resources and intelligence among local, state, and federal agencies to reduce drug activity and crime in specific areas of the country.

- Southwest Border Programs, or the creation of an integrated border management system that improves cooperation and coordination along the Southwest border to stop the flow of drugs but maintain the flow of legal immigration and commerce.

- Intelligence Architecture Support, or the ONDCP's plan to create a system of information and intelligence sharing among law enforcement agencies.

- Regional Interdiction Architecture, or an emphasis on the use of military resources to interdict drugs in Central America.

A Comprehensive, Long-Term Plan

The Anti-Drug Abuse Act of 1988 (PL 100-690) mandated the ONDCP to implement a national strategy for the creation of a drug-free America. The *National Drug Control Strategy, 1999* declared that

> *The National Drug Control Strategy* proposes a multi-year conceptual framework to reduce illegal drug use and availability by 50 percent. If this goal is achieved, just 3 percent of the household population aged twelve and over would use illegal drugs. This level would be the lowest recorded drug-use rate in American history. Drug-related health, economic, social, and criminal costs would also be reduced commensurately. The *Strategy* focuses on prevention, treatment, research, law enforcement, protection of our borders, and international cooperation. It provides general guidance while identifying specific initiatives. This document expresses the collective wisdom and optimism of the American people with regard to illegal drugs.

Some critics believe, however, that the program is fundamentally more of the same, which has done little to control the international supply of and demand for illegal drugs. Economic and social conditions are hardly mentioned. The program expresses no commitment to improve the economic situation of many of the nation's people living in inner cities.

Why do poor people turn to drugs? Why do rich people turn to drugs? What is it about American society that has led to the most serious drug problem in the developed world? Until these questions are confronted, critics think, it is likely that no drug-control program will ever be successful.

CHAPTER 11
LEGALIZATION

The United States suffers from a serious drug problem. The effects of drug use touch everyone. Crime rates rise, schools and neighborhoods deteriorate, police and courts are inundated with drug-related cases, potentially productive individuals become liabilities to themselves and their communities, health care facilities are overloaded, and innocent people become victims of drug transaction violence. Despite prevention programs that begin in elementary school; huge budgets for legal controls, interdiction, and international eradication; and a negative social attitude toward drug use, no end is in sight.

LEGALIZATION—WOULD IT SOLVE THE PROBLEM?

One of the more controversial approaches to the drug problem is the proposal to legalize or decriminalize presently illicit drugs. Legalization generally does not mean that all drugs would be available to all people. Laws would be made providing conditions under which drugs could be used, bought, and sold, just as laws regulate alcohol and tobacco. In this way, according to proponents of legalization, the purity and safety of drugs could be guaranteed. However, they often disagree on which drugs should be legalized.

Proponents of legalization include prominent people from different political backgrounds, including George Schultz, former U.S. secretary of state; Milton Friedman, Nobel Prize–winning economist; William F. Buckley, Jr., conservative political commentator; and Kurt Schmoke, mayor of Baltimore from 1987 to 1999. Schmoke asked his constituents to consider three questions: Do you think we've won the Drug War? Do you think we're winning the Drug War? If we keep doing what we're doing now, in 10 years, will we have won the Drug War? Presumably, "no" answers would indicate that drug policies need reform.

Arguments for Legalization

Proponents of legalization observe that billions of dollars have been spent on antidrug measures since 1972, when Richard Nixon launched the so-called "war on drugs." Opponents of the drug war argue that drug use and abuse in America are medical and social problems and that addiction is not curable through the criminal justice system. They think it is unreasonable to ask the public to spend increasing billions of dollars pursuing a failed policy that has caused states to build more jails and created an incarceration rate greater than that of any other country, except Russia.

Legalization supporters feel the criminality of drugs needs to be reconsidered. They point out that some crimes, such as murder, rape, and robbery, have always been considered wrong. Drug use, however, supporters claim, is not inherently wrong; it is seen as a crime because it has been labeled as such. There have been times when drug use was not considered dangerous. At the turn of the century, for example, opiates were sold in pharmacies and cocaine was used in small amounts in Coca-Cola. Furthermore, other activities that were once considered crimes, such as gambling or drinking alcohol, are now legal.

What benefits does legalization promise? First, the current status of prohibition creates a black market, or an alternative, illegal market, which inflates the price of drugs far beyond their natural value. If cocaine were legal, experts estimate that the price of a gram would be 1/20th or 1/25th the current price, reducing it to $3 or $4 a gram. This price would not be high enough to keep drug traffickers and dealers in business. Even William Bennett, the former director of the Office of National Drug Control Policy, who strongly opposes legalization, conceded in the *1989 Drug Strategy Report* that "to destroy the cocaine black market entirely, we would probably have to make the drug legally available at not much more than $10 a gram."

Legalization, proponents say, could be a boon to the criminal justice system. Presently, drug offenders clog the courts, pushing aside civil cases and non-drug-related criminal cases and monopolizing the time and attention of the police and the justice system.

Prisons and jails are overflowing with drug offenders, absorbing scarce resources to take care of the criminals and to build new incarceration facilities. Proponents say that half the cost of law enforcement and prisons is spent on drug-related crime. Of the total number of drug users, only a small percentage are addicts who commit crimes daily to support their "artificially expensive" habits. They are the robbers, car thieves, and burglars who make homes and streets unsafe. The majority of those incarcerated for drug-related crimes are sentenced for drug possession.

Proponents claim that with legalization, the billions of dollars spent on fighting the drug war could be redirected into drug education and treatment. A tax on drugs similar to taxes on tobacco and alcohol could further increase revenues for the government.

If the United States changed its attitude toward narcotics, marijuana, heroin, and even cocaine could be used for medical purposes. In the United Kingdom, heroin is used as a painkiller for terminal cancer patients, and marijuana has been found to help relieve the nausea associated with chemotherapy. Cocaine is already sold legally in small amounts to hospital pharmacies.

Legalization proponents see the drug problem as a public health issue, not a criminal problem. They believe that an enlightened society helps those with drug addictions; it does not punish them. The Tennessee Narcotics Act of 1913, for example, provided for the registration of addicts to satisfy their needs on a prescription basis through state-regulated pharmacists "to minimize suffering among this unfortunate class" and to keep "the traffic in the drugs from getting into underground channels."

CONSTITUTIONAL ISSUES. Many proponents of legalization believe that the war on drugs has threatened important individual rights guaranteed by the U.S. Constitution. They point to forfeiture procedures that allow prosecutors to confiscate homes, bank accounts, and other property of suspected drug users and dealers without due process, conviction, or just compensation. They point out searches of cars and schoolchildren's lockers without warrants. They believe that the random urine testing of many Americans, ranging from federal workers to football players, is an unnecessary invasion of personal privacy.

VESTED INTERESTS. Supporters of legalization point out that a number of groups have developed a vested interest in a continuing war on drugs. The rapid growth in prisons has provided tens of thousands of jobs, and many once-struggling cities and towns have become economi-cally reliant on new prisons built in their communities. Many police departments have become dependent on the money they confiscate from drug dealers and users. Proponents of legalization further note that, since the vast majority of illegal drug abusers use marijuana, if even only that drug were legalized, the number of abusers would be much smaller and the problem might be considered less serious. This could threaten the existence of the jobs tied to the war on drugs.

Arguments Against Legalization

Opponents of legalization base their arguments on the immorality of drug use and the dangers, particularly to impressionable children, of condoning such behavior. According to Drug Watch International, an information network and advocacy organization that opposes the legalization of drugs, drug abuse prevention

> Can take place only with positive societal norms which embrace and support healthy drug-free attitudes, environment, and activities, while reinforcing nonacceptance toward the presence of drugs and destructive behavior. These societal norms must be reflected in the accountability and enforcement of legal, medical, educational, community, and personal standards.

The DEA, which is totally opposed to the legalization of illicit drugs, believes that legalization in any form would likely

- Reduce the perception of the risks and costs of use.

- Increase availability of, and access to, harmful drugs.

- Increase demand, use, abuse, and addiction.

- Remove the social sanction against drug abuse that is reinforced by legislation.

In *Legalization: Panacea or Pandora's Box,* released by CASA (Center on Addiction and Substance Abuse, Columbia University, New York, 1995), Dr. Herbert Kleber, CASA executive vice president and medical director, and Joseph A. Califano, Jr., CASA chairman and president, outlined the problems and the gaps in drug legalization and decriminalization proposals. According to the report,

> Drugs like heroin and cocaine are not dangerous because they are illegal; they are illegal because they are dangerous. Legalization is a policy of despair, one that would write off millions of our citizens and lead to a terrible game of Russian roulette, particularly for children.

In "Voters Bamboozled into Legalizing Drugs" (*Human Events,* 1997) Califano blasted the advertising campaigns in Arizona and California leading to legalization legislation, saying

> Our children are at stake here. Those who make it through age 21 without using drugs, smoking or abusing alcohol are almost certain never to do so. Yet our record in keeping legal drugs out of the hands of children is

pitiful: five million children smoke cigarettes and millions more underage youngsters drink alcohol.

Opponents assert that legalizing drugs will not make the problem go away. Drugs are harmful, drug abuse is not a victimless crime, and legalization in other countries has been a failure. Legalizing drugs merely redefines the problem—it does not make it go away.

PERMITTING THE USE OF MARIJUANA FOR MEDICAL PURPOSES

In the November 1996 elections, California and Arizona voters approved referenda legalizing the possession of marijuana and other drugs for medical purposes. California Proposition 215, enacted as "The Compassionate Use Act of 1996," permitted patients and "primary caregivers" to possess and/or cultivate marijuana without fear of prosecution under state laws. Furthermore, physicians were allowed to recommend (not prescribe) the use of marijuana as a treatment for cancer, AIDS, anorexia, chronic pain, glaucoma, arthritis, migraine headaches, "or any other illness for which marijuana provides relief." More than half (56 percent) of California voters supported Proposition 215, while 44 percent opposed it.

In neighboring Arizona, 65 percent of the voters supported Proposition 200, enacted as the Drug Medicalization, Prevention, and Control Act, which provided that, in the case of medical necessity, marijuana and other drugs (including heroin and LSD) could be used in medical treatment. Two doctors would have to prescribe the use of these drugs. The law also called for probation and treatment rather than incarceration for first- and second-time nonviolent drug offenders. The Arizona legislature then amended the measure, saying voters had committed a grave error, and sent it back to the voters. In 1998 Proposition 200 again passed, this time with a 57 percent majority.

As of 2001 voters in nine states—Alaska, Arizona, California, Colorado, Hawaii, Maine, Nevada, Oregon, and Washington—had approved referenda that supported, in varying degrees, the medicinal use of marijuana. However, doctors are often afraid to write prescriptions because the federal government has threatened to prosecute them. Marijuana, a Schedule I drug, is illegal to buy and sell; it is also illegal to aid or abet someone who is trying to buy or sell it. A doctor writing a prescription for marijuana would be "aiding or abetting" a patient's ability to buy the drug. Doctors could lose their Drug Enforcement Administration (DEA) licenses, which allow them to prescribe Schedule II drugs such as cocaine, morphine, Demerol, and Percodan.

Is There a Medical Use for Marijuana?

Studies have shown that THC, the active ingredient in marijuana, can alleviate the nausea and vomiting caused by chemotherapy, a major procedure for fighting cancer.

Marijuana has also been found useful in alleviating pressure on the eye in glaucoma patients.

The drug has also been found effective in helping fight the physical wasting that usually accompanies AIDS. AIDS patients lose their appetites and slowly waste away because they do not eat, but using marijuana can restore the appetites of some AIDS patients. This has become particularly important with the development of new drugs for AIDS, many of which must be taken on a full stomach. On the other hand, further studies show that marijuana suppresses the immune system and contains a number of lung-damaging chemicals.

During the 1970s and 1980s the National Institute of Drug Abuse (NIDA) grew marijuana in Mississippi to supply the drug to experimental programs in six states. In 1986 the Reagan administration, feeling increasingly uncomfortable with this program and concerned that the growing AIDS epidemic might lead to increased demand for the medical legalization of marijuana, rushed through the approval of Marinol, a drug containing a synthetic form of THC, the active substance of marijuana. This soon led to the closing of the experimental state programs.

Opponents of the medical legalization of marijuana often point to Marinol as a superior alternative. However, many patients do not respond to Marinol. These patients claim that smoking marijuana allows them to better control the dosage they get. Although not legal, marijuana has been used, on the recommendation of doctors, by an unknown number of cancer and AIDS patients.

In its January 30, 1997, issue, the *New England Journal of Medicine* came out strongly in favor of the medical legalization of marijuana, saying, "A federal policy that prohibits physicians from alleviating suffering by prescribing marijuana is misguided, heavy-handed and inhumane." The journal recognized that marijuana use could cause long-term adverse effects and even lead to serious addiction. Nonetheless, the editors felt that these risks were irrelevant when the drug was used to combat uncontrollable nausea and pain in patients critically ill with AIDS, cancer, and other serious diseases. Doctors can prescribe morphine and other very strong drugs that can cause death, but with marijuana, there is no immediate risk of death.

The Response of the Clinton Administration

The passage of the medical legalization propositions in California and Arizona outraged the Clinton administration. In a December 30, 1996 press conference, General Barry McCaffrey, director of the Office of National Drug Control Policy; Attorney General Janet Reno; Secretary of Health and Human Services Donna Shalala; and a top DEA official all declared that the federal government would try to limit the effects of the two propositions.

Reno proclaimed that the U.S. Department of Justice "will not turn a blind eye to the enforcement of federal law. . . . We want to make clear that federal law still applies." Not only would any doctor who prescribed marijuana lose his or her or DEA license (which permits the physician to prescribe drugs), the doctor would not be able to participate in Medicare or Medicaid. This would make the doctor virtually unable to practice medicine.

Attorney General Reno thought that "the two initiatives . . . send the wrong message." General McCaffrey agreed that the propositions were "a terrible message. . . . This is the legalization of drugs we're concerned about. . . . Some very cunning people have displaced the argument for legalization—which Americans overwhelmingly reject—to one that is more acceptable."

Furthermore, observed McCaffrey, "Kids are hearing that marijuana is a medicine, that it can cure these various illnesses. How can anything that's medicine be that bad?" He accused the voters of California and Arizona of being "asleep at the switch [when they approved] hoax referendums." He concluded, "American medicine has gone way beyond smoking dope to manage pain," because of "smart physicians with good remedies [other than illegal drugs]."

A group of doctors and patients filed a class-action suit claiming that Attorney General Reno's threats interfered with the doctor-patient relationship in violation of the First Amendment of the U.S. Constitution. A federal district court granted an injunction in April 1997 barring the federal government from taking action to punish California doctors who recommended marijuana to their patients under the new law.

Institute of Medicine Report

Under pressure, General McCaffrey asked the Institute of Medicine (IOM), a private organization that advises the government on medical matters, to review the scientific evidence in order to assess the potential health benefits and risks of marijuana and its constituent cannabinoids. The review, which began in August 1997, culminated in March 1999 with the report *Marijuana and Medicine: Assessing the Science Base* (Janet E. Joy, Stanley J. Watson, Jr., and John A. Benson, Jr., eds., National Academy Press, Washington, D.C., 1999).

Cannabinoids, a group of compounds found in marijuana, contain THC, the primary psychoactive ingredient in marijuana. The IOM report drew the following general conclusions regarding cannabinoids:

- Cannabinoids likely have a natural role in pain modulation, control of movement, and memory.

- The natural role of cannabinoids in immune systems is likely multifaceted and remains unclear.

- The brain develops tolerance to cannabinoids.

- Animal research demonstrates the potential for dependence, but this potential is observed under a narrower range of conditions than with benzodiazepines, opiates, cocaine, or nicotine.

- Withdrawal symptoms can be observed in animals but appear mild compared with those of opiates or benzodiazepines such as diazepam (Valium).

The IOM report concluded that "the future of cannabinoid drugs lies not in smoked marijuana, but in chemically defined drugs that act on the cannabinoid systems that are a natural component of human physiology. Until such drugs can be developed and made available for medical use, the report recommends interim solutions."

John Benson and Stanley Watson, the report's principal investigators, determined that marijuana's effects are limited to symptom relief and that, for most symptoms, more effective drugs already exist. However, for patients who do not respond well to standard medications, cannabinoids seem to hold potential for treating pain, chemotherapy-induced nausea and vomiting, and the poor appetite and wasting caused by AIDS and advanced cancer.

The report noted that medical use of marijuana is not without risk. The primary negative effect is diminished psychomotor performance (control over movement). In some cases users may experience unpleasant emotional states or feelings. In addition, the usefulness of medical marijuana is limited by the harmful effects of smoking, which can increase a person's risk of cancer, lung damage, and problems (such as low birthweight) with pregnancies. Therefore, the report concludes, smoking marijuana should be recommended only for terminally ill patients or those with debilitating symptoms who do not respond to approved medications.

The report recommended that patients with no alternative to smoking marijuana be allowed to use it on a short-term, experimental basis. Both physical and psychological effects should be closely monitored and documented under medical supervision. Clinical trials of marijuana should be carried out parallel with the development of new delivery systems, such as inhalers, that are safe, fast-acting, and reliable, but which do not involve inhaling harmful smoke. Cannabinoid compounds that are produced under controlled laboratory conditions are preferable to plant products because they deliver a consistent dose.

Data collected in the review did not support the contention that marijuana should be used to treat glaucoma. Though smoked marijuana can reduce some of the eye pressure related to glaucoma, it provides only short-term relief that does not outweigh the hazards associated with long-term use of the drug. Also, with the exception of painful muscle spasms in multiple sclerosis, there is little evidence of marijuana's potential for treating migraines or movement disorders like Parkinson's disease or Huntington's disease.

TABLE 11.1

Recommendations for a government marijuana policy

Recommendation 1: Research should continue into the physiological effects of synthetic and plant-derived cannabinoids and the natural function of cannabinoids found in the body. Because different cannabinoids appear to have different effects, cannabinoid research should include, but not be restricted to, effects attributable to THC alone.

Scientific data indicate the potential therapeutic value of cannabinoid drugs for pain relief, control of nausea and vomiting, and appetite stimulation. This value would be enhanced by a rapid onset of drug effect.

Recommendation 2: Clinical trials of cannabinoid drugs for symptom management should be conducted with the goal of developing rapid-onset, reliable, and safe delivery systems.

The psychological effects of cannabinoids are probably important determinants of their potential therapeutic value. They can influence symptoms indirectly which could create false impressions of the drug effect or be beneficial as a form of adjunctive therapy.

Recommendation 3: Psychological effects of cannabinoids such as anxiety reduction and sedation, which can influence perceived medical benefits, should be evaluated in clinical trials.

Numerous studies suggest that marijuana smoke is an important risk factor in the development of respiratory diseases, but the data that could conclusively establish or refute this suspected link have not been collected.

Recommendation 4: Studies to define the individual health risks of smoking marijuana should be conducted, particularly among populations in which marijuana use is prevalent.

Because marijuana is a crude THC delivery system that also delivers harmful substances, smoked marijuana should generally not be recommended for medical use. Nonetheless, marijuana is widely used by certain patient groups, which raises both safety and efficacy issues.

Recommendation 5: Clinical trials of marijuana use for medical purposes should be conducted under the following limited circumstances: trials should involve only short-term marijuana use (less than six months); be conducted in patients with conditions for which there is reasonable expectation of efficacy; be approved by institutional review boards; and collect data about efficacy.

If there is any future for marijuana as a medicine, it lies in its isolated components, the cannabinoids and their synthetic derivatives. Isolated cannabinoids will provide more reliable effects than crude plant mixtures. Therefore, the purpose of clinical trials of smoked marijuana would not be to develop marijuana as a licensed drug, but such trials could be a first step towards the development of rapid-onset, nonsmoked cannabinoid delivery systems.

Recommendation 6: Short-term use of smoked marijuana (less than six months) for patients with debilitating symptoms (such as intractable pain or vomiting) must meet the following conditions:
- failure of all approved medications to provide relief has been documented;
- the symptoms can reasonably be expected to be relieved by rapid-onset cannabinoid drugs;
- such treatment is administered under medical supervision in a manner that allows for assessment of treatment effectiveness;
- and involves an oversight strategy comparable to an institutional review board process that could provide guidance within 24 hours of a submission by a physician to provide marijuana to a patient for a specified use.

SOURCE: Janet E. Joy, Stanley J. Watson, Jr., and John A. Benson, Jr., eds., "Recommendations," in *Marijuana and Medicine: Assessing the Science Base,* Institute of Medicine, Washington, DC, 1999

Table 11.1 lists the six recommendations made by the Institute of Medicine following their review.

REACTIONS TO THE IOM REPORT. The White House Office of National Drug Control Policy (ONDCP) thanked the IOM for its contributions to the debate on the medical efficacy and safety of cannabinoids and announced,

> We will carefully study the recommendations and conclusions contained in this report. We will continue to rely on the professional judgement of the Secretary of Health and Human Services, the Director of the National Institutes of Health, and the Surgeon General on all issues related to the medical value of marijuana and its constituent cannabinoids. . . . We look forward to the considered responses from our nation's public health officials to the interim solutions recommended by the report.

General McCaffrey, director of the ONDCP, declared that medical use of marijuana would remain illegal. Attorney General Janet Reno agreed that further "testing can give information that gives a medically sound approach" but declined to comment on whether federal law should be amended to decriminalize the use of marijuana for the terminally ill.

Mike Mitka, in "Therapeutic Marijuana Use Supported While Thorough Proposed Study Done" (*Journal of*

TABLE 11.2

Estimates of net returns per acre for Kentucky crops

Tobacco	$1,050
Processing tomatoes	$775
High fiber hemp*	$500
Low fiber hemp**	$200
Wheat and soybeans	$175
Soybeans	$100
Hay/silage	$100
Corn	$75

*High fiber hemp is grown more for its fiber.
**Low fiber hemp is grown more for its seeds and hurds than its fiber

SOURCE: Robert E. Frohling and Eric Staton, "Estimates of net returns per acre for Kentucky crops," in "Industrial Hemp: Fertile Dream or Legal Nightmare?" *NCSL Legisbrief,* January 1997

---

the American Medical Association, April 28, 1999), noted that the acceptance of marijuana "into the general population of prescribed drugs appears to be years away—if it happens at all."

Proponents of legalization believe the IOM report presents ample scientific evidence confirming the benefits of marijuana as medicine and proves General McCaffrey

TABLE 11.3

Attitudes towards the legalization of marijuana, by various demographic characteristics, selected years 1973–98

Question: "Do you think the use of maijuana should be legal or not?"

	1973 Should	1973 Should not	1975 Should	1975 Should not	1976 Should	1976 Should not	1978 Should	1978 Should not	1980 Should	1980 Should not	1983 Should	1983 Should not	1984 Should	1984 Should not	1986 Should	1986 Should not
National	18%	80%	20%	75%	28%	69%	30%	67%	25%	72%	20%	76%	23%	73%	18%	80%
Sex																
Male	22	75	25	69	32	64	34	63	30	67	25	71	28	68	23	75
Female	15	83	16	80	24	73	26	71	21	76	16	80	19	77	14	84
Race																
White	18	80	20	75	27	70	29	68	25	72	19	77	23	73	18	81
Black/other	18	79	22	71	33	60	38	59	27	71	28	69	22	75	19	77
Age																
18 to 20 years	42	56	34	56	57	39	51	48	45	52	33	67	36	62	16	82
21 to 29 years	38	60	40	54	49	48	49	49	42	56	29	68	34	62	27	71
30 to 49 years	14	84	18	79	25	72	29	69	27	71	21	76	27	68	20	79
50 years and older	9	89	9	86	16	81	16	80	13	84	13	83	9	87	12	87
Education[a]																
College	32	66	35	59	40	56	42	55	35	61	23	74	29	66	22	75
High school graduate	15	83	16	79	26	70	27	70	23	75	21	76	21	75	17	82
Less than high school graduate	6	94	5	89	11	86	13	84	3	88	9	87	7	91	8	91
Income																
$50,000 and over	NA	NA	NA	NA	NA	NA	NA	NA	NA	NA	NA	NA	NA	NA	NA	NA
$30,000 to $49,999	NA	NA	NA	NA	NA	NA	NA	NA	NA	NA	NA	NA	NA	NA	NA	NA
$20,000 to $29,999	NA	NA	NA	NA	NA	NA	NA	NA	NA	NA	NA	NA	NA	NA	NA	NA
Under $20,000	NA	NA	NA	NA	NA	NA	NA	NA	NA	NA	NA	NA	NA	NA	NA	NA
Occupation																
Professional/business	23	74	29	65	36	60	37	60	30	66	22	75	27	68	20	79
Clerical	15	83	20	76	26	72	27	71	23	75	18	79	22	72	16	82
Manual	17	82	17	79	25	71	28	69	23	74	22	75	20	77	19	79
Farmer	6	89	3	93	8	92	16	80	12	79	8	82	3	94	9	91
Region																
Northeast	22	74	26	70	32	64	33	62	27	70	20	76	24	74	20	80
Midwest	20	78	20	75	25	72	26	72	20	77	18	79	23	72	16	82
South	11	89	12	84	22	74	27	72	20	78	17	80	20	76	14	84
West	24	73	32	63	37	61	38	59	38	57	30	66	26	70	25	73
Religion																
Protestant	14	84	15	81	22	74	24	74	20	77	17	80	20	76	15	83
Catholic	18	81	21	73	32	64	31	64	26	71	17	78	20	76	18	80
Jewish	33	67	48	48	37	63	62	38	28	62	33	54	48	48	40	60
None	52	43	53	43	54	39	64	33	60	36	54	44	44	50	37	60
Politics																
Republican	11	87	12	86	20	78	19	80	18	80	15	82	17	80	13	86
Democrat	17	82	19	77	26	71	29	67	24	73	20	77	21	75	18	80
Independent	25	72	26	67	34	62	37	60	30	66	24	72	28	68	21	76

Note: The "don't know" category has been omitted; therefore percents may not sum to 100.

[a] Beginning in 1996, education categories were revised slightly and therefore are not directly comparable to data presented for prior years.

SOURCE: A. Pastore and K. Maguire, eds., "Table 2.82: Attitudes towards legalization of the use of marijuana," *Sourcebook of Criminal Justice Statistics 1999*, U.S. Bureau of Justice Statistics, Washington D.C., 2000

wrong in his statements opposing legalization. Advocates are calling for marijuana to be reclassified from Schedule I of the federal Controlled Substances Act to Schedule II, which would allow physicians to prescribe it.

Dr. Lester Grinspoon, then chairman of the National Organization for the Reform of Marijuana Laws (NORML) Foundation, a national advocacy organization for legalizing marijuana, said, "This report tries to find a middle ground between the political exigencies of an administration that wants to deny marijuana's medical value, and the reality that a growing body of the American public are using it successfully as a medicine." Grinspoon was one of the report's 13 peer reviewers. NORML Foundation Executive Director Allen St. Pierre added, "While the IOM report confirms marijuana's medical utility, it unrealistically suggests most patients wait years before using it as a medicine."

INDUSTRIAL HEMP

Industrial hemp and marijuana both come from the *Cannabis sativa* plant, but while marijuana can contain

TABLE 11.3

1987		1988		1989		1990		1991		1993		1994		1996		1998	
Should	Should not	Should	Should not	Should	Should not	Should	Should not	Should	Should not	Should	Should not	Should	Should not	Should	Should not	Should	Should not
16%	81%	17%	79%	16%	81%	16%	81%	18%	78%	22%	73%	23%	72%	26%	69%	28%	66%
19	78	21	74	20	76	19	79	23	74	27	68	27	69	30	66	34	60
14	83	14	82	14	84	14	82	14	81	19	76	20	75	22	72	22	71
17	80	17	80	18	80	17	80	18	78	22	73	23	73	26	69	28	65
12	84	18	75	10	85	13	82	16	76	20	75	24	71	22	70	24	70
21	74	16	74	19	75	22	78	21	79	24	69	50	50	38	60	34	64
25	70	24	70	21	76	19	76	25	73	25	70	24	71	30	66	34	59
19	79	19	78	19	78	19	79	22	74	27	67	26	70	28	67	30	63
8	90	12	86	11	86	12	85	10	86	15	81	17	78	19	75	21	73
21	75	20	75	20	77	18	79	21	74	25	70	26	69	27	68	32	62
13	84	16	80	15	82	16	81	16	81	19	76	22	74	24	71	23	70
10	88	12	88	9	88	12	87	8	88	19	80	10	84	22	72	22	72
NA	NA	NA	NA	NA	NA	NA	NA	NA	NA	23	72	24	70	25	70	27	68
NA	NA	NA	NA	NA	NA	NA	NA	NA	NA	22	72	21	76	25	71	29	67
NA	NA	NA	NA	NA	NA	NA	NA	NA	NA	27	69	20	77	27	68	32	61
NA	NA	NA	NA	NA	NA	NA	NA	NA	NA	23	73	27	69	29	66	26	68
20	77	16	80	20	77	21	77	19	76	24	71	26	69	26	68	31	64
11	83	14	82	10	88	9	87	16	80	19	75	18	79	23	71	23	72
16	81	20	75	17	80	16	80	17	79	24	71	24	72	26	69	28	65
2	95	6	94	25	75	6	88	15	80	5	90	15	82	26	71	42	45
18	78	19	76	14	80	12	84	18	77	24	70	19	75	26	67	28	65
14	83	18	78	14	84	16	81	13	83	19	77	19	76	23	74	27	66
13	85	12	86	14	83	12	84	15	81	19	77	22	74	24	70	22	72
23	72	23	72	26	72	29	71	30	66	28	64	32	64	31	64	37	58
13	85	13	84	13	86	12	85	16	80	18	78	19	77	19	74	21	73
16	81	16	80	16	80	15	84	15	82	21	75	21	74	29	68	27	66
40	55	52	44	35	65	33	60	36	59	30	60	42	49	37	54	56	44
42	51	38	55	40	49	44	51	40	52	47	45	46	49	42	54	48	44
13	84	14	84	14	85	11	86	16	80	14	84	15	82	20	77	19	77
15	82	18	78	16	81	18	79	16	80	28	68	24	73	24	69	29	65
19	76	20	75	19	76	18	78	21	75	23	69	29	64	30	64	31	62

tetrahydrocannibinol (THC) levels of 3 to 15 percent, cannabis plants grown for industrial hemp contain less than 1 percent of THC. Industrial hemp can be used to make many products, including rope, textiles, plastics, paper products, and oil.

U.S. law bans the cultivation of hemp but permits the sale of hemp products. Global hemp sales reached $75 million in 1997, $50 million of which were in the United States. The *Wall Street Journal* projected a 300 percent growth in hemp imports in 1999, to $250 million. Many agree with David Monson, a farmer and state legislator in North Dakota, who says, "We in North Dakota believe this [hemp] is a legitimate crop that can make us some money, help the environment, and maybe save some family farms." Growing hemp is legal in Germany, France, Spain, and Britain. Romania is the largest commercial hemp producer in Europe.

TABLE 11.4

High school seniors' attitudes toward the legalization of marijuana use, 1987–99

Question: "There has been a great deal of public debate about whether marijuana use should be legal. Which of the following policies would you favor?"

(Percent favoring policy)

Policy	Class of 1987 (N=3,330)	Class of 1988 (N=3,277)	Class of 1989 (N=2,812)	Class of 1990 (N=2,570)	Class of 1991 (N=2,515)	Class of 1992 (N=2,672)	Class of 1993 (N=2,768)	Class of 1994 (N=2,597)	Class of 1995 (N=2,574)	Class of 1996 (N=2,426)	Class of 1997 (N=2,585)	Class of 1998 (N=2,566)	Class of 1999 (N=2,285)
Using marijuana should be entirely legal	15.4%	15.1%	16.6%	15.9%	18.0%	18.7%	22.8%	26.8%	30.4%	31.2%	30.8%	27.9%	27.3%
It should be a minor violation like a parking ticket but not a crime	24.6	21.9	18.9	17.4	19.2	18.0	18.7	19.0	18.0	21.0	20.7	24.3	23.7
It should be a crime	45.3	49.2	50.0	53.2	48.6	47.6	43.4	39.4	37.3	33.8	34.0	32.6	32.5
Don't know	14.8	13.9	14.6	13.6	14.3	15.7	15.1	14.8	14.4	13.9	14.5	15.2	16.5

SOURCE: "A. Pastore and K. Maguire, eds., "Table 2.99: High school seniors' attitudes toward the legalization of marijuana use, United States, 1987–99, *Sourcebook of Criminal Justice Statistics 1999*, U.S. Bureau of Justice Statistics, Washington D.C., 2000

The changing economic fortunes of many of the nation's farmers have forced them to look to new alternatives. An acre of hemp can earn or return far more than an acre of wheat, soybeans, or corn. (See Table 11.2.) In 1999 the Virginia legislature approved the "controlled, experimental" cultivation of hemp. By 2001 Arkansas, California, Hawaii, Illinois, Maryland, Minnesota, Montana, North Dakota, Vermont, and Virginia had all passed legislation supporting either research into or cultivation of hemp.

The DEA opposes the cultivation of hemp for a number of reasons and has indicated that it will not register or permit it. The DEA indicates that it is hard to distinguish between a field of legitimate hemp and one of illegal cannabis. Since laboratory testing is needed to absolutely determine the difference, this would certainly slow down the process of fighting drugs. Finally, the DEA fears that legalizing hemp may be the first step on the way to legalizing marijuana.

OVERWHELMING MAJORITY OPPOSES LEGALIZATION

The National Opinion Research Center (Chicago, Illinois) asked Americans whether they thought "the use of marijuana should be made legal or not." In 1998, 66 percent indicated they thought marijuana should not be made legal, down from figures around 80 percent from 1986 through 1991. More than one-fourth (28 percent) of the 1998 respondents thought it should be legalized. (See Table 11.3.)

High school and college students were somewhat more likely to support the legalization of marijuana. The annual *Monitoring the Future* study, prepared by the University of Michigan Survey Research Center, asked high school seniors, "There has been a great deal of public debate about whether marijuana use should be legal. Which of the following policies would you favor?" In 1999 about 27 percent of the seniors thought "using marijuana should be entirely legal," while another 24 percent believed "it should be a minor violation like a parking ticket but not a crime." Approximately 33 percent thought "it should be a crime." (See Table 11.4.)

The annual *The American Freshman: Thirty Year Trends* and *The American Freshman: National Norms for Fall 1999,* prepared by the Higher Education Research Institute at the University of California at Los Angeles, found that in 1999, 33.9 percent of college freshman agreed that marijuana should be legalized. Males (39.2 percent) were more likely than females (29.4 percent) to support legalization. (See Table 11.5.)

In 1997 a CBS News Poll found that 62 percent of the American public supported a policy allowing physicians to prescribe marijuana to their seriously and terminally ill patients. Following the release of the 1999 Institute of Medicine report, the Gallup Organization conducted a poll on the use of marijuana for medicinal purposes. When asked whether they were for or against making marijuana legally available for doctors to prescribe in order to reduce pain and suffering, nearly three-quarters of the respondents (73 percent) supported the drug's medicinal use. Those age 65 and over were somewhat less supportive (63 percent). All three major political groups gave majority support, although Republicans were somewhat less inclined to do so (63 percent) than were Independents (79 percent) or Democrats (76 percent). (See Table 11.6.)

At the same time, as reported in the same Gallup Poll, a large majority of Americans continued to oppose the general legalization of marijuana. Sixty-nine percent opposed marijuana legalization, while 29 percent favored it. Attitudes were strongly related to age—44 percent of respondents under the age of 30 supported the legalization of marijuana, compared with 30 percent of those 30 to 49 years old, 21 percent of those 50 to 64, and only 11 percent of those 65 and older. (See Table 11.6.)

None of these polls asked if drugs such as heroin, cocaine, or methamphetamine should be legalized.

TABLE 11.5

College freshmen reporting that marijuana should be legalized, by sex, 1968–99

Percent indicating "agree strongly" or "agree somewhat"

| | Marijuana should be legalized | | |
	Total	Male	Female
1968	19.4%	21.4%	16.9%
1969	25.6	28.1	22.4
1970	38.4	41.0	35.2
1971	38.7	41.7	35.0
1972	46.6	49.6	43.0
1973	48.2	50.9	45.2
1974	46.7	49.7	43.4
1975	47.2	50.7	43.3
1976	48.9	51.6	46.1
1977	52.9	56.6	49.2
1978	49.5	52.1	47.1
1979	46.0	48.6	43.6
1980	39.3	42.1	36.6
1981	34.0	36.3	31.9
1982	29.4	32.5	26.4
1983	25.7	28.4	23.1
1984	22.9	25.8	20.3
1985	21.8	24.8	18.9
1986	21.3	25.0	18.0
1987	19.3	23.1	15.9
1988	19.3	22.8	16.4
1989	16.7	20.1	13.7
1990	18.6	21.7	16.0
1991	20.9	24.2	18.0
1992	23.0	26.6	19.9
1993	28.2	32.1	25.0
1994	32.1	36.4	28.3
1995	33.8	38.3	30.0
1996	33.0	37.2	29.6
1997	35.2	39.0	32.0
1998	32.4	38.6	27.2
1999	33.9	39.2	29.4

Note: These figures are taken from the Cooperative Institutional Research Program Freshman Survey, which is conducted annually by the Higher Education Research Institute (HERI) at the University of California, Los Angeles. The survey covers a wide range of student characteristics including demographic and background information, high school activities, college plans, values, attitudes, and beliefs. Each fall, the HERI surveys approximately 300,000 full-time students entering the freshman classes from a nationally representative sample of 2-year and 4-year colleges and universities in the United States. From 1966 to 1970, approximately 15% of the nation's institutions of higher education were selected by sampling procedures to participate in the program. Beginning in 1971, a stratified sample was selected from all institutions that have entering freshman classes and that respond to the U.S. Department of Education's Higher Education General Information Survey. An institution is considered eligible if it was operating at the time of the survey and if it had a full-time freshman class of at least 25 students. The data presented above are weighted estimates of all first-time, full-time students entering higher education institutions in the fall of each year. Response categories were "agree strongly," "agree somewhat," "disagree somewhat," and "disagree strongly." The text or format of the questions or responses may differ slightly in different years.

SOURCE: A. Pastore and K. Maguire, eds., "Table 2.101: College freshmen reporting that marijuana should be legalized, by sex, United States, 1968–1999," *Sourcebook of Criminal Justice Statistics 1999*, U.S. Bureau of Justice Statistics, Washington D.C., 2000

TABLE 11.6

Attitudes towards legalizing marijuana or legalizing marijuana for medical use, by age and political affiliation, 1999

Question: "Suppose that on election day this year you could vote on key issues as well as candidates. Please tell me whether you would vote for or against each one of the following propositions:"

	"For or against the legalization of marijuana?"			"For or against making marijuana legally available for doctors to prescribe in order to reduce pain and suffering?"		
	For	Against	No opinion	For	Against	No opinion
National	**29%**	**69%**	**2%**	**73%**	**25%**	**2%**
Age						
18 to 29 years	44	54	2	77	22	1
30 to 49 years	30	68	2	75	24	1
50 to 64 years	21	78	1	72	25	3
65 years and older	11	85	4	63	35	2
Politics						
Republican	22	77	1	63	36	1
Democrat	27	71	2	76	23	1
Independent	37	60	3	79	19	2

Note: These data are based on telephone interviews with a randomly selected national sample of 1,018 adults, 18 years of age and older, conducted Mar. 19-21, 1999.

SOURCE:"A. Pastore and K. Maguire, eds., "Table 2.81: Attitudes towards the legalization of marijuana," *Sourcebook of Criminal Justice Statistics 1999,* U.S. Bureau of Justice Statistics, Washington D.C., 2000

IMPORTANT NAMES AND ADDRESSES

AAA Foundation for Traffic Safety
1440 New York Ave. NW, Suite 201
Washington, DC 20005
(202) 638-5944
FAX: (202) 638-5943
URL: www.aaafts.org

Adult Children of Alcoholics
P.O. Box 3216
Torrance, CA 90510
(310) 534-1815
URL: www.adultchildren.org

Al-Anon/Alateen
Family Group Headquarters, Inc.
1600 Corporate Landing Parkway
Virginia Beach, VA 23454-5617
(757) 563-1600
FAX: (757) 563-1655
URL: www.al-anon.org

Alcoholics Anonymous
Grand Central Station
P.O. Box 459
New York, NY 10163
(212) 870-3400
URL: www.aa.org

American Association for World Health
1825 K St. NW, Suite 1208
Washington, DC 20006
(202) 466-5883
FAX: (202) 466-5896
URL: www.aawhworldhealth.org

Bureau for International Narcotics and Law Enforcement Affairs
U.S. Department of State
2201 C Street NW
Washington, DC 20520
(202) 647-4000
URL: www.state.gov

Center for Substance Abuse Prevention
National Clearinghouse for Alcohol and Drug Information

P.O. Box 2345
Rockville, MD 20847-2345
(301) 468-2600
FAX: (301) 468-6433
(800) 729-6686
URL: www.health.org

Center for Substance Abuse Prevention
Substance Abuse and Mental Health Services Administration
5600 Fishers Lane
Rockville, MD 20857
(301) 443-0365
FAX: (301) 443-5447
URL: www.samhsa.gov

Cocaine Anonymous
3740 Overland Ave., Suite C
Los Angeles, CA 90034-6337
(310) 559-5833
FAX: (310) 559-2554
URL: www.cocaineanonymous.org

Drug Enforcement Administration
Information Services Section (CPI)
2401 Jefferson Davis Highway
Alexandria, VA 22301
URL: www.usdoj.gov/dea

Drug Policy Foundation
4455 Connecticut Ave. NW
Suite B-500
Washington, DC 20008
(202) 537-5005
FAX: (202) 537-3007
URL: www.dpf.org

Nar-Anon
P.O. Box 2562
Palos Verdes, CA 90274-0119
(213) 547-5800

Narcotics Anonymous
P.O. Box 9999
Van Nuys, CA 91409

(818) 773-9999
FAX: (818) 700-0700
URL: www.narcoticsanonymous.org

National Council on Alcoholism and Drug Dependence
20 Exchange Place, Suite 2902
New York, NY 10005
(212) 269-7797
FAX: (212) 269-7510
URL: www.ncadd.org

National Drug and Alcohol Treatment Referral and Information Hotline
National Institute on Drug Abuse
National Institutes of Health
6001 Executive Blvd., Room 5213
Bethesda, MD 20892-9651
(301) 443-1124
URL: www.nida.nih.gov

National Organization for the Reform of Marijuana Laws (NORML)
1001 Connecticut Ave. NW, Suite 710
Washington, DC 20036
(202) 483-5500
FAX: (202) 483-0057
URL: www.norml.org

National Prevention Information Network
Centers for Disease Control and Prevention
P.O. Box 6003
Rockville, MD 20849-6003
FAX: (888) 282-7681
(800) 458-5231
URL: www.cdcnpin.org

National Resource Center on Women and AIDS Policy
Center for Women Policy Studies
1211 Connecticut Ave. NW, Suite 312
Washington, DC 20036
(202) 872-1770
FAX: (202) 296-8962
URL: www.centerwomenpolicy.org

National Women's Health Network
514 10th St. NW, Suite 400
Washington, DC 20004
(202) 347-1140
FAX: (202) 347-1168
URL: www.womenshealthnetwork.org

Office of National Drug Control Policy
Drug Policy Information Clearinghouse
P.O. Box 6000
Rockville, MD 20849-6000

FAX: (301) 519-5212
(800) 666-3332
URL: www.whitehousedrugpolicy.gov

Public Health Service
U.S. Department of Health and
Human Services
200 Independence Ave. SW
Washington, DC 20201
(202) 690-7694

(301) 443-4000 (Office of the
Surgeon General)
FAX: (202) 690-6960
URL: www.os.dhhs.gov/phs

Safe & Drug Free Schools Programs
U.S. Department of Education
400 Maryland Avenue, SW
Washington, DC 20202-0498
FAX: (800) 872-5327
URL: www.ed.gov

RESOURCES

The Drug Enforcement Administration (DEA) is the government agency responsible for controlling the use of illegal drugs and their flow into the country. The DEA releases many valuable publications on drug abuse, including *Drugs of Abuse* (1996 edition) and *Illegal Drug Price/Purity Report* (1999).

The Substance Abuse and Mental Health Services Administration (SAMHSA) of the U.S. Public Health Service monitors drug use in the United States. Among its important releases are the annual *National Household Survey on Drug Abuse, Annual Emergency Department Data, Annual Medical Examiner Data, Uniform Facility Data Set,* and the *Treatment Episode Data Set.* Other significant SAMHSA releases are the *Services Research Outcomes Study* (1998), *National Treatment Improvement Evaluation Study* (1997), and *National Expenditure for Mental Health, Alcohol, and Other Drug Abuse Treatment* (1998).

The National Narcotics Intelligence Consumers Committee (NNICC), a government consortium of a dozen government agencies involved in the "drug war," annually releases *The NNICC Report—The Supply of Illicit Drugs to the United States.* The *World Drug Report* (2001), prepared by the International Drug Control Programme of the United Nations, provides an excellent overview of the international drug trade.

The Office of National Drug Control Policy (ONDCP), in its annual *National Drug Control Strategy,* provides an overview of the nation's antidrug efforts. The yearly *Pulse Check—National Trends in Drug Abuse* also tracks the nation's attempts to control drug abuse. In conjunction with the Department of Health and Human Services, the ONDCP sponsored the study and subsequent report *Substance Use in Popular Movies and Music* (1999).

Among the many releases of the Bureau of Justice Statistics are *Correctional Populations in the United States, 1997* (1999) and *Prisoners in 1999* (2000). The National Institute of Justice (NIJ) prepares annually the *Arrestee Drug Abuse Monitoring Program* (ADAM), which shows the close connection between drug abuse and crime. *The Youth Gangs, Drugs, and Violence Connection* (1999) and "Highlights of the 1997 *National Youth Gang Survey*" (1999) study the level of street gang involvement in drug sales.

The United States Sentencing Commission's *Cocaine and Federal Sentencing Policy* (1997) studies the relationship between race and sentences for cocaine use and sales. The Federal Bureau of Investigation's (FBI) annual *Crime in the United States* provides arrest statistics.

The Bureau for International Narcotics and Law Enforcement Affairs of the U.S. Department of State, in its annual *International Narcotics Control Strategy Report,* monitors the antidrug activities of countries around the world to determine their commitment to fighting the international drug trade.

The Centers for Disease Control and Prevention (CDC) periodically releases the findings of the *Youth Risk Behavior Surveillance—United States,* the *Behavioral Risk Factor Surveillance System,* and the *HIV/AIDS Surveillance Report.*

The U.S. General Accounting Office has produced *Drug Control—An Overview of U.S. Counterdrug Intelligence Activities* (1998), *Drug Control—U.S.-Mexican Counternarcotics Efforts Face Difficult Challenges* (1998), *Drug Control—U.S. Counternarcotics Efforts in Colombia Face Continuing Challenges* (1998), *Drug Control—Observations on U.S. Counternarcotics Activities* (1998), *Drug Control—Update on U.S. Interdiction Efforts in the Caribbean and Eastern Pacific* (1997), *Drug Abuse—Research Shows Treatment Is Effective, but Benefits May Be Overstated* (1998), and *Drug Control—International Counterdrug Sites Being Developed* (2000).

The National Conference of State Legislatures publishes the *NCSL Legisbrief,* which has included "Drug-Free Workplaces" (February 1999) and "Industrial Hemp: Fertile Dream or Legal Nightmare?" (January 1997).

The annual *Monitoring the Future Study,* prepared by the Institute of Social Research of the University of Michigan and sponsored by the National Institute on Drug Abuse, is the most important study of drug use among the nation's students. The annual *PRIDE Questionnaire Report* (National Parents' Resource Institute for Drug Education), prepared by PRIDE Surveys (Bowling Green, Kentucky), has also become an important source for information about drug use among the student population. *Alcohol and Drugs on American College Campuses: A Report to College Presidents, 1995, 1996, 1997* (Core Institute, Southern Illinois University, Carbondale, Illinois, 1998) supplies information on alcohol use on college campuses.

The *National Survey of American Attitudes on Substance Abuse IV: Teens, Teachers, and Principals* (National Center on Addiction and Substance Abuse) and the 1998 *Partnership Attitudes Tracking Study* (Partnership for a Drug-Free America) provide information on attitudes toward drug use.

The Institute of Medicine studies important medical issues. *Marijuana and Medicine: Assessing the Science Base* (1999) investigates the use of marijuana for medical purposes, while *Dispelling the Myths About Addiction* (1997) looks at drug addiction. *Training About Alcohol and Substance Abuse for All Primary Care Physicians,* published by the Josiah Macy, Jr., Foundation (New York, 1995), provides insight into the medical community's growing recognition of the drug problem. *Mandatory Minimum Drug Sentences: Throwing Away the Key or the Taxpayers' Money?* (1997) and *Controlling Cocaine: Supply Versus Demand Programs* (1994), both published by the RAND Corporation, are useful resources.

Information Plus sincerely thanks all of the organizations listed above for the valuable information they provide.

INDEX

Page references in italics refer to photographs. References with the letter t following them indicate the presence of a table. The letter f indicates a figure. If more than one table or figure appears on a particular page, the exact item number for the table or figure being referenced is provided.

A

Abstinence as indicator of treatment success, 140
ADAM. *See* Arrestee Drug Abuse Monitoring Program (ADAM)
Addiction
    anabolic steroid, 40
    causes, 129–130
    definition, 129
    disease model, 130
    See also Treatment
ADHD. *See* Attention deficit hyperactivity disorder (ADHD)
Adult Patterns of Criminal Behavior, 87
Afghanistan, heroin production in, 114
Age
    admissions by substance of abuse and, 137t
    AIDS cases by, 148t
    club drug emergency department mentions by, 81f
    cocaine use by gender within age group, 27t
    cocaine use frequency by gender within age group, 28t
    crack use by gender within age group, 29t
    drug abuse deaths by, 37(t3.17)
    emergency room drug episodes by, 36t, 37(t3.16)
    hallucinogen use by gender within age group, 31t
    heroin use by, 30t
    illicit drug use by, 22t, 23(t3.2), 23(t3.3), 24t
    LSD use by, 32t
    marijuana use by gender and, 25t

marijuana use frequency by gender within age group, 26t
    PCP use by, 33t
    primary substance of abuse at admission, 138(f8.4)
    public opinion on legalizing marijuana for medical use by, 168t
    treatment clients by, 133t, 134
    treatment effectiveness by, 137–138
AIDS. *See* HIV/AIDS
AIDS Coordinating Committee, American Bar Association, 154
Alcohol
    consequences of use for students, 84t, 85
    use with drugs, 28, 35(f3.1)
    youth use, 71t
Alcohol and Drugs on American College Campuses—A Report to College Presidents: 1995, 1996, and 1997, 84–85
Alkaloids, 10
Alliance for Cannabis Therapeutics and Drug Policy Foundation v. Drug Enforcement Administration, 19–20
American Bar Association, 154
The American Freshman: National Norms for Fall 1999, 166
The American Freshman: Thirty Year Trends, 166
American Indians and Alaska Natives
    hallucinogen use, 2
    peyote use, 17
    See also Minorities; Race/ethnicity
Amphetamines, 15, 48
Anabolic steroids, 9t, 20, 39–42, 70, 78(f4.4)
Androstenedione, 43
Anorectic drugs, 16
Anslinger, Harry, 3
Anti-Drug Abuse Act of 1988, 155, 158
Arizona
    proposition for medical use of marijuana, 161–162
    treatment *vs.* incarceration, 144–145
Arrestee Drug Abuse Monitoring Program (ADAM), 88–91
Arrestee drug use, 88–91, 92t–93t, 94t–95t, 96t–97t

Attention deficit hyperactivity disorder (ADHD), 16
Availability, drug
    cocaine, 107
    late 19th-early 20th century, 2–3
    steroids, 42
    youth and, 68t, 69t, 70

B

Babies, drug exposed, 12, 31–39
Balkan route, heroin trafficking along, 115
Bank Secrecy Act of 1970, 126
Barbiturates, 13
Bayer Company, 2
Bennett, William, 159
Benson, John, 162
Benzodiazepines, 13
Black/African Americans
    attitude and involvement of parents, 80–81
    cocaine use, 24
    historic drug use, 3
    illicit drug use by age group and gender, 24(t3.4)
    racial makeup of state offenders, 93–94
    See also Minorities; Race/ethnicity
Black market, 159
Black tar heroin, 11, 114
Blumstein, Alfred, 98
Bolivia
    coca crops, 122
    eradication programs, 121
Border programs, 157
Bush, George W., 5

C

Califano, Joseph A., Jr., 160–161
California proposition for medical use of marijuana, 161–162
Cannabis, 18–20
    early use, 2
    uses and abuses, 9t
    See also Hemp, industrial; Marijuana
Cat. *See* Methcathinone
Certification process, drug, 124